Anderson County, Tennessee, County Court Minutes 1801–1809 and 1810-1814

Two Volumes in One

Transcribed by:
The Works Progress Administration
1936 and 1938

JANAWAY PUBLISHING, INC.
Santa Maria, California
2012

> *Notice*
>
> This book has been reproduced from carbon-copies of the original transcriptions of court records by the Works Progress Administration (WPA) in 1936. In many instances, the resulting text is light, the documents are physically flawed, and foxing (or discoloration) occurs. The pages of this reprint have been digitally enhanced and, where possible, the flaws and markings eliminated in order to provide clarity of content and a pleasant reading experience.

Anderson County, Tennessee, County Court Minutes
1801-1809 and 1810-1814
2 Volumes in 1

Originally transcribed by:

The Works Progress Administration (WPA)
1936 and 1938

Reprinted by:

Janaway Publishing, Inc.
732 Kelsey Ct.
Santa Maria, CA 93454
(805) 925-1038
www.JanawayGenealogy.com

2007, 2012

ISBN: 978-1-59641-042-8

Made in the United States of America

ANDERSON COUNTY, TENNESSEE
COUNTY COURT MINUTES
1801-1809 and 1810-1814

Two Volumes in One

Works Progress Administration
1936 and 1938

This book consists of two volumes: Volume One covers the period 1801-1809, and was produced in 1936; Volume Two covers the period 1810-1814, and was completed in 1938. The original page numbers, which are located at the top of the page, have been retained. Each volume has an index, located at the beginning of the volume.

Unfortunately, these indexes directed the reader to the page number of **THE ORIGINAL COUNTY RECORD BOOK FROM WHICH THE INFORMATION IN THIS BOOK WAS EXTRACTED, AND NOT THE PAGE NUMBER OF THIS WORK YOU ARE NOW READING.**

Fortunately, the page numbers of the original record have been included within the text of both Volume One and Two. In Volume One, the Original County Record Book page number is located on the left side of each individual page. In Volume Two, the Original County Record Book page numbers are shown in parenthesis throughout the text. For example, on page 7 of Volume One, you find the notations "14", "15", and "16' in the left margin, which indicates the information following the notation has been transcribed from page 14, page 15, or page 16 of the Original Record Book. In Volume Two, you will find the insertions "(P-12)" and "(P-13)", which indicates the information following the notation has been transcribed from page 12 or page 13 of the original record. Since both volumes of this book were transcribed sequentially, locating these original page numbers within the text will not be difficult.

RECORDS OF ANDERSON COUNTY

TENNESSEE

COURT RECORD

1801 - 1809

COPYING HISTORICAL RECORDS PROJECT

WORKS PROGRESS ADMINISTRATION

Official Project No. 165-44-6502

MRS. JOHN TROTWOOD MOORE

STATE LIBRARIAN & ARCHIVIST, SPONSOR

MRS. ELIZABETH D. COPPEDGE

STATE DIRECTOR OF WOMEN'S & PROFESSIONAL PROJECTS

MRS. PENELOPE JOHNSON ALLEN

STATE SUPERVISOR

MRS. MARGARET HELMS RICHARDSON

SUPERVISOR FIRST DISTRICT

WORKER:

Mrs. Anna Roe Mims

November 25th, 1936.

INDEX

(NOTE: page numbers in this index refer to those of the original volume from which this copy is made. These numbers are carried in the left hand margin of this copy.)

ANDERSON COUNTY

COURT MINUTES VOL. 1, 1801 - 1809

A	Abbott James	4-5-131-143-147
	Adair John	12-33-54-57-72-77-94-112-114-213
	Adair Thomas	37-47-86-102-103-123-147-150-191-194-223-228-252-272-275 276-279-295-297-315-318-319-353-368-371-402-408
	Adair Robert	217
	Adair James	73-77
	Adair Alexander	73-112-114
	Adair Oliver	78
	Adkins James	3-5-48-49-65-77-103-136-237-303-317-367
	Adkins Roberts	25-37
	Adkins Joseph	305
	Adkins Bartlett	97
Aj	Ajey Isaac	61
Ald	Aldredges Ford	8-16-22-62-168-183-185-236-247
	Aldredge William	5-7-11-24-25-26-50-53-78-95-100-101-119-125-238
	Aldredge Nathan	26-68-167-178-179-181-197-198
	Alderson John	237-262
	Allbright John	141
Ale	Alexander Hugh	148-174-242-318
	Alves Galven	190
	Alves Walter	37-155-171-190-287
	Allen John	280
	Allen William	280
	Alred Solomon	256-347
	Alred Thomas	134
	Anderson County	21-22-24-31-38-40-43-47-50-53-63-64-67-68-71-72-74-78 81-84-88-90-94-95-96-97-100-101-104-105-114-117-118-120 125-131-133-135-137-150-162-166-173-174-176-180-189-192 193-194-199-203-208-210-211-215-216-221-222-227-228-229 242-262-264-266-269-275-279-284-289-294-296-297-299-300 310-311-317-320-322-330-346-359-365-375-381-387-391-396 398
	Andrews Road Branch	156
	Anderson Stewart	146
	Anderson Peter	141-143
Ar	Arbuckle James	67
	Archer Richmond	194
	Armstrong M.	255
	Armstrong John	7-21-36
	Armstrong Robert	17-28-35-38-62-80-146-162
	Arnold William	10-32-33-47

	Arnold Wm. Senr.	91
	Arnold John	59
Ash	Ashlock William	10-11-12-19-23-25-35-50-53-73-135-178-186-217-229-259 263-272-289-291-295-300-303-306-308-309-318-322-282 392-408
	Asher Robertson	217-232-252-265-282-284-304-306-311-327-356-397-407
	Ashurst John	160-176-198-206-210-242-310-311-340-346-350-360-
	Asher Nolman	374
	Asher Charles	332
	Asher John	36-81-84-85-86-88
	Asher William	397
	Asher Susannah	397
	Asher Milly	46-332
	Asher Richmond	119-125-130-135
	Ashlock Obediah	153
Aus	Austin William	5-6-7-34-38-40-46-55
	Austin John	38-46-211-213
	Austin Hezekiah	38
	Austin Betsy	195-375
	Austin Robe	38
	Austin Elizabeth	38
	Austin Joseph	38-173
	Austin Zachariah	38-46
	Austin Phebe	46
	Austin Nathaniel	46-55-78
	Austin Hannah	46
	Austin Daniel	38-46
	Austin Nancy	38
Ave	Avery Peter	7-9-21
Aye	Ayers Chastly	248
	Ayers David	248
B	Baid William	377
	Bailey Christopher	94-339
Bak	Baker Mary	282
	Baker Robert	76-88-173
	Baker Samuel	173
	Baker James	312
	Baker Wm.	141
	Baker John	78-80-81-106-111-147;165-173
	Baker Christopher	138-149-150-273-276-279-288-313-318-319-352-365-386-397 401-403-409
Bas	Ball James V.	141
	Barron Joseph	206-223-228-232-337
Bar	Barton Hugh	204-205-214-253-261-279-282-283-287-291-295-299-300-301 303-306-307-309-315-318-329-334-337-340-345-346-348-353 356-358-360-363-381-390-399-401-404-408
Bas	Bashaw Johathan	206-210-219
	Bashaw Jonath	149

Page 2

Bau	Baumgerter George	88-167-169-217-236-243-248-257-261-279-282-286-309 310-316-319-324-344-358-389
Bea	Beatty Martin	144-164-168-183
	Beard Joseph	391
	Beaver Creek	56
	Beaver Creek Road	332-361-362
	Beasley James	259-264-268-269-271
	Belew Jesse	76-95-103-106
	Blew Robert	95
	Biesly James	352
	Bemcombe Countz	91-95
	Bennet William	238
	Benson Thomas	5-26-183-216-233
	Benham Tophley	368-370-372-373-374
	Berry John	248
	Bickerstaff Henry	163-164-168-169-170-184-203-242
	Bickerstaff John	248-249-271-273
Big	Big Buffalo	20-49-139-212
	Big Creek	62-111-149-221
Bel	Belew Robert (?)	95
	Belew Jesse (?)	76-95-103-106
Bee	Beesly James	352
Ben	Benson Thomas (?)	5-26-183-216-233
Bic	Bickerstaff Henry(?)	163-164-168-169-171-184-203-242
	Bickerstaff John (?)	248-249-271-273
Big	Big Buffalo (?)	20-49-139-212
	Big Creek (?)	62-111-149-221
	Big Valley	26-49-172-185-196-208-391
	Big Valley (?)	26-49-172-185-196-208-391
Bir	Bird Mrs.	104
	Bird Charles Lee	141
Bis	Bishop William	203-205
Bla	Black Oak Ridge	186-220-270-277-403
	Black House	110
	Black John	139-157
	Blain Robert	231
	Blagges John	156
Ble	Blevens John	85
	Boletourt County	189
Boo	Bookout Charles	110-138-149-150-191-198
	Bookout Joseph	406
	Bookout Marmaduke	49-131-138-143-149-179-240-257-258-268-276-279-300 313-340-353-356-358-360-362-273-383-386-395-408
	Bookout Jesse	283-406
	Bookout William	370
Bot	Botelor William	292
	Boteler Thomas	292
Bou	Bounds Obediah	95
	Bounds James	95-149-191-194-240-
	Bounds John	6-24-40-43-85-95-97-103-119-125-240
Bow	Bowling Sally	90
	Bowling Benjamin	314-409
	Bowling Joel	8-26-33-35-73-96-100-147-158-167-176-197-205-213-223-228-248
	Bowling Larkin	255-259-274-307-314-317-327-351-365-367-369-370-372-

		373-374-389
	Bowman Sherwood	406
	Bowman John	26-65-71-154
	Bowman Henry	72
	Boyd William	6-22-24-25-190-248-347-383-397
	Boyd John	179-190-205-207
	Boyd Jordon	238
Bra	Braden Andrew	206-210-248-265-272-288-289-291-303-309-311-320-327-333-337-342-369-371-377-381-384-397
	Bradley John	131-143-388
	Bradberry John	11-19-20-25-175
	Branham Ephram	259
	Brazelton Isaac	7-21-22-33-40-43-59-60-65-71-76-86-88-91-103-111-114-153-157-186-248-270-304
	Brazeale D. W.	181
	Brazle William	40-43-45-47-48-59-81-84-85-90-91-103-121-183-191-194-307
	Brazle Robert	7-8-48-64-75-85-88-115-121-197-216
	Brazle Valentine	5-67
	Brazle Richard	77
	Brazle Taylor	173
	Brazle George	34-37-65-71-77-173-342
	Brazle Nancy	398
	Bray James	54-59
	Brewer Sylvanus	265
Bro	Brown John	167-176-178-179-181-195-308-358
	Brown Reuben	215
	Brown Jack	173
	Brown Claiborn	94-256
	Browner William	77-161
	Brock Robert	220
	Brocks Mill	148
	Brock Sherard	119-125-131-134-136
	Brockeuridge James	189
	Brummett Elijah	341
	Brummett John	342-349
	Brummett George	173
	Brummett James	173
	Brumly William	361
	Brumly Judah	217
	Brummly John	141
	Brumley Nancy	63
	Bruton James	167-178-179-181-1820187-250-257
	Bruton John	261
Buc	Buckman Josiah	237
	Buckham Valley	272
	Buck Horn Valley	186
Buf	Buffalo Creek	14-15-51-130-196-271-272-404
	Buffalo Creek Ford	342
Bul	Bullock N. Leonard	40-68
	Bullock David	164-240
	Bullock Richard	192
Bun	Bunkham County	61

Bur	Burk W. Mary	223
	Burres Jesse	212
	Burris Elijah	383
	Burton Robert	44-115-117-129-152-158-161-195-197-283-308-407
	Burton Thomas	190-246-259-288-300-311
	Burton Hutchens	167-191-211
	Burville	39-43-44-48-49-51-53-56-71-73-74-76-79-82-84-86-87-88-92-100-102-107-111-118-121-123-125-128-129-136-140-143-144-145-146-167-169-172-174-210-215-217-224-228-238-242-247-262-266-269-271-272-278-279-285-286-290-299-300-302-309-313-314-316-318-322-324-331-332-338-344-345-346-347-348-351-357-359-361-381-390-392-396-399-401-410
But	Butler Thomas	229
	Butler James	4-7-9-11-13-22-25-27-29-31-34-37-38-50-53-58-61-62-64-71-74-76-79-80-82-85-88-105
	Butler Elizabeth	85-88
	Butler Jacob	202-215-236-257-304-366-381-384
	Butler Isaac	384-387
	Butler Henry	206-259-264-268-269-271-273-275-310-381
	Butler William	312-329-331-333-336-337-401-403
	Butler William Senr.	288-322
	Butler William Junr.	386-397
	Butcher Bornabas	277-408
Byr	Byrans Fork	15-49-59-110-140-179-190-257-272-293-332-335-406-
	Byrans Aulden	15
	Byran Eleenezer	3

C

Cai	Cain Creek	28-62-97-186
Cam	Campbell County Line	331-332-351-359-361
	Campbell County	246-247-257-293-296-299-302-395
	Campbell Thomas	2-4-27-31-33-177-199-206-210-219-220
	Campbell Lewis	340-346-350-353-356-358-360-408
	Campbell John	408
	Campbell Patrick	115-216-277-281-320-356
	Campbell Richard	352-382
Can	Canlerberry Daniel	173
	Canlerberry John	191
Cop	Cope Andrew	75
Car	Carbrough Charles	147-152-167-176-179-182-187-282-283-285-286-309-337-344-352
	Carlock Henry	106-124-145-177
	Carlock Abraham	6-9-82
	Carlock Sarah	61
	Carlock Mary	61
	Carlock Jacob	173
	Carnal Thomas	295-300-340-346
	Corney Lewis	408
	Carpenter Thomas	46-85-91
	Correll Elizabeth	68
	Correll Polly	203-203
	Carwile John	273-288
Cap	Captain Davis	11-29

	Captain Underwood Co.	240
	Captain Sinclair Co.	218-240
	Captain Tunnell Co.	230-240-290
	Captain Martains Co.	266
	Captain Mc Guire Co.	240-294
	Captain Silas Co.	35-50-186
	Captain Adair Co.	240-299
	Captain Clouds Co.	29-35-50-166-240
	Captain Huffakers Co.	240
	Captain Chapman Co.	235-239
	Captain Oliver Co.	240
	Captain Lays Co.	240
	Captain Huffakokers Co.	214-215
	Captain Bowling	364
	Captain England	2
	Captain George	166
	Captain Graham	11
	Captain Griffith	407
	Captain Hill	76
	Captain Heard	166
	Captain Hoggs	166
	Captain Hart	130-166
	Captain Halfaires	166
	Captain Hawkins	35-50-58-159-166
	Captain Hale	11-29
	Captain Hoggs	170
	Captain Jeffery	7-11-29
	Captain Linville	35-50-103
Cha	Champbers Charles	382
	Chandler Richard	68
	Chaney Jacob	35-40-43-50-53
	Chandler William	115-324
	Chandler Shadrach	85
	Chapman John H.	261-268
	Chapman John	269-317
	Chesnut Ridge Mutirghouse	185
	Chesnut Ridge	8-15-49-92-156-179-184-185-202-206-257-270-277-332-397-406
	Cheatham Thomas	342
	Childress John	352
	Chiles ~~Charles~~ John	351
	Chiles Rowland	106 (205)
	Childress Michael	401
	Chitwood James	8-12-13-73
Cho	Choat Christopher	69
	Choat Austin	67-202-302-305
Chr	Christenberry Joshua	357
	Chressman Isaac	62
Cla	Claiborn Line	111-149
	Claiborn County	10-148-193
	Clapp Ludowick	180
	Clack Spencer	122-126-104
	Clapier Lewis	244-299

	Clardy Michael	144-149-191-194-202-204-205-265-276-279-293-297-310-381-384-387-398-402-406-408-409-410
	Clark Saml.	349
	Claxton Constance	10-21-60-86-102-149-152-211-217-223-228-230-232-243-285-310
Cle	Clear Peter	245-249
Cli	Clinch River	8-9-14-15-22-26-37-39-48-51-62-73-79-87-90-97-107-110-111-121-129-135-148-172-180-182-184-186-191-194 200-203-212-216-220-221-270-271-286-315-332-335-349-361-262-391-395
	Cloudfetler John	69-68
	Clodfetler Jacob	331-340-345-351-402
	Cloud Jason	11-19-22-25-26-36-50-53-56-64-69-71-101-102-102-107-110-117-118-121-130-140-143-148-150-151-158-160-164-166-169-170-171-190-194-197-198-202-203-204-211-212-214-220-222-223-237
	Cloud Jeremiah	224-230-243
	Clouds Ford	26-110-121-130-180-194-270
Cob	Cobb William	44-182-281
	Cobb Pharoon	182
	Cobb Richard H.	20
	Cobb Sally	182
	Cobb Caswell	15-391
	Cobb Richard C.	49-50-53-59-65-69-71-74-96-101-102-107-132-148-163-166-179-189-195-196-199-214-236-240-245-246-249-259-270-271-292-298-311-315-330-334-349-359-367-379-390-404-409
Coo	Cook Joseph	69
Col	Cold Creek	21-72-76-88-186
	Cold Creek Ford	406-409
	Cole John	199-266
	Cole Alexander	78-162-240-247-381
	Collinsworth John	199
Com	Combs Philip	92
	Combs Job	47
Con	Conner James	391
	Conner Archebald	105
	Coney Jesse	3
	Conway Charles	352
	Coons John Senr.	45
	Coonce John Senr.	235
Cop	Copper Ridge	8-74-119-184-185-203-206
	Cooper Thomas	8-33
	Cooper William	191-230-361
	Cooper John	185-223-232-276-310-340-346-350-353-356-368-377-381-383-408
Cor	Cormack Patrick	223-238
Cou	Counts John	48
	Counce John Senr.	147
	Counce John	173
	Counce John Junr.	147
	County Line Knox	78
	County Line Anderson	88-107-110-111-139-179-184-185-186-277-290-342-406
	Countz John	150

Cot	Cotter William	46-63-78-79-87-91-107-110-116-119-122-149-170-290-293-331-376-379
	Cotton James	67
Cov	Cove Road	183-326-329
	Cove Creek	90-111-211-247-252
Cow	Cowan Alexander	78-80-106
Cox	Cox Joel	238, 119 — COX, Jacob 131-136
	Cox John	274
	Cox Joab	119-131-136-238
Cra	Crain James	162-164
	Crain Isaac	135-137
	Crackins James M.	200
	Crabough Charles	198-248-255-271-273-274
	Crawford Samuel	9-45-63-74-92-97-127-235-207
Cre	Creely William	17-67
Cri	Cristman Isaac	117
Cro	Croffroth Conrod	402-404
	Cross Joseph	101-158-198
	Cross Roads	342
	Cross Britian	385
	Cross Cynthia	327
	Cross Mountain	193-201-246
	Cross Micajah	47-80-106-119-125-159-161-171-176-177-220-255-282-297-307-320-327-329-356-368-374-402
	Crozier John	182-280-323-330-334-345-354-355-369-371-373
	Crozier Arthur	46-65-74-80-82-87-97-101-105-107-109-111-114-123-125-126-127-136-138-143-145-146-149-151-156-162-163-167-169-171-178-179-187-189-190-195-196-200-202-204-207-209-214-219-223-224-228-234-241-243-245-255-258-260-261-262-279-280-282-284-286-290-292-293-295-301-303-306-309-311-312-315-317-318-319-321-322-323-324-330-331-334-342-343-344-345-346-350-354-355-356-357-358-360-363-364-369-371-372-373-374-377-379-383-387-389-390-395-396-399-400-410
	Crouch William	236
	Crouch Solomon	222
	Crouch Nancy	222
	Crowley Berry	123-136
	Crowley James	158-191
	Crowley Littleberry	223-228-237
Cum	Cumblerland Mountain	326
	Cumberland Thomas	394
	Cumberland Ford	9-22-36-45-47-62-127-200-335
Cun	Cunninghams Mill	191
	Cunningham David	87-163-164-168-169-171
	Cunningham Moser	47-116-135-145
	Cunningham James	6-11-19-25-49-79-87-206-210-219-220-252-259-264-291-295-300-301-304-306-311-316-324-350-377
	Cunningham Jonathan	15-27-28-31-32-38-50-51-53-55-59-62-67-73-78-81-84-85-119-125-131-134-136-139
	Cunningham Jacob	141
	Curtis Samuel	200-223-228
	Curry Samuel	1-91-
	Curry Thomas	1

D

Dar	Dardis Thomas	101-107-128-277
Daf	Daffron George	26
Dal	Dalton Bradley	199-207-234-265
Dav	Davis William	45
	Davis James	141
	Davis Nathaniel	2-4-5-8-36-39-38-50-53-65-69-71-72-86-88-112-114-119-127-131-173-183-184-216-410
	Davis Thomas	281
	Davis Samson	367
	David Sampson	193-200-201-211-214-220-222-226-230-232-234-240-245-247-291-295-296-297-298-301-302-303-304-305-306-307-308-309-310-311
	Davidson William	7-8-34-54-104-112-114-117-121-135-162-198-206-207-218-219-251-340-346-353-356-357-358-360-378
	Davidson Jacob	406
	Davidson James	117-154-162-168-253-256
Day	Day Daniel	273
	Day John	2-4-5-20-24-39-40-45-65-71-87-96-100-101-119-131-134-136-167-176-201
	Day Joseph	179-261
	Day Magor	49
	Days Ford	20-252-329-399-401
Dea	Deaton Mathew	156
	Deaton Zadock	156
	Delap Robert	195
	Delk Jordon	389
	Delk John	389
Den	Denham Joseph	2-4-14-16-17-144-168-169-179-198-218-242
	Denham Joseph Junr.	33-48-50-
	Denham Joseph Senr.	39-48-53-76-82-87-90-96-97-100-101-102-106-108-123-124
	Denon John	104-121-190
	Denton Jonas	27-31-50-53-69-81-84-85-87
	Denton Abraham	286
Der	Derrott J. C.	340-346
	Derrick Joseph	102
	Derrick Samuel	145
	Derrick Simon	186-232-260-264-314-319-331-333-351-375-382-393-401-404
	Derrick Jacob	293, 102
	Derrick William	150-191-194-217-240-259-295-300-327-336-404-
Dew	Dew Robert	87-128-129-131-143-147-152-167-176-179-211-216-218-219-220-243-245-248-249-253-255-263-267-274-286-288-295-296-298-299-322-327-330-332-346-347-358-359-362-363-373-379
Dis	District of Columbia	337
Div	Divers John	72
Dod	Dodd Jacob	403-409
	Dodd Joab	295-340-346-353-360-385-386-397-401
	Dodson Oliver	81-84
Doh	Doherty Helen	
	Doherty Eli	363
	Doherty Andrew	238
	Doherty Francis	223

	Doherty James	5
	Doherty Devisus	134
Dal	Dalton Oliver	24
Don	Donelson Stockley	63-90-157-213-391
	Dotson Oliver	45-50-54-85-101-112-114-149-211-230
Dou	Double Springs	61
Dow	Dowlin Amas	340-346
Dra	Drake James	314-336
	Drake George	305
	Dry Buffalo	277
Duc	Duckworth John	121-158-221
	Duckworth Margaret	158
	Duckatt James	5-7
Dun	Dun John	369
	Dunn Samuel	249-269-271-273-282-285-319-352-369-385-402-407-409
	Duncan Joseph Junr.	38
	Duncan Stephen	267
	Duncan John	141
	Duncan Stockley	32
	Duncan Polly	245-249
	Duncan Raleigh	340-346-350-353-356-358-408
	Duncan Rawley	4-17-27-31-81-84-85-110-131-140-145-198-240-259-276-279-281
	Dunnaven John	153
Dur	Durratt John J.	243-245-249-252-255-259-310
	Durrick William	275
	Durrick John G.	386-397-401-403-409
	Duggins John	68-76-108-150-304-317
	Dew Robert	399
	Dwiggins(?) John	106-147-164-168-169-205-220-303

E

Eag	Eagle Ford	8-26-39-48-92-183-185-203-206-272-329-338-400-410
Eas	Easter Goldman	173
Edw	Edward Samuel	87-107-148-366
	Edward Mary	148-357
Ell	Elliot Amos	102-103-147-167-176-179-218-224-228-232-236-241
Eng	English Joshua	195
	English John	191-193-194
	England John	35-162-191-192
Ent	Entery Vickory	24
Eva	Evans William	215
	Evans Thomas	164-173
	Evans Walter	90-115
	Evans John	141

F

	Fan Richard	104
Far	Farmer Frederick	69-141
	Farmer Andrew	187-222-228-276
	Farmer William	33-186-206-210
	Farmer Abner	229-366
	Farmer Henry	2-4-7-11-19-88-112-114-119-125-134-135-136-170-186-285-372-382-394-402
	Farmer Henry Junr.	206-210-229-248-289

	Farmer Henry Senr.	20-21-27-31-32-36-81-84-85-86-97-229-408
	Farmer John	187-229-238-330-333-337-342-394-408
	Farmer John Senr.	149-322-323
Fel	Felix Gilbert	158
Fen	Fen Richard	190
Fer	Ferrell	27-31-54-176
	Ferry Road	383
Fil	Filpot Richard	206-210-214
	Finley James	86-111-116-129-147-161-177-191-194-200-286-292-295
	Fish Trap Island	249
Fle	Fleenor Elizabeth	387
For	Ford of Cold Creek	7
	Forrest Richard	12-24-61-73-91-108-112-114-115-149-170-217-224-227-238-256-258-291-292-299-310-352
Fos	Foster Edward	217
	Foster Enoch	91-129-147-206-210-214-217-277-288-319-332-362
Fou	Fourner Doctor	350
Fre	Freels Anderson	291
	Freels Thomas	305
	Freels Edwards	131-143-145-146-152-215-216-241-261-276
	Freels Isaac	124-133-167-176-202-301-386-396
	Freels Edward	159-180
	Freels Edward Senr.	149-167-176-281-313
	Freley Caleb	2-4-14-22-25-27-28-31-34-75-79-96-100-167-213-215
	Freley Reuben	238
	Freley Charles	37-131
Fro	Frost Thomas Senr.	48-54-115-119-256-265-292
	Frost Thomas Junr.	44
	Frost Edward	26-27-31-32-131 143-147-150-152-271-283
	Frost Elijah	147-185-268-269-276-279-280-281-287-295-300-325-330-349-368-372-408-409
	Frost Joshua	295-300-301-304-306-309-340-346
	Frost Micojah	48-56-74-115-398
	Frost Samuel	5-11-17-19-35-36-37-50-53-56-74-112-114-117-121-122-123-124-127-131-143-158-167-179-183-185-190-203 223-228-276-280-281-307-323-325-352-365-367-373
	Frost Joseph	54
	Frost John	240-244-256-276-280-281-283-298-320-325-333-338-339-350
	Frost John Senr.	323
Fry	Fry John	253-268-338-375-381-
	Fry Philip	11-19-20-79-81-84-87-92-106-156-296-338-364
Ful	Fulton Thomas	67
	Fulton John	144
Fun	Funk Abraham	20
Fur	Furguson John	297
	Furguson Samuel	189
Gal	Galbreath Robert	351-365-369-367-374-
	Galbreath James	115-155
	Galbreath Thomas	85-86-155-243

	Galbreath Alexander	54-112-114-115-131-180-181-201-258-275-312-322-329-331-336-337
	Galbreath Samuel	119-125-155-201-206-211-232-236-252-254-286-287-288-290-293-305-308-309-317-326-328-329-337-376-384
Gam	Gamble John	243-310-408
	Gamble William	215-289-295-300-322-357-381
Gar	Garner John	216-289-322-327-331-333
Gas	Gastin Alexander	27-31-33-35-36- 37-48-88-101-102-108-114-117-118-120-122-123-124-127-128-136-137-160-164-166-168-169-171-176-177-179-181-182-187-193-194-205-218-219-232-236-241-245-248-249-263-288-297-298-301-307-309-310-311-319-329-330-343-350-358-362-365-370-374-381-387
Gen	Gentery Isaac	375
Geo	George Cratha	234
	George James	234
	George Travis	96-100-101-113-331-138-145-150
	George Shutters Mill	272
	George Henry	400
Gib	Gibbs John	54-288-332-340-346-350-353-356-358-361-362-366
	Gibbs Jacob	134-357
	Gibson John	67
Gil	Gilbreath Samuel	300-301-34-310-311-312-386-389
	Gilbreath Alexander Junr.	289-386-396
	Gilbreath Thomas	310-381
	Gilbreath Robert	295-300
	Gilbert Felix	45-59-62-150-152-179-199-206-210-214-219-220-234-268-272-305-315-366-368-384
Gle	Glenns Robert	193-201
Go	Goad John	192
	Goad Ayers	54
	Golher Joseph	2-4-20-65-71-81-84-85-87-91-94-191-194-198-202-203-205-207-276-279-289-295-300-305-322-335
Gol	Goloher George	265-347
	Goloher James	253-347
	Goloher John	2-4-347
	Golson John	11-20-71-125-111
	Golston John	65-119-121-240-229
	Golston Reuben	216-279-282-287-288-315-319-335-386-396-397
	Gonson Henry	310
	Gordon George	132-267-305-382-391
	Gordon Robert	195
	Gordner Joseph	310
	Gorchain James	55
Gar	Garner John	50-75-119-125-149-169-183-184-336-337-342-375-377-383-
Gra	Grants Creek	139
	Granger County	51-288
	Grantsbrough	38-47-51-61-62-73-79-115-148-119-233-257-258-270-272-293-332-361
	Grantsbrough Road	12-14-68-110-138-139-140-149-150-179-332
	Graham Joseph	118-183
	Graham George	177

	Graham Spencer	1-4-11-20-34-35-45-50-51-53-59-63-65-73-78-81-84-96-101-105-111-120-128-131-133-134-136-137-160-163-164-166-178-179-190-191-202-203-204-205-214-230-240
	Graham Alexander	170-259-263-272-286-289-310-322-325-332-338-351
	Grant James	2-9-11-12-13-15-16-17-24-25-26-28-29-31-34-37-41-45-47-49-50-51-53-58-61-64-69-71-72-73-75-79-81-82-84-86-89-90-94-96-98-100-102-104-105-107-108-114-115-117-120-121-122-124-130-131-132-136-137-138-142-143-148-157-158-160-163-164-168-169-170-171-172-174-182-187-189-190-191-192-193-194-196-197-198-200-201-203-204-205-207-209-210-213-214-218-219-221-222-224-226-227-232-234-236-237-240-241-242-268
	Grants Farry	51
	Grandner John	119
	Gray John	55
	Grayson Joseph	1-5-21-27-48-112-114-131-143-148-185-203-206-210-219-220-225-323
Gre	Gregsby Simion B.	85
	Green James	38-62-80
	Green William	245-249
	Greenwood Henry	152
	Greenwood Caleb	205
	Greenwood H. B.	149-183-203-206-210-215
	Greenwood Bailey	27-31-50-53
	Greer Joseph	21-306-350
Gri	Griffee Thomas	54
	Griffey William	9-22
	Griffin Landrum	173
	Griffith William	45-50-53-59-62-96-182-187-188-201-211-289-312-322-329-331-333-336-337-382-384-387-408
	Grills Elliot	11-19-54-119-125-145-253
	Grimes George	2-199
Gus	Guess Aron	7-22-36-55
	Guess John	22-55-173
Gur	Gurthery John	256
	Gurthery Boyce	257-292
	Gurthery William	256

H

Hac	Hackett John	54-115
	Hackworth Necocdemus	62
	Hackworth Augustine	10-11-25-48-85-95-127
	Hackworth Austins	50-53-104-112-114-117-119-122-123-124-127-163-164-168-171-184-190-194-291-293-296-298-381-384-385-387-408
Hag	Hagler Jacob	2-4
	Hagler Abraham	31-33-34-36-50-53-59-62-87-94-96-100-101-111-121-149-289-322-329-330-331-333-336-337-342-386-408
Hai	Hailey David	213
Hal	Halbert Joel	408
	Hall David	59-62-76-77-81-84-85-90-91-92-94-163-164-168-169-171-183-184-185-197-216-236-377-383
	Hall Luke	327
	Hall Richard	249-307

	Hale Nathan	3-5-22-23-40-43-45-47-62-111-112-114-121-131-143-162-191-194-198-204-205-234-265-275-276
	Hale Mathew	352
Ham	Hamilton District	8-63-132-284-386
	Hamilton John	192
	Hamton Robert	128
Han	Hancock John	157-160-163-164-170-171-172-228-255
	Hancock Thomas	340-346
	Hancock Joel	17-174-179-241-259-261-287-289-290-295-298-309-310-323-330-339-341
	Hancock William	73-143-145-150-161-233
	Hancock William Junr.	79
	Hancock William Senr.	7-14-15-35-55-111-114-131-148
	Hankins William	55
	Hannah John	27-31-36-65-71-119-125-127-136-167-178-179-181-182-183-187-190-216-240-255
	Hannah James	59-296-303-307-311
Har	Harbin Jarrett	38-76-82-91-92-97-131-147-152-159-190-199-241-398-401-402-407-408-409
	Harbison James	306
	Harbin Gibson	11-20-24-29-87-89-250
	Hardin Amos	250-347
	Harless Henry	27-31-32-44-119-125-126-235-240-332-361
	Harless Philip	126-332-351-369-365-368-369-374-408
	Harless David	49
	Harman Thomas	371
	Harman Powell	87
	Harman Gidson	106
	Harman Lewis	154-280-281-310-323-352-336-338-349-352-358-370-372-376-377-391-392-399-401-408-410
	Harman Paul	20-107-128-130-131-194-219-259-263-289-291-293-297-298-322-330-333-337-342-347-386-396
	Harris John	173
	Harris William	134-163
	Hart Joseph	97-121-137-154-174-198-201-203-204-205-207-209-218-233-240-263-318-326-358-359-362-399
	Hart Thomas	92-205-262-263-266-276-312-318-320-327-338-363-389-399-405-407
	Hart Nathanuel	44-68-137
	Hart David	201-218-226-320
	Hart James	166
Has	Haskins William	233
Hat	Hatchett John	215
	Hatfield James	173
	Hatfield Joseph	173
	Hatfield John Senr.	173
	Hatfield John	92-94-102-103-106
	Hatmaker Francis	291-293-297
	Havens William	78-101-103-107-110-128-130-170-306-326-341-359-366
	Harvey Robert	189
	Hawkins County	91
	Hawkins Edward	198-243-310-381

	Hawkins Mathew	154-156-204-205-206-210-215-288-340-346-350-356-358-360-386-396-397-398-401-403-404
	Hays James	155-369-392-394-402-404
	Haynes Richard	156-386-396-401-403-404
	Haynes Stephen	236
	Haynes Christopher	199
Hea	Heard Stephen	8-46-51-74-109-162-176-218-234-283-294-299-322-324-325-326-351-373-410
	Heard James	141
	Heath Mathew	150-266-280-
	Heath John	268
	Heath Johnson	288-356-357-358-359-361-400-401-402-403-404
Hel	Hellums Jonathan	110-164
	Helton Jesse	199-295-297
	Helton Peter	198-259-264-271-273-275-361
Hen	Henderson James	384
	Henderson Jesse	154-185
	Henderson Archebald	24-25-161
	Henderson & Company	200-216-308
	Hendrix Carter	295-300-329-335
	Hendrix Squire	161-167-176-256-281-328-397-401
	Hendon Elijah	175-249-310-370-373-377-381-383-408
	Henley David	299
	Henry Farmers Mill	217
	Henry Ezekiel	161
	Henry William	65-161-320
Hib	Hibbs John	243-245-249-252-255-259-310
	Hibbs Malon	145-152-168-169-171-282-288-306-333-337-340-386-394-400
	Hibbs Samuel	400
Hic	Hickman John	150-240-276-279-280-282-287-288-313-315-318-319-352-361-381-404
	Hicks Henry	173
	~~Hicks~~ Heath Johnson	264-267-269-273
	Hicks James	259-263
	Hickory Valley	110
Hil	Hill Delilah	366
	Hill Thomas Senr.	75
	Hill Thomas	111-118-121-127-128-131-132-138-159-160-164-166-240-245-247-249-250-295-296-300-301-303-307-311-352
	Hill Thomas W.	1-15-81-101-105-109-
	Hill James	131-138-143-149-150-206-210-219-220-240-259-276-279-283-287-288-295-300-301-303-307-309-347-386-379-401-403-409
	Hill Henry	281-366
	Hinds Creek	15-49-59-79-87-110-138-149-179-205-230-272-288-293-326-332-335-349-399-406
	Hinkle Henry	338
Hob	Hobbs Richard	19
	Hobbs Enos	173
	Hobbs James	67
	Hobbs Curtis	76-88
	Hobbs Joel	11-19-20-21-26-55-67-86

Hog	Hogg Joseph	6-78-90-91-144-145-150-170
	Hogg James	37-171
	Hogshead Ann	273
	Hogshead William	8-10-17-23-25-33-39-40-43-44-49-59-62-78-79-87-92-96-100-101-102-106-108-119-121-129-143-152-167-168-169-172-181-186-198-199-204-205-235-237-250-273-283-297-299-306-307-309-338-342-344-350-357-362-376-377-388
Hol	Holt Michael	376
	Holt William	27-31-67
Hom	Homas John	306
Hor	Horn Thomas	87
Hop	Hope Thomas	60
	Horton Joseph	77-119-157-257
	Horton James	146-178-324
	Horton Isaac	381-384-387
	Horton William	40-43-45-47-60-64-77-80-102-119-128-157-178-198-217-229-252-281-289-291-295-296-303-309-311-322-333-337-342-351-365-392-410
Hos	Hoskins George	146-167-176-211-217-230-289-310-322-329-330-331-333-336-337-342-351-365
	Hoskins	91-118-149-211-217-230-232-295-327
	Hoskins John	248-276-279-282-287-319-352-369-381
	Hoskins Elias	97
	Hostler Michael	32-45-50-53-97-100-101-102-103-201-211-289-322-281
	Hostler George	67
	Houston	6 7
	Houston Robert	1-9-44-128-157-213-217-308-347-366
How	Howard	7-16-44-46-93-97-187-211-241
Hug	Hughes Francis	147
Hun	Hunley William	238
	Hunter Maleun(?)	149
	Hutcherson Reuben	150-238
Hyn	Hynds Ridge	406
Ind	Indian Trace	28-111
	Indian Boundary	227
	Indian Creek	16-51-73-199-222
Ing	Ingam Puma?	375
	Indland	237-276-329-340-346-350-356-360
	Inglish John	2-4-11-19-20-40-43-65-67-71-73-123-129-136-149-198-200-201-203-205-207-224-247-259-302-308
	Inglish Richard	238
	Inglish Joshua	11-19-20-40-43-47-119-125-126-149-201-221-240
	Inglish Joseph	163
	Ingram Purnell	164
Ise	Iseley Christain	33-34-47-58-75-76-149-168-312-337
Isl	Island F Road	111-186
	Island Ford	9-12-16-21-22-28-45-72-76-79-87-88-107-111-186-278-290
Jac	Jack John F.	1-9-46-47-91-92-264-294-312
	Jackson Andrew	23
	Jackson Jacob	295

	Jackson Churchekl	143-197-198
	Jacksbrough	332-361
	Jacobs Jeremiah	77
	Jacobs Perry	78-173
	Jacobs Joseph	48
	Jacobs Zachariah	62
	Jacobs Edward	67
Jam	Jameson John	88-101-147-176
Jef	Jeffery Joseph	40-43-77-81-84-85-86-90-91-94-103-106-117-121-137-186-213-226-229-252-272-276-285-293-313-354-363-370-372
	Jeffery Jermiah	2-4-5-6-7-11-12-23-33-40-43-60-65-71-77-91-119-121-125-146-271-307-313-315-318-354-362-363
Jem	Jemmison John	21-53-60-62-86
Jen	Jenkins Aaron	48-75-78-115-119-125-127-167-176-183-248-259-263-280-281-289-322-323-377-387-388-404-408-410
	Jenkins Nancy	323
	Jennings Daniel	56-74-295-300
Joh	John Simpson Tan Yard	274
	Johnson Mill Branch	202
	Johnson Thompson	335
	Johnson Seth	197-198
	Johnson Curtis	383
	Johnson Noble	32
	Johnson John	50
	Johnson Andrew	173
	Johnson Craven	2-4-86-102-112-114-123-206-212-217-230-232-259-263-282-381-384-387-389-402
	Johnson Aquillia	9-10-22-27-31-32-33-38-81-84-85-90-91-92-94-108-111-119-127-160-164-165-166-176-170-180-197-198-202-210-211-214-237-242-302-357
	Johnson Kinza	1-5-7-21-45-48-49-60-86-88-91-118-156-176-185-187-225-232-340-345-386-389-396-399-402-404
	Johnson William	38-50-53-69-167-176-182-187-238-259-285-352
	Johnson Samuel	128-167-176-265-268-269-272-291-295-300-303-309-364-366-382-385-392-399-401
Jon	Jones Cloe	169
	Jones Thomas	6-258-275-276-312
	Jones Solomon W.	324
	Jones Lewis	12-61-173
	Jones Abraham	139-218-240-261-289-322-332-336-361-381-
	Jones Samuel	117
	Jones Moses	117
	Jones Mathew	67
	Jones Sugar	351-365-367-369-374
Joy	Joy Elijah	192
Jul	Julian John	63-117
	Julian George	65-71-86

K

Kee	Kee Sarah	118
	Kee Zachariah	203-206-210-259-263
Kea	Kean John	242
	Keaths Old Cabbin	180-211

	Keath Johnson	192
	Keath Necodemues	104-121
Kel	Kelcherside Thomas	259-264-268-269-271-273-275
	Kelley William	400
	Keeling William	137-199-200-213-263
	Keener Rodham	152
	Keeney Joseph	72-80-103-151-195-204-205-240-264-267-268-269-271-273-275-277-285-286-290-291-293-296-298-313-314-330-331-342-386-387-389-401-408-409
	Keeney Joseph Senr.	323
	Kenney Joseph Junr.	323
	Keentz Adam	63
	Keentz John	63-179
	Kentucky Line	308
Kill	Killerson George	34-45-59-
Kirb	Kirby Richard	375
	Kirby Francis	49-62
	Kirby John	4-8-9-10-28-31-33-37-39-48-50-55-74-84-86-87-88-100-102-104-109-111-117-122-124-127-137-144-147-151-160-168-170-183-187-202-203-204-205-207-209-219-220-240-244-253-261-263-269-271-273-277-284-290-293-295-297-298-315-317-321-330-334-344-349-352-359-387
Kir	Kirk Elijiah	243-257-293-314
	Kirk John Senr.	288
	Kirk John	243-257-259-313-332-408
	Kirkpatrick Alexander	23-235
	Kirkpatrick James	259-263-338-344-345-355
	Kirkpatrick John	235-255-261-295-299-311-338-344-355-370-372-377-384-393
Kin	Kincaid Thomas	5-11-25-50-53-69-81-87-96-100-101-111-149-322-329-331-333-336-337
	Kincaid Thomas Senr.	289
	Kincaid John	5
	King John	189-231-276-330-340-346
	King William	182-187-206-210-230
	King & Crozier	207-249-304
	King Wigton	231
	Kitchen John	57
Kno	Knox County Line	8-26-48-268-288-293
	Knox County Line	156-183-332-335-338-361
	Knox Road	183-332-361
	Knoxville	48-50-132-136-172-185-293
L		
Lak	Lakey Hugh	153-243-310-386
Lam	Lamb John	2-4-11-20-22-40-43-119-125-136-149-240
	Lamb Henry	178-179-202-204-205
	Lamor William	176-224-228-232-241-286-289-295-300-301-304-306-309-322-327-330-332-333-337-338-351-365-367-369-374-379-402-405
Lan	Lander Jacob	206-243-295-310
	Landrum Thomas	199
	Landville Richard	1-2-4-5-27
	Lanes Branch	247
	Lane John	406
	Lantrum Thomas	108
Las	Laswell David	185-186

Lat	Latham John	5
	Latham Samuel	67
Lau	Laughford Minon(?)	256-333-350
	Laurel Branch	351
Law	Lawe Aquilla	91
	Lawe Isaac	265-275-279-287-310-317-328-334-335-348-374-397-409
	Lawler John	81-84-85-110-114-117-121-122-123-124-131-202-203-205-207-223-228-232-236-237-276-279-282-284-287-310-315-318-348
	Lawler Levi	210-214-219
	Lawson William	402
	Lawson Robert	352-365-369-374
Lax	Laxton Thomas	380-396
Lay	Lay John	141-206-238-244-289
	Lay Joel	238
Laz	Lazell Lucreta	282
	Lazell Abner	164-202-247-274-282-286-294
Lea	Lea Lach T.	81
	Lea James	7-144-146
	Lea Robert	106
	Lea Luke Senr.	119-125
	Lea Luke Junr.	144
	Lea Luke	131-134
	Lea John	144
	Lea Lackey	12-114
	Lea William	1-7-27-28-31-32-34
	Lea Zachariah	27-28-31-34-37-77-84-85-112-131-143-144-146
	Lea David	65-76-81-84-96-100-101-131-143-145-150-152-194
	Lea Jesse	7-12-16-28-34-35-38-65-67-77
	Lea Joseph	31-32-65-70-86-102-103-119-125-131-134-136-149-163-176-185-223-230-236
	Leatch James	92-186-206-210-260-276-279-291-295-296-314-340-368-386-396-402
	Leatch Nancy	233
	Leatch John	62-80-275-293-295-296-297-298-309-317-337-351-358-389
	Lear George B.	181
Lef	Leftridge Jesse	173
Lib	Lieb John Junr.	283-365-386-396
	Leib John Senr.	289-306-329-351
	Leib John	27-31-32-39-48-62-66-125-127-129-131-144-164-165-168-170-171-174-193-197-204-205-216-239-268-272-287-291-299-303-316-318-322-348-388-392-410
	Leibs Mill	309-392-399
	Leib John Wm.	75-82-97-108-119-121
	Leinart Jacob	21-40-43-59-96-100-101-119-125-149-159-211-241-289-322-331-365-386-397-401-403-409
	Lender Jacob	340-346-381-408
	Lett Mathew H.	406
	Lewis John	67
	Leevis Stephen	69
	Leevis James	82
	Lewis William	141
	Lewis Thomas	141
Lic	Lick John	141
	Linder Jacob	14-26-55

	Linder Mary	14-55
	Linder Anthony	14
	Linder Andon	21
	Linder William	21
	Lenville Richard	12-28-29-31-33-34-37-38-48-51-67-73-75-91-96-101-107-109-111-122-123-125-127-128-130-134-136-177-199-200-201-214-230
	Lipe John	12-13-16-21-23
	Little Buffalo	139-140-199-218
	Lively John	91-173-381-384-387
Lol	Lollor John	72-112-167
Lon	Long John	45-68
	Long John Junr.	146
	Long John Senr.	146
	Long Robert	73-106-171
	Long Edward	118-392
	Long James	67
	Long Tobias	16-38-63-78-123-124-164-168-170
	Loonly David	129-130-131-133-147-159
	Loonly Peter	317
Lov	Love Charles	90-105-120-128-123-161-177-197-224-320
	Love Samuel	85-90
	Love John	9
	Love Ford	379
	Love Hazekiah	91-106-111-152-333-373
	Lovers Lain	9-21-22
	Loy John	386-396-403
Lua	Luallen Betsy	151
	Luallen Richard	11-19-20-37-50-103-119-121-125-160-161-163-172-187-194-204-205-207-242-283-297-329-362-405
Luc	Lucas Hezakiah	370
	Lucas Betsy	138
	Lucas & Parker	68
	Lucas Elizabeth	64-197-266-316
	Lucas George	352
Lum	Lumpkins Robert	316-403
	Lumby Benjamin	94
	Lush Andrew M.	75
Lyn	Lynn John	314-406
	Lynch John	224-243-245-255-259-309-310-343-351
	Lynch Jacob	351
	Lytle Thomas	243-310
M	Macey Robert	96-100-101-103-106-108-110-122-123-124-249-150-157-167-191-194-197-198-202-203-204-205-207-224-241-243-266-287-304-310-315-318-319-342-350-392-394
	Maccum Stephen	62
	Made James	167-191-194-204-215-
	Made Thomas	204-205
	Madison John H.	78-86-105-124-147-189-231-247-317
	Maloby John	252
	Mankins William	7-20-33-35-77-167-176-186-259
	Manley Ansell(Ancil)	229-235-276-279-292-351-365-367-369-374
	Manley Caleb	292

	Marcus Josiah	35-47-49-145
	Marcum Jacob	173
	Marrisons Capt.	3
	Marshall Samuel	301
	Markham Arthew	173
	Markham William	238-282
	Martin Capt.	317
	Martin Daniel	241-243-245-247-249-252-255-258-274-286-291-292-295-302-308-310
	Martin Jess	270-342
	Masterson	243
	Masterson John	88
	Masterson John P.	197-198-240-252-253-269-295-310-319-333-340-386
	Massengill(Massengale Massengile) Allen	180
	Massengale Alfred	105-227-238
	Massengile James	352
	Massengale Solomon	1-4-14-25-35-44-58-57-90-104-118-128-136-137-149-160-163-154-181-196-202-205-206-221-225-235-242-248
	Mattox Daniel	265
	Mattox Jacob	333
	Mattox John	286-333
	Maury County	155
	Maxviell David	79-87-97
	Maxwell George	199
	May David	191-194
	May Francis	117
	Mayo John	206
	Mayberry	307
	Mayberry-Ferry.	156-338
	Mayberry Francis	141-177-199-231-312
	Mayberry George	37
	Mayberry Isaac	272-286-289-295-300-301-304-319-322-332-350-352-365-378-399-408
	Mayson Edmund	224
	Mayson Nathaniel	173
	Mcampbell John M.	264-284-285
	Mc Intire John	255-271
Me	Medlin Capt.	11-29-35-50-57
	Medlin,(Madlin) Hardy	40-45-110-119-121-125-191-221-240-276-279-282-288-318-319-340-346-350-353-358-360-386-396
	Medlin Henry	404
	Medlin Richard	2-4-5-20-26-40-43-65-71-72-96-100-112-114-130-150-167-178-340-346-348-350-353-358-360
	Medlin Robert	11-19-20
	Medlin William	11-19-20-21-26-49-67-68
	Medlin William Owen	27-31-Meloney John
	Meloney John	67
	Menefee John	8-3-9-232
	Meneffs(Menefee) Mill	56-185-
	Meneffee Thomas	117-224-228-232-276-279-284-285-291-293-295-298-299-302-303-307
	Meredith Frederick	67
	Miller Frederick	2-4-8-9-11-19-28-29-53-54-55-58-61-157
	Millers-Ford	139-212
	Miller Hugh	35

Mo	Miller John	26-28-409
	MillsAjays	139
	Mills Molley	370
	Montgomery Col.	41-76
	Montgomery Hugh	2-4-7-12-13-16-27-28-31-34-37-40-45-48-49-50-58-63-64-71-81-90-94-96-97-98-100-102-107-109-114-117-118-120-121-122-127-128-130-133-134-136-143-145-148-150-159-163-164-168-171-172-176-177-178-179-181-182-187-189-190-193-194-196-200-201-221-225-228-230-242-246-288-290-292-295-298-299-304-311-367-372-378
	Montgomery Lemonerl	261
	Montgomery P.	317
	Morris Absplom	33-191-194-234
	Morris Capt.	111-127-161-
	Morris Sherdrick	2-4-12-28-50-65-67-73-76-80-105-112-114-117-119-128-131-132-136-169-171-176-205-220
	Morrison William	170
	Morgan Milly	137
	Moore Joseph	4-50-53-69-81-84-85-87-104-243-272-310-338
	Moore William	61
	Morse Reuben	139-195
	Morton(Mortin) Daniel	119-131-159-173
	Morton James	161-173
	Morton Quin	154-156-276-279-283-301-303-314-324-329-351-357-358-360-365-370-374-386-387-397-402-404
	Moss Marcelles	190-191
	Moss Reuben	79-191
	Moser Adam	408
	Moser Abraham	351-381
	Mosers Jacob	273-288-289-313-322-329-330-333-337-367-391-409
	Moser Mill	272-409
	Moser Nicholas	223-228-276-323-340
	Moser Robert	392
Mu	Murrays(Murrah) James	156-199
	Murray William H.	3-51-65-67-73-116-338
	Murphy John	216
	Murphy-Road	12-16-72
	Murphy William	6-7-10-77-216
Mc	Mc Adoo John	2-4-5-20-35-46-50-53-79-81-84-85-87-112-114-115-131-143-167-178-179-181-189-190-201-224-228-232-236-259-264-279-281-286-295-300-301-304-306-309-310-317-332-358-359-362-363-374-376-379-396-399-401
	Mc Amey(McAmy) Capt.	11-20-29-35-58
	Mc Amey John	1-8-11-16-23-24-29-43-50-56
	Mc Amey(McAmy) John	58-62
	McAmey Robert	27-35
	Mc Amy William	1-4-6-9-13-23-27-31-33-34-38-45-47-49-50-57-71
	Mc Anelly Littleberry	238
Mc B	Mc Bird John	7-21-43-72-81-84-85-92-112-114-122-123-124-126-158-178
	Mc Bird Pleasant	273-276-279-288-318-319-408-409
	Mc Bird Thomas	87
	Mc Bird William	140
	Mc Bride John	206-245-247

Page 22

	Mc Campbell John	287-324-341-359-388-390
	Mc Ampbell Thomas	119-125 Mc C
	Mc Commas (Mc Commess) Stephen	87-151-186-247-302-310
	Mc Coy(Mc Kay) Annanias	90-120
	Mc Coy Samuel	81-84-101-110-121-130-138-164-166-180-219-220-221-233-271-273-277-402-403-406
	Mc Coy Sequire	110
	Mc Cracken John	216-223
	Mc Daniel Archibald	78-145-159-206-210-233-240-241
	Mc Entire (Mc Intire) John	35-46-62-116-119-129-130-141-147-159-177-195-290-311-331-402
	Mc Entire John F.	273-314-319-337-344-370
	Mc Entire John Junr.	248-320-391
	Mc Entire John Sen.	233-236-241-248-255
	Mc Entire Mololine	381-384-387
	Mc Farland George	141-238
	Mc Farland James	106-150-238
Mc G	Mc Ghee James	144-240-307
	Mc Ghee William	188
	Mc Graw Elizabeth	274
	Mc Graw Michael	343
	Mc Griff Thomas	67
	Mc Guire William	51-67-73-240
Mc K	Mc Kamey Andrew	116-167-180-192-194-223-228-259-364-289-310-322-351-365-368-369-386-396-401-403-409
	Mc Kameys Bridge	276
	Mc Kamey Capt.	118-166-188
	Mc Kamey Henry	191
	Mc Kamey John	71-77-84-100-135-147-153-170-180-191-194-223-233-237-258-259-276-279-287-289-312-315-318-366
	Mc Kamey Robert	161-179-197
	Mc Kamey William	72-80-82-84-88-89-94-100-102-117-118-122-123-125-133-134-137-143-145-148-151-152-160-166-168-169-176-177-178-179-181-182-185-189-190-194-196-210-214-218-219-222-223-228-237-241-242-243-245-255-256-257-261-267-268-271-274-275-282-284-287-291-293-295-303-306-307-308-309-310-311-313-319-328-331-346-351-353-356-357-358-360-365-367-376-383-384-386-389-390-391-396-399-400-401-409
	Mc Kenney Henry	194-229-291-295-296-298-302-308
	Mc Kenley Joseph	101-143-300-
	Mc Kenley Samuel	77-191
	Mc Krakin(Mc Crackin) James	11-19-92-96-100-101-102-103-106-108-119-125-228-232-237-241
	Mc Krakin John	216-223
	Mc Kay(Mc Coy)? Samuel	195-240-264-267-269-273-317-329-332-334-346-348-361-371-409
	Mclellan John	32-128-135-
	Mc lung Charles	32-104-121-188-205-308-397-398
	Mc Mahan Barnard	231
	Mc Mullin Joseph	160
	Mc Murry James	72-94
	Mc Nutt- Ford	277

Mc Nutt James	4-17-81-84-85-119-124-131-134-136-139-157-212-351
Mc Affray Terence	47
Mc Peters Joseph	48-62-76-91-95-102-103-106-145-155
Mc Wharters Ferry	39-
Mc Wharter James S.	309-319-344-363
Mc Wharter John	27-31-39-66-123-131-124-146-183-197-198-203-214-283-295-316-318-320-324-329-353-360-377-386-402-404
Mc Whorter Lain	400
Mc Whorter Moses	2-4-11-17-19-20-50-53-63-79-81-84-85-106-108-115-116-149-156-173-179-167-168-170-181-182-187-198-233-272-275-286-289-307-322-325-332-338-345-351-352-365-396-402
Mc Whorter Samuel	299

N

Neel William	144
Neely Isaac	351
Nemo David	34
New * River	396
Newman John	173
Nickason Jeremiah	408
Noble (Nobles) David	75-92-276-279-282-288-314-319-334-386-408
Nobles Lewis	35
Noble William	75-91-92-106-108-131-250-278-409
Noel John	215
Noel Michalas	215
Nolurtson James	374
Norma Henry	289-295-300
Norman Aron	276-279-289-322-330-337-342
Norman Eli	56-74
Norman Henry	40-43-56-74-81-84-85-90-91-94-158-322-329-331-333-336-337-340-342-408
Norman Isaac	40-43-48-56-74-88-119-125-183-191-194-198-202-203-205-207-240-259-263-289-301-333-352-365
Norton John H.	328
North- Baranch	190-194
North Carolina	61-91-95-
Norris Lemuel	173
Norris Samuel	121-180
Nunnery Henry	9-23-105

O

Oak- Ridge	
Oakes Isaac	238-383-408
Oliver Capt.	334
Oliver Charles	91-128-153-258-289-304-312-322-328-337-386-363-396
Oliver Douglas	53-63-119-124-125-128-131-134-135-136-149-153-164-180-189-201-211-229-232-234-236-240-252-261-263-267-273-286-288-290-291-297-300-304-305-306-307-328-331-363-366-368-373-381-396-397
Oliver Lunsford	135-210-258-281-295-305-317-340-346
Osborne Squire	282
Overtone Joseph	179-295-300-313-335-366-406
Owens David	259-311-330

	Owen William	238
	Owen Willis	173
P		
	Pain Robert H.	101
	Bain Thomas H.	152-172-201-238-284-285-319-326-343
	Pankey Edward	59-146
	Pankey James	86-92-103-137
	Pankey Smith	368
	Pankin Stephen	67-176-186
	Parks Benjamin C.	384
	Parks Capt.	397
	Parks James	154
	Parks John	20-40-43-55-65-112-114-118-130-131-143-185-210-229-259-264-271-283-294-328-345-366-369-382-388-408
	Parks William	154
	Parker Benjamin C.	21-68-105-181-211-217-219-240-249-251-253-255-271-272-273-279-282-283-286-292-293-295-296-306-311-315-318-319-332-341-346-356
	Parker Richard	150-342
	Parsons Robert	26
	Parsons Thomas	26-106-154-159-241
	Parson William	26
	Pate Nathon	173
	Patterson James	65-71
	Patterson John	389
	Patterson William	20-27-35-76-86-102-168-170-171-176-301
	Pawpaw	133
	Paw paw- Ford	111
Pe	Peak(Peek) Jacob	71-77-91-108-119-125-145-149-179-191-194-201-211-223-228-241-259-276-279-287-292-328-333-346-397-398
	Peak(Peek) Joseph	9-11-20-23-65
	Peak(Peek) Zacharial	259-310
	Perry George	290-331-362
	Peery James	92
	Peery John	179-301-303-304-305-307-314-340-346-350-353-356-358
	Perry Robert	340-346
	Pepper James	107-158-189-232-341-359
	Peters Henry	149-215-295-300-381-384-387
	Peters Tobias	72-111-117-121-131-143-276-279-282-287-288-315-319-352-365
	Petty John	150
	Petty Witson	150
	Philips Robert	141
	Philips Thomas	59-75
	Philpot Isaac	179
	Philpot Richard	219-220
	Pilot-Knob	222
	Pine - Ridg	87-185-186-187-326
	Poages Encampment	247
	Poore Peter	195-342
	Pol Lindsey	171
	Pollock John	179-181
	Pollock Robert	9-11-14-29-37-40-53-58-62-71-75-78-80-90-92-106-202-206-207-210
	Pollock William	141

	Poplar- Creek	59-77-186-320-344-391
	Porter James	2-9-17-22-38-45-65-71-75-77-78-80-124-134-139-161-182-187-256-401
	Portwood Page	2-4-5-8-35-37-40-55-61-86-90-91-92-94-112-114-149-167-169-179-187-203-206-210-235-257-266-303-374-375-378-393-398-403-408
	Portwood James	375
	Portwood John	375
	Portwood Micajah	375
	Potter Benjamin	400
	Potter Vsary (?)	187
	Powells - River	11-12-14-15-28-51-72-73-139-195-200-221-270
	Powells - Valley	14-26-28-40-51-79-103-129-139-158-195-200-201-207-222
	Powells Valley Road	191-193-314-326-351-395
	Prett Thomas	67
	Prior Samuel	381-384-387
	Pruett Charles	126-168-169-193-203-204-207-382
	Pruett James	197
	Pruett Gabriel	137
	Puckett Claiborn	141-173-192
	Puckett Drury	37-233
	Puckett James D.	20-21-38-88-115-118-120-134-144-146
	Puckett(Pecket) Stephen	67
	Purdon John	116-119-147-159-177-241
Q		
	Queener Daniel	164-179-182-187-190-308
	Queener Jacob	149-164-206-252-308
R		
	Raccoon - Valley	183-184-185-216-236-314
	Ragland Britain	71-77-131-143-
	Ragland Reuben	11-19-20-21-35-40-50-53-92-97-130-145-148-206-210-214-266
	Ragland William	10-26-40-43-55-65-71-131-143-229-240-289-322-330-333-337-402
	Ragsdale Britton	65-110-112-114-121-145-248-367-391
	Rains John	45-47-199-370
	Rains Jonathan	55
	Rains Newman	177
	Rains William	199
	Rams Isaac	403
	Ramsay Andrew	32
	Ramsay George	23-36-47-59-62-77-87-139
	Ramsay James	141
	Ranly George	23
Re	Ready(Reedy) Isaac	192-194
	Ready Nicholas	191-194-221-222-240-242
	Ready(Reedy) Shedrack	11-14-19-51-79-108-117-148-181-192-200-209-220-222
	Rector John	295-300-301-304-306-311-351-365-367-374
	Rector Landon	84-116
	Rector W. M.	81
	Reed - Branch	133-202
	Reed Elizabeth	134-357
	Reed John	173

	Reed Thomas	350
	Reed William	37-72-357
	Reins Henry	48-57-77
	Reynolds Margaret	219
	Reynolds Thomas	386-396-401-403-409
	Reynolds Furney	238
	Rhea Jacob	78
	Rhea John	54-156-170-338-402
	Rice Thomas	67
	Rich Hallow	61-72
	Richards Lewis	45-243-248-257-261-310
	Ridenour Henry	61
	Ridenour John	20-96-100-115-157-158-221-222-245-249-301-332-261
	Ridenour John Senr.	51-61-101-408
	Ridenour Joseph	218
	Ridenours - Ferry	79
	Ridenour Martin	61-212-245-252-335-368
	Rippeto William	22-40-43-45-46-47
	Rippetoes(Rippetoes)William 9-	
Ro	Roan - County	10-289
	Roan - County line	335
	Robbins Capt.	11-29-35-50-63
	Robbins Isaac	48-78-91-130-147-400
	Robbins John	104-122-126
	Robbins Michael	90-198-410
	Robbins William	192
	Roberson Charles	305
	Robertson Carnelius	238
	Robertson Henry	189
	Robertson James	67-136-147-352-365-367-369-373
	Robertson(Roberson) Joseph	2-77-112-114-119-148-184-307
	Robertson(Roberson) Stephen	67-68
	Robertson(Roberson) William	9-21-22-40-43-46-48-49-65-71-96-100-101-118-124-134-180-201-292
	Robbinson William	211-225-248-252
	Roberts Archibald	312
	Roberts Benjamin	152
	Roberts Collins	153
	Roberts James	238
	Roberts John	152.
	Roberts Moses	78-170-271-340-346-366-393
	Roberts Nathan	12-23-25-35-40-62-78-117-198
	Roberts Reuben	45-47-75-90-91-94-116-119-130-147-164-165-171-176-186-187-193-195-199-217-229-255-259-283-284-287-309-327-332
	Roberts Robert	272
	Rogers James	163-346
	Rogers Joseph	198
	Ross Anguis	27-31-32-96-100-108
	Ross James	178
	Ross Robert	218-240-333
	Rosses - Spring	129

		Roysdon Jess	10-14-54-56-95-105-119-195-207-222-252-268-271-274-275-289-299-309-314-327-337-341-359-366
		Roysdon Robert	117-156-340-346
		Ruben Williams- Sprang branch 210
		Ruckman Isaiah	34-61
		Russell Bryel	300
		Russell Henry	2-4-5-20-40-43-65-71-110-112-114-121-131-143-167-179-182-187-188-196-206-210-214-219-220-404
		Russell James	300
		Russell John	169
		Russell William	160-168-169-192-210-219-220-295-300-304-307-311-351-365-367-369-373-374-408
		Rutheyford James	76-91-102-106
		Ryan Harris	27-28-31-32-54-85-119-125-131-134-136-216-
		Ryan John	141-173
		Ryan William	26-59
S			
	Sa	Sadler Fredrick	21-181-279
		Sallar Levi	206
		Salter Robert	55
		Sampson David	275
		Sartin David	179-250-233
		Sartin John	28-33-48-56-97-121-172-266-280-283-309-316-329-334-364-392
		Sartin Nancy	250
		Sartin Right	250
		Sartin Rosey	250
	Sc	Scarbra(Scarbrough) David 329-330-331-333-335-336-337-342
		Scarbro James	40-43-44-62-72-96-101-107-108-110-111-121-128-131-134-135-143-147-150-160-164-176-178-180-291-301-302-330-335-356-358
		Scarbro John	180-293-296-298
		Scarbro Milley	106
		Scarbro Robert	159
		Scarbro William	116-131-133-134-145-152-159-164-177-180-322-329-331-333-335-336-337
		Scarbrough David	289
		Scarbroughs - Ferry 62-135-202
		Scarbrough James	40-5-6-8-22-35-72-191-202-210-214-219-223-234-237-243-245-248-252-254-255-263-275-357-358
		Scarbrough John 240
		Scarbrough Robert 241-244-
		Scarbrough William 215-224-228-232-241-275-289-385
		Scoggins Jonas	238-271
		Scott Edward	236-301
		Scruggs John	8-20-25-27-31-32-49-65-71-77-87-107-110-138-147-156-179-217-224-228-243-248-252-257-288-310-315-316-332-347-351-354-357-362-365-372-382-376-401-403-404
	Se	Sears James	344-345
		Severs -- County	122
		Severs(Sevoers) John 101-211
		Sevrs Philip	372
		Severs(Sevors) William 48-68-112-114-123-124-186-191-194-204-205-207-240-276-279-282-315-316-318-319-340-346-350-356-358-400

	Seward John	333
	Seward William	261-295-315-318-352
Sh	Shannon Andrew	335
	Sharp Aaron	149-157-179-212-224-228-232-236-243-310
	Sharp Benjamin	144
	Sharp Conrad	27-54-157-195-212
	Sharp George	199-218-361
	Sharp Henry	119-125-176-199-213-
	Sharp Henry Senr.	55-65-71-77-78-137
	Sharp Jacob	296-310
	Sharp John	44-50-53-153-182-190-332-361
	Sharp Joseph	2-4-5-38-50-51-53-67-73-81-84-96-100-101-105-119-131-143-144-145-155-152-201-223-228
	Sharp Richard	69
	Sharp - Station	20
	Sharp Thomas	168
	Sharp William	176-206-213-224-232-237-276-277-323-240-345-351-361-386-396
	Shelly Thomas	166-190-205
	Shelton(Shelters) James	160
	Shelton(Shelters) George	27-31-110-138-149-150-230-240-273-280-288-342-386-396-400
	Shelton Gobriel	68
	Shelton Palaliah	259
	Shinliver Charles	21-27-31-32-65-71-75-86-102-156-168-178-179-181-187-190-206-210-211-219-230-230-259-363279-326-331-351-365-386-396-401-403-404
	Shoemake(Shoemaker) David	163
	Shoemake(Shoemaker) Elizabeth	63
	Shoemaker(Shoemake) Robert	45-67
	Shoemaker(Shoemake) Thomas	173
	Shoemaker William	134
Si	Siler(Silor) John	160-163-165-217-227-252-254-295-
	Silvedge Milhael	26-59-141
	Silvey William	67
	Simmons John	324-361
	Simpson George	311
	Simpson John	167-179-182-187-190-197
	Sinclair(Sindair) Charles	206-210-240-243-268-269-291-293-298-310-341-351-359-365-368-370-373
	Sinclair John	110
	Sinclair Joseph	3-4-5-6-9-11-13-23-24-25-26-28-29-34-38-39-40-43-45-47-49-53-61-64-65-71-73-84-90-98-100-102-104-107-108-109-116-117-118-120-121-122-123-124-128-130-131-133-134-136-137-144-147-151-158-160-162-163-168-170-171-177-179-181-187-190-193-198-202-203-204-205-214-218-222-224-231-236-241-243-251-252-269-279-286-287-288-291-292-295-296-297-298-303-304-306-307-323-338-353-356-357-358-362-365-367-368-369-370-374-381-383-384-392-396-409
	Sinclair Robert	71-77-81-112-114-115-131-143-144-150-152-247-299-302
Sl	Slover Aron	162-223-249-351-365-369-374-386-396-
	Slover John	159

Sm	Smith Genl. Benj.	37-38
	Smith James	34-165-168-169-177-244
	Smith John	173
	Smith Joseph	20-67-184
	Smith Lathan(Layton)	11-20-50-53-56-74-81-84-85-90-91-92-149-185-259-263
	Smith Richard	173
	Smith Robert	119-179-307-319-
	Smith Samuel	173
	Smith Thomas	50-53-59-62-72-125-192
	Smith William	212
	Smythe Thomas	119
Sn	Snoderly John	143-148
	Southerland(Southerlin)	
	Southerlands - Ferry	377
	Southerland George	261-309-344-357-386-389
	Southerland John	164-183-185-216-218-223-233-258-284-285-295-307-312-314-324-326-343-355-356-377-383-
	Southerland John Junr.	361
Sp	Spencer John	179-197-206
	Spessard John	21-96-100-101-129-187-211-218-230-271-273-326-331-351-408-409
St	Standfer Abraham	256
	Standefers - Branch	211
	Standefer Israel	21-40-43-202-232-375-385-393-401
	Standefer James	61-104-146-202-205
	Standefer Jereal	7
	Standefers - lane	276
	Standefer Samuel	243-391-373-374-310-370
	Standefer William	4-6-9-11-13-16-21-23-24-31-48-49-62-63-71-79-100-107-108-120-125-135-143-153-160-154-166-168-178-179-180-201-202-203-204-223-227-225-228-236-237-258-304-312-328-340-346-347-397
	Standoford	223
	Stanley Garland	233-250-297-306
	Stanley Harris	149
	Stanley Nathan	108-179
	Stanley Reuben	91-92
	Stanley Rhodes	186-240-276-279-290-330-351-381-395-405-408
	State of Virginia	144
	Steekley Chrisley	265
	Steeley George	265
	Steels Capt.	11-29-35-50-164-166
	Steele George	106-136-146-202-207
	Stephens Godson	67
	Stephen Lewis	106-138-149-150-181-187-280-313
	Stephenson Edward	27-31-32-106-144
	Stewart(Steward) Andrew	156-313-369-390-404
	Stewart(Stuart) James	275-288-289-297-314-322-369-372-375-393-401-402
	Stewart(Stuart) John	119-124-131-136-145-168-178-190-283-287-318-362-400
	Steuart(Steward) William	307
	Still George	378
	Still James	340-346
	Still Trulman	81-340-347-399
	Stinnett Isham	40-43-45-47-55-71-131-143-144

	Stinnett William	5
	Stirman Jennima	81
	Strader Jacob	11-19-25-26-112-114-117-122-133-143-148-223-228-232-236-237-241-
	Strader William	118
	Strong John	255-259
	Stone David	193
	Stone John	134-159-163-190-240-257-269
	Stone William	197-198
	Stoncipher Michail	386-396-397
	Sugar - Hallow	221
	Sullins Nathan	188
	Sullins Zackareah	188
	Sutton Robert	199
	Swanson Dewsey	68
	Swanson Gordon	68
	Swanson Mary	68
	Swanson Mildred	68
	Swanson Sarah	68
	Swaggerty Abraham	357
	Sweeton John	103
	Sweeton Robert	238
	Sweeton William	69
	Sycamore - Spring	129
	Sylor John	260
Slaves	Slave Alse	35
	" Daniel	375
	" Diel	27
	" Frank	361
	" Hanna	372
	" Isbell	35
	" Jacob	316
	" James	35
	" Jess	316
	" Jim	233
	" Lige	352
	" Patty	160-233
	" Peter	383
	" Polly	160
	" Same	356
	" Seen	270
	" Seal	316-334
	" Spencer	372
	" Wenn	316
Ta		
	Tan Vats	78-88-314
	Tate William	155
	Taylor Euan	150
	Taylor Henry	119-131-136
	Taylor Isaac	28
	Taylor James	44-56-78-96-100-101-102-103-106-108-117-119-125-131-134-158-162-191-194-278-314-319-331-359-408-409
	Taylor John	278-314-351-356-368-369
	Taylor Walter	314-351-394-400

	Teague(Tleague) William	238-408
	Terry Capt.	82
	Terry John	24-90-91-139-146-159-160-176-190-202-206-210-230-259-264-267-340
	Terry Joseph	45-59
	Terry Samuel	39-92-179
	Testament William	393
Th	Thacker Alias	81
	Therman Philip	163-164-168-169-171
	Thomas Christopher	238
	Thomas James	45-144-183-184
	Thomas John	17-93-122-123-124-180-206-210-241-269
	Thomas William	158
	Thompson John	360-368-371-373
	Thompson Joseph Terry	251
	Thompson William	104-110-131-137-138-149-179-180-191-194-224-228-232-236-237-245-249-260-263-295-300-313-314-332-335-359-360-361
	Thornberry Richard	284-351-365-637-369-372-374-385-389
Ti	Tilman Tobias	20-119-125-131-134-136-244
	Timlett Mary	60-62
	Tipton Samuel	400
	Tipton Shedrick	48-163-198-259-264-275-408
	Tobery Thomas	149
	Tolbert Eli	346
	Tovera Dorcas	302
	Tovera Jane	302
	Tovera John	153-279-302-307-384-370-371-373-381-384-387
	Tovera Philip	153
	Tovera Robert	302
	Tovera Thomas	115-191-208-240-245-248-307
	Trace Philip	23-61
	Trimble James	154-218-274-277-303-314-317-337-344-374
	Tudor Harris	206-210-214-218-220
	Tunnell Capt.	326
	Tunnell James	153
	Tunnell John	62-149-153-168-170-191-194-213-259-269-330-340-346-353-360-386-396
	Tunnell Robert	272-276-289-322-348
	Tunnell William	86-91-94-103-125-140-186-317-318-382
	Tunnell William Junr.	81-84-85-119-295-297-298-310-365-386-396
	Tunnell William Senr.	36-60-65-71-86-103-140-223-237-351
	Turner George	406
U		
	Underwood Capt.	166
	Underwood James	156-165-243-286-297-303-310-315-316-338-410
	Underwood John	1-4-13-24-31-51-53-67-68-71-78-80-81-84-100-104-109-114-122-125-126-140-141-143-154-162-173-174-176-178-191-192-193-194-195-207-209-214-215-216-234-243-266-267-279-294-298-299-300-306-310-316-320-322-326-344-345-346-347-349-352-362-363-364-365-367-372-375-376-379-381-389-390-391-396-407

Underwood William	2-4-9-11-13-15-19-26-28-29-35-37-43-45-49-50-61-63-65-71-79-80-81-96-97-98-100-102-104-107-108-110-121-122-123-124-132-139-147-151-168-170-171-174-179-180-181-187-190-193-196-197-198-202-203-204-205-207-213-214-218-219-220-222-231-232-234-236-237-238-241-245-248-249-251-252-256-257-258-263-264-267-269-271-273-277-278-286-287-288-291-293-295-296-297-298-303-304-305-306-308-309-311-313-315-318-319-321-322-326-328-331-332-334-342-344-345-349-350-356-357-360-361-362-363-368-369-370-384-391-400-401-402-403-406-408-409
Umstead John	24-37-47-143-195-268
Upton David	164
Ussery Robert	37
Ussery Samuel	25-37-75-78
Ussery Thomas	54
Ussery William	167-176-185

V

Valley - Mill	379
Valley - Road	138-179-183-187-315-342
Vance Thomas	265
Vanay Jesse	16-58-65-147-150-151
Vanay Jonathan	173
Vanderpool John	200
Vaught Andrew	141
Vaugn Edmund	198
Virginia State of	144
Virginia Court House	189
Vernon Isaac	150
Vowell Manapage(Manpage)	33-45-50-53-115-122-127-145-152-160-220-242-275-325-336

W

Wallace John	87-107-129-131-138-143-147-150-152-167-179-182-187-190-240-271-273-295-300-301-305-309
Wallace John Senr.	314
Wallace - Mill	399
Wallan John	301-303
Walling - Bridge	7-9
Walls John	151
Walker George	126
Walker Polly	313-390
Walker Thomas	58-117-256-282-306-309-329
Walnut - Cave	12-16-51-73-76-87-90-107-129-290-299-308-320
Wamock Jesse	37
Warren Benjamin T.	170-171-297-303
Warren John	289-322-330-331-333-336-337-391
Warren Robert	54-150-168-179-195-202-205-213-307-366
Warwick John	28-138-149-276-279-282-288-286-287-288-313-315-318-319-342-398-400-406-409
Warwicks Meetin house	138-149-150-270
Warick Willie	406
Warwick Wiley	277

	Wasson Elisha	6-67
	Watker West	154
	Watson Josiah	32-68
We	Webb John	155
	Webb Mosely	237
	Wear Robert	122
	Weaver Jacob	223-228-244-289-322-342-
	Weaver Joseph	2
	Weeks Charles	236-257-258
	Wenningham John	78
	Wheeler Benjamin	105-128-161-177-224
	Wheeler Polly	348
	Wheeler Thomas	246-247-291-292-293-298-302-308
	White Andrew	198-219
	White Daniel	2-16-40-96-100-101-103-149-163-192-202-214-233-234
	White Hugh L.	231
	White Joel	62
	White & Lynch	253-281-337-339-353-373-378
	White Moses	242
	White - Oak	312
	White Sampson	201
	White Thorn	133
	Whithead William	109
	Whitman Jacob	139-167-178-179-181-190-191
	Whitton Elijah	130-197-266-
	Whitton Robert	26-136-179-180
	Whitton William	102-103-110-121
	Whitreal William	73-146
	Whorton Isaac	352
Wi	Widener Lewis	68
	Widow Wilsons	247
	Wildon Jess	297
	Wildon John	151-159-163-164-168-170-171-241-285-292-343
	Willhite(Willhights) Conright(Conrite)	27-28-31-32-35-51-81-84-85-86-112-119-125-127-130-192-199-222-229
	Willhite Conrad	173
	Willhite Elijah	173
	Willhite Elizabeth	229
	Willhite Ezekiel	173
	Willhite Simon	229
	Williams Alexander	289-322-330-333-337-342-348
	Williams Amby	126
	Williams Benjamin	49
	Williams David	67
	Williams Edward	149-240-260-263-270-271-293-296-298-386
	Williams Evan	173
	Williams James	126-149
	Williams John	67-85-141
	Williams Mathias	230-290
	Williams - Ridge	187
	Williams Ruben	116-167-176-229-236-258-291-295-296-298-312-328-351-365-386-396-408
	Williams Ruben Spring	210-281
	Williams Spring	22-77-139

	William Standefers - lane	276
	Williams Thomas	377-381
	Williams William	265-310
	Willing Thomas	311
	Willis Owen	55
	Wilkinor John	17
	Wilson Benjamin	192
	Wilson Capt.	11-29-35-50-63-106
	Wilson David	288-383
	Wilson Jess	108-179-183-187-241-341-364
	Wilson Nancy	180
	Wilson Samuel	34-40-43-61-76-90-106-122-234-240-246
	Wilson Saml. Senr.	96-100-158
	Wilson Thomas	8-40-48-65-71-85-88-140-169-183-185-203-206-240
	Wilsons Widow	302
	Wime Martha	162
	Winton Moss	374
	Winters Moses	236
	Wisdom(Wisdon) James	248-311
	Witson Thomas	314-361-383
	Woods Benjamin	375
	Woods John	238
	Woods Mathew	238
	Woods Obediah	5-6-62-81-84-85-102-103-120-122-123-124-204-205-217-229-243-268-269-283-310-409
	Woods Sampson	5-14-176-289-322-329-331-333-336-337-342
	Woods William	56-141
	Woods Young	397
	Wolls John	336
	Womack Cloe	37
	Worthington Conright	4-5-12-
	Worthington George	24
	Worthington James	60-126-191-194-215-237-255-259-264-268-269-270-275-297-309-315-319-356-357-368-409
	Worthington Samuel	115-119-124-125-126-164-186-215-216-258-270-312-340-346-350-356-358-360-368
	Worthington Samuel Junr.	62-383
	Worthington Samuel Senr.	2-4-5-7-12-22-23-35-36-40-43-60-62-65-71-77-87-110-180-305-373
	Worthington Thomas	11-23-25-38-115-116-146-148-164-223-228-295-300-368
	Worthington William	368
	Wright Thomas	323
	Wright William	323-370-376-390
	Wyatt Joseph	197
	Wyatt Samuel	259-263
	Wyatt William	139-153-197-198-200-203-205-210-215-256-281-300-325
X		
Y	Young Edward	45
	Young Henry	35-123-124-129
	Young Robert	7-33
Z		

Anderson County Court Record, 1801 - 1809.

1 English for 320 acres of land was proved in open Court by Spencer Graham one of the subscribing witnesses List as registered.

From Samuel Curry to Richard Lendville for 500 acres of land was proved in open court by Thomas Campbell the subscribing witnesses. Let it be registered.

Received the acknowledgment of a conveyance from Solomn Massengale to John Underwood in open court for 100 acres of land. Let it be registered. W. John Finley Jack was then unanmously appointed Solicitor for the County of Anderson and take the necessary oaths.

W. Joseph Grayson was unanimously appointed Cornor for Anderson County and offered Robert Houston and John Menefee as his securties who were received by the court. W. Grayson then took the necessary oaths.

The court then proceeded to elect a register and it appeared on counting out the votes that Kenza Johnson was duly elected, who offered William McDrug and John Love as his securties, who were approved by the Court. He then took the necessary oaths.

The Court then proceeded to elect a ranger and it appeared on counting out the costs that John McArny was duly elected who offers Robert Houston and William McArny as his securties that were approved of by the Court then Adjourned till Tomorrow 9 o'clock.

2 Wednesday 16th Dec. 1801 ---

The Court met - present James Grant, Hugh Montgomery, William Underwood, & Frederick Miller.

Ordered that Hugh Montgomery Esquire have & Brand record. Which is for cattle a cut in right ear and the left ear a whole crop and a slit, the right ear an half crop and slit. Hogs and sheep the same ear marks as cattle. Horses branded thus .

Ordered that William Mays M. Clung be appointed constable for Captain Englands Company, who offered Joseph Denham & Moses McWhirter his securties who were received by the court. He was then qualified.

Ordered that George Grimes be appointed constable for Captain Grahams company who offered Joseph Denham Seivor and Daniel White as his securties, who were approved of by the court. He then took the necesary oaths.

The Court appointed the following persons as jurors to March term 1802.

1 James McNutt
2 James Abott
3 Henry Russell
4 Richard McEntire
5 John Gallaher
6 Spencer Graham
7 Conright Willhight
8 Richard Lendville
9 Thomas Campbell
10 Rolly Duncan
11 Nathaniel Davis
12 John Day
13 Majes McWhoeter
14 John McAdoo
15 Joseph Moore
16 James Pater
17 Joseph Gallaher
18 Samuel Worthington
19 Jacob Hagler
20 Craven Johnson
21 Henry Farmer
22 Jermiah Jeffery
23 Nathan Hale
24 James Scarbrough
25 Shadrack Morris
26 John English
27 Joseph Sharp
28 John Laent
29 Caleb Friby
30 Page Partwood.

3 Ordered that James Adkins be appointed constable for Captain Morrisons Company who offered William H. Murray & Jesse Vancy as his securties who were approved of by the court. He then took the necessary oaths.

  Ordered that William Mays McClung be constable to wait on the court.

  Joseph Sinclair acknowledged a Bill of sale to Ebecnezor Bryam for a negro girl, which was ordered to be recorded.

  William H. Murray was qualified as deputy sheriff for Anderson County. The Court then Adjourned until Court in Course

          James Grant chairman.

4 At a court begun and held for the county of Anderson at the house of Joseph Denham Sevior on the second Monday of March in the year of our Lord 1802.

      Present.

Hugh Montgomery	Wm. Standep
John Kerby	Frederick Miller
Wm. McAiny	Wm. Underwood
Joseph Sinclair	Solomn Massengale
James Butler	

  John Underwood Esquire high sheriff of the county of Anderson returns that he has executed the venire facias on the following persons (viz.)

1	James McNutt	16	James Potter
2	James Abott	17	Joseph Gallaher
3	Henry Russell	18	Saml. Worthington
4	Richard Medlin	19	Craven Johnson
5	John Gallaher	20	Henry Farmer
6	Spencer Graham	21	Jeremiah Jeffery
7	Conright Willhight	22	Nathan Hale
8	Richard Lendville	23	James Scarbrough
9	Thomas Campbell	24	Shadrach Morris
10	Polly Duncan	25	John English
11	Nathaniel Davis	26	Joseph Sharp
12	John Day	27	John Crab
13	Mosses McWharter	28	Calex Freley
14	John Maccadoo	29	Page Partwood
15	Joseph Moore	30	Jacob Hagler - not found

of whom the following are appointed Grand Jurors. (viz.)

5

1	John Maccadoo (foreman)	8	Jeremiah Jeffery
2	Richard Medlin	9	Conright Willhight
3	Nathan Hale	10	Richard Lendville
4	James Scarbrough	11	Joseph Sharp
5	Page Partwood	12	John Day
6	Nathaniel Davis	13	James Abott
7	Samuel Worthington	14	Henry Russell.

  James Adkins constable sworn to attend Grand Jury at this Term-

  Ordered that Kinza Johnson have his mark recorded which is a crop off each ear, and under bib out of each ear.

  Deed of Conveyance from John Lathom to Obadiah Wood for 100 acres proved in open court by Sampson Wood one of the subscribing witnesses thereto- Let it be registered.

  Ordered that James D. Puckett have his mark recorded which is a crop and a slit in the right ear-

  Deed of conveyance from Valentine Brazel to Thomas Benson was proved in open court by William Aldredge one of the subscribing witnesses thereto -- 100 acres of land---

Received the acknowledgment of a conveyance from Joseph Grayson to Samuel Frost in open court for 100 acres of land. Let it be registered.

Conveyance from James Doherty to Thomas Kinkaid for 500 acres of land was proved in open court by Thomas Kincaid one of the subscribing witnesses. Let it be registered.

Conveyance from William Stinnett to William Austin for 80 acres of land was proved by Joseph Sinclair one of the subscribing witnesses in open court. Let it be registered.

6   Deed of conveyance from William Boyd to Thomas Jones for 250 acres of land was proved in open court by William Standefer Esquire one of the subscribing witnesses therto - Let it be recorded --

Ordered that Obadiah Wood have his mark recorded which is a Smoothe crop and an hole in each ear --

Ordered that Joseph Sinclair have his mark recorded which is a smooth crop off the left ear and one hold in the right ear.

Ordered that James Scarbrough have his mark recorded which is a swallow fork in the right ear and an under bit in the left.

Deed of conveyance from William Murphy to John Bounds for 150 acres of land was proved in open court by William Aldredge one of the subscribing witnesses. Let it be registered.

Conveyance from William Stinnett to William Austin for 80 acres of land was proved by Joseph Sinclair one of the subscribing witnesses in open court. Let it be registered.

7   Deed of conveyance from William Boyd to Thomas Jones for 250 acres of land was proved in open court by William Standerfer Esquire one of the subscribing witnesses thereto. Let it be registered.

Ordered that Obadiah Wood have his mark recorded, which is a smooth crop and an hole in each ear --

Ordered that Joseph Sinclair have his mark recorded, which is a smooth crop off the left ear, and an hole in each ear.

Ordered that James Scarbrough have his mark recorded which is a swallow fork in the right ear and an under bit in the left.

Deed of conveyance from William Murphy to John Bounds for 150 acres of land was proved in open court by Jeremiah Jeoffery one of the subscribing witnesses hereto let it be registered

Ordered that John Bounds have his ear mark recorded which is a crop and a slit in the right ear a crop off the left ear and two slits in the underside thereof.

Ordered that William Austin have his mark recorded which is two small crops and an under keel in the right ear.

Ordered that James Cunningham have his ear mark recorded which is a crop off the left ear and an hole in the right.

Ordered that William McArny have his mark an Brand recorded which is a crop off each ear and two slits in the left his brand thus -W

Ordered that Elisha Wasson be appointed constable for McAmys Company who gave John Law and Isaac Braselton securties and was qualified-

James Puckett was appointed constable for Captain Jefferies who gave Samuel Worthington William Davis as securties and was qualefied.

Robert Brasil was appointed constable for Captain Davis old company who gave James Butler & William Davidson security & was qualified-

John Howard was appointed a constable for Captin Jefferys old company, who gave Wm. Austin and Jeremiah Jeffery his securties and was qualified accordingly -

Deed of Conveyance from Robert Young to William Murphy was proved in open court by James D. Puckett one of the subscribing witnesses thereto for 200 acres - Let it be registered -

Deed of conveyance from James Lea to Jesse Lea for 250 acres of land was proved in open court by William Lea one of the subscribing witnesses thereto - Let it be registered.

The last will and Testament of Aaron Guest was proved in open court by Hugh Montgomery Esquire one of the subscribing witnesses thereto & ordered to be recorded.

Ordered by the court that the following persons be appointed a jury to view and lay out a road from the Island ford Road near the ford of Cole Creek, to the lower line of Anderson County between Peter Avery's house & the foot of Wallings Ridge and make report to the next court - (Viz.) John McBride, Isarel Standefer, Henzy Johnson, John Armstrong, William Mankins, Henry Farmer & Isaac Brazleton.

William Hencock was appointed Deputy sheriff for the county of Anderson & gave bond and security & was qualified.

8   Ordered by the court that James Chitwood have to keep an House of Public entertainment who gave bond accordingly to law with William Davidson & John McAmy securties who were approved of by the court.

Ordered by the court that James Scarbrough, William Hogshead and William Davidson be appointed to serve as jurors at March Term of the superior court for Hamilton District to be holden at Knoxville on the fourth Monday of March Instant.

The petition of Joel Boling who was read in open court praying hat the court would grant him a writ of certeorai to bring up into court proceedings had before Fredrick Miller Esquire in a certain suit had before the said Fredrick, who in Thomas Cooper is Plaintiff & the said Joel Boling is Defendant and also that they would grant him a writ of Supercedas commanding all officers Ardies & Abittus to stay all other & further proceedings in large cause which is granted.

Stephen Heard gave bond as the law requires to be accountable for the public monies that may come into his hand & gave Nathaniel Davis & John Scruggs securties.

Ordered that Page Partwood by overseer of the road leading from John Menefee to the Eagle Ford from the top of the Chestnut Ridge to Clinch river & that John Kerby Esquire point out the hands.

Ordered that Thomas Wilson be overseer of the road leading from John Menefee to Clinch River from the top of the copper ridge & that John Kerby point out the hands.

Ordered that Robert Brazle be overseer of the road leading from John Menefees, from S. Ford to Blazes Branch & that John Kerby esquire points out the hands.

Court adjourned till tomorrow 10 o'clock.

9   Tuesday March 9th 1802.
Court met according to adjournment
Present ---

James Grant	Wm. McAmy
James Butler	Frederick Miller
John Kerby	Robert Pollock &
Wm. Underwood	Wm. Standefer.
Joseph Sinclair	

W. Sawiel Crawford gave Bond accordingly to law as a surveyor for the county of Anderson, Robert Houston & John Love securties- He then took the necessary oaths.

Ordered that the following persons be appointed a jury to view and lay out a road from the old Cumberland fork on Clinch river to intersect the road leading from the Island ford road near the ford of Cole Creek to the lower line of Anderson County between Peter Averys house & the fact of Wallings Ridge, at the lower line of Anderson County (viz.) Aquella Johnson, James Porter, Henry Nunnery, William Robertson, Jacob Peak, William Rippetaco and William Griffery.

Ordered by the court that John F. Jack esquire be allowed fifteen dollars for each term he may attend as Solicitor for Anderson County.

10   Rec. Acknowledgment of conveyance from Aqualla Johnson to Augustine Hackworth for 50 acres of land- Let it be registered.

Ordered by the court that a Tax for the year 1802 be served on all taxable property for Anderson County in the following manner. (viz.)

	cents
On each hundred acres of land	$6\frac{1}{4}$
On each white pole	$6\frac{1}{4}$
On each black pole	$12\frac{1}{2}$
On each stud horse kept for mares	25
On each Lott	$12\frac{1}{2}$

Ordered that William Hogshead be allowed the sum of ten dollars for running the line between the county of Anderson & Clauborne as pr. account exhibited.

Ordered by the court that Jesse Raepdon be allowed the sum of sixteen dollars for running & John Kerby Eight dollars for marking carrying the chain in extending the line between the County of Anderson and Roane as pr. account exhibited.

Ordered that Constant Claxton have his mark recorded which is an under keel in each ear.

Ordered that William Arnold have his mark recorded which is a crop and under bit in each ear and an over slit in the right ear.

Deed of conveyance from William Murphy to William Ashlock for 215 acres of land was proved in open court by William Ragland one of the subscribing witnesses. Let it be registered.

11   The following is a list of jurors to attend at June sessions 1802 for Anderson County.

1	John Bradberry	16	Augustine Hackworth
2	William Medlin	17	Thomas Kincaid
3	Henry Farmer	18	John Galson
4	Robert Medlin	19	Spencer Graham
5	William Ashlock	20	John Lamb
6	Richard Lewallen	21	John English
7	Shadrack Rudy	22	James McCrackin
8	Jacob Strader	23	Joshua English
9	Jason Cloud	24	Philip Fry
10	Samuel Frost	25	Elliott Cunningham
11	William Aldridge	26	Moses McWhorter
12	Lathau Smith	27	Douglas Oliver
13	Jacob Peek	28	Joel Hobbs
14	Douglas Oliver	29	Reuben Ragland
15	Thomas Worthington	30	Caswell Cobb

Ordered by the court that the following persons be appointed to take lists of taxalbe property for the year 1802 (viz.)

James Grant for the Company in the fork of Powels River.
Frederick Miller for Capt. Medlines Company.
Wm. Underwood for Capt. Wilsons & Robbins Company.
Joseph Sinclair for Capt. Jefferys Company
John McAmy for Capt. McAmys Company.

Robert Pollock for Capt. Steels & Grahams Companies.
Gibbson Hardin --- for Capt. Hales company.
James Butler -- for Capt. Davis's Co.

Ordered that William Standefer have his mark recorded which is a swallow fork in each ear & an under bit in each ear. Ordered that James Butler Esq. have his mark recorded which is a swallow fork in the right ear an and under square or half crop in the left.

Ordered Jermiah Jeffery have his mark recorded which is a crop in the right ear and a swallow fork in the left.

Ordered by the court that the following persons by appointed as a Jury to view a road from Burrville to the upper dive of Anderson County, where the old trace near sharpo Station intersects the same, Richard Medlin Henry Russell, John Bradberry, John McAdoo, John Day, Elliott Grills and Richard Lewallen ---

Ordered by the Court that the following persons be appointed to view a road from Burrville to James Childwood -- John Jesse Richard Forrest, William Ashlock, Jeremiah Jeffery, Samuel Worthington, Nathan Roberts, and Douglass Oliver ---

The Grand Jury dismissed from further attendance at this term.

Ordered by the court that the following persons be appointed a jury to view a road leading from Burreville to where the road leading from the Island ford to the Walnut Cave intersects the old trace (viz.) Wm. Lea, Tack Lea, Shadrach Morris, Hugh Montgomery, Conright Willhight, Jesse Lea, Richard Lenville.

Ordered that John Adair be overseer of the road from the mouth of Powels River into Mayberrys road in the rich hollow and to open the same as ordered and marked out by a Jury under a former law and that James Grant Esquire point out the hands to keep open said road.

Court adjourned till tomorrow 9 o'clock.

Wednesday March 10th 1802.
The court met according to adjournment.
Present   )
Wednesday)   James Grant
                    James Butler
                    Wm. Standefer
                    Hugh Montgomery
                    Joseph Sinclair
                    Wm. McAmy
                    Wm. Underwood

John Underwood high sheriff of Anderson County gave bond and security according to law for the collection of the Taxes for the county aforesaid & was qualified accordingly in open court --

Ordered by the court that John Jesse build a pound at Burrville for the use of Anderson County and that he be allowed by the court for the same.

The worshipful court of Anderson County other than the following regulations shall be abscured in doing business in said county (viz.)

Ordered that the first day of each court to be held in and for the county of Anderson aforesaid shall be appropriated and set apart for receiving probates of deeds of conveyance and all other instruments of writing directed and required by law to be proved in open court - and also for hearing and determining all causes carried up into court either by appeal or writ of certearari ordered that the second and third days of said court be appropriated and set apart for the purpose of hearing & determining all other civil causes not above mentioned.

14   3 Ordered that the fourth and fifth days of said court be appropriated and set apart for hearing and determining all State causes.

4 Ordered that the sixth day of said court be appropriated and set apart for the purpose of hearing and determining all motions for new trials, all reasons on arrest of Judgment, all other argument causes and taking all necessary rules on the Docket of said Court.

5 Lastly ordered that if the witness apportioned as above for particular days can be got through in less time as abofe shall be taken up.

The last will & Testament of Anthony Lindar deceased was proved in open court by Joseph Denham and Jesse Raysdon two of the subscribing witnesses thereto.

Also a codicil thereto annexed by Sampson Wood & Jesse Raysdon the subscribing witnesses thereto and Mary Lendar and Jacob Lendar were then qualified as Executors of said last will and testament and leadeath in open court.

Ordered that Calet Friby be overseer of the Grantsborough Road from where the road leading from the mouth of Powels river intersects the same into the Powels Vally road at the county line and that Robert Pollock Esquire point out the hands to keep open said road.

Ordered that Shadrach Reedy be overseer of the road from the South Bank of Clinch River at Wm. Hancocks ford to Buffalo Creek & that Solomn Massingale Esq. point out the hands to keep open said road.

15   Ordered that Riahard Caswell Cobb be overseer of the Road from Buffalo Creek to Byram & fork of Hinds creek & that Wm. Underwood Esquire point out the hands to keep open said road.

Ordered that A. Byram be overseer of the road from Bryants fork of Hinds creek to the county line on the chestnut ridge and that William Underwood Esquire point out the hands to keep said road open.

Ordered that Jonathan Cunningham be overseer of the road from the North Bank of Clinch River at William Hancocks ford to where the road leading from the mouth of Powells river intersects the same, North of Powells River - and that James Grant Esquire point out the hands to keep open said road.

Ordered by the court that the following rates be observed by those licensed to keep public houses in Anderson County (Viz.)

	Dol. cents
For a comfortable Breakfast with good coffee	.16 2/3
for good comfortable dinner	.25
for good comfortable supper	.12 1/2
For comfortable lodging	.06 1/4
For keeping horse 24 hours with barn and fodder or hay	.25
For 1/2 pt. good proof whiskey	.08 1/4
For 1/2 pt. good Peach or Apple	.12 1/2 brandy
For 1/2 pt. good French Brandy	.25
For one Quart good cider, metheglin or Beer	.08 1/3
For Quart good cyder Royal	.12 1/2
For corn & oats pr. gallon	.06 1/2

16   Ordered that John McAmy have his mark recorded which is a crop and under Bit in the left ear, and two under bits in the right ear.

Ordered by the court that John Howard be appointed constable to wait and attend on the court.

Ordered that Jesse Lea be appointed overseer of the road from the Island ford intersects the South West point road to Thomas Hills in the Walnut Cave & that Hugh Montgomery Esquire point out all the hands.

Ordered that James Adkins be appointed overseer of the road from Thomas Hills to Indain Creek & that Hugh Montgomery point out the hands to work on said road.

  Ordered that Tobias Long be overseer of the road from Aldredges Ford to Wm. Standefers & that John McAny Esq. point out the hands to work on said road.

  Ordered that Joseph Denham be allowed the sum of five dollars for the use of an house for the court to set in, firewood etc.

  Court then adjourned till court in sourse to the house of John Jesse --- James Grant chairman

17

State	)	March sessions 1802
vs.	)	Charged - plea - not guilty
Jesse Vaney	)	Jury sworn - (viz.)

1 Polly Duncan   7 Joseph Denham
2 James Porter   8 Moses M. Whorter
3 James McNutt   9 John Thomas
4 Robert Armstrong 10 John Wilkerson
5 Joel Hancock   11 Samuel Frost
6 Wm. Creely   12 Wm. Hogshead.

  Mistrial Plea of not guilty with drawn- Prisoner submits to the court & is fined 25 cents- James Grant Chairman --

  Page 18 Blank

19 At a court began and held for the county of Anderson at Burrville on the second Monday of June in the year of our lord 1802

  Present: William Underwood
        Fred Miller
        Wm. McKamey
        Joseph Sinclair

  John Underwood high sheriff of the county Anderson, returns that he has executed the Venire facias on the following persons (viz.)

1 John Bradberry   16 Augustin Hackworth
2 William Medlin   17 Thos. Kincaid
3 Robt. Medlin   18 John Galsan
4 Wm. Ashlock   19 Spencer Graham
5 Richd. Lewallen   20 John Lamb
6 Shadrach Reedy   21 John English
7 Jacob Strader   22 James McCracken
8 Henry Farmer   23 Joshua English
9 Jason Cloud   24 Philip Fry
10 Saml. Frost   25 Elliott Grills
11 Wm. Aldridge   26 Jas. Cunningham
12 Laton Smith   27 Moses McWhorter
13 Jacob Peek   28 Reuben Rageland
14 Douglas Oliver   29 Joel Hobbs
15 Thos. Waithington 30 Richd. E. Cobb.

of whom the following are elected grand Jurors.

20 1 Douglas Oliver, foreman 8 John Galson
  2 Henry Farmer   9 John Lamb
  3 Richard Lewallen   10 Moses McWhorter
  4 Laton Smith   11 Wm. Medlin
  5 Joshua English   12 Spencer Graham
  6 Jacob Peek   13 Joel Hobbs
  7 John English   14 Robt. Medlin

15 Reuben Ragland
Who being sworn & charged, retired to Enquire --

    Deed of conveyance from Abraham Funk to Joseph Golaher for 500 acres of land was proved in open court by Gibson Harden one of the subscribing witnesses thereto - Let it be registered.

    A deed of conveyance from William Hankin to William Patterson for 150 acres of land was proved in open court by James D. Puckett one of the subscribing witnesses thereto - Let it be registered.

    John McAdoo, John Day, Richard Lewallen, Richard Woodlen, John Bradberry, and Henry Russel who were appointed as a Jury of view from Burriville to the upper line of Anderson County near Sharps Station, report that they have marked and laid out the road nighest and best way and the court have appointed Richard Lewallen, overseer on said road from Burrville to Days ford Clinch   Joseph Smith who said Ford to John Scruggs, John Parks from Scruggs to Richard C. Cobb, William Underwood, William Medlin from said Cobbs to big Buffalo & Tobias Tilmare from big Buffalo to the county line.

    Ordered that Paul Harmon have his mark recorded which is a crop and a slit in the left ear and a slit in the right ear.

    Ordered that John Ritenour have his mark recorded which is a smooth crop in the left ear.

21   John McBride, Hinza Johnson, John Armstrong, Henry Farmer, Isaac Brazleton, and Isarel Standfer, who were appointed a Jury to view and lay off a road from the Island ford road near the ford of Cole Creek, to the lower line of Anderson County near the house of Peter Avery Report that have laid out said road according to their order.

    And the court have appointed John McBribe overseer on said road from the upper end to his own house, John Specered from John McBribe to Kenza Johnsons Constant Claxton, from there to John Jemmesons, James D. Puckett, from there to the upper end of Isaac Braghtons field, and John Lively from there to the lower line of Anderson County. And Wm. McKamey will point out the hands.

    A deed of conveyance from Benjamin C. Parker, William Macklin & Joseph Greer, to Frederick Sadler, for six hundred & forty acres was proved in open court by John Leit, one of the witnesses and Jacob Leinart. Let it be registered.

    A deed of conveyance from Andon Lyon and Wm. Linder to Joel Hobby for 132 1/2 acres was proved in open court by Reuben Ragland one of the subscribing witnesses thereto. Let it be registered.

    Deed of conveyance from Frederick Sadler, to John Shepheard for one hundred and twelve acres was acknowledged in open court. Let it be registered.

    A deed of conveyance from Frederick Sadler, to Jacob Lemar for one hundred and fity one acres was acknwoedged in open court.
Let it be registered.

    A deed of conveyance from Isaac Brazleton to Charles Shinliver for 315 acres 130 poles was acknowledged in open court. Let it be registered.

    A deed of conveyance from John Leit to Henza Johnson, Wm. Standefer Wm. Robertson, Joseph Grayson & Hugh Montgomery commissioners for 40 acres, was acknowledged in open court. Let it be registered.

22   A deed of conveyance from Robert Burton to Cabel Freley was acknowledged in open court for 500 acres of land. Let it be registered.

    Ordered by the court that James Scarbrough have leave to keep a public ferry on clinch river adjouning his own land and that he shall observe the following rates.

	Dols.
Waggon & team	$1.00
Pleasure Carriage of 4 wheels & horses	1.00
Pleasure carriage 2 wheels & horses	.50
Man & Horse	.08 1/3
Led horse	.06 1/4
cattle, hogs & sheep each head	.03
Single person	.06 1/4

A deed of conveyance from Robert Burton to John Lamb for 131 acres of land was acknowledged in open court. Let it be registered.

Ordered that Jason Cloud & John Guest be qualified as executors of the last will & testament of Aaron Guest deceased they having given bond and security accordingly to law.

Ordered that Austin Hackworth Aquilla Johnson, Saml. Worthington, Senior, James Scarbrough, Nathan Hail, Sam. Worthington Jr. & James Butlet be appointed a Jury to view & lay off a road from Scarbroughs ferry on Clinch to Alderidges Ford on Clinch & make report to the next court.

Aquilla Johnson, Henry Nunnery, James Porter, Wm. Griffith, Wm. Rippeto, & William Robertson who were appointed a jury to view a road from the Cumberland ford on Clinch river to where it intersects The Island Ford Road near the lower line of Anderson County.

23 Report that they have viewed and marked the same - and the court have appointed Nathan Hale overseer from the river to Geo Ramseys, Jacob Peek, from there to the head of Williams Spring Branch and Joseph England from there to the end near Mr. Averies and that Wm. Standerfer point out the hands to Clark on the same.

Douglass Oliver, Jermiah Jeffery, Nathan Roberts, John Pipe and Saml. Worthington who were appointed a jury of view to lay out a road from Burriville to James Chilwoods Report that they have reviewed and marked the same the nearest and best way to the best of their knowledge and the court have appointed Richard Forrest overseer of the same from Burrville to Wm. Ashlocks, and Thomas Worthington from Ashlocks to Philips Trace, and that Joseph Sinclair Esquire point out the hands. And James Chilwood from Philips Trace to his own house and that John McKamey Esquire point out the hands.

A deed of conveyance from Andrew Jackson to Alexander Kirkpatrick for fifty one acres of land was proved in open court by William Hogshead one the subscribing witnesses. Let it be registered.

The court then adjourned until tomorrow morning 9 o'clock.

24 Tuesday 15th June 1802.
The court met according to adjournment.
Present
William McKamey
Joseph Sinclair
Gibson Harden
William Standfer
John McKamey

A deed of conveyance from John Bounds to Nathan Aldridge for 50 acres of land was proved in open court by Wm. Aldridge. Let it be registered.

A deed of conveyance from James Grant Esquire attorney for John Winstead to George Worthington Campbell Esquire for lott N. B. Nineteen in the town of Grantsborough was acknowledged in open court by said James

Grant Esquire. Let it be registered.

This day John Underwood high sheriff of Anderson County came into court and enters his protest in exoneration of any escapes that may happen for want of a public goal.

A deed of conveyance from Robt. Burton Ex. and from Robert Burton Att. in fact for Archibald Henderson one other Ex. to John Day for 175 acres was acknowledged in open court. Let it be registered.

Ordered that Oliver Dotson have his mark recorded which is a crop and under bit in the left & swallow fork in the right ear.

Francis Vickory Entry taken Anderson County was qualified to the necessary oaths & entered into Bond & gave security according to Law. Court adjourned until 2 o'clock.

25   Court met according to adjournment.
    Present   James Grant
              Joseph Sinclair
               Solomn Nassingale

State   )
vs.   ) Challenge, charged, pleads not guilty.
Saml. Ussery)

Whereupon came a jury (Viz.)

1 Jason Cloud   7 Thomas Kincaid
2 Jacob Strader   8 Augustin Hackworth
3 John Bradberry   9 Philip Fry
4 Thos Worthington   10 James Cunningham
5 Wm. Ashlock   11 Nathan Roberts
6 Wm. Aldridge   12 Robert Atkins.

Who say the Defendant is not guilty in manner or form as charged in the Bill of Indictment. Rule to Tax the prosecution with the cost - discharged.

A deed of conveyance from Robert Burton, Caleb Friley for two hundred and twenty five acres of land was acknowledged in open court. Let it be registered.

A deed of conveyance from Robert Burton Ex. and Robert Burton Att. in fact for Archibald Henderson one other Ex. to John Scruggs for 200 acres of land was proved in open court by Wm. Hogshead one of the subscribing witnesses. Let it be registered.

26 State   )
   vs.   ) Charged plead guilty & submitted to the court.
   Robert Pearson) Wm. Pearson is fined five dollars and costs &
   & Wm. Pearson) Robert Pearson one dollar and costs.

   State   )
   vs. A. B.   ) Charged, Pleads not guilty Plea with drawn &
   Thos. Pearson) submits to the court- & fined fifty cents & costs.

Ordered that the following persons are appointed a jury of view to lay off a road from or near the Black House on the road leading up the big valley by Captain John Miller the nearest & best way to Clouds Ford _____ er, thence across the river to where it will intersect the _____ kville across Clinch river near to Grantsborough into Pow-

Robert Whitton, Richd. Medlin, William Medlin, Jacob Strader, Wm. Ryan, Jason Cloud, Joel Bowling.

The Court then Adjourned till tomorrow morning 9 o'clock.

27   Wednesday 16th June 1802
      Present   James Grant Esquire
                Joseph Sinclair
                James Butler
                Wm. Underwood
                Wm. McKamey.

The following are a list of Jurors to attend at September Sessions 1802.

1 Conard Sharp
2 William Holt
3 Wm. Owen Medlin
4 Henry Harless
5 John Scruggs
6 Polly Duncan
7 Jonah Denton
8 Calet Friley
9 Barley Greerwood
10 Tachariah Lea
11 Wm. Lea
12 Henry Farmer Sen.
13 Joseph Lea
14 Thomas Campbell
15 Richard Lindville
16 Geo Shutters
17 John McWhorter
18 Alexander Gaston
19 Conright Willright
20 Anguish Ross
21 Jonathan Cunningham
22 John Hannah
23 Abraham Hagler
24 Aquilla Johnson
25 Harris Ryan
26 Charles Shinliver
27 Charles Ferrel
28 Edward Stephenson
29 John Leib
30 Edward Frost

A bill of sale from William Patterson to William McKamey for a negro girl slave named Dice about four years old was acknwoledged in open court & ordered to be recorded.

Ordered that Robert McKamey have his mark & brand recorded which are, a crop off each ear an underbit out of each ear and a hole in the right ear. His brand thus R. and 7 -

28   Ordered by a majority of the court that Joseph Grayson be allowed fourteen dollars & fifty cents for work & material furnished for an house for the court to sit in as pr. as filed.

Ordered that Wm. Underwood have his mark recorded which is a crop slit and under keel in the left ear.

William Lea, Richard Lenville, Jesse Lea, Tachariah Lea, Shadrach Morris, Conright Willright & Hugh Montgomery who were appointed a jury of view to mark to lay out a road from Burrville to where the Island ford Road intersects. Report that they have laid off the same. Ordered by the court that John Sarton be overseer from Burrville to Isaac Taylors on Cain Creek ' that John Kerby point out the hands. And that Robert Armstrong be overseer from Isaac Taylors to where the said road intersects Powells valley road, and that Joseph Sinclair point out the hands.

Ordered that Harris Ryan be overseer of the road leading to Powells valley from the north Bank of Powells river where Jonathan Cunningham leaves off, to the top of the ridge where Calet Friley oversees it, and that James Grant Esquire point out the hands.

Ordered that John Warrick be overseer of the road leading from the Block house to Captain John Millers to the County line & that Fred Miller Esquire point out the hands to work on the same.

29   Received the following tax lists from the following Justices Esq. James Grant Esq. for Capt. Clouds Co. Wm. Underwood for Robins & Wilsons.

Gibson Harden for Hales Company. Fred Miller for Medlins Co. John McAmy for McKameys' Co. Robt. Pollock for Lenvills & Steels. Joseph Sinclair for Jefferys' Co. James Butler for Davis Co.
   Court then Adjourned until court in course.
             James Grant Chairman.
Page 30 Blank ----

31   At a court begun and held for the county of Anderson at Burrville on the second Monday of September in the year of our Lord 1802 --
Present) James Grant
      Hugh Montgomery
      William Standefier
      John Kerby
      Wm. Underwood
      Wm. McKaney
      James Butler

   John Underwood high sheriff of the county of Anderson returns that he has executed the Venire facias on the following persons (viz.)

#	Name	#	Name
1	William Holt	16	Alex Gastin
2	Wm. Owen Medlin	17	Joseph Lea
3	Henry Harless	18	Conright Willright
4	John Scruggs	19	Angus Ross
5	Rolly Duncan	20	Jonath Cunningham
6	Jonah Denton	21	John Hannah
7	Cabel Friley	22	Abr. Hagler
8	Bailey Greerwood	23	Aquilla Johnson
9	Tachariah Lea	24	Harris Bryan
10	Wm. Lea	25	Chas. Shinliver
11	Henry Farmer Sen.	26	Chas. Ferrell
12	Thomas Campbell	27	Edw. Stephenson
13	Richard Lenville	28	John Leib
14	George Shetter	29	Edw. Frost
15	John McWhorter		

   of whom the following are Grand Jurors ----

32
#	Name	#	Name
1	Wm. Lea, foreman	8	John Leib
2	Conright Willright	9	Edward Stephenson
3	Angus Ross	10	Edward Frost
4	Harris Bryan	11	John Scruggs
5	Joseph Lea	12	Aquilla Johnson
6	Chas. Shinliver	13	Henry Harless
7	Jonathan Cunningham	14	Henry Farmer, Sen.

   Who being sworn and charged, retired to inquire.
   A deed of conveyance from Joseph Watson to Andrew Williams Ramsey and William Ramsey under the firm of Andrew & William Ramsey for nine hundred and three acres and one quarter was produced in open court with sufficient protest & ordered to be registered.
   A deed of conveyance from Charles McClung to Michael Hosler for 200 acres of land was proved in open court by Nobble Johnson one of the subscribing witnesses. Let it be registered.
   Wm. Reed gave in two hundred acres of land for Taxes & was sworn to it.
   A deed of conveyance from John McClellan as Att. in fact Stockley Donelson & from Stockley Donelson himself both beginning it to Isaac Brazleton was proved in open court for one hundred acres by Aquilla Johnson & William Arnold. Let it be registered.
   A deed of conveyance from John McClellan as att. in fact for Stockley Donelson himself to Issac Bragelton for two hundred & fifty acres

of land was proved in open court be Aquella Johnson and William Arnold the subscribing witnesses. Let it be registered.

Thomas Cooper)
vs. appeal) On motion of Deft. Att. in this case the court ordered
Joel Bowling) that proceedings should be quashed for irregularity.

William Franklin)
vs. Att.)
Robert Young) Where upon came a Jury (viz.)

Richard Lenville, Thomas Campbell, Alexander Gastin, William Hogshead, John Sartin, Manpage Vowel, Thomas Adair, Abraham Hagler, Jeremiah Jeffery, Absolom Morris, Joseph Denham, Sen., and Christian Isely who being duly sworn do say they find for the Plaintiff and assess his damages one hundred and forty one dollars and eighty eight cents.

William Farmer returns one Poll for taxes.

Ordered that the following persons be appointed as Grand Jurors to the next superior court September Term (viz.) William McKamey, John Kerby Esq.

The court then adjourned till tomorrow morning 9 o'clock.

34   Tuesday 14th September 1802. Court met according to adjournment.
       Present   James Grant
                  Hugh Montgomery
                  James Butler
                  Joseph Sinclair
                  Wm. McKamey

A deed of conveyance from Wm. Lea to Samuel Wilson for four hundred acres of land was acknowledged in open court.

A deed of conveyance from Wm. Lea to Samuel Wilson for two hundred and seventy four acres of land was acknowledged in open court.

Conveyance from Jesse Lea to Stephen M. Comsus for 100 acres of land was acknowledged in open court.

Spencer Graham)
vs. Appeal)
George Kellins) Whereupon came a Jury(Viz.)

Richard Lenville, Abraham Hagler, William Davidson, George Brazle, James Smith, Tachariah Lea, William Austin, John Terry, David New, Isaiah Ruckmean, Calet Failey, Christian Isely, who being duly sworn say they find for the Defendant - Rule for new trial. Rule made absolute.

35   Ordered that Spencer Graham be appointed a valuer or property owner execution for Capt. Linvills Company, Conright Willright for Capt. STeels Co. William Hancock Sen. for Capt. Clouds Co. Reuben Ragland for Capt. Aldredges Company, Samuel Worthington Sen. for Capt. McKameys Co. James Scarbrough for Captain Hawkins Company, Robert Armstrong & William Ashlock for Captain Coles Co. John McAdoo for Captain Robbins Co. William Underwood Esq. for Capt. Wilson's Co. & Solomn Massingale Esq. for Capt. Medlins Co.

A Bill of sale from William Patterson to William Mankins for two negros one named Alse the other Isbelle was acknowledged in open court.

State)
vs.)
Joseph Marcum & orther.) Whereupon came a Jury towit Jesse Lea, Nathan

Roberts, Lewis Nobles, William Leinar, Robert McKamey, Henry Young, Jacob Chawey, Alexander Gastin, John England, Samuel Frost, Page Partwood, & Joel Bowlin who being duly elected and sworn say they find the Defendant not guilty in manner or form as charged in the bill of Indictment. Rule to show cause why the prosecutor not be taxed with the costs.

A bill of sale from Hugh Miller, John McEntire and William Lemar for a certain negro man named James with a condition annexed was proved in open court by Robert Armstrong who say Hugh Wills & John McEntire sign it and Robert McKamey who saw William Lamar sign it.

A deed of conveyance from John Armstrong to John Asher for one hundred and sixty three acres was acknowledged in open court.

Ordered that Abraham Hagler have his mark recorded which is a crop in the right ear and an hole in the left ear.

Ordered by a majority of the court that William Tunnell Sen. Saml. Worthington Sen. Sam. Frost, Henry Farmer, Sen., Capt. Nathaniel Davis, Alexander Gastin, and John Hannah be a jury of view in consequence of a petition from a number of Inhabitians praying to have the road discontinued in the bounds of Nathaniel Hale from the old Cumberland ford to George Ramseys to view & report to next court, the best way and the most convenient between those two points.

Jason Clouds exhibits an Inventory of the Estate of Aaron Guess deceased which is ordered to be recorded.

Court then adjourned till tomorrow 9 o'clock.

Wednesday 15th September 1802.
Court met according to adjournment.
Present   Hugh Montgomery
           James Butler
           Wm. Underwood &
           Robert Pollock.

Returned by John Kerby Esq. 1000 acres of land No. of Clinch river opposite the mouth of Bull run.

James Grant Esquire returns the following lands for taxes for the year 1802.
James Hagg   8847
John Unstead   4032
Gen. Benj. Smith   1342
Walter Alves two lots 10, 750.

State
vs.
Jesse Womack, Cole Womack, his wife, Chas. Friley, Samuel Friley, & Drurey Puckett.

Whereupon came a Jury (vix.)
Richard Linville, Alexander Tastin, Tachariah Lea, Thomas Adair, George Brazle, Richard Lewallen, Robert Adkins, Wm. Ussery, Robert Pollock, Jr. Saml. Ussery, Page Portwood, & George Mayberry, who say they find Druery Puckett not guilty. Rule to tax prosecutor costs so far as respects Druery Puckett. Guilty as to Jesse Womack, Cole Womack his wife, Charles Fribey, Samuel Friley and they are fined two costs each.
Rule to Tax prosecuts with the costs discarged respecting Drury Duckett.

Ordered that Jared Harbin have leave to keep an ordinary or house of public entertainment in Burrville he having entered into Bond & given security as the law directs.

A deed of conveyance from Aquella Johnson to James Porter for 100 acres of land was acknowledged in open court. Let it be registered.

Ordered that James Butler, Wm. McKamey and Joseph Sinclair Esquire be appointed to make an equal division of the hands working on the roads under Thomas Worthington, Tobias Long and James D. Puckett.

Ordered that William Austin bring the orphan children he in named which were presented by the grand Jury (viz.) Joseph Austin, Elizabeth Austin, Zachariah Austin, Hezekiah Austin, John Austin, Daniel Austin, Pobe Austin, & Nancy Austin to the next court to be held for the county of Anderson on the second Monday of December next to be disposed of as court may think proper.

Ordered that William Johnson have his mark recorded which is a crop off the right ear and an under bit out of each ear.

Ordered by a majority of the court that the following persons be appointed a jury to view and lay off a road from the cave road at James' Greens to Grantsborough (viz.) Jesse Lea, Joseph Denhem, Robert Sinclair, Rich Lenville, Jonathan Cunningham, Joseph Sharp, Robert Armstrong or any given of them the best & most convenient way.

39 Ordered by a majority of the court that John McWhorter and John Leib have leave to keep a public ferry on the river Clinch opposite Burrville they having given bond & security as the law requires-- and that the following rates be observed.

	Dols.	cents--
waggon & Team	1.	
Pleasure carriage of 4 wheels and horses	1.	
Man & horses		.8 1/3
Pleasure carriage of 2 wheels & horses		.50
Led horse		6 1/4
Cattle, Hogs, and sheep each head		.3
Single persons		.6 1/4

Ordered by a majority of the court that the following persons be appointed a jury to view and lay off a road from Burrville to Leibs and McWhorters ferry the nearest and best way and from the ferry to intersect the road leading from Menefies to the Cagle ford the most convenient way. (viz.) John Kerby, Capt. Nathaniel Davis, John McWhorter, John Leib, Joseph Sinclair.

Ordered by a majority of the court that the following persons be a jury to view and lay off a road the nearest & most convenient way from the Eagle ford to Burrville (viz.) Joseph Denham, Sen., Wm. Hogshead, John Day, John Kerby & Joseph Sinclair.

Ordered that Samuel Terry have to keep an ordinary at this house in Burrville he having given Bond and security as the law requires.

40 Ordered by the court that the road leading through Oliver Dotsons field be vacated & that the said Oliver Dotsons keep open and in good repair a road around his fence into the road again.

The Court Adjourned till tomorrow morning 9 o'clock

Thursday 16th Sept. 1802 - Court met according to adjournment.
Present - Hugh Montgomery
         Joseph Sinclair
         Robert Pollock

Ordered that page Portwood have leave to keep an ordinary or house of public Entertainment he having given bond and security as the law requires.

Ordered that the following persons be appointed as Jurors to attend at the next court to be held for the County on Anderson on the second Monday of Dec. 1802.

1 Isaac Norman	17 Jacob Leinard
2 Henry Norman	18 James Scarbro
3 Thomas Wilson	19 Nathan Hale
4 Isham Stennett	20 Nathan Roberts
5 Wm. Austin	21 John Day
6 Wm. Ragaland	22 Wm. Horton
7 Richd. Medlin	23 Henry Russell
8 Hardy Medlin	24 Jeremiah Jeffery
9 John English	25 Saml. Worthington
10 John Lamb	26 Joseph Jeffery
11 John Parks	27 Wm. Hogshead
12 Wm. Brazle	28 Joshua English
13 Jacob Chainey	29 Wm. Rippetoe
14 Wm. Robertson	30 Saml. Wilson
15 Isaac Brazleton	31 John Bounds.
16 Isarel Standefer	

41   Col. Montgomery returned 5375 acres of land the property of the heirs of Leonard H. Bullock for Taxes for the year 1802.

Ordered by the court that Danl. White have leave to keep an ordinary at his house in Powells valley he having given bond & security as the law requires.

The court then adjourned until Court in course. James Grant Chairman.

Page 42 Blank ---

43   At a court begun and held for the county of Anderson at Burrville on the second Monday of December in the year of our Lord 1802 -

Present - - Joseph Sinclair Esquire
            William McKaney
            William Underwood
            John McKaney

John Underwood high sheriff of the county of Anderson, returns that he has executed the Venirie facias on the following persons (viz.)

1 Isaac Norman	15 Jacob Leinard
2 Henry Norman	16 James Scarbro
3 Isham Stinnett	17 Nathan Hale
4 Wm. Ragland	18 John Day
5 Richard Medlin	19 Wm. Horton
6 Hardy Medlin	20 Henry Russell
7 John English	21 Jeremiah Jeffery
8 John Lamb	22 Saml. Worthington
9 John Parks	23 Joseph Jeffery
10 Wm. Brazle	24 Wm. Hogshead
11 Jacob Chainey	25 Joshua English
12 Wm. Robertson	26 Wm. Rippeto
13 Isaac Brazleton	27 Saml. Wilson
14 Isarel Standifer	28 John Bounds

of whom the following are appointed Grand Jurors.

1 William Hogshead	8 John English
2 Richard Medlin	9 Henry Russell
3 Jeremiah Jeffery	10 Joseph Jeffery
4 Nathan Haile	11 Wm. Ragland
5 Saml. Worthington	12 Jacob Leinard
6 Isaac Brazleton	13 John Parks
7 John Bounds	14 John Day
	15 John Lamb

And the following are traverse Jurors – Wm. Rippeto, Isaac Norman, Joshua English, James Scarbro, Wm. Horton, Wm. Brazle, Isham Stenitt.

44 Ordered by the court that Robert Barton be released from the payment of the state and County Tax on three Black polls for the year 1802.

Robert Houston returns six thousand acres of land the property of Nathaniel Hart reliable to taxation for the year 1802.

A deed of conveyance from William Cobb to Henry Harless for four hundred and forty eight acres of land was proved in open court by Thomas Frost Jr. one of the subscribing witnesses & ordered to be registered.

A deed of conveyance from Wm. Cobb to John Sharp for four hundred and twenty three acres of land was proved in open court by Solomn Massengale one of the subscribing witnesses.

A deed of conveyance from Wm. Hogshead to James Taylor one hundred and twenty five acres of land was proved in open Court by John McBribe.

Ordered by the court that James Taylor have his mark recorded which is a slit in the right ear and an half crop off the underside of the left.

Ordered by the court that John McBribe have his mark recorded which is a crop & slit in each ear.

Ordered by the court that James Scarbro have leave to keep an ordinary at his house he having given bond & security as the law requires.

A deed of conveyance from the commissioner of town of Burrville to William Tunnell for lott No. 42, was proved in open Court by John Howard to be registered.

45 Joseph Terry produced his commissioner from the Governor as Entry taker and entered into bond as the law directs and took the necessary oaths.

The Court then adjourned until Tomorrow morning 9 o'clock.

Tuesday 14th Dec. 1802. The Court met according to adjournment.

Present – –James Grant
    Joseph Sinclair
    Wm. Underwood
    Hugh Montgomery

Robert Shewmaker)
vs. ）
Wm. Davis) In this case the Defendant prefered a petition for writs of certeorari & superdeas which was granted.

A deed of conveyance from John Long to Kenza Johnson & others for five acres & fifty poles was proved in open court by Samuel Crawford and ordered to be registered.

Spencer Graham)
vs. appeal)
George Kelluns) Whereupon came a Jury (towit) William Rippeto, Wm. Houston, Wm. Brazle, Isham Stinnett, Manpage Vowel, Reuben Roberts, Lewis Richards, James Thomas, John Rains, John Coons Sen., Edward Young, and Felix Gilbert, who say they find for the Defendant – – Rule for to show cause why a new trial should be granted. Rule made absolute.

Ordered that Nathan Hale be fined in the sum of two dollars for a contemp in wearing his hat in open court and that the clerk issue Execution for the same Instance.

46 Ordered by the court that the following persons be appointed to

view and lay out a way from the Road so as to go either below or above Hostlers Mill pond as they may think best (viz.) Douglass Oliver, James Pater, Thomas Carpenter, Michael Hostler, Wm. Griffith, Wm. Rippito, & Wm. Robertson, & that they report to next court.

John F. Jack Esquire returns 1000 acres of land subject for the taxes of the year 1802 - the property of Francis Mayberry.

A deed of conveyance from John McEntire to William Cotter for two hundred and twenty acres of land was acknowledged in open court and ordered to be registered.

Ordered by the court that Hannah Austin and Nathaniel Austin have the Administration of all and singular the goods and chattles rights & credits of William Austin deceased they having entered into Bond in the sum of one hundred dollars and give Arthur Crozier and John Howard - - Securties - they were qualified accordingly -

Ordered by the court that John McAdoo be released from the payment of the state and county tax on one Black Poll he having made oaths that he has none.

Ordered by the court that Arthur Crozier have Hezekiah Austin a Boy Born Feby. 17th 1787 Bound to him until he attanes the age of twenty one years. That John Howard have John Austin a Boy Born 26 Oct. 1789 until he attanes to the age of Twenty one and that Sthephen Heard have Daniel Austin a Boy Born 16 October 1793 until he shall attain to the age of twenty one years.

Ordered by the court that Hannah Austin be allowed the sum of ten dollars for keeping the children of Milley Austin (viz.) John Austin, Daniel Austin, Nancy Austin, Phebe Austin, from September Term 1802 to December.

The court then Adjourned until Tomorrow morning 9 o'clock.

Wednesday December 15th 1802 -
The Court met according to adjournement.
Present - James Grant (Esquire)
           Hugh Montgomery
           Joseph Sinclair
           Wm. McKamey.

Ordered by the court that Nathaneil Hale be overseer of the road from the old Cumberland ford to George Ramseys the upper way it being in the opinion of the Jury to view the nearest and best way & that the open and keep it open according to Law --

State   )
vs.   )
Moses Cunningham &)
Job Combs   )   Whereupon came a Jury towit, John Rains, Joseph Harkin, Francis Kerby, William Rippeto, Joshua English, William Horton, William Brazle, Isham Stinett, William Arnold, Christian Isely, Reuben Roberts, Thomas Adair, --
It was moved by John F. Jack that he have leave to enter a Nolleproseque as far as respects Job Combs which was refused. Who say they find the Defendant not guilty - Rule to Tax prosecutor with the costs as far as respects Job Combs - Rule discharged -

John Armstrong by James Grant his attorney come into open court and acknowledged a deed fo conveyance for one town lott in the town of Grantsborough to Terence McAffray Whereupon the same was ordered to be registered -

Ordered by the court that Micajah Cross have leave to keep an ordinary or house of public entertainment at his house in Anderson County, he having given Bond & security as the law requires -

48 State)
vs.)
James Adkins) Charged- Pleas not guilty whereupon came a Jury towit, William Severs, Richard Lenville, Aaron Jenkins, John Sartin, Henry Revis, Shadrach Tipton, Joseph McPeters, Augustine Hackworth, Joseph Jacobs, John Counts, Isaac Robbins, Joseph Denham, Sen., who say they find the Defendant guilty & fined by the court the sum of fifty dollars.

A deed of conveyance from Kinza Johnson, William Stanefer, William Roberson, Joseph Grayson, & Hugh Montgomery, for lott No. 39 in the town of Burrville to William Brazle was proved in open court by Robert Brazle one of the subscribing witnesses - and ordered to be registered.

Ordered by the court that John Leib be overseer of the road from Burrville across Clinch River to intersect the Eagle ford Road as viewed and marked & that John Kerby point out the hands.

Ordered by a majority of the court that the following persons be appointed a jury of view to lay off a Road from the old Tan Vats near the house of Aaron Jenkins on the road leading from the Eagle ford to Knoxville so as to meet the road of a Jury of view from Knox. County at the Knox Line - Agreeable to the prayer of the petition. (towit) Nathaniel Davis, Alexander Gastin, Isaac Norman, Thos. Wilson, Thos. Frost Sen., & Micajah Frost - and that they report to next court.

Ordered by a majority of the court that Joseph Denham Sen. be overseer of the road leading from Burville to the Eagle Ford.

49 Ordered by the court that James Adkins one of the constables here to fore appointed by this court be suspended from any longer exercising any of the duties annexed to the office of the constable, he having been conveled of any high misdemeanor.

The Court then Adjourned till Tomorrow morning 9 o'clock.

Thursday Dec. 16, 1802.
Present James Grant
         Joseph Sinclair
         Hugh Montgomery
         Wm. Mc Kamey
         Wm. Underwood.

Ordered by the court that Joshia Marcum have his mark recorded which is an half crop in each ear.

A deed of conveyance from Hugh Montgomery, Kenza Johnson, William Robertson, & William Standifer for lott No. 8 in the town of Burrville to Benjamin Williams was proved in open court by Wm. Hogshead one of the subscribing witnesses & ordered to be registered.

Ordered by the court that David Harless be appointed overseer of the road from Richard C. Cobbs on the Road leading up the Big valley to Big Buffalo in place of William Medlin.

Ordered by the court that Maronduke Bookout be overseer of the road from Bryan's fork of Hind's Creek to the county line on the chestnut ridge in place of Alden Bryan.

Ordered by the court that James Cunningham be overseer of the road from Clinch river at Major Days South side to John Scruggs.

50 Ordered by the court that James Grant Esquire take the list of Taxable property & polls in Captain Jason Clouds Company for the year 1803. Solomn Massingle for Capt. Medlins Company.
William Underwood Esquire for Capt. Wilsons & Robbins Co.

John Kerby for Aldridges Co.
Wm. McKamey for Capt. Coles Co.
James Butler for Capt. Hawkins Co.
John McKamey for McKamey's Co.
Hugh Montgomery Esquire for Capt. Steels & Lenvilles Co.

Ordered by the court that the following persons be appointed as Jurors to attend at March Term 1803 (viz.)

1 Nathaniel Davis
2 Laton Smith
3 Wm. Aldridges
4 John Jameson
5 Wm. Johnson
6 Wm. Ashlock
7 Michael Hostler
8 Wm. Griffith
9 Douglas Oliver
10 Manpage Vowel
11 Jacob Cheney
12 Abraham Hagler
13 Bailey Greerwood
14 Thos. Kincaid
15 Joseph Moore
16 Joseph Denham Sen.
17 John McAdoo
18 Moses McWhorter
19 Joseph Sharp
20 John Sharp
21 Saml. Frost
22 Reuben Ragland
23 Oliver Dotson
24 Jonathan Cunningham
25 Richd. C. Cobb
26 Spencer Graham
27 Thomas Smith
28 Jonah Denton
29 Jason Cloud
30 Austin Hackworth.

Ordered by the court that Richard Lewallen have his mark recorded which is a crop off the left ear and slit in the right ear.

Ordered by the court that a Tax for the year 1803 be levied on all taxable property for Anderson county in the following manners. (viz.)
on each white poll twelve and one half cents.
on each black poll twenty five cents
on each hundred acres of land twenty five cents.
on each stud horse kept for covering mares twenty five cents.
on each town lott twnety five cents.

Ordered by the court that John Garner have his mark recorded which is a crop & under keal in each ear.

Ordered by the court that Stephen Heard clerk be allowed the sum of forty dollars for his ex office services for the year 1802.

Ordered by the court that John Underwood sheriff be allowed the sum of Fifty dollars for his ex offices services for 1802.

Ordered by the court that John Ridenhour Sen. be appointed overseer of the road from the Junction of Powells and Clinch Rivers of Grants Ferry leading to Knoxville and to ppen it accordingly to law to Buffalo Creek where the Burrville road crosses the same and that James Grant point out the hands to work under him.

Ordered that Shadrack Reedy have leave to keep a ferry at the junction of Clinch & Powells river, and that he receive the same rates as was allowed by the county court of Grainger under the same regulations.

The commissioners having received the public gaol in the town of Burrville have surrendered the keys of said gaol to the court who put them in possession of the sheriff.

Ordered by a majority of the court that a Jury of view be appointed to mark out a road from where William Murrah now lives in the Walnut Cave by William McEntire Cotton machine on Indian Creek the nearest and best way into the road that leads from Grantsborough by the mouth of Powells river into Powells valley, and that Shadrack Morris, Conright Willright, Spencer Graham, Richard Lenville, Joseph Sharp, Jonathan Cunningham, & William McEntire be appointed to view a road & report to next court.

The court then adjourned until court in course.

James Grant, Chairman

Page 52 blank.

53   At a court began and held for the county of Anderson at Burrville the second Monday of March in the year of our Lord 1803.

Present   James Grant, Esquire
          James Butler
          Frederick Miller
          Joseph Sinclair
          Robert Pollock.

John Underwood Esquire high sheriff of the county of Anderson returns that he has executed the venirie bacias, on the following persons (viz.).

1 Nathaniel Davis   16 Joseph Denham Sen.
2 Laton Smith   17 John McAdoo
3 William Aldridge   18 Moses M. Whorter
4 John Jimmerson   19 Joseph Sharp
5 Wm. Johnson   20 John Sharp
6 Wm. Ashlock   21 Saml. Frost
7 Michael Hostler   22 Reuben Ragland
8 Wm. Griffith   23 Jonathan Cunningham
9 Douglas Oliver   24 Richd. C. Cobb
10 Manpage Vowel   25 Spencer Graham
11 Jacob Chaney   26 Thomas Smith
12 Abraham Hagler   27 Jonah Denton
13 Bailey Underwood   28 Jason Cloud
14 Thomas Kincaid   29 Austin Hackworth.
15 Joseph Moore

of whom the following were appointed grand Jurors (viz.) Reuben Ragland, Michael Hostler, Wm. Ashlock, John McAdoo, Manpage Vowell, Saml. Frost, Austin Hackworth, Wm. Aldridge, Moses M. Whorter, John Jimmerson, Jacob Chancy, Joseph Sharp, Spencer Graham, Douglas Oliver, Layton Smith who being sworn retired to enquire.

54   A deed of conveyance from Thomas Upery to Robert Warren for 100 acres of land was proved in open court by Benjamin T. Warren one of the subscribing witnesses & ordered to be registered.

A deed of conveyance from Joseph Frost to Benjamin T. Warren for one hundred acres of land was proved in open court.

A deed of conveyance from James Bray to Ayers Goad for eighty four acres of land was proved in open court by Thos. Frost Sen. one of the subscribing witnesses thereto fore and ordered to be registered.

A deed of conveyance from John Adair Administrator to Oliver Dratson for two hundred and sicty five acres of land was acknowledged in open court ordered to be registered.

A deed of conveyance from John Hackett to Alexander Galbreath for three hundred acres of land was proved in open court by Wm. Davidson, one of the subscribing witness & ordered to be registered.

A deed of conveyance from John Rhea to Oliver Dotson for two hundred and sixty five acres of land was proved in open court by Elliott Grills & ordered to be registered.

A deed of conveyance from Charles Ferrell to Thomas Griffer, for three hundred acres of land was proved in open court by Harris Ryan one of the subscribing witnesses & ordered to be registered.

A deed of conveyance from John Gibbs to Conrad Sharp for three hundred and ninety five acres was proved in open court by Frederick Miller and ordered to be registered.

55   A deed of conveyance from Joel Hobb to John Park for two hundred &

forty acres of land was proved in open court by Wm. England & Saml. Crawford and ordered to be registered.

A deed of conveyance from Wm. Hawkins to Henry Sharp for one hundred & ninety seven acres was proved in open court by Fredrick Miller esqr. and ordered to be registered.

A deed of conveyance from William Hawkins to Frederick Miller for two hundred acres of land was proved in open court by Henry Sharp one of the subscribing witnesses & ordered to be registered.

A deed of conveyance from William Hawkins to Isham Stunnett for eighty acres of land was proved in open court by Nathaniel Austin, one of the subscribing witnesses and ordered to be registered.

A deed of conveyance from James Graham & John Gray Blount Executors of Robert Satler deceased was proved in open court sufficiently certefied authenicated to Johathan Cunningham and was ordered to be registered, for two hundred & Ninety acres.

A deed of conveyance from William Hawkins to Tobias Tillman for one hundred and Eighty Seven acres of land was proved in open court by Fridrek Miller Esqr. and ordered to be registered.

Jacob Lender & Mary Lendar give bond for the due administrator of the Estate of Anthony Linder deceased and gave Page Portwood & John Kerby security.

William Hancock Duputy sheriff made oath in open court that the taxes returned on due by the following persons could not be collected they having removed out of the county (viz.) John Guess, Owen Willis, Jonathan Rains, for the year 1802 --

56 Ordered by the court that Jason Cloud of the Executors of the last will and testament of Aaron Guess deceased have leave to sell the property belonging to said Estate agreeable to the tenor of the will -

Ordered by the court that John Sartain have leave to keep an ordinary or house of public entertainment in Burrville he having give bond and security as the law requires and taken the necessary oaths.

Ordered by the court that James Taylor have leave to keep an ordinary or house of entertainment he having given bond and security as the law requires.

Ordered by the court that William Wood be appointed constable for Capt. Aldridge Company he having given bond and security as the law requires and having taken the necessary oaths.

Ordered by a majority of the court that Micajah Frost, Layton Smith, Isaac Norman, Henry Norman, Eli Norman, Daniel Jennings, & Samuel Frost be appointed to view & lay off a road to the nearest & best way from Burrville to Menefees mill on Beaver Creek so as to go by the saw mill on Bull Run & that make report to next court.

Court then adjourned for one hour.
Court met according to adjournment.

57 Ordered by the court that John Kitchen be appointed a constable for Captain Medlins Company he having given bond and security as the law requires & having taken the necessary oaths.

Ordered by the court that Joseph Adair be admitted Defendant instead of Henry Revis Tenant in possession he having given bond and security as the law requires, on condition that he confess lease, Entry, & ouster and rely on his title only.

Received of Solomn Massingale Esquire the list of Taxable property & polls in Capt. Medlins Company for the year 1803.

Wm. McKamey Esq. returns the list of Taxable property & polls in Capt. Coles Company.

Court adjourned till tomorrow morning 9 o'clock.

58   Tuesday March 15th 1803
      The Court met according to adjournment.
      Present   James Grant Esquire
                Hugh Montgomery "
                Robt. Pollock   "
                Frederick Miller "

Ordered by the court that Christain Isely have his brand recorded which is C E and also his ear mark which is an under keel in the left ear and two square pieces out of the right.

James Butler Esquire returns the list of taxable property & polls in Capt. Hawkins Company for the year 1803.

Ordered by the court that Jesse Vanoy have his mark recorded which is a smooth crop & under bit in the left ear and a half cross in the right ear.

James Grant Esq. returns the Tax list for Capt. Clouds Company for the year 1803 also the list of Taxable of a member of (non residents)

59   Spencer Graham)
      vs.   )
      George Kellums) Whereupon came a jury (viz.) Thomas Smith, Jonathan Cunningham, Wm. Griffith, Abraham Hazler, James Bray, John Arnold, Thomas Walker, Thomas Philips, Michael Aldridge, Jacob Leinard, David Hall, & William Hogshead who being duly sworn say they find for the Defendant - appeal prayed --

Ordered by the court that George Ramsay have leave to keep an ordinary or house of public entertainment at his house on poplar creek he having given bond and security as the law requires.

Edward Pankey returns 150 acres of land & one poll for 1803.

Ordered by the court that Felix Gilbert be overseer of the road in room of Richard C. Cobb from Byrans Fork of Hinds creek to little Buffalo.

      State   )
      vs.   )
      Joseph Tirry) Plea not guilty-- whereupon came a Jury (viz.) Thomas Smith, Abraham Hagler, Thomas Walker, Thomas Philips, Michael Selvidge, Jacob Leinard, David Hall, & William Hogshead, William Brazle, and Isaac Brazleton, James Bray & James Hannah, William Ryan who say they find the defendant guilty in manner & form as charged in the bill of indictment fine five dollars and cost.

60   A deed of conveyance from Jeremiah Jeffery to James Worthington for 150 acres of land was acknowledged in open court and ordered to be registered.

A deed of conveyance from Samuel Worthington to Jeremiah Jeffery for fifty acres of land was acknowledged in open court and ordered to be registered.

Ordered that Saml. Worthington Sen. have his mark recorded which is a slit & half penny in the left ear and a smooth crop off the right.

A deed of conveyance from Wm. Horton to William Tunnell for three hundred acres of land was acknowledged in open court & ordered to be registered.

Ordered that William Tunnell have his mark recorded which is an half crop in the right ear and a slit and over bit in the left.

Thomas Holt returns one pole for Taxes for the year 1803.

A deed of conveyance from Kenza Johnson to Constant Claxton for two hundred and thirty acres of land was acknowledged in open court &

ordered to be registered- Rowland Lee returns one white poll for taxes for the year 1803.

Isaac Brazleton four hundred & and fifty acres of land one white poll and one black poll for taxes for the year 1803.

Ordered by the court that John Jimmerson be allowed the sum of thirty dollars for keeping a considerable time when alive and burying when dead, a certain old woman named Mary Timlett.

61 Ordered by the court that James Stanifer be appointed overseer of the road from Phillips Trace to Double Springs in room of James Chiltwood.

Ordered by the court that Isacah Ruchman, Sarah Carlock, Mary Carlock, & Isaac Carlock be released from their recognizance & farther attendance.

Ordered by the court that Martin Ridenhour & Henry Ridenour be released from their recognizance & farther attendance in the suit the State vs. Wm. Brumley -

Court adjourned until Tomorrow morning 9 o'clock.

Wednesday 16th March 1803-
Court met according to Adjournment.
Present   James Grant, Esq.
           William Underwood
           Frederick Miller.

Ordered by the court that Isaac Ajey be appointed overseer in the room of Levie Jones from Mayberrys road in the rich hollar to the Grantsborough Road- and that James Grant Esquire point out the hands.

Ordered by the court that Samuel Wilson have a commissioner to take the deposition of William Moore in the state of North Carolina, Bunkham county at the court house in Bunkham county, and that he give the Defendant thirty days notice.

Ordered by the court that Joseph Sinclair Esq. John Kerby, Esq. & James Butler Esq. be appointed an equable distribution of the hands between Page Portwood & Rich Forrest.

62 Jonathan Cunningham, Robert Armstrong who were appointed a Jury of view to lay off a road from James Greens to Grantstore report that they have laid off the same and John Leach is appointed overseer from James Greens to Love Creek. Joel White from there to Big Creek and Isaac Chrissman from there to Grantsborough. It is recommended that the same be marked & opened only as a Bidle way and that Robert Pollock Sen. point out the hands.

Ordered by the court that on reconsideration that the order made yesterday allowing John Jimmerson the sum of thirty dollars for keeping when alive and burying when dead a certain old woman by the name of Mary Timlett be rescended and that the said John Jimmerson by allowed the sum of twenty dollars only --

State   )
vs   )
Stephen Marcum)   Pleads not guilty-

Whereupon came a Jury (viz) Thomas Smith, William Griffith, Abraham Hagler, Jonathan Cunningham, William Hogshead, Nathan Roberts, Obadiah Wood, John Leib, Felix Gilbert, Francis Kerby, Tachariah Jacobs, & Joseph McPeters, who say they find the defendant not guilty.
Rule to show cause why the prosecutors should be taxed with the costs-
Rule discarged - James Butler Esq. Nathan Hale, James Scarbro, Samuel Worthington, Saml. Worthington Junr. who were appointed a jury to view & lay off a road from scarbro Ferry to Aldridges Ford & from thence to Samuel Worthington. Report that they have renewed & marked out the same. And Necodemus Hackworth be overseer from where it intersects the road leading from the Cumberland Ford on Clinch to George Ramsays to David

Halls, and John Funnell from there to Samuel McKameys & that James Butler Tom Standifer, Wm. Standifer & John McKamey, Esquire make an equal distribution of the hands between the said overseers.

63 A deed of conveyance from Stockley Donelson to John McEntire for one thousand acres of land was proved in open court by William Cotter one of the subscribing witnesses and ordered to be registered.

Samb. Crawford returns one white poll, and six hundred and forty acres of land the property of the heirs of Watson Reed for taxes for 1803.

William Underwood returns the list of taxable property & Polls in Capt. Robbins Co. & Wilsons for the year 1803.

Adam Keintz came into court and entered into bond to keep the county of Anderson indemnified an free from the maintance of a bastard child begotten by him on the body of Nancy Brumley and gave John Keinty & Moses McWhorter Securties himself in the sum of five hundred dollars & the securties in two hundred an fifty dollars each.

John Julian came into court and entered into Bond in the sum of five hundred dollars and gave Nathan Aldridge and Tobias Long as securties bound in the sum of two hundred and fifty dollars each to keep the county of Anderson free and indemnified from the maintance of a bastard child begotten by him on the body of Elizabeth Shoemaker.

Ordered by the court that William Standifer, Douglas Oliver and Hugh Montgomery be appointed as Jurors to attend at the superior court at next March term for Hamilton District.

Ordered by the court that Spencer Graham have his mark recorded which is a crop a slit in the right ear and a swallow fork in the left.

64 It is considered by the court that Hugh Montgomery Esq. and John Kerby Esq. have to the last day of April next to return into the clerks office the list of taxable property & polls in the companies assigned them they having given satisfactory reasons to the court for not have taken them previously.

William Horton was fined in the sum of thirty seven and one half cents for swearing profoundly which is paid to the treasurer.

John Kerby ordered and paid in open court five dollars the amount of a fine paid by Elizabeth Lucas for Bastardy & refusing to swear which is paid to the county treasurer.

Ordered by a majority of the acting Justices that Robert Brazle be allowed one dollar for every day he has attended as constable of the court & Grand Jury --

Court adjourned until tomorrow morning 9 o'clock.

Thursday March 17th 1803.
Court met according to adjournment.
Present   James Grant Esq.
           Hugh Montgomery
           John Kerby
           Joseph Sinclair
           James Butler.

65 Ordered by the court that the following persons be appointed as a Jury to attend the next court of pleas & Quarter sessions to be held for the county of Anderson on the second Monday of June next ---- (viz.)

1 Jason Cloud   6 Richd. C. Cobb
2 Joseph Galoher   7 Thomas Wilson
3 John Colston   8 John Bowman
4 Nathan Davis   9 Wm. Rayland
5 James Porter   10 John Day

11 John Hannah
12 John Scruggs
13 Wm. Tunnell
14 George Julian
15 Jacob Peak
16 Wm. Robertson
17 Isaac Brazleton
18 James Patterson
19 Joseph Lea
20 Chs. Shinliver
21 Robert Sinclair
22 Geo. Brazle
23 Jeremiah Jeffery
24 Richd. Medlin
25 Henry Russell
26 Henry Sharp Sen.
27 John English
28 Britain Raysdale
29 Saml. Worthington Sen.
30 Isham Stinneld.

Arthur Crozier produced his commission from the governor as entry taker pro tem in open court and gave bond as security as the law requires and was qualified accordingly.

Ordered by a majority of the court that William Underwood make an equal distribution of the hands between the overseers John Parks and Felix Gilbert.

Ordered by that Jesse Vancy be appointed overseer in the room & stead of James Adkins.

Ordered by a majority of the court david Lea be appointed overseer of the road in stead of Jesse Lea who is removed.

A deed of conveyance from William Henry to Shadrack Morris for one thousand acres was proved in open court by Wm. H. Murrah & ordered to be registered.

66 Ordered by a majority of the justices on reconsideration that the following rates of Ferriage be abserved by John Leib and John McWhorter. (viz.)

	dols	cents
for waggon and team		.75
Pleasure carriage of four wheels & horses	1.00	
" " " two " " "		.50
Foreman & horse		.06 1/4
Led horse		.06 1/4
Footman		.06 1/4
cattle, hogs & sheep pr. head		.03

Ordered by a majority of the Justices that the following rates be observed by those who have obtained license for keeping ordinaries & retailing Spirituous Liquors ------------

	cents
for good comfortable breakfast with coffee	.16 2/3
For a good comfortable dinner	.25
" " " " supper	.16 2/3
" " " " lodging	.06 1/4
For keeping an horse 24 hours with corn & fodder or hay	.25
for 1/2 pint good prof. whiskey	.08 1/3
for 1 qt. " " . "	.25
for 1/2 pt. good peach or apple brandy	.12 1/2
for 1/2 pt. " french brandy	.25
for good west Indian Rum pr. 1/2 pt.	.25
for country made rum " " "	.12 1/2
for 1 qt. cyder	.12 1/2
for 1 qt. good malt beer	.12 1/2
" " " " Cyder Royal	.16 2/3
for corn or oats per gallon	.06 1/4

67 Ordered by the court that an alias order to Spencer Graham, Shadrack Morris, Wm. McEntire, Jonathan Cunningham, Joseph Sharp, Richard Levnille & John English issue as a jury of view.

William Murrah report to the following persons to the court as delinqushment in paying their taxes for the year 1802 & is sworn as the law requires that he could find no property to make the tax of (viz.) James

Long 18 3/4 cents. James Arbuckle 56 1/4 Richard Sharp 18 3/4 cents.

John Underwood high sheriff for the county of Anderson reports the following persons as delinquements in paying their taxes for the year 1802 and is qualified as the law requires that he can find no property to make the taxes of (viz.)

Godson, Stephen	18 3/4	Frederick Merdith	18 3/4
William Holt	18 3/4	Joseph Book	18 3/4
John Lewis	18 3/4	Austin Cheat	18 3/4
Stephen Lewis	18 3/4	Christopher Choat	18 3/4
Wm. Medlin	18 3/4	John Juston	18 3/4
Stephen Pickett	18 3/4	Matthew Jones	18 3/4
Clodfeller, John	18 3/4	Stephen Robertson	18 3/4
Frederick Farmer	18 3/4	Silvey William	18 3/4
George Hostler	18 3/4	Elisha Wasson	18 3/4
Jesse Lea	18 3/4	Samuel Latham	18 3/4
Panken Stephen	18 3/4	Thomas M. Griff	18 3/4
James Cotton	18 3/4	John Rice	18 3/4
John Gibson	18 3/4	David Williams	18 3/4
Joel Hobbs	18 3/4	John Williams	18 3/4
James Hobbs	18 3/4	William Nelson	18 3/4
Edward Jacobs	37 1/2	Jas. Roberson	18 3/4
John Meloney	18 3/4		
Thomas Pratt	18 3/4		

68   John Underwood Esquire sheriff reports the following tracts of land returned for the year 1802 on which the taxes have not been paid & that he can find no personal property to make the tax of. It is therefore ordered by the court that the same be advertised according to law(Viz.)

	Acres	Dols.	Cents
Gen. Benjamin Smith	8668	16.	28 3/4
Heirs of Leonard Bullock	8625	16.	17 1/8
Parker & Lucas	10,000		
John Duggins	640		
John Clodfeller	200		
John Long	700		
Benjamin Parker by his Att. Wm. Medlin	3500		
Lewis Widener	600		
Stephen Roberson	150		
RichD. Chan Gersasseynee) 2 town lots Grantsboro)			
Nathan Hart	6000		
Josiah Watson	2015 5/8		

Ordered by the court that Gabriel Shelton bring forward to the next court to be held for the county of Anderson a girl by the name of Elizabeth Carrell, who was presented by the grand Jury as improvided for.

Ordered by the court that Maloby bring forward William Sears to the next court to be held for the county of Anderson who is presented by the grand Jury as unprovided for.

Ordered by the court that Mary Swanson bring forward to the next court to be held for the county of Anderson the following children (viz.) Mildred Swanson, Dewsey Swanson, Gordon Swanson & Sarah Swanson who have been presented by the Grand Jury, as unprovided for.

69   Ordered by the court that Richard Sharp, William Sweeton & Abraham Learlock be released from the payment of poll Taxes on account of their unability.

Jason Cloud, Nathaniel Davis, Thomas Kincaid, William Johnson, Joseph Moore, & Richard C. Cobb and John Denton were on application to the court excused from werving as Jurors at the present term.

Court adjourned until court in course.

James Grant Chairman --

Page 70 Blank

71   At a court begun and held for the county of Anderson at Burrville on the second Monday of June in the year of our Lord 1803 --

    Present
- James Grant Esq.
- William Underwood Esq.
- Hugh Montgomery "
- James Butler "
- Joseph Sinclair "
- Wm. McKamey "
- Robert Pollock "
- John McKamey "
- Wm. Standifer "

John Underwood Esquire high sheriff of the county of Anderson returns that he has executed the venirie facias on the following persons (viz.) those marked thus x

1. Jason Cloud
2. Joseph Goloher x
3. John Gotson
4. Nathan Davis
5. James Porter
6. Richd C. Cobb
7. Thomas Wilson
8. John Browmar
9. Wm. Bagland
10. John Day
11. John Hanna
12. John Scruggs
13. Wm. Tunnell
14. George Julian
15. Jacob Peak
16. Wm. Roberson x
17. Isaac Brazleton
18. James Patterson x
19. Joseph Lea
20. Charles Shinliver
21. Robert Sinclair
22. George Brazle
23. Jeremiah Jeffery
24. Richd Medlin
25. Henry Russell
26. Henry Sharp Sen.
27. John English
28. Britain Raysdale
29. Saml. Worthington
30. Isham Stunnett

of whom the following are appointed grand Jurors (viz.) William Ragland foreman- Isaac Brazleton, Richard Medlin, John Bowman, Nathaniel Davis, Jeremiah Jeffery, Robert Sinclair, George Julian, Jacob Peak, John Hanna, Isham Stunnett, Henry Russell, John Gotson, John Day.

72   The Ballance are Graverse Jurors- Harry Sharp Sen. Richd. C. Cobb, Geo. Brazle, Saml. Worthington, Joseph Lea, Charles Shinliver, Britain Cross, James Porter, & John Scruggs.

    A deed of conveyance from James Scarbrough to Tobias Peters for one hundred and twenty acres of land was acknowledged in open court and ordered to be registered.

    A deed of conveyance from William Reed to James Scarbro for two hundred acres of land was proved in open court by Tobias Peters & ordered to be registered.

    Ordered by the court that Joseph Keeny be overseer of the road laid out from the Island ford road near the ford of Coal creed to the lower line of Anderson County, from the upper end thereof to John McBrows house in the room & stead of John McBribe & that Wm. McKamey point out the hands.

    A deed of conveyance from Nathaniel Davis to John Dever, for two hundred & thirty seven acres of land was acknowledged in open court & ordered to be registered.

    A deed of conveyance from Richard Medlin to John Collar for one hundred and two acres of land was acknowledged in open court and ordered to be registered.

Thomas Smith surrendered James McMurry for whom he was bail in exgneration of himself who was ordered incustody of the sheriff.

A deed of conveyance from Nathaniel Davis to Alexander Gastin for one hundred and twenty seven acres was acknowledged in open court & ordered to be registered.

Ordered by the court that Henry Bowman be overseer of the road from the mouth of Powells river, into Mayberrys Road in the Rich Hollow in room of John Adair & that James Grant Esq. point out the hands.

Ordered by the court that Joel Bowling be overseer of the road from the north bank of Clinch River at William Hancocks ford to where the road leading from the mouth of Powels river in stead of Jonathan Cunningham and that James Grant Esquire point out the hands.

Ordered by the court that William Whitial be overseer of the road leading from Burrville to James Shiltwoods from Burrville to William Ashlocks instead of Richard Forrest and that Joseph Sinclair Sen. point out the hands. *[margin: Chitwood]*

A deed of conveyance from James Adair to Alexander Adair for five hundred acres of land was proved in open court by John Adair one of the subscribing witnesses there to & ordered to be registered.

William McEntire, Spencer Graham, Joseph Sharp, Richard Lenville, Jonathan Cunningham, Shadriah Morris & John English who were a Jury appointed to view an mark out a road from where Wm. Murrah lives in the Walnut Cave by McEntire, Cotton Machine to Grantsborough, Report they reviewed an marked out the same and Wm. McEntire is appointed overseer of the same from the valley road to Indian Creek and that John Whitman be overseer of the same from said Creek to Grantsborough- and that Robert Pollock Esquire & Hugh Montgomery Esquire point out the hands of the said overseers.

Received from Wm. McKamey Esquire the sum of two dollars & fifty cents as fines for Sabbath breaking-- which sum is paid to the county treasure.

Ordered by the court that Robert Long have his mark recorded which is a swallow fork in each ear.

Ordered by the court that Richard C. Cobb, Arthur Crozier & Samuel Crawford be appointed commissioners to settle with the treasure of Anderson County.

Saml. Frost, Micajah Frost, Layton Smith, Isaac Norman, Henry Norman & Daniel Jennings who were appointed as a Jury to view & open a road from the top of the copper ridge by the sawmill on Bull run into the road leading to Burrville. Report that they have reviewed and opened the same & that John Kerby Esq. point out the hands.

Ordered by the court that Arthur Crozier, Samuel Crawford and Stephen Heard be appointed to lay off the prison Bounds in the town of Burrville according to law and mark the same.

The Court then adjourned till Tomorrow Morning 9 o'clock.

Tuesday June 14th 1803.
Court met according to Adjournment.
Present   James Grant   Esquire
           Robert Pollock   "
           James Butler   "

Andrew M. Lush Esquire produced his Sience to practice as an attorney in the several courts of law and Equity in this state and took the necessary oaths.

Robert Brazle
   vs.

Thomas Philips) Whereupon came a Jury (viz.) Charles Shinliver, James Porter, Richard Linville, Reuben Roberts, Calet Friley, Christian Isely, John Garner, John Leib, Andrew Cape, David Noble, William Noble, Thomas Hill Sen. who being duly sworn say they find for the plaintiff and assess his damage to six cents. Rule for a new trial- Rule Discharged.

Robert Brazle)
vs)
Thomas Philips) Saml. Upery, ' Aaron Jenkins, who were regularly summoned to attend as witness in the above cause on part of the Defendant being solemnly called came not wherefore it is considered they forfeit accordingly to act of assembly in such case made & provided.

76

Jesse Belew)
vs)
Joseph McPeters) John Duggins & Garret Harbin who were securties in the afore mentioned suit for the Defendant surrendered him in open court in discarge of themselves. The Deft. then gave Joseph Denham Senr. & Shadrach Morris as his securties. Who acknowledged themselves indebted to the Plff. in the sum of four hundred dollars to be void on condition the Deft. appear at next term of court to our few the plff.

James Rutherford)
vs.)
Joseph McPeters) John Druggins & Garret Harbin who were securties for the defendant surrendered him in open court. The Defendant gave Joseph Denham Sen. & Shadrach Morris as hhs securties for the who acknowledged themselves indebyed to the James Rutherford in the sum of one hundred dollars to be void on condition the Defendant appear at next court to answer the complaint of said Plff.

Ordered by the court that Robert Baker have leave to administer on the Estate Curks Hobbs deceased he having entered into Bond in the sum of five hundred dollars and gave Wm. Patterson & Shadrack Morris his securties & was qualified accordingly.

Ordered by the court that David Lea be released from his omership from the fork of the island ford road and the Burrville road above Cole Creek to Capt. Hills in the Walnut Cave and that Saml. Worthington be overseer in his stead & that Col. Montgomery point out the hands.

A dded of conveyance from Isaac Brazleton to David Hall for one hundred acres of land was proved in open court by James Butler Esquire & ordered to be registered.

77

James Adkins)
vs.)
Christian Isely) Whereupon came a Jury (viz.) John Scruggs, Joseph Lea, Samuel Worthington, Britian Ragsdale, Henry Sharp Sen. George Brazle, David Hall, Richard Brazle, William Brawney, William Mankins, Jeremiah Jacobs & Henry Revis who being duly sworn say they find for the Defendant ---

Ordered by the court that James Porter be overseer of the road from George Ramsays on the East fork of Poplar Creek to Reuben Williams Spring instead of Jacob Peak and that John McKamey Esquire point out the hands.

A deed of conveyance from John Adair administrator of James Adair to Samuel McKinley for one hundred acres of land was proved in open court by

John Adair & ordered to be registered.
 Court adjourned for one hour-
 Court met according to adjournment.
 A deed of conveyance from William Murphy to Joseph Jeffery for two hundred acres of land was proved in open court by Jeremiah Jeffery & ordered to be registered.
 A deed of conveyance from George Brazle to Joseph & Wm. Horton for one hundred acres was acknowledged in open court and ordered to be registered.
 A deed of conveyance from Jesse Lea to Robert Sinclair for one hundred and eighty seven acres of land was proved in open court by Tachariah Lea & ordered to be registered.

78 A deed of conveyance from John Underwood high sheriff of Anderson County to William Aldridge was acknowledged in open court and ordered to be registered for six hundred & forty acres of land.

Temple & Russell)
 vs.   )
Spencer Graham) Whereupon came a Jury (viz.) Perry Jacobs, Tobias Long, James Taylor, William Harvers, William Hogshead, Archibald McDaniel, Nathan Roberts, Samuel Ussery, Joseph Hogg, Alexander Cole, Aaron Jenkins & James Porter, who being duly sworn say they find for the defendant hath not paid the debt in Declaration mentioned and assess the damages of the plaintiff by reason of the detention thereof to seven dollars and twenty five cents. Reasons filed in arrest of Judgment by John H. Maddison attorney for the Defendant- Reasons overruled --

 Ordered by the court that an Alias order issue to the Jury of view appointed to view the road from the Tan Vats to county Line of Knox & that they report to next court.

Isaac Robbins)
 vs.   )
William Cotter) Whereupon came a Jury (towit.) Henry Shark, John Wenningham, Jonathan Cunningham, William Aldridge, Robert Pollock, Nathaniel Austin, Jacob Rhea, John Baker, Samuel Ussery, Alexander Cowan, Alexander Cole, & Moses Roberts, who being duly sworn say they find for the Defendant --

79 Ordered by the court that James Cunningham, Moses McWhorter, Arthur Crozier, David Maxwell, William Hogshead, Philip Fry, & John McAdoo, be appointed a Jury to view & lay off a road from Burrville crossing the river at William Hogshead, near the mouth of Hinds Creek & leading from thence to Cotton, Williams, where it will intersect the Island ford road and that they report to next court.
 Court adjourned till tomorrow morning 9 o'clock.

 Wednesday 15th 1803.
 Court met according to Adjournment.
 Present James Grant Esquire
     James Butler "
     William Standifer "
     William Underwood "

 Ordered by the court that Wm. Hancock Senr. be overseer of the road from the South Bank of Clinch River to where it intersects the road opened by Ridenour from the ferry instead of Shadrach Reedy- and that James Grant Esq. point out the hands.
 Ordered by the court that Reuben Hoss be overseer of the road lead-

ing to Grantsborough from the Powels valley road across the first high ridge to the foot of it instead of Caleb Bailey and that James Grant Esq. point out the hands.

80   Ordered by the court that William McKamey Esq., Joseph Sinclair Esq. & Robert Pollock Esq. or any two of them be appointed to make an equitable distribution of the hands between Robert Armstrong, Joseph Keeny, and John Leach the said Justices to meet at James Greens.

Ordered by the court that John Baker have his mark recorded which is a swallow fork in the left ear and a half crop in the right ear.

Ordered by the court that Alexander Cowan have his mark recorded which is a crop off the left ear and a slit in the right.

Ordered by the court that Shadrack Morris have his mark recorded which is a crop & under keel in the left ear and two underkeels in the right.

Ordered by the court that James Butler Esq. William Underwood Esq. & Arthur Crozier be appointed inspectors of the next ensuing election for governor members of congress an members of the Genl. Assembly.

A deed of conveyance from James Porter to William Horton for one hundred acres of land was acknowledged in open court & ordered to be registered.

A deed of conveyance from John Underwood sheriff to Micajah Cross for three thousand six hundred and sixty six acres of land was acknowledged in open court & ordered to be registered.

81   The following persons are appointed Jurors to attend at September sessions 1803 (viz.)

1 John Asher
2 Oliver Dotson
3 James McNutt
4 Samuel McCoy
5 John McBribe
6 Joseph Jeffery
7 Jonah Denton
8 Wm. Tunnell Jr.
9 David Hall
10 Joseph Golloher
11 Aquella Johnson
12 Wm. Brazle
13 Thos. Kincaid
14 Henry Norman
15 Obadiah Woods
16 Henry Farmer Senr.
17 Layton Smith
18 Conright Willright
19 Joseph Sharp
20 Spencer Graham
21 David Lea
22 Lacky Lea
23 John McAdoo
24 Moses McWhorter
25 Philip Fry
26 Polly Duncan
27 John Lawler
28 L. Rector
29 Joseph Moore
30 Jonathan Cunningham.

Ordered by the court that Robert Sinclair have his mark recorded which is a crop off the left ear and an hole in the right.

Ordered by the court that Thomas Hill have his mark recorded which is a swallow fork and an upper and under keel in the right ear- and two upper keels and two under keels in the left.

Freeman Stilt comes into open court and enters into bond in the sum of five hundred dollars and give Robert Sinclair & John Baker securties to keep the county of Anderson indemnified from the maintance of a child by him begotten on the body of Jenna Sterman alias Thacker.

John Underwood high sheriff of the county of Anderson entered into bond in the penal sum of five thousand dollars and gave James Grant Esq. Hugh Montgomery Esq. & William Underwood Esquire securties for the collector of the public & county tax.

82   Court Adjourned for half an hour.
Court met according to Adjournment.
Present -- James Grant Esq.
        James Butler "
        Wm. McKamey "

Ordered by the court that Jarrott Harbin be appointed as constable in Burrville in Captain Terry's Company he having given bond & security as the law requires (viz.) Joseph Denham Sen. & Arthur Crozier, & took the necessary oaths.

Ordered by the court that Abraham Carlock & James Lavis be executed from the payment of poll tax in consequence of theretofore & debitated state.

Ordered by the court that John Leib be allowed the sum of forty dollars for the use of this court house for the court to sit up and during June sessions 1803. On condition that Leib give the use of the house for the ensuing Election and next court provided by the court house is not ready for holding said Election & court

James Grant Chairman

Page 83 Blank---

84 At a court began and held for the county of Anderson at Burrville on the second Monday of September being the 12th in the year of our lord 1803.

Present James Grant Esquire
Joseph Sinclair "
John McKamey "
John Kerby "
& William McKamey Esquire

John Underwood Esquire high sheriff of the county of Anderson returns that he has executed the Venirie Facias on the following persons. (viz.)

1 John Asher
2 Oliver Dodson
3 James McNutt
4 Saml. McCoy
5 John McBribe
6 Joseph Jeffery
7 Jonah Denton
8 Wm. Tunnell Jr.
9 David Hall
10 Joseph Golloher
11 Aquella Johnson
12 Wm. Brazle
13 Henry Norman
14 Obadiah Wood
15 Henry Farmer Sen.
16 Layton Smith
17 Conright Willright

18 Joseph Sharp
19 Spencer Graham
20 David Lea
21 Tachariah Lea
22 John McAdoo
23 Moses McWhorter
24 Philip Fry (excused)
25 Polly Duncan
26 John Fowler
27 Landon Rector
28 Joseph Moore
29 Jonah Cunningham

of whom the following are grand Jurors.

85 1 John McAdoo
2 John Fowler
3 Joseph Moore
4 Tachariah Lea
5 Jonah Denton
6 Samuel McCoy
7 Conright Willright
8 Jonathan Cunningham

9 Moses M. Whorter
10 Oliver Dotson
11 Landon Rector
12 Polly Duncan
13 Obadiah Wood
14 John McBribe
15 James McNutt.

The remainder are Traverse jurors (viz.)
Wm. Brazle, Layton Smith, Henry Farmer sen. Henry Norman, Wm. Tunnell Sen. Joseph Tolloher, John Asher, David Hall, Joseph Jefferies, Aquilla Johnson.

A deed of conveyance from Thomas Carpenter to John Williams for seventy five acres of land was acknowledged in open court & ordered to be registered.

Ordered by the court that Elizabeth Butler widow & relect of James Butler deceased and Robert Brazle have leave to administer on the Estate of the said James Butler they having entered into Bond with Augustin Hackworth & William Brazle in the sum of eight hundred dollars & qualified as the law requires.

A deed of conveyance from John Belevens to Harris Ryan for two hundred acres of land was proved in open court by Shadrach Chandler & ordered to be registered.

A deed of conveyance from Thomas Galbreath to Thomas Wilson for two hundred acres of land was acknowledged in open court & ordered to be registered.

Simon B. Greysby & Samuel Love produced their license to profile law in open court and took the necessary oaths.

86   A deed of conveyance from Joel Hobbs to Thomas Talbreath for two hundred acres of land was proved in open court by Nathaniel Davis & ordered to be registered.

A deed of conveyance from John Umstead by James Grant his attorney for one hundred and seventy acres of land was acknowledged in open court & ordered to be registered.

A deed of conveyance from John Kerby to Page Portwood for two hundred and thirty nine acres of land and three fourths was acknowledged in open court & ordered to be registered.

Ordered by the court James Finley be appointed a constable in Captain Bakers Company he having given Conright Willright & John H. Madison his securties & entered into Bond & qualified as the law requires.

Ordered by a majority of the court that John Asher, Constable Claxton, Charles Shinliver, Kenza Johnson, Joseph Lea, Wm. Patterson & John Jimmerson be appointed a Jury to view & lay off a road leading from the house of Craven Johnson to Burrville & that they make report to next court.

Ordered by the court that John Bounds, George Inland, Wm. Tunnell, Sen., James Pankey, Joseph Jeffery, and Isaac Brazleton be appointed a Jury toview and lay off a road from the valley road near Henry Farmers to where it will intersect the road at Thomas Adairs & that they report to next court.

87   A deed of Thomas McBribe to Jonas Denton for one hundred and forty seven acres was proved in open court by David Cunningham & ordered to be registered.

Ordered by a majority of the court that John Scruggs, Powell Harmon, Samuel Edwards, Major John Day, Robert Dew, John McAdoo, John Wallace be appointed a Jury to view and lay off a road from the Walnut Cave to the Island Ford on Clinch river and from thence to William Cotters & that they report to next court.

Arthur Crozier, William Hogshead, Philip Fry, James Cunningham, and David Maxwell, who were appointed jurors to view and lay off a road leading from Burrville crossing the river at William Hogshead, near the mouth of Hinds Creek and leading thence to William Cotters, Report that they have viewed and marked the same to cross the river Clinch at the mouth of Hinds Creek on the lower side and from thence to the house of Wm. Cotter be appointed overseer on the south side of said river and William Hogshead on the north side and that John Kerby Esq. point out their hands.

Ordered by the court that Joseph Gollohere, Abraham Hagler, Thomas Kincaid, Thomas Horn, and Joseph Moore be appointed a Jury to view and lay off a road from the house of Gibson Harden Esquire the nearest and best way to strike the Gap of the pine ridge at George Ramsays and from thence to intersect the Burrville road near Saml. Worthington & that they report to next court.

A deed of conveyance from Stephen M. Commus to Joseph Denham for one hundred acres of land was acknowledge in open court & ordered to be registered.

88   Elizabeth Butler Administrator and Robert Brazle administrator of the Estate of James Butler deceased produced an inventory of the same in open court & had leave to sell the same.

Ordered by the court that John Asher be appointed overseer in the room of Constant Claxton, of road laid out and leading from the Island ford road near the ford of Cole Creek to the lower line of Anderson county from Kenza Johnsons to Jimmerson.

Ordered by the court that Henry Farmer be overseer of the road instead of James D. Puckett from John Jimmerson.

A deed of conveyance from the commissioners of the town of Burrville for a tract of land containing fifty square poles in the town of Burrville to John Masterson was proved in open court by George Baumgertner, & ordered to be registered.

Received of Wm. McKamey Esq. forty seven cents for fines for profane swearing.

Isaac Norman, Thomas Wilson, Nathaniel Davis, & Alexander Gastin who were appointed a Jury to view the road from the Tan vats to the county line, Report that they have reviewed the same and Nathaniel Davis is appointed overseer of the same, and John Kerby Esquire is to point out the hands.

89   Ordered by the court that James Grant, William McKamey and Gibson Hardin Esquires, be appointed Jurors to the next superior court to be holden for the district of Hamilton.

Court adjourned till tomorrow morning 9 o'clock.

90
Tuesday 13th September 1803.
Court met according to adjournment.
Present   James Grant Esquire
          Hugh Montgomery   "
          Joseph Sinclair   "

Samuel Wilson   )
     vs.   )
Michael Robbins) A Jury sworn (towit) Wm. Brazle, Layton Smith, Henry
                  Norman, David Hall, Joseph Jeffery, Aguella Hohnson,
Reuben Roberts, Robert Pollock, John Terry, Page Portwood, Reuben Stanley, and Joseph Hogg who say they find for plaintiff sixty nine dollars forty seven cents and one half of a cent costs & 6¢ cost Rule for a new trial- Rule discarged- Appeal prayed Reason filed appeal granted   appeal bond entered into & filed.

Ordered by the court that Walter Evans be bound in the sum of five hundred dollars who gave Joseph Denham Sen. & Solomn Massingale his securities to indemnify the county from the maintance of a Bastard child begotten on the body of Sally Bowling.

Ordered by a majority of the acting Justices in Anderson county on motion of Saml. Love attorney for Charles.
J. Love have leave to file a petition for the rectifying & alluring several mistakes or errors in making a survey of 3150 acres of land also in making out the plates & certificates for the secretaries office by the surveyor & also several other mistakes & errors as mentioned in said petition which said tract of 3150 acres of land lays in what was then Hawkins county & now the county of Anderson on the north side of Clinch ri-

ver on Cave Creek in a place known by the name of Walnut Cave which tract of land was surveyed for Stockley Donelson by Annanias McCoy a deputy Survey under said Donelson who was the surveyor of the Eastern district.

91
Samuel Curry)
30 vs. Debt)
Richd. Lenville) A Jury sworn (towit) Wm. Brazle, Layton Smith, Henry Horman, David Hall, Joseph Jeffery, Aquella Johnson, Reuben Roberts, John Terry, Page Portwood, Reuben Stanley, Joseph Hogg, and Enoch Foster who say they find the Deft. hath not paid the debt in the declaration mentioned & assess his damages by reason of the detention thereof to Eleven dollars and eighty eight cents costs.

James Rutherford)
vs.)
Joseph McPeters) Ordered by the court on motion of John F. Jack that a commissioner issue to the state of North Carolina Buncombe county the Defendant to take depositions, with twenty days notice.

Ordered by the court that Isaac Brazleton be appointed overseer of the road in place of John Lively from Isaac Brazletons fence to Thomas Carpenter.

A deed of conveyance from Isaac Brazleton & Aquella Low to Jesse Hoskins for two hundred acres of land was proved in open court by Kenza Johnson & ordered to be registered.

Garrett Harbin)
vs.)
Wm. Noble) A Jury sworn, (towit) Henry Horman, Wm. Tunnell, Joseph Golloher, Isaac Robbins, Jeremiah Jeffery, Hezekiah Love, Richd. Forrest, Jacob Peak, Reuben Roberts, Charles Olive, Wm. Arnold Sen. William Cotter who say they find for the Defendant rule to show cause why a new trial should be granted- Rule made absolute motion to ammend declaration.

92 Jarett Harbin)
vs.)
Wm. Noble) David Noble surrenders William Noble in discarge of himself and he is prayed in custody of the sheriff which is granted.

A deed of conveyance from William Hogshead to John McBribe for two hundred acres of land was acknowledged in open court & ordered to be registered.

James Pery)
vs. Appeal)
Robert Pollock) A Jury sworn (viz.) Wm. Brazle, Layton Smith, David Hall, Aquella Johnson, Page Portwood, Ruben Stanley, John Hatfield & David Noble, Philip Fry, James Leach, Stephen Pankey, Thomas Hart who say they find for the plaintiff five dollars & six cents Costs.

A deed of conveyance from the Commepioners of the town of Burrville for the equal half part of Samuel Crawford of Burrville was proved in open court by Samuel Terry ordered to be registered.

Ordered by the Court that Reuben Rayland be appointed overseer in the place and stead of Page Portwood from the top of the chestnut ridge to the Eagle Ford.

A deed of conveyance from Philip Combs to James McCracken for three hundred acres of land was proved in open court by John F. Jack & ordered to be registered.

93   A deed of conveyance from Isham Stinett to John Thomas for eighty acres of land was proved in open court by John Howard and ordered to be registered.

Court adjourned until Tomorrow 9 o'clock.

94   Wednesday 14th September 1803.
Court met according to adjounrmnet.
Present   James Grant   )
               Hugh Montgomery &   )
               William McKamey   ) Esquires

A deed of conveyance from John Adair to Abraham Haglen for one hundred and ninety two acres of land was acknowledged in open court & ordered to be registered.

State   )
   vs.   )
James M. Murry   )   Jury sworn (towit) William Brazle, Henry Norman, Wm. Tunnell, Joseph Golloher, David Hall, Joseph Jeffery, Aquilla Johnson, Reuben Roberts, Page Portwood, Christiopher Bailey, Benjamine Hurley, & Claiborn Brown who say the Defendant guilty whereupon it is considered by the court that James M. Murry receive three lashes on his Bare Back at the public whipping post of Anderson County to be executed by the Sheriff thereof between the hours of two & four o'clock of this day Rule to show cause why a new Trial should be granted Rule discharged- appeal prayed and Reasons filed.

Ordered by the court that John Hatfield be appointed constable who enters into Bond and gives Cols Montgomery security & is qualified as the law requires.

Ordered by the court that Aquella Johnson have his mark recorded which is an under slope in each ear.

95
Jesse Benten   )
   vs.   )
Joseph McPeters) Ordered that a commission issue for Plff. to Buncomb County North Carolina to esamin Robert Belew and others twenty days notice-

Ordered by a majority of the court that Jesse Rayson be allowed the sum of one dollar pr. day for last court & the same for each day he may attend the court in future.

Ordered by the court that Augustie Hackworth have his mark recorded which is a crop and a slit in the right ear.

Ordered by the court that James Bounds enter into Bond in the sum of six hundred dollars who gave John Bounds & Augustice Hackworth securties of keep the county of Anderson indemfied from the maintaince of three megiehmate children by name James Bounds, Obadiah Bounds, & Stacey Bounds.

Court then adjourned until Tomorrow morning 9 o'clock.

96   Thursday 15th September 1803.
Court met according to adjournment.
Present   James Grant   )
               Hugh Montgomery)
               Wm. Underwood   ) Esquire.

Ordered by the court that the following persons be appointed as grand Jurors to attend at the next court of pleas & Quarter sessions to be held for the county of Anderson on the second Monday of December next (viz.)

1 Saml. Wilson Senr.
2 Richard Lenville
3 James McCracken
4 Spencer Graham
5 Joseph Sharp
6 Daniel White
7 David Lea
8 Constant Claxon
9 John Shepheard
10 Abraham Hagler
11 Thomas Kincaid
12 Jacob Lenard
13 Wm. Hogshead
14 Wm. Robejon
15 Michael Hattler
16 Wm. Griffith
17 Jas. Scarbro
18 Jas. Taylor
19 Richd. C. Cobb
20 John Day
21 Richard Medlin
22 Gravis, George
23 Robert Macey
24 Wm. Aldridge
25 Jacob Cheney
26 Joseph Denham
27 John Ridenhour
28 Anguish Ross
29 Caleb Friley
30 Joel Bowling

The commissioners who were appointed to lay off and the prison Bounds in Anderson County report that they have laid off said Bounds they also presented a plff. thereof to the court which was received and approved. It is ordered by the court that the commissioner have a post set up at each corner of the Bounds four feet above the surface of the earth.

97 Ordered by the court that James Grant and Hugh Montgomery Esq. be appointed to apportion the hands amongst all the overseers on the North side of Clinch River in Anderson county from Cove Creek to the upper line of Anderson county.

State   )
   vs.   )
Elias Hoskins)   Bartle M. Adkins who was one of the securties for Elias Hoskins delivered him up in open court in discarge of himself.

Ordered by the court that Arthur Crozier and Saml. Crawford who were appointed commissioners to settle with collector & Treasurer enter into bond, who gave Reuben Ragland & John F. Jack securties.

Court Adjourned until 3 o'clock
Court met according to Adjournment
Present.   James Grant   )
           Wm. Underwood &   )
           Joseph Sinclair   )   Esquires.

State   )
vs   )
Elias Hoskins) Jury sworn to wit) Joseph Denham Sen. John Bounds, Reuben Ragland, Arthur Crozier, Henry Farmer Sen., Samuel Crawford, John Howard, John Leib, David Maxwell, Garrett Harbin, Joseph Hart, John Sartin who say they find that Elias Hoskins the Defendant came accidently by a wool hat some time in the month of May or June in the county of Anderson & State of Tennessee which was after proven to be the property of Amos Eliott and afterwards sold said hat but we do not determine whether he knew said hat belonged to said Eliott at the time he sold said hat to Hatfield. If the coming of said hat in manner aforesaid is by law made petit Larceny we find the said Hoskins guilty, if the law is

otherwise we find the said Elias Hoskins not guilty. It appearing that the court were divided in opinion on the above special verdict. The prisoner Elias Hoskins was discarged on proclamation- Rule to tax prosecutor with the cost ruled discarged.

98   Court adjourned for one Hour.
Court met according to Adjournment.
Present   James Grant   )
           Hugh Montgomery   )
           Joseph Sinclair   )
           Wm. Underwood   )   Esquires.

Court adjourned till tomorrow morning 7 o'clock.

Friday 16th Sept. 1803—
Court met according to Adjournment
Present   James Grant   )
           Hugh Montgomery   )
           Wm. Underwood   )
           Joseph Sinclair   )   Esq.

Court then adjourned until court in course.
                                        James Grant, Chairman.

Page 99 Blank ---

100   At a court begun and held in and for the county of Anderson on the second Monday of December in the year of our Lord 1803.
Present: Hugh Montgomery, William McKamey, William Standifer, Joseph Sinclair, John McKamey, & William Underwood Esquires.
The court then adjourned for one Quarter of an hour to meet and open at the Court House in Burrville. The Court met according to Adjournment.
Present) James Grant, Hugh Montgomery, William Standifer, John Kerby, Joseph Sinclair, William McKamey, & William Underwood.
John Underwood Esquire high sheriff of the county of Anderson returned the Venirie facias executed on the following persons (Viz.) Samuel Wilson Sen., James McKrakin, Joseph Sharp, Daniel White, David Lea, Constant Claxton, John Shepheard, Abraham Hagler, Thos. Kincaid, Jacob Lenard, Joseph Denham, Sen., Anguis Ross, William Hogshead, William Robisson, Michael Hostler, William Griffith, James Taylor, John Day, Richard Medlin, Travis George, Robert Macoy, William Aldridge, Jacob Cheney, John Ridenhour Senr. Caleb Friley, Joel Bowling.

101   Of whom the following are grand Jurors (viz.) William Robisson, foreman, Daniel White, Jacob Cheny, Thos. Kincaid, William Aldridge, Abraham Hagler, John Ridenhour, Gravis George, Joseph Sharp, David Lea, John Day, Jacob Leinard & Constant Claxton- who being empannelled and Sworn returned to enquire.
The following are traverse Jurors (viz.) James Taylor, John Shepheard, William Hogshead, James McKrackin, Robert Macey, Michael Hostler, Joseph Denham Sen.
A deed of conveyance from Joseph McKinley, to Joseph Cross for two hundred and fifty acres of land was proved in open court by Oliver Dotson & ordered to be registered.
Thomas Dardis and Thomas H. Paine Esquires produced in open court their License to practice law in the several courts & Law and Equity in the state and took the necessary oaths.

A commission from his Excellency John Sevier with the Great Seal of the State annexed appointing Arthur Crozier, Spencer Graham, Samuel McCoy, William Havens, James Scarbro, Alexander Gastin, Richd. C. Cobb, Thomas Hill, Richard Lenville, and Jason Cloud, Justices of the peace in and for the county of Anderson, was produced in open Court, who were all qualified accordingly except William Havens.

102   Ordered by the court that Wm. Horton have his mark recorded which is a swallow fork an over bit and under bit in the right ear, and a smooth crop off the left.

Charles Shinliver, John Jimmerson, Constant, Claxton, Joseph Lea and William Patterson, who were appointed a jury to view and lay off a road from Craven Johnsons to intersect the Burrville Road near Thomas Adairs, Report that they have viewed and laid out the same- and William McKamey Esquire is to point out the same and Thos. Adair is appointed overseer of the same and William McKamey Esquire is to point out the hands. The Court then adjourned till tomorrow morning 9 o'clock.

Tuesday 13th December 1803.
Court met according to Adjournment.
Present James Grant, Hugh Montgomery, Joseph Sinclair, William Underwood, Richd. C. Cobb, John Kerby, Jason Cloud and Alexander Gastin Esquires.

James Rutherford)
  vs.)
Joseph McPeters) A jury sworn (towit) James Taylor, William Hogshead, James McKraklin, Michael Hostler, Joseph Denham Sen. John Hatfield, William Whitton, Obadiah Wood, Joseph Lea, Amos Elliott, Thomas Adair, & Jacob Derrick, say that they find the Defendant hath not paid the debt in the declaration mentioned before the issuing of the original writ and assess the damages by reasons of the detention thereof to five dollars and twelve cents.

103   Ordered by the court that Joseph Keeny have his mark recorded which is a smooth crop off the right ear and an under and over keel in the same ear. Also his brand which is a Roman I on the nigh shoulder and K on the nigh Buttock.

Ordered by the court that Daniel White be appointed a constable in Captain Lenvills Company who entered into Bond and gave James Adkins and John Sweeton securties, and took the oaths required by law.

Jesse Belew)
  vs.)
Joseph McPeters) A jury sworn towit, James Taylor, James McKarckin, Robert Macy, Michael Hostler, John Hatfield, William Whitton, Wm. Brazle, Obadiah Wood, Joseph Lea, Amos Elliott, Thomas Adair and William Lamar, who say they find the Defendant did assume within three years, and assess the Plaintiffs damages to fifty one dollars. Appeal prayed. William Tunnell, John Bounds, William Tunnell, Sen., Joseph Jeffery, Isaac Brazleton, and James Pankey, who were appointed a jury of view to lay off a road from Thomas Adairs to intersect same and Joseph Jeffery, is appointed overseer thereof from Adairs to his own House, and James Pankey from there to the intersection.

William Havens came into court and was qualified as a Justice of the peace in presurvance of a commissioner from his excellency the governor.

104   As an election for the office of high sheriff of the county of An-

derson it appeared on counting out the votes that John Underwood was duly elected who entered into Bond and took the necessary oaths required by Law.

At an election held for the office of Cornor in and for the county of Anderson, it appeared that Solomn Massingale was duly elected who entered into Bond as the Law requires and took the necessary oaths.

The Court then Adjourned for one hr.
Court met according to Adjournment.
Present: James Grant, Joseph Sinclair, William Underwood & John Kerby Esquires.

John Underwood)
   vs.)
John Robbins) In this case William Thompson being summoned as a garnishee deposed in open court that he has no property of the Defendant in his hands. And that he has reason to believe there is property of the Defendant in the hands of Spencer Black and Mrs. Berd of Sevier County. It is therefore ordered on motion of Plaintiffs Attorney that an Alias Judicial attachment issue to be levied in the hands of the said Spencer Black and Mrs. Bird.

John Den on the demise of Charles McClung
   vs
Richd. Fan with notice to Nicodemus Keith of al. Tenants in possession. James Standifer who was one of the securties for Nicodemus Keith surrendered him in discarge of himself. The said Keith then gave William Davidson and Austin Hackworth as his securties, who acknowledged themselves indebted to the Plaintiff in the sum of four hundred dollars to be void on condition the said Nicodemus Keith do appear at next term to answer the Plaintiff complaint.

105   A deed of conveyance from Henry Nunery to Joseph Moore for fifty acres of land was proved in open court by Jesse Raysdon and ordered to be registered.

Court then adjourned till tomorrow morning 9 o'clock.

Wednesday 14th December 1803.
Court met according to adjournment.
Present. James Grant, Arthur Crozier, Joseph Sinclair, Spencer Graham, & Thomas Hill Esquire.

A supplementary Inventory and amount of sales of the property of James Butler deceased was produced & filed by order of the court.

On motion of John H. Madison it is ordered by the court that Thomas Hill, and Shadrach Morris be admitted to contest the petition of Charles J. Love filed at last Term.

Benjamin C. Parker, and Benjamin Wheeler came into court and acknowledged themselves indebted to the Defendant in the sum of one hundred and twenty five dollars each. It was then continued until next term.

Alfred Massingale came into court and was sworn as deputy sheriff for the county of Anderson.

106 State)
   vs)
Hezekiah Love) In this case Milly Scarbro who was summoned as a witness being solonmly called where upon it is considered by the court that she forefet accordingly to act of assembly.

State
   vs.

Hezekiah Love) Whereupon came a Jury (towit) James Taylor, James Mc-
Kracken, Henry Carlock, John Baker, Joseph Jeffery,
Alexander Cowman, Thomas Parsons, Gideon Harmon, Robert Long, John Hatfield,
George Steele, & John Dwiggins who being duly sworn say they find the defendant not guilty.

State)
vs)
James McFarland) A jury sworn towit, Robert Macy, William Hogshead,
Lewis Stephens, Saml. Wilson, Joseph Denham, Sen.,
William Noble, Robert Pollock, Reuben Roberts, Edward Stephenson, Micajah Frost, Moses McWhorter, & Philip Fry who say they find the Defendant not guilty, in manner & form as charged in the bill of Indictment.

In the cases Jesse Belew vs. Joseph McPeters and James Rutherford & Joseph McPeters, Joseph Denham Sen., and Shadrach Morris his securties delivered him upon in open court in discarge of themselves.

Ordered by the court that Archibald Conner be appointed constable in Capt. Wilson's Company who gave bond and security and was qualified as the law requires.

107 The court then adjourned for one hour.
Court met according to adjournment.
Present Arthur Crozier, Joseph Sinclair, William Standifer & William Underwood.
The court then adjourned till Tomorrow morning 9 o'clock.

Thursday 15th December 18 03.
The court met according to adjournment.
Present- James Grant, William Underwood, Joseph Sinclair, James Scarbro, Richard C. Cobb, William Standifer, Jason Cloud, Richard Lenville & Hugh Montgomery-- John Scruggs, Paul Harmon, Robert Dew, John Wallace and Saml. Edwards who were appointed a Jury to view & lay off a road from the county line to the Island Ford on Clinch River and from there along the old waggon road to the Burrville road and from thence to the same Walnut Cave. Report that they have viewed and laid out the same and Paul Harmon is appointed overseer from the Island ford to William Cotters, and James Pepper from the Island ford to the Burrville road and William Havens to point out the hands to each.

108 John Sinclair)
vs)
Wm. Hogshead) A Jury sworn (towit) Joseph Denham Sen., James Taylor,
James McKracken, John Leib, Shadrach Reedy, Anguis Ross, Wm. Nobble, Robert Macey, Moses McWhorter, Jesse Wilson, Jacob Peak and Thomas Landrum - who say they find for the Plaintiff and assess his damage to eight dollars & costs.

Nathan Stanley)
vs)
William Hogshead) A Jury sworn (towit) Joseph Denham Sen., Jas. Taylor, James McCrackin, John Leib, Shadrach Reedy,
Anguis Ross, Robert Macey, Moses McWhorter, Jacob Peak, Richard Forrest, John Duggins & Richard Lewallen, who say they find for the Plaintiff and assess his damages to twelve dollars & costs.

Ordered by the court that Aquella Johnson have leave to keep a ferry immidiately below the mouth of his mill creek. He having given Bond and security as the law requires.

Court adjourned for one hour.
Court met according to adjournment.
Present- James Grant, William Underwood, Joseph Sinclair, James Scarbro, Wm. Standifer, and Alexander.

109 Ordered by a majority of the court that Joseph Sinclair and John Kerby Esquire assign to William Whitial his hands.

Ordered by a majority of the court that Stephen Heard Clerk be allowed the sum of fifty dollars fro ex office services for the year 1803.

The court then adjourned till tomorrow morning 9 o'clock.

Friday 16th December 1803.
Court met according to adjournment
Present---- Hugh Montgomery, Arthur Crozier, John Kerby, Thomas Hill, and Richard Lenville Esquires.

110 Ordered by the court that Jonathan Hollums be overseer of the road from Squire McCoys, to the top of the Red Oad Ridge, and that Saml. McCoy Esquire point out the hands.

Ordered by the court that William Cotter be overseer of the road from the mouth of Hinds Creek to the County Line and that William Havens Esquire point out the hands.

Ordered by the court that the road leading from Saml. Worthingtons to intersect another road near James Scarbro Esquire be discontinued.

Ordered by the court that the following persons be appointed a jury to view & lay off the road from the Black House to Clouds ford on Clinch River, and from thence to Jason Clouds House (viz.) Polly Duncan, Saml. McCoy, Esquire Henry Russell, Brittian Ragsdale, Hardy Medlin, Jesse Fowler, and Wm. Whitton.

Ordered by the court that the following persons be appointed a jury to view and lay off a road from the House of George Shelters thro the Hickory Valley, crossing the Grantsboro Road at Wm. Thompson, crossing Bryant fork near William Underwoods thence to the gap where John Sinclair formerly lived. Thence to the valley road at John Scruggs, George Shelters, Charles Bookout, Robert Macey, Wm. Thompson, Wm. Underwood, & John Scruggs.

111 Ordered by the court that the following persons be appointed a Jury to view & lay off a road from James Scarbro's Ferry on Clinch River to intersect a road leading from the Pawpaw Ford, to the county line (viz.) John Golson, Nathan Haile, Tobias Peters, Hezikiah Love, Thomas Kincaid, & Aquella Johnson.

Ordered by the court that James Finley have leave to resign the office of constable.

Ordered by the court that John Baker be appointed a constable in Captain Morris Company who gave Bond and securties as the law requires and took the necessary oaths.

Ordered by the court that Spencer Graham Esq. make an equal distribution of the hands to work on the road from Big Creek to the Claiborne Line; That are north of Clinch river and that Richard Lenville Esq. make an equal distribution of the hands who are between Big creek and Cove Creek; and that Thomas Hill Esquire made and equal distribution of the hands from Cove Creek to where the Island road intersects the old Indian Trace and that Arthur Crozier & John Kerby Esq. make an equal distribution of the hands from the Island ford road to Burrville.

112 The following are a list of Jurors to attend at March Term 1804 (viz.)

1 John Adair   4 Jacob Strader
2 Alex. Adair   5 Robert Sinclair
3 Wm. Hancock Senr. 6 Conright Willright

```
      7  Shadrich Morris           19  Joseph Roberson
      8  Alexander Golbreath       20  Oliver Dotson
      9  Isaac Brazleton           21  Craven Johnson
     10  Austin Hackworth          22  Richard Forrest
     11  William Davidson          23  John McBribe
     12  Nathan Hale               24  John McAdoo
     13  Henry Farmer              25  Wm. Sevors
     14  Tachariah Lea             26  John Parks
     15  Joseph Grayson            27  Henry Russell
     16  Samuel Frost              28  Richard Medlin
     17  Page Portwood             29  Britian Ragsdale
     18  Nathaniel Davis           30  JohnLallor
```

113   Gettysburg.

114   At a court begun and held for the county of Anderson on the second Monday of March being the 12th in the year of our Lord 1804.
           Present --- James Grant   )
                       Hugh Montgomery)
                       Arthur Crozier)
                       Alexander Gastin) Esquires.

John Underwood Esquire high sheriff o the county of Anderson returned that he had executed the Venirie Facias on the following persons (viz.) John Adair, Alexander Adair, Wm. Hancock, Sen., Jacob Strader, Robert Sinclair, Shadrach Morris, Alex Galbreath, Isaac Brazleton, Austin Hackworth, Wm. Davidson, Nathan Hale, Henry Farmer, Lachy Lea, Joseph Grayson, Saml. Frost, Page Portwood, Nathaniel Davis, Joseph Roberson, Oliver Dotson, Craven Johnson, Richard Forrest, John McBribe, John McAdoo, Wm. Seviors, John Parks, Henry Russell, Richard Medlin, Britain Ragsdale, John Fowler, of whom the following are grand Jurors (viz.) Joseph Grayson, John Parks, John McAdoo, Tachariah Lea, Richard Medlin, Wm. Hancock Sen., Nathan Hale, John McBridge, Page Portwood, Joseph Roberson, Isaac Brazleton, Alex Adair, Henry Russell,

115 Robert Sinclair & Richard Forrest. The Ballance are Traverse Jurors.

A deed of conveyance from Manpage Vowell to Thomas Tovera & for one hundred and fifty acres of land was proved in open court by James D. Puckett & ordered to be registered.

A deed of conveyance from Walter Evans to John Ridenhour for a town lot No. five in the town of Grantsborough was proved in open court by James Grant Esquire & ordered to be registered.

A deed of conveyance from Thomas Forst Sen. to Micajah Frost for two and twenty five acres of land was acknowledged in open court and ordered to be registered.

A deed of conveyance from Micajah Frost to Aaron Jenkins for two hundred and twenty five acres of land was acknowledged in open court and ordered to be registered. D.

A deed of conveyance from Patrick Campbell to William Chandler for forty acres of land was proved in open court by Robert Brazle & ordered to be registered. D.

A deed of conveyance from Wm. Worthington to Thomas Worthington for one hundred and seventy acres of land was acknowledged in open court and ordered to be registered.

A deed of conveyance from John Hackett to James GAlbreath for five hundred and thirty one acres of land was proved in open court and ordered to be registered.

A deed of conveyance from Robert Burton to John McAdoo for forty acres of land was proved in open court by Moses McWhorter & ordered to be registered.

116   Ordered by the court that Thomas Worthington have his mark recorded which is a smooth crop in the left ear and a slit and under bit in the right.

A deed of conveyance from William, Reuben to Landon Rector for ten acres of land was proved in open court by Alexander Galbreath and ordered to be registered.

A deed of conveyance from John Hackett to Landon Rector for two hundred acres of land was proved in open court by Joseph Sinclair Esquire and ordered to be registered.

Ordered by the court that James Finley who was a constable pay to Moses Cunningham, who was the informer against William H. Murrah, five dollars of the Ten in which he said Murrah was fined under the act of assembly Entitled an act to prevent excessive gaming.

A deed of conveyance from Andrew McKamey to William Scarbro for two hundred acres of land was acknowledged in open court and ordered to be registered.

John Purdon & Reuben Roberts who were Bail for John McEntire in a suit William Cotter against John McEntire, surrendered said McEntire in open court in Discarge of themselves.

The Court then adjourned till tomorrow morning 9 o'clock.

117   Tuesday 13th March 1804.
Court met according to Adjournment.
Present- James Grant, Hugh Montgomery, Jason Cloud, Joseph Sinclair, & William McKamey Esq.

Thomas Emmerson Esquire proceeded a license authorising him to practice as an attorney in the several courts of law and Equity in this state and took the necessary oaths, and is admitted as an attorney of this court.

Ordered that Robert Burton have his mark recorded which is a crop and under keel in the left ear and over half crop in the right ear.

Ordered that Shadrach Reedy have his mark recorded which is a smooth crop off the left ear and a slit in the right ear.

A deed of conveyance from Wm. Davidson for six hundred and forty acres of land was acknowledged in open court & ordered to be registered.

Francis May)
   vs.)
Thomas Walker)   Present: James Grant, Hugh Montgomery, Jason Cloud, William McKamey, Alexander Gastin, Joseph Sinclair & John Kerby---- Whereupon came a jury to wit, Samuel Frost, Jehu Fowler, Austin Hackworth, Jacob Strader, Shadrach Morris, John Julian, Isaac Chrisman, Tobias Peters, Robert Raysdon, Joseph Jeffery, Nathan Roberts, Thomas Menefee, who being empannelled and sworn say they find for the Plaintiff and assess his damages to twenty six dollars eighty seven cents and costs.

Ordered that James Taylor have leave to keep and ordinary or House of entertainment at his House in Anderson County he having given Bond & security as the law requires.

118   A deed of conveyance from Kenza Johnson, William Stander, William Roberson and Joseph Grayson commissioner of the town of Burrville for lott No. 24 in Burrville to Edward Long was proved in open court and ordered to be registered.

The following persons were drawn by Ballot agreeable to Law as

Grand Jurors to the next superior court for Hamilton District (viz.) Solomn Massingale, John Peeks, and Hugh Montgomery - Esquire- fifteen justices of the peace for Anderson being present, they proceeded to Ballot for a commission of the Reverence when it appeared on counting out the votes that Jason Cloud was duly elected, who was then qualified as the law requires.

Thomas Hill Esquire was Elected Trustee for the county of Anderson who entered into Bond and gave security as the law requires.

Ordered by the court that Sarah Kee an orphan girl of the age of nine years be bound to Tachariah Kee until she arrives at the age of Eighteen years.

The Court then adjourned for one hour.
Court met according to adjournment.
Present: Joseph Sinclair, Alexander Gastin, & Wm. McKamey- Esq.-

Ordered by the court that James D. Puckett be appointed a constable in Captain McKameys Company who gave Bond and Security and was qualified as the law requires.

Ordered by the court that Jesse Hoskins have his mark recorded which is a swallow fork in the right ear and a crop off the left ear.

William Cotter)
   Vs.   )
James McEntire) John Purdon, William Hogshead, & Reuben Roberts appeared in open court and undertook for the Defendant John McEntire that in case he shall be cast in this suit he shall pay and satisfy the condemnation or surrender his body in execution for the same or that they said John Purdon, William Hogshead & Reubin Roberts will do it for him.

A deed of conveyance from Joseph Horton to William Horton for forty five acres of land was proved in open court by Jesse Raysdon and ordered to be registered.

The following is a list of Jurors appointed at June session 1804 (viz.) Conright Willright, Joseph Sharp, John Lamb, Joshua English, James McCracken, Thomas M. Campbell, Micajah Cross, Luke Lea Sen., Richard Luallen, James Taylor, Jacob Lenard, Joseph Lea, Jeremiah Jeffery, John Day, John Leib, Tobias Tilman, James McNutt, Henry Sharp, Douglas Oliver, Jacob Peak, Samuel Galbreath, Henry Harless, Elliott Grills, Aaron Jenkins, John Hanna, Henry Farmer, John Garner, Isaac Norman, Wm. Aldridge, Saml. Worthington, William Tunnell Sen., Hardy Medlin, John Goulston, Jonathan Cunningham, Shepheard Brock, Harris Ryan, Thomas Smythe, Richmond Archer, and John Bounds.

Moses McWhorter & Robert Smith who were bail for John Stewart surrendered him in open court in discarge of themselves.

Daniel Martin and Shadrach Morris of this county appeared in open court and undertake for the Defendant John Stewart, that in case be shall be cast in this suit he shall pay and satisfy the condemnation, or surrender his body in execution for the same or that they the said Danl. Martin and Shadrach Morris will do it for him-- Joal Cox vs. Henry Taylor, & John Stuart.

Ordered that Aaron Jenkins, John Hanna, Austin Hackworth, Aquella Johnson, John Garner, Nathl. Davis, & Thomas Frost Sen. be appointed a jury to view and lay off a road from the road on the Copper Ridge crossing at Joseph Robersons to where it will witness the said road again near Aquella Johnson mill & that they report to next court.

Court adjourned till tomorrow morning 9 o'clock.

Wednesday 14th March 1804.
Court met according to adjournment
Present -- James Grant, Hugh Montgomery, Joseph Sinclair, Alexander Gastin, Spencer Graham, & William Standifer Esq.

Ordered by the court that a Dedimus Potestatem issue to Hugh Montgomery Esquire authorising him to take the deposition of Aminiah McCoy, de bene esse on the petition of Charles L. Love.

The Court then proceeded to lay a tax for the county of Anderson for the year 1804 as follows (viz.)

for public Buildings on each 100 acres of land	.12½
on each white poll or male servant	.12½
on each stud horse kept for mares	.50
on each town lot	.25
For weight and measures	
on each white poll and male servant	.04
on each Black poll	.08
on each stud horse kept for mares	.12½
For county purposes	
On each 100 acres of land	.12½
On each town lot	.25
On each white poll & male servant	.12½
On each Black poll	.25

On each stud Horse a sum equal to the season of a mare --

The State Tax the same as the county Tax except the owners for retail States Hawkers and Pedlars, who are to pay five dollars each.

Ordered by the court that John Sartin have leave to keep an ordinary or house of public entertainment at his house in Burrville, he having given bond and security as the law requires.

John Dew on the necedinmus of

Charles M. Clung)
vs.)
Nicodemus Keith & al) Present, James Grant, Hugh Montgomery, Samuel McCoy, Joseph Sinclair, William Underwood, and Thomas Hill Esquires.

Whereupon came a jury (towit) John Fowler, Samuel Forst, Obadiah Wood, Robert Brazle, Wm. Brazle, William Hogshead, John Leib, Jeremiah Jeffery, Richard Lewallen, Joseph Hart, Joseph Jeffery, and James D. Puckett who being empannelled and sworn do say the Defendant is guilty of the Trespasses in Ejectment as the Plaintiff hath alledged in his Declaration and assesses the Plaintiffs damage to six cents and Six cents costs. Ordered by the court that a writ of possession issue.

John Fowler, Henry Russell, Samuel McCoy, Britian Ragsdale, Hardy Medlin, and William Whitton who were appointed a jury of view to lay off a road from Samuel McCoys Esquire to Jason Clouds Esquire. Report that they have viewed and laid out the same in pursuance thereto- and Robert Whitton is appointed overseer of the same from Samuel McCoys to Clouds Ford on Clinch River and Samuel Norris from there to Clouds old place.

Nathan Hale, John Golston, Tobias Peters, and Abraham Hagler who were appointed a jury to view and lay out a road from James Scarbro's Ferry on Clinch River to the lower end of Anderson County- Report that they have viewed and marked the same. Old Colonel William Davidson is appointed overseer thereof-

Court then adjourned till Tomorrow morning 9 o'clock.

Thursday 15th March 1804.

The Court met according to Adjournment.

Present -- James Grant, Hugh Montgomery, William Underwood, William McKamey, Joseph Sinclair, and John Kerby Esq.

Hugh Montgomery)
vs.)
John Duckworth) James Grant, William Underwood, Joseph Sinclair, Wm. McKamey, John Kerby, Alex. Gastin, and Richard Lenville-- Whereupon came a jury (towit) Manpage Vowell, John Thomas, Austin Hackworth, Samuel Frost, John Fowler, Wm. Cotter, Tobias Long, Samuel Wilson, Obadiah Wood, Robert Macey, Jacob Strader, and John McBribe, who being empannelled and sworn do say they find for the Plaintiff and assess his damage to ten dollars and costs.

The Court then adjourned for one hour.

John Underwood)
vs.)
John Robbins) In this cause Robert Wear Sheriff of Sevior County having made return on the Alias Judicial attachment that he had summoned in writing Spencer Black to appear at this term of our said court, and give in an oath as a garnisher what of the goods and Estate of said Robbins he hath in his hands, or knows to be in the hands of any other person and being solomnly called and failing to appear on the fourth day of this term. It is ordered by the court that a conditional Judgment be entered up against the said Spencer Black for the whole of the damage alledged in the Plaintiffs declaration, to be subject to the judgment and costs of said Plaintiff against the said Robbins and that a Scria facias issue directly him to appear at our next court and give in an oath what of the goods and Estate of said Robbins he has, or to shew cause why final judgment should not be entered against him for the whole of the Plaintiffs Judgment & costs.

123   Court met according to adjournment.

Present) Alexander Gastin, Wm. McKamey, Wm. Underwood, Joseph Sinclair, and Arthur Crozier.

Ordered by the court that Thomas Adair be overseer of the road laid out from Craven Johnsons to Burrville.

The Court then Adjourned for half an hour--

Court met according to Adjournment.

Present-- James Grant, William Underwood, Hugh Montgomery and Joseph Sinclair Esquire-

John English)
vs.)
Berry Crowley) Present-- James Grant, Wm. Underwood, Hugh Montgomery, Joseph Sinclair, Alexander Gastin, and Richard Lenville Esquire---

Whereupon came a jury (towit) John Thomas, Austin Hackworth, Samuel, Frost, John Fowler, Obadiah Wood, Robert Macey, John McBridge, Wm. Seveirs, Henry Young, Tobias Long, John McWhorter, and Joseph Denham Sen. who being empannelled and sworn do say they find that the Defendant hath not kept and performed his covenants and assess the Plaintiffs damage by reason thereof to two hundred & ninety three dollars & ninety four cents and two thirds of a cent and costs.

John English)
vs.)
Berry Crowley) Present: James Grant, Wm. McKamey, Wm. Underwood, Jo-

seph Sinclair, Arthur Crozier, Hugh Montgomery, Richard Lenville, and Alexander Gastin Esquires.

Whereupon came a jury (towit) John Thomas, Austin Hackworth, Samuel Frost, John Fowler, Obadiah Wood, Robert Macey, John McBride, William Sevoirs, Henry Young, Tobias Long, John McWhorter, and Joseph Denham Sen. who being empannelled and sworn say they find for the Plaintiff one hundred and thirty three dollars and one third of a dollar to be discarged by sixty eight dollars and ninety three cents & costs..

124
John Stewart)
  vs.)
Henry Carlock) Present) James Grant, John Kerby, Wm. Underwood, Joseph Sinclair, & Alexander Gastin Esquires.

Whereupon came a jury (towit) John Thomas, Austin Hackworth, Samuel Frost, John Fowler, Obadiah Wood, Robert Macey, John McBride, William Sevoirs, Henry Young, Tobias Long, John McWhorter, & Joseph Denham Sen. who being empannelled and sworn or return into court and being called Eleven only to answer therefore a mistrial.

John Stuart)
  vs.)
Henry Carlock) In this case John Sweeton a witness for the Defendant and legally summoned being solomnly called, came not, therefore it is considered he hath forfited according to the act of Assembly.

Ordered that John H. Madison Esquire have his mark recorded which is two Smooth Crops.

Ordered by the Court that Douglass Oliver, William Roberson, Saml. Worthington, and James Porter be appointed to lay of view on oath an Acre of the land of Isaac Freels for the purpose of erecting a grit mill and that a summons issue to the said Isaac Freels to appear at next court. Court Then adjourned till Tomorrow morning 9 o'clock.

125   At a court begun and held for the county of Anderson at the Court House in Burrville on the second Monday of June in the year of our Lord 1804.

Present-- Arthur Crozier, Richard Lenville, William McKamey, and William Standifer.

John Underwood high sheriff of Anderson County returned the Venire Facias executed on the following --

1 Conright Willright
2 John Lamb
3 Joshua English
4 James McKracken
5 Thomas Campbell
6 Micajah Cross
7 Luke Lea Sen.
8 Richard Luallen
9 James Taylor
10 Jacob Leinard
11 Joseph Lea
12 Jeremiah Jeffery
13 John Day
14 Tobias Tilman
15 John Leib
16 James McNutt
17 Henry Sharp
18 Douglas Oliver
19 Jacob Peak
20 Saml. Galbreath
21 Henry Farless H
22 Elliott Grills
23 Aaron Jenkins
24 John Hanna
25 Henry Farmer
26 John Garner
27 Isaac Norman
28 Wm. Aldridge
29 Saml. Worthington
30 Wm. Tunnell Jr.
31 Hardy Medlin
32 John Gotson
33 Jonathan Cunningham
34 Sherard Brock
35 Harris Ryan
36 Thomas Smith

37 Richmond Archer
38 John Bounds

of whom the following are grand Jurors (vi&.) Aaron Jenkins foreman, John Bounds, Wm. Tunnell, John Leib, Isaac Norman, Saml. Worthington, Thomas Smith, John Golson, Wm. Aldridge, Henry Sharp, Joshua English, Jacob Linard, John Garner, Jeremiah Jeffery, James McKrackin, who being empannelled and sworn retired to enquire.

126   A deed of conveyance from Henry Harless to Philip Harless for one hundred and one acres of land was acknowledged in open court and ordered to be registered.

John Underwood)
  vs   )
John Robbins   ) Spencer Black who was summoned as a garnishee in the above cause, being sworn in open court, deposed that he had none of the effects of the Defendant in his hands at the time of being summoned or fined.

Ordered by the court that James Worthington have his mark recorded which is a smooth crop in the right ear and an half crop and under bit in the right.

Ordered by the court that Samuel Worthington have his mark recorded which is a crop off the right ear and half crop in the left.

Ordered by the court that Charles Pruett have his mark recorded which is a crop and slit in the left ear and a crop and under keel in the right.

A deed of conveyance from Joshua English to George Walker for fifty acres of land was acknowledged in open court and ordered to be registered.

Ordered by the court that Amey Williams have leave to administer on the estate of her late husband James Williams she having given bond in the sum of two hundred dollars and given John McBride security and took the oath required by law. Court then adjourned till Tomorrow Morning 9 o'clock.

127   Tuesday 12th June 1804.
Court met according to adjournment.
Present) Hugh Montgomery, Arthur Crozier, Thomas Hill, Richard Lenville, Esquires ---

Ordered by the Court that Conright Willright be appointed a constable in Captain Morris's Co. who gave bond and security and was qualified as the law requires.

Ordered by a majority of the Justices that Manpage Vowell be allowed the sum of seventeen dollars for building a pound on the public square for the purpose of holding Estrays.

Aquella Johnson, John Hanna, Aaron Jenkins, Nathaniel Davis, Thomas Frost, John Garner, & Augustine Hackworth who were appointed a jury to view and lay off a road from near Joseph Robersons, to intersect the road leading to the Cumberland ford near Aquella Johnsons mill report that they have viewed and marked out the same.

Austin Hackworth is appointed overseer of the same- and John Kerby and Alexander Gastin Esquires are to assign his hands. It was then considered by the court that it be laid over until the next term.

Ordered by a majority of the justices that Samuel Crawford one of the commissioners appointed for laying out the gaol Bounds be allowed the sum of four dollars for running out and making a Plff. thereof; and that John Leib be allowed the sum of nine dollars for settling up Sassafras posts.

128 Charles J. Love)
     vs.   )
     Thomas Hill &   ) Petition for rectipeation of Survey --
     Shadrach Morris) On motion of Thomas Dardis Esquire attorney for the
                        petition for a continuance on the affidavid Benjamin
Wheeler the consult on consideration refused it. The petition then came
on to be heard, Present, Hugh Montgomery, Joseph Sinclair, Richard Lenville, Solomn Massingale, Alexander Gastin, Spencer Graham, James Scarbro & William Havens Esquires, when it appeared to the court that suffcent evidence was not adduced they therefore refused to grant the prayer of the petition - an appeal was then prayed reasons filed Bond & security given and appeal granted.

 A deed of conveyance from the commissioners of the town of Burrville to Saml. Johnson for a lot in said town No. 12 was proved in open court by William Horton and ordered to be registered.

 A deed of conveyance from John M. Clellan to Douglas Oliver for one hundred and forty acres of land was proved in open court by Charles Oliver & ordered to be registered.

 A deed of conveyance from Robert Horton to Robert Dew for five hundred acres of land was proved in open court by Paul Harmon & ordered to be registered.

129 A deed of conveyance from Robert Dew to John Wallace for two hundred and fifty acres of land was acknowledged in open court and ordered to be registered.

 A deed of conveyance from John Wallace to Enoch Foster for two hundred and fifty acres of land was acknowledged in open court and ordered to be registered.

 A deed of conveyance from the commissioners of town of Burrville to John Leib for one acre of land on the north side of Clinch River adjoining the town of Burrville was proved in open court by John Shepheard and ordered to be registered.

 A deed of conveyance from Robert Burton to Henry Young for one hundred acres of land was proved in open court by William Hogshead and ordered to be registered.

David Looney)
   vs.   )
John McEntire) In this case William Hogshead surrendered the Defendant
                 in open court in discarge of himself.

 Ordered by a majority of the Justices that the main waggon road now leading from the first deep Hollow South of where John English now lives in the Walnut Cave be discontinued and that the overseer of said road open away direct from said Hollow to the mouth of or near the mouth of Rosses Spring Branch from thence a direct course along a ridge to where James Finley now lives, and from thence along said ridge between the old waggon way and Sycamore Spring until a direct course will intersect with the Pow-
130 ells Valley Road - - between Willrights field and Carlocks field.

 Ordered by a majority of the justices that part of the road leading from Samuel McCoys Esq. to Jason Clouds ford running from a point on the north side of Buffalo, and thence down the said creek to the lower ford leaving Elijah Whittons Plantation on the north side of said Road be discontinued.

 Ordered by the court that Paul Harmon be appointed a constable in Captain Harts Co. he having given Bond and Security as the law requires, and taken the necessary oaths.

David Looney)
   vs.)
John McEntire) Isaac Robbins and Reuben Roberts appeared in open court
and undertake for the Deft. John McEntire that in case
he shall be cast in this suit he shall pay and satisfy the condemnation,
or surrender his body in execution for the same or that they will do it for
him.
    Ordered by the court that Samuel Crawford, Reuben Rayland & John
Parks be appointed commissioners to settle with these who hold or received
County monies- Who gave bond and security as the law requires.
    Court then adjourned for one hour.
    Court met according to adjournment.
    Present, James Grant, H. Montgomery, Joseph Sinclair, Wm. Havens,
& Richard Lenville.

131 Jarrett Harbin)
   vs.)
William Noble) Present, James Grant, Joseph Sinclair, Thomas Hill,
Richard Lenville, & Spencer Graham.
    Whereupon came a jury (towit) Joseph Lea, Sherard Brock, Richmond
Archer, Harris Ryan, John Lamb, Douglass Oliver, James Taylor, Tobias Tilman, John Day, James McNutt, Luke Lea & Jonathan Cunningham who being duly
sworn say they find for the Defendant --
    A deed of conveyance from James Scarbro to William Scarbro for twenty seven acres and ninety five poles of land was acknowledged in open court
and ordered to be registered.

Jacob Cox)
   vs.)
John Stewart &)
Henry Taylor) In this case Shadrach Morris and Daniel Martin surrendered John Stewart in discarge of themselves as Bail-
    The following is a list of Grand Jurors to attend at the next court
to be held for the county of Anderson on the second Monday of June next,
William Hancock Sen., Jacob Strader, John Snoderly, James Abbot, Richard
Medlin, John Fowler, Henry Russell, William Scarbro, Tobias Peters, Nathan Hale, John McAdoo, Tachariah Lea, William Robbins, David Lea, William
Thompson, Marmaduke Bookout, James Hill, Travis George, Joseph Sharp,
Caleb Friley, Robert Sinclair, Britian Ragsdale, Saml. Frost, Joseph Grayson, William Ragland, Edward Frost, Robert Dew, John Wallace, Nathaniel
Davis, Edward Freels, John Bradley, Alexander Galbreath, Rawley Duncan,
John Parks, John McWhorter, Powell Harmon & Isham Stunnett.

132 Chas. L. Love)
   vs.)
Thomas Hill)
Shadh. Morris) In this case George Gordon who was summoned to attend
as a witness being solemnly called came not wherefore
it is considered that he forefit according to act of assembly.
    The court then proceeded to Ballott for jurors to attend at the
next superior court to be held for the District of Hamilton at Knoxville.
When it appeared that James Grant, William Underwood, and Richard C. Cobb
Esq. were duly elected---
    Court then adjourned till tomorrow morning 9 o'clock.

133   Wednesday 13th June 1804.

Court met according to adjournment.

Present) James Grant, Hugh Montgomery, Richard Lenville, Joseph Sinclair, Spencer Graham, & Wm. McHamey, Esq.

The Freeholders who were here-tofore appointed to value an acre of the land of Isaac Freels return the following report.

Pursuant to an order directed to us from the worshipful court of Anderson County for the purpose of laying off one acre of the land of Isaac Freels and also an acre of the land of William Scarbro for the purpose of erecting of a grist mill thereon do report and say that we have proceeded to lay off view and value upon oaths, one acre of land belonging to the said Isaac Freels. Beginning at a dogwood standing on the north east side of a large branch known by the name of Reeds branch thence up the several menders of said branch forty poles to a stake thence north forty five degrees east four poles to a stake, Thence a line paralled to the first line forty poles to a stake thence to the beginning. And say that the said acre is worth four dollars and fifty cents; and also do lay off view and value upon the oath one acre of land for William Scarbro, Beginning opposite the aforesaid beginning corner at a pawpaw and what standing on the north west side of said Reeds Branch thence up, the several meanders of said Branch twelve poles to a stake, thence south forty five degrees west thirty poles and twenty five links, to a stake, thence a line parallel to the first line twelve poles to a stake, thence a direct line beginning and say that the said one acre is worth five dollars and fifty cents.

Signed by the jury of review who were appointed. This 11th day of June 1804 (signed) Douglass Oliver, William Roberson, Saml. Worthington, James Porter.

Which was ordered to be recovered the valuation paid by William Scarbro, and leave granted to erect a grist mill.

State)
  vs.)
James D. Puckett) Present: James Grant, James Scarbro, Joseph Sinclair, Spencer Graham, Hugh Montgomery, Wm. McKamey, and Richard Lenville- Jury sworn to wit, Joseph Lea, Sherad Brock, Harris Ryan, John Lamb, Douglass Oliver, James Taylor, Tobias Tilman, John Day, James McNutt, Luke Lea, Jonathan Cunningham, & Henry Farmer, who being duly sworn do say they find the Defendant guilty.

John Stone &)
Doherty Devisees)
  vs.)
Thos. Alred, Wm. Harris &)
David Shoemaker) In this case Elizabeth Reed a minor is admitted Defendant and Jacob Gibbs appointed her guardian to defend for her, who enters into the common rule, and gave James McNutt and Henry Sharp, security who came into open court and undertakes for the Defendant that in case he shall be cast in the suit he shall pay the condemnation & costs or surrender his body in execution for the same, that they will do it for him.

It is further ordered by the court that Samuel Crawford be appointed to survey the land in dispute, and make return thereof to next court.

A deed of conveyance from John McClellan to Douglass Oliver for two hundred and eighty acres of land was proved in open court by Linsford Oliver and ordered to be registered.

Ordered by the court that Isaac Crane be put in the stocks and continue there the space of two hours for constable to the courts.

Henry Farmer was excused on application to the ? for non attendance as a Juror at Last Term.

Ordered by a majority of the justices that John McKamey, Wm. Standifer, and James Scarbro apportion the hands among the different overseers from Ashlocks to the lower end of the county on the north side of Clinch and that it may be done either of the said Justices provided it be the knowledge of the other two.

Ordered by a majority of the court that William Davidson be overseer of the Road from the first ford above Scarbro Ferry to the lower end of Anderson County.

Ordered by the court that Moses Cunningham have leave to amend his peition for writs of supersides, & Artearari and that alias writs issue.

136 George Steele)
    vs.)
Robert Whitton) Present, James Grant, Hugh Montgomery, Solomn Massingale, Joseph Sinclair, Alexander Gastin, Richard C. Cobb, Richard Lenville & Spencer Graham Esq.

Whereupon came a Jury to wit, Joseph Lea, Sherard Brock, Richmond Arthur, Harris Ryan, John Comb, Douglas Oliver, Tobias Tilmon, John Day, James McNutt, Jonathan Cunningham, Henry Farmer and John Hanna who being duly sworn could not agree whereupon a mistrial was consented to by the attornies on each side.

A conveyance from John English to Berry Crawley for one hundred and fifty acres of land was acknowledged in open court & ordered to be registered.

Jacob Cox)
    vs.)
John Stuart)
& Henry Taylor.) In this case Shadrach Morris, James Adkins, and James Robertson came into open court an undertake for the defendant that in case he is lost in this suit he shall pay the condemnation and costs or surrender his body in execution for the same or that they will do it for him.

137   Ordered by the court that William Keeling an aged infirm blind man be allowed the sum of three dollars pr. month for his support for the space of twelve months if he shall so long need it and that Henry Sharp Senior take care of him and support him.

Ordered by the court that Joseph Sinclair and William McKamey apportion the hands to the over seer Joseph Jefferies and James Pankey.

Court then adjourned for one hour and half.

Court met according to adjournment.

Present) James Grant, W. McKamey, Alex. Garten, Spencer Graham & Solmon Massingale.

A deed of conveyance from Nathaniel Hart executor of Nathaniel Hart deceased to Wm. Thompson for three hundred & twenty five acres of land was proven in open court by Joseph Hart and ordered to be registered.

Ordered by the court that Isaac Crane be committed to the common gaols of Anderson county thereto remain until the rise of the court until he makes satisfaction for the fees for his disorderly behavior.

Joseph Sinclair paid into office thirty one and 1/4 cent the fine imposed upon Gabriel Pruitt for intoxaction.

John Kirby esquire paid into office six dollars the fine imposed on Milly Morgan for refusing to swear a bastard child.

Court adjourned until tomorrow at 9 o'clock.

138   Thursday 14 day of June 1804.
         Court met according to adjournment.
         Present) James Grant, Arthur Crozier & Thomas Hill Esquires.

Ordered by the court that John Wallace be voerseer of the road from the valley road near John Scruggs to the Grantsborough Road at William Thompsons. And that the following hands work on the same under him (viz.) Robert Dew, David Sartin, Nathan Stanley, Thos. Stanby, Robert Smith, Joseph Day, Amos Elliott, Joel Hancock, Jessee Wilson, Benjamin Wilson, Wm. Underwood, hands Isaac Philpot & Felix Gilbert.

Ordered by a majority of the justice that the road leading from William Thompsons to George Shetters mill be discontinued and that the following persons be appointed to view and lay off a road from the Grantsborough road near William Thompsons up Hincless creek by Lewis Stephens mill to intersect the road leading from Samuel McCoys Esquire near Warnicks meeting house (viz.) Marmaduke Bookout, James Hill, Charles Bookout, Lewis Stephen, Travis George, Christian Makes & John Warnick & that they report to next court.

139   William Underwood Esquire paid into office six dollars twenty five cents the fine imposed on Betsy Lucas for refusing to swear a Bastard child.

Ordered by the court that John Black be appointed overseer of the road from Millers ford to the county line on the north side of clinch river.

Ordered by the court that James McHuff be overseer of the road from Millers Ford on the south side of Clinch river to Big Buffaloe.

Ordered by the court that John Terry be overseer of the Grantsborough road leading to Powells valley from the north Bank of Powells river to the top of the dividing ridge to where Reuben Morse ends.

Ordered by the court that Abraham Jones be overseer of the Grantsborough road from the ferry at the south Bank of Clinch river to Little Buffaloe.

Ordered by the court that Jacob Whitman be overseer of the Grantsborough road from the north bank of clinch river at the ferry the best way and nearest into the Powells Valley road crossing Grants Creek near Cunningham or Ajeys mills.

Ordered by the court that William Myatt be overseer of the road from George Ramsays to Reuben Williams spring in place of James Porter.

140   Ordered by the court Rowley Duncan be overseer of the Grantsborough road from Little Buffaloe to Byranes Fork.

A deed of conveyance from the commissioners of the town of Burrville to William Tunnell for two lotts in said town No. 41 & 43 was proven in open court & ordered to be registered.

Ordered by the court that William Tunnell Senior have his mark recorded which is a <u>Sht</u> in the right ear and a small bit off the upper side of the left ear.

Ordered by the court that William McBride be appointed overseer of the road instead of Saml. Wilson.

John Underwood was appointed collector of the public & county tax for the year one thousand eight hundred and four and entered into bond in the sum of three thousand dollars and gave security as the law requires and took the necessary oath.

Ordered by the court that Jason Cloud Esq. have his mark redorded which is a cross and slit in the right ear and a swallow fork in the left.

Jason Cloud Esq. who was appointed commissioner to take the lists of taxable property in Anderson county returned the same in open court.

141   John Underwood Esquire reports the following tracts of land town lots

and polls upon which the tax has not been paid for the year 1803.

	No. OK Acres	Polls	Dr.	Cents
Francis Mayberry	1111111	11	3	75
John McEntire	111111	11	3	75
John Duncan	11111			37 1/2

Town lotts

		Dr.	Cents
Major Thos. Lewis 1 lott Grantsbro		50	50
Chas. Lea Bird four lotts "		2	"
James V. Mall 2 Do Do		1	
Robt. Philips	1		25
Geo. Gentry	1		25
James Hurd	1		25
James Rowsdy	1		25
Clabiorne Puckett	1		25
Frederick Farmer	1		25
Michael Selerdge	1		25
Peter Anderson	1		25
John Williams	1		25
John Evans	1		25
Jacob Cunningham	1		25
John Dick	1		25
James Davis	1		25
Wm. Pollock	1		25
Andrew Vaught	1		25
John Wood	1		25
John Allbright	1		25
John Brumley	1		25
Wm. Lewis	1		25
John Lacy	1		25
Geo. McFarland	1		25
Nimrod Teague	1		25
Wm. Baker	1		25
John Bryan	1		25

142   The court then adjourned until court in course
                    James Grant, Chairman.

143   A court began and held in and for the county of Anderson at the court house in Burrville on the second Monday of September in the year of our lord 1804.
    Present, Hugh Montgomery, Arthur Crozier, William McKamey, William Standifer, Joseph Cloud, Samuel McKoy, James Scarbro and Joseph Sinclair Esquires.
    John Underwood high Sheriff of Anderson county returned the Venire facias executor over all except John Bradley of whom the following are Grand Jurors (viz.) Joseph Grayson, John McAdoo, John Parks, Marmaduke Bookout, Nathan Hale, Isham Stinnett, James Hill, William Ragland, John Snodderly, Tobias Peters, Henry Russell, Zachariah Lea, Jacob Strader, Samuel Frost and John Lawlese.
    The following are petit Jurors (viz.) John Wallace, Robert Sinclair, Robert Dew, Edward Frost, James Abott, Joseph Sharpe, Edward Freels, David Lea, Briton Ragsdale, William Scarbro, Rowley Duncan, Travis George and William Hancock.
    A deed of conveyance from John Unstead by James Grant his attorney to Jacob Strader for one hundred and twenty five acres and one half of land was proved in open court by William Hancock & ordered to be registered.

A deed of conveyance from William Hogshead to Joseph McKinley for two hundred and fifty acres of land was proved in open court by Churchill Jackson & ordered to be registered.

144   A deed of conveyance from Edward Stephenson to Michael Clardey for one hundred and fifty acres of land was acknowledged in open court & ordered to be registered.

A deed of conveyance from Jasan Stinnett to Michael Clardy for one hundred and fifty acres of land was proved in open court by John Kerby Esq. & ordered to be registered.

A deed of conveyance from James and Zachariah Lea, to Luke Lea Juriors for six hundred and forty acres of land was proved in open court by John Lea and ordered to be registered.

Martin Beatty)
vs.)
James Thomas and)
Joseph Sharp.) Ordered by the court that a Dedimus Patestatew issue to take the Testimoney of James McGee at Lea court house in the State of Virginia directed to Benjamin Sharp, William Neel and John Fulteon and that twenty days notice be given.

A deed of conveyance from the commissioners of the town of Burrville to John Leib for four lotts in said town (viz.) No. 1, 3, 14, & 29 was proved in open court by James D. Puckett and ordered to be registered.

A deed of conveyance from Joseph Denham to Charles Sinclair for seventy five acres of land was proved in open court by Robert Sinclair & ordered to be registered.

Ordered by the court that Joseph Hoge have his mark recorded which is an hole in the right ear and an under keel in the left.

145   Ordered by the court that Reuben Ragland have his mark recorded which is a cross and over keel in the right ear and a Slit and under Keel in the left.

Ordered by the court that Manpage Vowell have leave to keep an ordinary at his house in Burrville he having give bond and security as the law requires.

Ordered by the court that Jacob Peake be overseer for non attendance as a Juror at June Session 1804.

Court then adjourned till tomorrow 9 o'clock.

Tuesday 11th September 1804.
Court met according to adjournment.
Present -- Hugh Montgomery, Arthur Crozier and William McKamey Esq.

John Stuart)
vs.)
Henry Carlock) In the case Jasen Marcus? and Joseph McPeters who were witnesses being solemly called were not whereupon it it considered by the court that the perfect according to act of assembly.

Archibald McDaniel)
vs.)
Elliott Grills) Whereupon came a jury to wit Joseph Sharp, Edward Freels, David Lea, Briton Ragsdale, William Scarbro, Rowley Duncan, Travis George, William Hancock, Joseph Haze, Moses Cunningham, Malin Hibbs, & Simon Derick, who being duly sworn say they find for the defendant -

146   A deed of conveyance from James D. Puckett to George Hoskins for one hundred and fifty acres of land was acknowledged in open court and ordered to be registered.

A deed of conveyance from the commissioners of the town of Burrville to John McWhorter for lott No. 15 in said town was proved in open court by George Bumgertner & ordered to be registered.

A deed of conveyance from William Lea to Zachariah and James Lea and proved in open court for six hundred and forty acres and ordered to be registered by George Steele.

A deed of conveyance from John Long Junior for John Long, Sen. to John McWhorter for one hundred and seventy five acres of land was proved in open court by Arthur Crozier and ordered to be registered.

Ordered by the court that James Hortone be overseer of the road instead of William Witnal.

Ordered by the court that Jermiah Jeffery be overseer of the road instead of Thomas Worthington.

Ordered by the court that Edward Freels be overseer of the road instead of James Standifer.

A bill of sale from Robert Armstrong to John Terry was acknowledged in open court and ordered to be registered.

A conveyance from Edward Parsley to Stewart Anderson for one hundred and fifty acres of land was proved in open court by James D. Puckett and ordered to be registered.

147   John D. Wiggins)
vs.)
Jessee Vanoy &)
James Robertson)   Whereupon came a jury (towit) John Wallace, Robert Dew, Edward Frost, James Abbott, John Coence? Jun., John Coence? Sen., Joel Bowling, Enoch Foster, John Jameson, Elyah Frost, James Finley & Amos Elliott who being duly sworn say they find for the plaintiff and assess his damage to seven hundred and five dollars and costs appeal prayed.

Ordered by the court that Thomas Adair have his mark recorded which is a cross and slit in the right ear and a cross and under keel in the left.

The court then adjourned for one hour.

The court met according to adjournment.

Present William Underwood, John Kirby, Hugh Montgomery, James Scarbro, William McKamey and Joseph Sinclair Esqrs.

Francis Hughes)
vs.)
Charles Crabaugh)   in this case Travis Hughes by John H. Madeson his attorney moved for a judgement against John --- makes a constable and his securties for nine dollars and twenty two cents with interest from March term 1804- Judgment was thereupon given by the court accordingly.

David Looney)
vs.)
John McEntire)   in the case Isaac Robbins & Reuben Roberts who were bail for the defendant surrendered him in open court in discharge--- of themselves and John Burdock, Jarett Harbin---came into open court and undertook that the Defendant should pay the Plaintiff his debt

and costs or surrender his body in discharge of the same or that they will pay it for him.

148   Ordered by a majority of the acting Justices that James Grant, John Snodderly, William Hancock, Jacob Strader and Shadrach Reedy view and mark out a road the nearest and best way from the ----- in the fork of Powells and Clinch rivers, through the town of Grantsbrough in the main street and continue on until it intersects the road that goes up between the said rivers into Claiborne county near Brocks mill and make report to next court.

The report of a Jury relative to a road to Joseph Robersons is confirmed and it is ordered by the court that he have leave keep a public Ferry on the river Clinch he having given bond and security as the law requires.

Mary Edwards came into open court and had leave to administer on the Estate of Samuel Edwards her late husband deceased and entered into Bond with security in the sum of five hundred dollars and was qualified as the law directs.

Ordered by the court that Joseph Grayson be appointed overseer instead of Reuben Ragland.

Ordered by the court that Hugh Alexander be appointed overseer from John Scruggs to Richard C. Cobbs.

The court then adjourned till tomorrow 9 o'clock.

Wednesday 12th Sep. 1804.

Court met according to adjournment Hugh Montgomery, Joseph Cloud, Joseph Sinclair and William McKamey.

149   The following is a list of Jurors for December term 1804.

1 Abraham Hagler
2 Thomas Kincaid
3 Henry Peters
4 Joseph Lea
5 Constant Claxon
6 Thos . ?
7 And. Farmer
8 Jacob Linard
9 Oliver Dodson
10 Michl. Clardy ?
11 John Farmer Jun.
12 Jessee Hoskins
13 Rich. Forster
14 James Bounds
15 Lewis Stephens
16 John Wanick ?
17 George Shettert?
18 John Tunnell
19 Thos. Worthington
20 Edw. Freels Jun.
21 Edward Williams
22 Aron Sharp
23 Wm. Thompson
24 Robert Macey
25 Jacob Queenes
26 Christan Isley
27 James Mode
28 Joshua English
29 John English
30 H. B. Greenwood
31 John Garner
32 Layton Smith
33 Jacob Peak
34 Malcum Hunter
35 Jonath Bashaw
36 Harris Stanley
37 Page Portwood.

Renewed inventory of the Estate of James Williams deceased order of sale is granted to the administratrix.

Ordered by the court that John Lamb be appointed overseer of the road from big creek to the county line of Claiborne instead of Daniel White.

Ordered by the court that Moses M.cWhorter be appointed overseer instead of William Cotter and that he shall have the same hands.

Ordered by the court that Arthur Crozier, Dauglas Oliver and Solomn Massengale be appointed suspector of the election for electore?

James Hill, Charles Bookout, Lewis Stephens, Christian Baker, Marmaduke Bookout & John Warmick who were appointed a jury to view & mark out a road from Hinless creek at the Grantsborough road to Warmicks meeting house report that they have done it and it is ordered that Charles Bookout be overseer to open the lane, from the Grantsborough Road to ane quarter of a mile above his own house and the following hands are to work under him. James Hill, Evan Tayler, John Retty, Robert Warren, Wilson Petty, Robert Maceys hands & John Bookout.

Ordered by the court that Lewis Stephens be appointed overseer to open the road from where Charles Bookout stops to Warricks meeting house and that the following hands work under him Mamhew Heathe, Reuben Hutchinson, John Hickman, Travis George, Christian Makes, George Shetter, Richard Parker, James McFarland & Isaac Vernon.

Ordered by the court that James Scarbro have leave to keep an ordinary at his house in Anderson county he having given bond and security as the law requires.

State)
vs.)
Jesse Vanoy) Whereupon came a Jury (to-wit) John Wallace, Robert Sinclair, Edward Frost, Joseph Sharpe, David Lea, William Derrick, John Countz, Joseph Hage, John Dwiggins, Felix Gilbert, Richard Medlin, Thomas Adair who being duly sworn do say they find the defendant Guilty in manner and form as charged in the Bill of indictment whereupon it is considered by the court that he pay a fine of fifty dollars and be imprisoned for the space of one month and continue therein until the fine and foes are paid an appeal was then prayed.

Ordered by the court that Jason Cloud the commissioner of the revenue have leave to correct certain error by committee in making a return of the taxable property & polls in Anderson County.

Ordered by the court that William Hancock be appointed constable in Jason Clouds company he having given bond & security as the same requires and also taken the necessary oaths

Court then adjourned until tomorrow morning 9 o'clock.

Thursday 13th September 1804.
Court met according to adjournment.
Present, H. Montgomery, Joseph Sinclair, John Kirby and William McKamey, Arhtur Crozier & Jason Cloud Esquires.

A bill of sale from John Watts to Ercuis Anderson was acknowledged in open court and ordered to be registered.

Ordered by the court that Stephen McOmess be appointed overseer of the road instead of Joseph Keeney.

A recognizance in which John Weldone was bound, charged with begetting a Bastard child on the Body of Betsy Luallen was returned to court and the court on hearing Testimoney concerning the premisses were of opinion that John Weldon is the father of said child whereupon it was ordered by the court that John Weldon entered into bond with security in the sum of five hundred dollars.

The Grand Jury then discharged by the court.

State)
vs.)
Jesse Vanoy) In this case the court on reconsideration were of the opinion that one half of the fine be remitted and that his imprisonment should continue only until the end of the present term.

The court then adjourned till tomorrow morning 9 o'clock.

Friday 14 September 1804.
The court met according to adjournment
Present--- Hugh Montgomery, William Underwood and William McKamey Esquires.

(Part of a paragraph left out of page 151)
quarterly yearly for the support and maintaince of said child until it shall attend to the age of eight years which was done accordingly and it is considered by the court that the money be paid to Arther Crozier esquire.

152   Ordered by the court that Janet Harbin have leave to resign his office of constable.

John Roberts Assign of)
Benj. Roberts)
  vs.)
William Hogshead) In case John Roberts by T. H. Payne his att. moved for judgement against Jarrett Harbin constable and his securties for twenty two dollars and eighty cents which was granted by the court.

William Scarbro came into court and entered into bond with security and was qualified as the law directs as an inspector of cotton.

Rodham Keener)
  vs.)
Hezihiah Love) Whereupon came a jury (to wit) John Wallace, Robert Dew, Edward Frost, Joseph Sharp, Robert Sinclair, David Lea, Felix Gilbert, Malen Hibbs, Edward Freels, Constant Claxon, Manpage Vowell and Charles Scarbrough who being duly sworn do say they find for the plaintiff and assess his damage to sixty nine dollars and forty four cents & costs.

Robert Burton)
  vs.)
Henry B. Greenwood) Whereupon came a jury (to wit) John Wallace, Robert Dew, Edward Frost, Joseph Sharpe, Robert Sinclair, David Lea, Felix Gilbert, Malin Hibbs, Edward Freels, Constant Claxtone say the defendent hath not paid the debt in the declaration mentioned and assess the plaintiffs damage by reason forty one cents and costs.

153   Ordered by the court that John Sharp have his mark recorded which is a swallow fork in the left and a smooth cross and under bit in the right.

A deed from Briton Cross to Obadiah Ashlock for seventy two and an half acres of land was proved in open court by John & James Tunnell and ordered to be recorded registered.

Ordered by the court that John Tonera be overseer of the road instead of Philip Teoners & have the same bonds.

A deed from William Standfer to Collins Roberts for four hundred acres of land was proved by Charles T. Oliver & John McKamey and ordered to be registered.

A deed from William Wyatt to Hugh Lackey for fifty one and half acres of land was proved by Douglas and Charles Oliver, and ordered to be registered.

Ordered by the court that John Denham be overseer of the road in place of Isaac Brazelton and the same hands.

154   A deed from John Bowman to John Cooper for two hundred acres of land was proved by John Oks and Jesse Henderson and ordered to be registered.

A deed from Guin Marton and William Parks for one hundred and seventy four acres of land was acknowledged and ordered to be registered.

James Trimble)
  vs.)
Samuel and James Henderson) In this case Thomas Carsons, Sam Davidson surrendered the defendant in. discharge of himself and bail and Mathew Hawkins and West Walker come in to open court and undertook that he should pay the plaintiff his debt of cost in the action or surrender his body in discharge of the same or that they would do it for him.

State)
  vs.)
Lewis Harman) This was for Bastardy and the defendant came into open court acknowledged himself indebted to the State of Tennessee the sum of one hundred dollars and John Underwood, Joseph Hart and Robert Dew, acknowledged himself indebted to said state in one other hundred dollars jointly to be levied off their respective goods and chattles lands and tenements but to be void on condition said Lewis Harman appears from day to day to answer said charge at the court house.

Court then adjourned until tomorrow morning at 9 o'clock.

155   On motion of William Tate by his attorney to enter a judgment given against Spencer the sheriff of Maury county for the sum of one hundred and thirty eight dollars and twenty four and one half cents the principal and costs of an execution put into his hands at the suit of William Tate against Joseph McPeters issued from the court returnable to March term 1809 and it appearing to the satisfaction of the court that said sheriff had received the same more than thirty days before the return day and that he had failed to make return of the same.

It is considered by the court that the said William Tate recover of the said Spencer the sum aforesaid and costs and that execution issue accordingly.

A deed from Walter alves to John Webb for two hundred and sixty acres of land was proved in open court & ordered to be registered.

A deed from James Hays to Thomas Galbreath for three hundred and fifty nine acres of land.

And a deed from James Galbreath to James Hays for three hundred and fifty nine acres of land.

And a deed from James Galbreath to Samuel Galbreath for two hundred and twelve one acres was proved in open court & ordered to be registered.

156

Andrew Stewart)
  vs.)
Quin Morton) In this case Ainza Johnson, Charles Shinliver, Matthew Hawkins, John Scruggs and Richard Haynes who were appointed arbitrators do say award & determine in favor of the defendant.

Bounds for William Lamon overseer (to wit) Moses McWhorter hands thence to Matthew Deatons leaving Philip Fry's hands to John Rhea from Deatons to James Murrays hands thence to Thomas Harts thence to John Blaggs on the b ---- thence to the beginning.

Bounds for John Rhea including Fry's hands thence to where James Underwood lived taking Tadock Deaton thence to the top of the chesnut ridge at the head of Andrew Reads Branch thence down the ridge to the Knox line taking in Robert Raysdon thence to Mayberrys ferry and all others who may hereafter move within their bounds.

Arthur Crozier.

Court adjourned until court in cause.

C. A. C.

157 A deed from John Izly to Isaac Braziel for one hundred acres of land was proved in open court by Ely Frost.

A deed from Frederick Miller to James McNutt for two hundred acres of land was proved in open court by Coward Sharp & ordered to be registered.

A deed from James McNutt to John Black for one hundred and ninety three acres of land was acknowledged in open court and ordered to be registered.

A deed from Robert Macey to John Ridenour for one hundred and fifty six poles. And sixty acres of land was proved in open court by James Grant and ordered to be registered.

A deed from Stokley Davidson to Conrad Sharp for two hundred acres of land was proved in open court by James McNutt and ordered to be registered.

A deed from Stockley Davidson to Aron Sharp for two hundred acres of land was proved in open court by James McNutt and ordered to be registered.

A deed from Robert Houston attorney in fact for Robert for one hundred and eighty acres of land was proved in open court by John Hancock & ordered to be registered.

A deed from William Horton to Joseph Horton for one hundred acres of land was proved in open court and ordered to be registered.

A deed from Joseph Horton for one hundred acres of land was proved in open court and ordered to be registered.

158 Ordered by the court that James Pepper and Charles Sinclair have leave to administer on the estate of William Thomas dec's who entered into bond in the sum of one thousand dollars each and their securties each in five hundred that is John Ridenour and Saml. Wilson Jun. They were then qualified as the law directs.

A bill of sale from John W. Duckworth to Margart Duckworth for two improvements in Powells Valley and other property was acknowledged in open court and ordered to be registered.

Ordered that James Crowley be overseer of the road in the palce of Joel Bowling and that James Grant & Jason Cloud esq. part out of his hands.

Ordered that Samuel Frost be appointed overseer of the road instead of Henry Norman.

Received from the admix. an inventory of the estate Joseph Cross deceased.

A deed from Robert Burton to James Taylor for one hundred and twenty five acres of land was proved in open court by John McBride.

Ordered that Burton to John McBride for two hundred acres of land proved in open court by William.

159 A deed from John Stone to John Ferry for two hundred acres ofland was acknowledged in open court & ordered to be registered.

David Looney)
vs.)
John McIntire) In this case John Purdon and Jarett Harbin who were bail for the defendant surrendered here in open court in discharge of themselves- and William Lamar - and Archibald McDaniel came into

open court and undertook that the defendant John McIntire should pay to the plaintiff his debt and damages or surrender his body in discharge of the same or that they would do it for him.

A deed from John Stone to Robert Scarbro for one hundred and twenty acres of land was acknowledged in open court.

Ordered by the court that Thomas Parsons be appointed a constable in Captain Hawkins company who gave bond and security and was qualified as the law requires.

Jacob Linard who failed to attend at last term as a juror was excused on affadavit.

Ordered by the court that Micajah Cross be appointed overseer of the road instead of Daniel Martin and that Hillon Gooseberry, R. Thos. Hill point out his hands.

Ordered by the court that the following person be a jury to view the road from off the road near Edwards Freels to where Shellys line called Keeths Old Cross Wm. Scarbro, John Wildoke

Ordered by the court that a boy named Joseph M. Miller bound as an apprence to William Russell. The boy he attends to the age of twenty one years supposed now to be twelve years old on the twenty fourth day of June next.

Court then adjourned until tomorrow morning 9 o'clock.

Thursday 12th March 1805.
Court met according to adjournment.
Present, James Grant, Solomon Massingale, Thomas Hill, and James Scarbro Esquires.

James Grant Esquire paid into office five dollars the amount of a fine imposed on Nicholas Reedy for gambling which was immediately paid to the treasurer.

John Ashurst)
vs.)
Manpage Vowell) Present, James Grant, William Standifer, Jason Cloud, Aquella Johnson, Joseph Sinclair, William Spencer, Thomas Hill, John Kirby.

A deed from Robert Burton Executor and Robert Burton attorney in fact for Archibald Henderson one other Executor to Richard Luallen for one hundred and ten acres was proved in open court by William Hancock.

William Browner was fined in the sum of five dollars and stands committed until the fine is paid for a comtempt to the court.

A deed from William Henry Woodson, D. Francis and Ezekeil Henry for two thousand acres of land was acknowledged in open court.

A deed from Charles J. Love by his attorney in fact Benjamin Wheeler to Micajah Cross for two hundred and nine acres and twenty poles was proved in open court by James Firley.

A bill of sale from Thomas Shelby to Robert McKamey for two negro girls Polly and Patty was proved in open court by James Porter and John McKamey and ordered to be recorded.

A deed from James Porter to squire Hendrix for one hundred acres of land was acknowledged in open court.

Ordered by the court that James Martin be appointed constable in Captain Morris' company who entered into Bond with security & was Qualified as the law requires.

William Davidson)
vs)
Robert Armstrong and James)
Davidson by his next friend)
vs)
Robert Armstrong) In the aforementioned causes Nathan Hale

and James Crain were bail for the defendant surrendered here in open court in discharge of themselves.

And John England and James Crow came into court and undertook that the defendant should pay to the plaintiffs their damage or surrender his body in discharge of the same or that they will do it for him.

Ordered by a majority of the acting justices of Anderson county that Stephen Heard clerk be allowed the sum of forty dollars and John Underwood Sheriff fifty dollars for their ex office services for the year 1804.

Ordered by the court that the sum of three dollars per month be appropriated for the support of Martha Wine an object of charity so long as she shall or need it.

Ordered by the court that James Taylor have leave to keep an ordinary at his house in Anderson county he having given bond and security as the law requires.

Ordered by the court that Alexander Cole be appointed overseer instead of Aron Slover and that Joseph Sinclair and Arthur Crozier point out his hands.

163   Soloman Massengale, Arthur Crozier and Richard Cobb, Esquires were elected as Grand Jurors to the next Superior court.

A deed from Joseph English to Daniel White for one hundred and thirty five acres of land was proved in open court by Spencer Graham.

```
John Slover and Dohertys )
Denises Jessee           )
    vs                   )
William Harris           )  Present James Grant, Joseph Sinclair and Rich-
                            ard C. Cobbs Esq.
```
Whereupon came a Juror to wit -- David Cunningham, David Hill, John Hancock, Henry Bickerstaff, Austin Hackworth, Richard Luallen, Joseph Lea, James Robers, Shadrach Tipton, John Tilor, Philip Thermon, John Weldon who being duly sworn say they find that the defendant is quilty in manner and from as charged in the plaintiffs declaration in ejectment.

```
Sane             )
   vs            )
David Shoemaker  )  Present James Grant, Joseph Sinclair and R. C. Cobb
                    Esquires.
```

The same Jury as above, who being duly sworn say they find the defindant is quilty in manner and form as charged in the plaintiff declaration in ejective.

Court adjourned till tomorrow morning 9 o'clock.

Wednesday 13th March 1805.

Present, James Grant, Hugh Montgomery and Richard C. Cobb Esquires.

164   Ordered that David Bullock be appointed overseer of the road instead of Jonathan Hellens and that Solo. Massengale and Saml. McCoy point out his hands.

A deed from Hugh Montgomery to David Queener & Jacob Queener for two hundred and fifty two acres of land was acknowledged in open court.

Ordered by the court that David Upton be appointed overseer of the road instead of Tobias Long and that Wm. Standfer point out his hands.

```
State          )
   vs          )
Reuben Roberts )  Present James Grant, Thomas Hill, James Scarbro, Aqu-
                  illa Johnson, Jason Cloud, Alexander Gaston & Spencer
```

Graham.

Whereupon came a jury (towit) David Cunningham, David Hall, John Hancock, Henry Buckerstaff, Austin Hackworth, Philip Herman, John Waldon, John Leib, James Crain, Parnell Ingram, Thomas and Samuel Worthington. Who being duly sworn say they find the defendant guilty and is fined fifty cents.

A deed from John Dwiggins to John Southerland for six hundred and forty acres of land was proved in open court by Douglas Oliver.

Received from Marten Beatty Administrator an inventory and amount of sales of the estate of Thomas Evans deceased.

165 Ordered by the court that Abner Lezell be appointed a constable in Capt. Steels old company who gave bond, and security as the law requires & took the company oath.

Ordered by a majority of the court that John Leib have charge of the court house public pound and stodes that he be allowed the sum of eight dollars annually for so doing.

Ordered by the court that William Scarbro be appointed guardian to James Smith a minor and that Aquella Minor also.

Ordered by the court that John Baker who has heretofore been appointed a constable in   be suspended from the exercise of said office for misconduct in the same.

Ordered by the court that John Silor be appointed a constable in Capt. James Underwood company he having given bond & security and qualified as the law requires.

A deed from Reuben Roberts to John Leib for fifty acres of land was acknowledged in open court.

166 Ordered by the court the following tax be laid and collected in the county of Anderson for the 1805.

	cents
For each white pole	.12 1/2
For each Black pole	.25
For each hundred acres of land	.12 1/2
For each town lott	.25
For each Stud horse half the season of one mare.	
For each merchant pedlar or hawker.	

Ordered by the court that the Justices afternamed be approved to take lists of taxable property or polls in the different companies hereafter mentioned (to wit) ---

Capt. Hawkins Compy.	Aquella Johnson
McKameys Compy.	Wm. Standifer
Hayes Compy.	Wm. McKamey
Heards Compy.	A. Gastin
Harts Compy.	J. Hart
Underwoods Compy.	R. C. Cobb
Georges Compy.	Saml. McKay
Clouds do.	J. Cloud
Halfaere Compy.	S. Graham
Steels Compy.	T. Hill

167 Ordered by the court that the following persons be appointed as Jurors to in 1805.

Moses McWhorter, John Day, Joel Bowley, John Brown, Jacob Whitenor, John Supson, James Bruton, Danl. Queener, Hutchins Burton, James Mode, Caleb Friley, William Johnson, William Moukin, George Hoskins, Page Portwood, Saml. Frost, Elijah Hendore, John Hoence, Aron Jenkins, William Ussery,

Charles Crabough, Charles Shinliver, Saml. Johnson, Edward Freels Sen., Reuben Williams, Isaac Freels, Squire Hendrix, Nathan Aldridge, Wm. Laware, John McAdoo, Andrew McKamey, Amos Elliott, Robert Dew, John Wallace, Richard Medhee, Henry Russell, John Lollere.

A deed from the commissioners of the town of Burrville to Robert Macey for lotts No. 33, 34, 35, 36, 37, 38, and 44 was proved in open court by Geo. Baumgrentner.

Ordered by the court that the ferry where William Hogshead lives be an established or public ferry and that the following rates of ferriage be a bill road to wit;

For a waggon and team	1	---
For town wheeled pleasure carriages	2	---
For a cart	---	.50
For two wheeled pleasure carriages	1	.08 1/3
For each cow		.02
For each led horse		.06 1/4
For each hog or sheep		.01

And that William Hogshead be appointed ferryman of the same who entered into bond and security as the law directs.

Court then adjourned till tomorrow 9 o'clock.

168   Thursday 14th March 1805.
Court met according to adjournment.
Present Arthur Crozier, Joseph Sinclair, Wm. Underwood, Wm. McKamey and Wm. Standefer Esquires.

John Stewart)
   vs.)
H. Montgomery) Present James Grant, Joseph Sinclair and William
                  Standefer Esquires.

Whereupon came a jury to wit David Cunningham, David Hall, Henry Bickerstaff, Austin Hackworth, Wm. Hogshead, Joseph Denham, Albert Long, John Dewiggins, Malon Hibbs, James Smith, James Davidson and Charles Pauett who being duly sworn say they find four dollars, twenty four and three fourth cents.

Back for a new trial made absolute.

Martin Beatty)
   vs)
Thomas & Sharp) Present James Grant, John Kerby, Arthur Crozier and Joseph Sinclair whereupon came a jury (to wit) Philip Therman, John Wildon, John Leib, John Hancock, John Tunnell, William Russell, William Patterson, Tobias Long, Moses McWhorter, Alexander Gastin, Benjamin T. Warren and Christian Isely.

Who being duly sworn say they find the defendant have not kept their covenant and assess his damages by reason thereof to one hundred and ninety seven dollars and eighty two cents & costs.

169   Ordered by the court that David Hall be appointed overseer of the road from aldridges ford to where it intersects the road near Thomas Wilsons in place of John Garner and that Alex. Gastin point out his hands.

John Russell)
   vs.)
Shad Morris & James Patterson.) Present James Grant, John Kirby, Arthur Crozier & Joseph Sinclair Esquires.

In the case judgment was confessed by Shadrack Morris according to Specalty.

Cloe Jones)
vs)
Elisha Wasson) Present James Grant, Jason Cloud, Joseph Sinclair, Arthur Crozier, & William McKamey Esquires.

Whereupon came a jury (towit) David Cunningham, David Hall, Henry Buckestaff, Wm. Hogshead, Joseph Renhaw, William Russell, John Dwiggins, Malon Hibbs, James Smith, Charles Pruett, Philip Thermon and Page Portwood who say they find for the plaintiff and assess her damage to twenty six dollars and twenty five cents Rule to shew cause why a new trial should not be granted Rule discharged.

A deed of conveyance from the commissioners of the town of Burrville to George Baumgertner for L. H. N 31 was acknowledged in open court.

170 William Morrison)
vs appeal)
Wm. Cotter) Present James Grant, Jason Cloud, John Kirby & John McKamey Esquires.

Whereupon came a Jury (towit) John Waldon, John Leib, John Hancock, John Tunnell, William Patterson, Tobias Long, Moses McWhorter, Alexander Graham, Benjamin T. Warren, Moses Roberts, Joseph Hayes and Henry Farmer who being duly sworn say they find for the defendant- Rule to shew cause why a new trial should not be granted Rule discharged.

John Rhea)
vs)
George Shatters) Present Wm. Underwood, Joseph Cinslair and Jason Cloud Esquires.

The same Jury as above who being duly sworn say they find for the plaintiff the debt in the declaration mentioned and assess his damage by reason of the detention thereof to twenty eight dollars.

Received from the administrator an inventory of the estate of Wm. Havens deceased and an order of sale was granted.

Ordered by the court that Richard Forrest be appointed a constable in Captain Hayes company who gave bond and security and was qualified as the law requires.

The court then adjourned to morrow 9 o'clock.

171 Friday 15th March 1805.
The court met according to adjournment.
Present James Grant, Arthur Crozier and William Underwood Esquires.

Micajah Cross's Lessee)
vs Executor)
William Patterson.) In this case a motion was made to have leave to amend the Decleration which was then made by the Defendants counsel to dismiss the suit which was made absolute.

A letter of attorney from James Hogg to Walter Alves was produced in open court with the proper certificate and ordered to be recorded.

A deed of conveyance from Walter Alves Esquire to James Grant Esquire was acknowledged in open court and ordered to be registered.

Shad'h. Morris
vs.

Lindsey Pol) Present, James Grant, H. Montgomery, Joseph Sinclair, Jason Cloud and A. Gastin Esqrs.

Whereupon came a jury (towit) David Hall, David Cunningham, John Haccock, Henry Buckerstaff, A. Hackworth, Philip Therman, John Weldon, Benjamin T. Warren, Robt. Long, Reuben Roberts, Malon Hibbs, John Leib, who being duly sworn say they find for the defendant.

172   Ordered by the court that John Sartin have leave to keep and ordinary at his house in Burrville he having given bond and security as the law directs.

A deed from William Hogshead to Richard Luallen for thirteen acres of land was proved in open court by Thos. H. Payne and ordered to be registered.

Ordered by the court that John Hancock be appointed overseer of the road from the south bank of Clinch River at the ford near said Hancocks leading into the big valley to where the said road intersects the road from the junction of Powells and Clinch river leading to Knoxville and that James Grant Esqr. point out the hands to work under him.

The court then adjourned till tomorrow 9 o'clock.

Saturday 16th March 1805
Court met according to adjournment.
Present, James Grant, H. Montgomery, Arthur Crozier & Jason Cloud, Esqr.

173   John Underwood Esquire high Sheriff of Anderson County returns the following delenquents who have not paid their poll tax for the year 1804, (to wit) --

Joseph Austin	Perey Jacobs
Samuel Baker	Andrew Johnson
Robert Baker	Samuel Smith
John Baker	Taylor Brazle
Enos Hobbs	John Harris
Arthur Maskham	John Lively
John Newman	Claiborne Puckett
John Reed	Edward Parkey
Jonathan Vanoy	Jessee Leftridge
Evan Williams	Nathaniel Mayson
George Brazle	Nathan Pate
Goldman Eastes	John Smith 1 black pole

Carlock Jacob	Willhite Elijah
Conce John	Willhite Conrad
Evans Thomas	Brown Jack
Griffin Landrum	Couterberry Daniel
Hatfield James	Davis Nathanel
Hatfield John Jun.	Guest John
Hatfield Joseph	Hicks Henry
Marcum Job	Jones Levi
Martin Daniel	Norris Larence
Brummett George	Owens Willis
Brummett James	Ryon John
Bradley John	Shoemaker Thomas
Lewis John	Smith Richard
Willhote Ezkiel	

174   Ordered by the court that Joel Hancock be appointed as overseer of

the road instead of Hugh Anderson that William Underwood and Joseph Hart Esqrs. point out the hands and that he work in the same bounds that said Alexander was to do.

John Underwood high sheriff of Anderson county returned a list of the different tracts of land upon which the taxes have not been paid for the year one thousand eight hundred and four, which the court ordered to be advertised as the law requires.

Ordered by the court that John Leib receive of the treasurer of Anderson county the sum of sixty dollars for the purpose of proceiving a standard of weight and measure. He having entered into bond with security in the sum of one hundred and twenty dollars and qualified as keeper of the same.

Ordered by the court that James Martin be suspended from the office of constable because of his being under age.

The court then adjourned until court in cause.

James Grant Chairman.

175 At a court began and held in and for the county of Anderson at the court house in Burrville on the second Monday of June in the year of our Lord one thousand eight hundred and five.

Present Hugh Montgomery, James Scarbro, Wm. McKamey, Alexander Gastin- Aquella Johnson Esquires.

John Underwood Esquire returned the Venire facias executed on all except Caleb Friley of whom the following were elected as grand Jurors (viz.) Aron Jenkins, Reuben Williams, Robert Dew, William Harkin, Samuel Johnson, Elijah Hendon, John Day, William Ussery, Amos Elliott, William Johnson, William Lavar, Joel Bowling, Edward Freels, Sen., George Hoskins Squire Hendrix who being empanelled & sworn retired to enquire.

The following are traverse Jurors (to wit) Moses McWhorter, John Simpson, John Brown, Charles Shinliver, James Bruton, Jacob Whitenor, Charles Crabough, Samuel Frost, John Hanna, John Wallace, Daniel Queener, Nathan Aldridge, Andrew McKamey, Henry Russell, Richard Medlin, John Mcadoo, Isaac Freels & Page Portwood.

176 Tobias Tilman was excused for his non attendance at March term 1805.

Isaac Freels was exeused from attending as a juror at the present term.

A deed from Charles Fenell to John Terry for six acres of land was proved in open court by John Brown and ordered to be registered.

A conveyance from Stephen Heard to Sampson Wood for one hundred and thirty two and one half acres of land was acknowledged in open court and ordered to be registered.

Ordered by the court that Joseph Lea be appointed overseer of the road instead of John Ashurst from Hinza Johnson to John Jameson.

A conveyance from Micajah Cross to Charles Crobough for one hundred and fifty acres of land was acknowledged in open court and ordered to be registered.

William Mankin and Stephen Pankey who were security for William Patterson surrendered him in open court in discharge of themselves.

And Reuben Roberts and Shadrack Morris came into open court and undertook that in case the plaintiff should recover he should pay him his costs and damages or surrender his body in discharge thereof or that they would do it for him.

A conveyance from Henry Sharp to William Sharp for one hundred and ninety seven acres of land was acknowledged in open court & ordered to be registered.

177 A conveyance from Benjamin Wheeler attorney in fact for Charles &

leave to James Firley for one hundred and Eighty two acres of land was proved in open court by Hugh Montgomery Esquire and Micajah Cross and ordered to be registered.

Ordered by the court (towit) Hugh Montgomery, Joseph Sinclair, William McKamey and Alexander Gastin that William Scarbro be appointed guardian to James Smith a minor who gave bond with security in the sum of five hundred dollars also that Aquella Johnson be appointed guardian to William Smith a monor who gave bond & security in the same sum.

A conveyance from John McIntire to John Purdon for six hundred and forty acres of land was acknowledged in open court and ordered to be registered.

A conveyance from Francis Mayberry to George Graham for three hundred and twenty acres of land was acknowledged in open court and ordered to be recorded.

A conveyance from Richard Lenivlle to Henry Carlock for fifty acres of land was proved in open court by Thomas Campbell and ordered to be recorded.

A conveyance from Travis Mayberry to Newman Rains for one hundred acres of land was proved in open court by Thomas Campbell and ordered to be registered.

178 Ordered by the court that William Ashbeck be appointed overseer of the road instead of James Horton.

Court then adjourned until tomorrow morning nine o'clock.

Tuesday 11th June 1805.
Court met according to adjournment.
Present Hugh Montgomery, William Standfer, James Scarbro and Spencer Graham Esquires.

John Stuart)
  vs.)
Hugh Montgomery) Present William Standfer, James Scarbro, Spencer Graham, William McKamey and Arthur Crozier Esquires.

Whereupon came a jury (to wit) Moses McWhorter, John Brown, James Bruton, John Houisa, Jacob Whitman, Richard Medlin, John McAdoo, Nathan Aldridge, Charles Shinliver, Henry Lamb, William Horton and Jacob Eheney who being duly sworn say they find for the plaintiff and assess his damage to eight dollars and fifty cents an appeal was then prayed by the defendant.

A conveyance from John McBride to James Ross for two hundred acres of land was proved in open court by John Underwood and ordered to be registered.

179 John Spencer)
  vs.)
John Boyd) Present Hugh Montgomery, Spencer Graham, William Underwood, Joseph Sinclair and Alexander Gastin Esquires.

Whereupon came a jury (to wit) Page Portwood, John Simpson, Charles Crabough, Samuel Frost, Daniel Queener, Henry Russell, John Wallace, John Keintz, Robert Warren, John Peery, Aron Sharp and Jacob Peak, who being duly sworn say they find for the plaintiff and assess his find damage to five dollars besides his costs.

Ordered by the court that Amos Elliott be appointed overseer of the road from the valley road near John Scruggs to the Grantsborough road at William Thompsons in the place of John Wallace and that the following hands under him (viz.)
Robert Dew, David Sartin, Nathan Stanley, Thomas Stanley, Robert Smith, Jo-

seph Day, Amos Elliott, Joel Hancock, Jesse Wilson, Isaac Philpot, & Felix Gilbert.

Ordered by the court that Joseph Overton be appointed overseer of the road from Byrams Fork of Hinds creek to the county line on the chesnutt ridge and that the hands of Marmaduke Bookout and William Underwoods hands work under hands.

Samuel Terry)
   vs.)
Joseph Denham) Present Arthur Crozier, William Standfer, Richard C. Cobb, Joseph Sinclair, William McKamey, Alexander Gastin and Spencer Graham Esquires.

Whereupon came a jury (towit) Moses McWhorter, John Brown, James Bruton, John Hanna, Jacob Whitman, John McAdoo, Nathan Aldridge, Charles Shinliver, Henry Lamb, John Pollock, Robert Whitton and Robert McKamey who being duly sworn say the find for the plaintiff and assess his damage to one hundred dollars besides his costs - an appeal bond given.

A deed from William Thompson to William Underwood for one hundred and seventy five acres of land was acknowledged in open court and ordered to be registered. The appeal was then granted.

Ordered by the court that Soloman Massengale Esquire be bound in recognizance in the sum of five hundred dollars for Allen Massengale a minor to endemnify the county of Anderson from the maintainance of a bastard child begotten on the body of Nancy Wilson by the said Allen Massesgale.

Ordered by a majority of the acting justices that the following persons be appointed a jury to review the road from the upper corner of Edward Freels fence to the house where Thomas Shelly lives called Keeths Old ----- (viz.) John Scarbro, William Scarbro, William Roberson, Alexander Galbrath, Andrew McKamey, Douglas Oliver, John McKamey, Samuel Worthington Sen., Aquella Johnson and James Scarbro and that they report to next court.

Ordered by a majority of the acting justices that Aquella Johnson and William Standfer Esquires assign the hands to work under Edward Freels Jun. an overseer of the road.

Ordered by the court that Landwick Clapp be overseer in place of Robert Whitton and John Thomas in place of Samuel Morris that is to say Landwick Clapp from Samuel McKoys to Clouds ford on Clinch river and John Thomas from them clouds old place.

Court adjourned till tomorrow morning 9 o'clock.

Wednesday June 12th 1805.
The court met according to adjournment.
Present Hugh Montgomery, Alexander Gastin, William McKamey and Joseph Sinclair Esquires.

A conveyance from Benj. C. Parker to Frederick Sadler for fifteen acres of land was acknowledged in open court and ordered to be registered.

William Hogshead)
   vs. Attachment)
D. W. Breazeale) Ordered by the court that an Execution issue to sell the land on which said attachment was levied.

State)
   vs. Larceny)
George B. Lear) Present Hugh Montgomery, William Underwood, & Solomon Massengale.

Whereupon came a jury (to wit) Moses McWhorter, John Brown, James

Bruton, John Hance, Jacob Whitman, John McAdoo, Nathan Aldridge, Charles Lewis, Shadrack Reedy, William Hogshead, John Pollock, Lewis Stephens who being duly sworn say they find the defendant is not guilty. A rule to shew cause why the prosecution should be taxed with the costs which rule or argument was discharged.

182 Pharoah Cobb & Sally Cobb
Admon & Admix of the Estate of
William Cobb deceased for the use
of William King and John Crozier
        vs
John Sharp.

    Present, James Grant, Hugh Montgomery, Arthur Crozier, Alexander Gastin & William McKamey Esquires.
    Whereupon came a jury (to wit) Page Portwood, John Simpson, Charles Crobough, Daniel Queener, Henry Russell, John Wallace, William Griffith, James Porter, William Johnson, Moses McWhorter, John Hanna and James Bruton who being duly sworn say they find that the defendant hath not paid the debt in the declaration mentioned as by pleading he hath alledged and assess the plaintiffs damage by reason of the detention of said debt to fifty one dollars besides his cost.

Pharoah Cobb &nSally Cobb
Admon & Admin of the Estate of
William Cobb deceased for the use
of William King & John Crozier
        vs
John Sharp----

    Present, James Grant, Hugh Montgomery, Arthur Crozier, Alexander Gastin and William McKamey Esquires.
    Whereupon came a Jury (to wit) Page Portwood, John Simpson, Charles Crobough, Daniel Queener, Henry Russell, John Wallace, William Griffith, James Porter, William Johnson, Moses McWhorter, John Hanna and James Bruton who being duly sworn say they find the defendant hath paid the debt in the declaration mentioned except eighty two dollars which sum they find the defendant hath not paid and assess the plaintiffs damage by reason of the detention thence to three dollars and sixty nine cents besides his costs.

183   Ordered by the court that the following persons be appointed a jury to view the old Knox Road from the Eagle ford on Clinch river to the Knox line (towit) John McWhorter, John Kirby, Joseph Grayson, Samuel Frost, Aron Jenkins, Thomas Wilson, and Isaac Norman and that the report to next court.
    Ordered by the court that the following persons be appointed ajury of view from the fork of the road in the racoon valley to Alldridge ford on Clinch river (towit) John Sotherland, David Hall, Thomas Benson, William Brazle, John Garner, John Hanna, & Nathanel Davis, and that they report to next court.
    Ordered by a majority of the court that the road formerly extablished leading from the valley road to where it intersects the cove road be discontinued.

Jesse Wilson   )
  vs Demurrer   )
Henry B. Greenwood & James Thomas.) This cause coming on to be heard on
                                                       argument it was considered by the

court that demurrer be over ruled and that the plaintiff recover off the Defendants the debt in the declaration mentioned together with the sum of dollars, for his damages for the detention of the debt together with his costs.

184 Martin Beatty)
    vs)
James Thomas)
& Joseph Sharp) In the cause on the motion of Joseph Sharp to enter a Judgement against James Thomas for the amount of the principal and costs and it appearing to the satisfaction of the court that Joseph Sharp was the security of said James Thomas and that said Joseph was sued for said debt by said Plaintiff by suit in the county court of Anderson andthat said Joseph Sharp had paid on said Judgement as security for said James Thomas one hundred and ninety seven dollars and eighty two cents and the sum of twenty dollars and thirty four cents for costs in all two hundred and eighteen dollars sixteen and one half cents.

This therefore considered by the court that said Joseph Sharp recover of said James Thomas according to the Tenor and effect of the act of assembly in such case made and provided the said sum of two hundred and eighteen dollars and sixteen and one half cents and Execution to issue for the same accordingly.

Ordered that by a majority of the court that the following bounds be observed by the overseers.

Nathaniel Davis Bounds beginning at the Tan vats in the racoon valley running at the foot of the chesnet ridge to David Halls from thence crossing Bull run so as to include John Garner thence to the top of the copper ridge so as to include John Hanna & Henry Buckesstaff.

Austin Hackworth Bounds beginning at said Hackworth running up Clinch river to Joseph Robersons from thence to the top of the copper ridge at the county line thence to the mouth of Bull run so as to include John Buckerstaff and the Hightowers thence crossing clinch so as to include the plantation of the Widow Butler from thence running the chesnut ridge to the
185 head of Johnsons Mill Branch.- - thence down said branch to the river thence up the river to the beginning.

David Halls Beginning at Aldridges Ford on clinch including Southerlands thence down clindh to the mouth of Bull run thence up the Racoon Valley to David Halls thence across the chesnut ridge to include Tankard Vandew thence across the Pine ridge and big valley to the lost ridge to include John Cooper thence along said ridge to the beginning.

Joseph Graysons beginning at the Eagle ford on Clinch thence down the said river to Henry Farmer excluding Hortons and Clardys hands thence across the last ridge to include John Parks from thence to the chesnut ridge meeting house thence to the mough of little dismal including Joseph Grayson thence to the beginning.

Saml. Frost beginning at the mouth of little dismal running up Clinch to Henderson & Co line & with said line running up Clinch to Henderson & Co line & with said line to Bull run thence to the mill thence to include Layton Smiths thence to the forks of Knoxville & Mucesses Mill road.

Thos. Wilson from the top of the chesnut ridge to Mcusses mill to include Jerkins and Kirkland thence with the county line to the top of the copper ridge to run so as to include Wm. Ussery & Elijah Frosts place thence to the beginning.

Joseph Lea's beginning at Kinza Johnsons including all the hands on the north side of the road as far down as William McKameys thence across said road to the pine ridge thence along the said ridge to include David Laswell.

186   Henry Farmers beginning at Tazwells thence down the valley including all the hands in said valley to Isaac Brazletons.

Brazeltons bounds beginning at said Brazeltons thence the pine ridge including Kee thence down poplar creek including Alexander Galbraith thence across poplar creek running down said creek to the county line.

Wm. Mankins beginning at William Farmers thence down Poplar creek on the north side including William Tunnell thence across to the pine ridge to include Samuel Worthington.

Joseph Jefferys beginning at said Ashlocks thence running up the Branch to the Buckhorn Valley thence up said valley to Reuben Roberts thence to Burrville thence down Clinch river to the beginning including Horton & Clardys hands.

McAmmuss from the fork of the island ford road to hwere Ross lives from Nolles down to Cole Creek from the mouth of Cole Creek to Greens including Jackson thence direct course to Bosses including the Stiles & James Leech.

Capt. Coles from James Greens to Simon Derricks including Rhodes Stanley thence to the pine ridge.

Wm. Sevoris from the mouth of Cave creek leaving Simon Derrick and Stainley in Coles bounds and a direct line to include Low and James.

Joseph Dehham what one in Bentville.

Wm. Hogshead those who live on his place.

187   Rich. Luallen to have Lynch and Cormick or any that come in their place.

Reuben Roberts- Beginning on the south side of the valley road including William Johnson down said road to including McKamey thence to include Andrew Farmer & J. Farmer thence to said Roberts thence to include Ureah Potter thence to said Johnsons.

John Shepards beginning at John McBrides including all the hands between the pine ridge and Wallens ridge so far down as to include Kinza Johnson and Shinliver.

John Howard   )
  vs   )
Jesse Wilson   )   Present James Grant, Arthur Crozier, William Underwood, Joseph Sinclair, John Kirby, William McKamey, Hugh Montgomery and Alexander Gaston Esqr.

Whereupon came a jury (to wit) Page Portwood, John Simpson, Charles Crobough, Daniel Queener, Henry Russell, John Wallace, William Griffith, James Porter, William Johnson, Moses McWhorter, John Hanna and James Bruton who being duly sworn say they find that the Defendant hath not paid the debt in the declaration mentioned as by pleading he hath alledged and assess the plaintiffs damage by reason of the detention thereof to three dollars fifty cents besides his costs.

King & Crozier)
  vs.   )
Lewis Stephens)   Present James Grant, Alexander Gastin, William McKamey, Joseph Sinclair, Willlam & Underwood.

Whereupon came a jury (towit) Page Portwood, John Simpson, Charles
188 Crobough, Daniel Queener, Henry Russell, John Wallace, William Griffeth, James Porter, William Johnson, Moses McWhorter, John Hanna and James Bruton,

who being duly sworn do say they find the defendant hath paid the debt in the decleration mentioned except one hundred and eight dollars and eight cents and assess the plaintiffs damage by reason of the detention of that sum to four dollars and eighty six cents and also find that the bill single in the declaration mentioned was assigned.

A conveyance from Nathan Sullins to Zacarah Sullins for one hundred acres of land was acknowledged in open court and ordered to be registered.

A conveyance from Charles McClung to William Griffeth for one hundred and thirty six acres of land was proved in open court by Nathan Sullins and ordered to be registered.

A conveyance from Charles McClung to Nathan Sullins for two hundred and fifty acres of land was proved in open court by William Griffeth and ordered to be registered.

Ordered by the court that Henry Russell be discharged from farther attendance as a juror at the present term.

Ordered by the court that William McGhee be appointed a constable in Capt. McKameys old company he having given bond and qualified as the law requires.

The grand jury were then discharged and
The court adjourned till tomorrow morning 9 o'clock.

189 Thursday 13th June 1805.
The court met according to adjournment.
Present James Grant, Arthur Crozier and Hugh Montgomery esquires.

James Pepper)
  vs   )
John H. Madison) In this case it is ordered that a dedemus potestatum issue to take the depositions of Samuel Ferguson and John King at Bottetourt court house in Virginia for the plaintiff and that a dedemus potestatum issue for the defendant to take the depositions of the same persons at the same place each giving thirty days notice.

John H. Madison)
  vs   )
James Pepper   ) In this case it is ordered that a commission issue to Botetourt county in Virginia to take the depositions of Samuel Ferguson, Henry Roberson, Robert Hamey, John King and James Brookeridge for the plaintiff and a commission to take the depositions of the same persons at the same place for the defendant each giving thirty days notice.

Ordered that Douglas Oliver, Richard C. Cobb and John McAdoo be appointed inspectors of the ensuing election for members to congress, governor and members of the General assembly in Anderson County.

190 John Ferry)
  vs   )
John Boyd   ) Present James Grant, Hugh Montgomery, Arthur Crozier, Spencer Graham, William Underwood and Jason Cloud Esq.

Whereupon came a jury (towit) Page Portwood, John Simpson, Samuel Frost, John McAdoo, John Wallace, John Hanna, Daniel Queener, Jacob Whitman, James Bruton, Charles Shinliver, Moses McWhorter and John Brown who being duly sworn say the find for the Defendant.

A Conveyance from John Stone to William Boyd for three hundred acres of land was proved in open court by John Boyd and ordered to be registered.

John Dew on the demise)
& Walter & Gauin Alves)
      vs   )
Rich'd Fer---- with notice)
to John Sharp)   Present James Grant, William Underwood, Jason Cloud, Joseph Sinclair, Arthur Crozier, William McKamey and Spencer Graham Esquires--- At this term--- in this case plea & issue was joined & the trial came on by consent.

     Whereupon came a jury (towit) Page Portwood, John Simpson, Samuel Frost, John McAdoo, John Wallace, John Hanna, Daniel Queener, Jacob Whitman, James Bruton, Charles Shinliver, Moses McWhorter and John Brown who being duly sworn say they find the defendant guilty in manner and form as charged in the plaintiffs declaration in ejectment.

Jarret Harbin)
    vs   )
John Stuart) Present James Grant, William Underwood, Jason Cloud, Joseph Sinclair, Arthur Crozier, William McKamey and Spencer Graham Esq. Whereupon came a jury (towit) Page Portwood, John Simpson, Samuel Frost, John McAdoo, John Wallace, John Hanna, Daniel Queener, Jacob Whitman, James Briton, Charles Shinliver, Moses McWhorter, and John Brown who being duly sworn say they find for the plaintiffs damage to thirteen dollars and sixty three cents besides his costs.

191   Ordered by the court that William Cooper be overseer of the road instead of Jacob Whitman on the Grantsborough road from the north bank of Clinch river at the ferry into the powells valley road and that James Grant Esquire assess to him his hands.

    Ordered by the court that Marselles Mass be appointed overseer of the road instead of Reuben Mass on the road from the Powells Valley road by Burtons to the path that goes to Cunninghams Mill and that Spencer Graham point out the hands.

    Ordered by the court that the following persons be appointed to attend as Jurors at next term (towit) Richard Luallen, Wm. Seveirs, Jacob Lynard, Thomas Towery, Jacob Peak, John McKamey, John Tunnell, James Worthington, James Bounds, Thomas Adair, Austin Hackworth, John England, Joseph Galaher, John English, James Finley, Henry McKamey, William Thompson, Robert Macey, Nathan Haile, Charles Bookout, Hutchens Burton, Absalom Morris, David May Lamb, James Taylor, William Derrick, Nicholas Reedy Mode, Michal Clardy, David Lea & Aron Sharp.

192   Ordered by the court that John Underwood Esquire be released collector from the payment of the tax on the following property and polls for the year 1804 (towit)

	Free poles	B poles	acres
John Hamilton	11	11	10,000
Richard Bullock			9,625
John England	4		
John Good	1		
Samuel McKinley	1		
Conrite Wilhite	11	11	100
Claiborne Puckett			150
William Russell	11	1	
William Robbins	11	11	200
Elijah Jay	11		400
Benjamin Wilson	1	11	150
David Lea	1		

	Free pole	B poles	acres
David Bullock	1	11	
Johnson Keath	1	11	
Thomas Smith	1	11	
Daniel White	11	11	200
Andrew McKamey	1	2	11

it appearing to the court from the certificate of the sommissioner that they have been unproperly returned.

Ordered by the court that James Grant Esquire be appointed Chairman of the county court of pleas and quarter session of the county of Anderson.

Ordered by the court that Shadrack Reedy bring to court on the second Monday of September next an orphan boy by the name of Isaac Reedy that the court may enquire into his situation and do what they may think best respecting him.

193 Ordered by the majority of the acting Justices that the following persons be appointed a Jury to view and lay off a road the nearest and best way up Powels Valley from the cross mountain to the Claiborne county line near Robt. Glenns, passing near to Sampson David's Store (to wit) Hugh Montgomery, James Grant, John English, Arthur Crozier, Richard Lenville, Joseph Sinclair and John Leib. And that they make report to next court.

John Underwood entered into bond in the sum of two thousand dollars and gave Hugh Montgomery and William Underwood as security for the collection of the public and county tax for the year 1805 and was qualified.

The court then adjourned until court in cause.

James Grant Ck. (to wit)

194 A a court began and held in and for the county of Anderson at the court house in Burrville on the second Monday of September in the year of our Lord one thousand eight hundred and five. Present James Grant, Alexander Gastin and William McKamey Esquires.

John Underwood Esquire high Sheriff of the county of Anderson returned the venire facias executed on all except David Lea of whom the following persons were appointed, Grand Jurors (to wit) James Worthington foreman David May, William Thompson, William Brazle, John Tunnell, Henry McKimey, William Derrick, James Taylor, James Bounds, Jacob Peak, James Firley, Nicholas Reedy, Austin Hackworth, Thomas Adair, & Absolam Morris who being duly sworn retired to enquire.

The following are traverse Jurors (to wit) Robert Macy, John English, John English, John Fowler, Isaac Norman, Joseph Galaher, William Severis, Richard Luallen, Michael Chardy, Nathan Hale & James Mode.

John McKamey was excused from attending as a juror in consequence of sickness in his family.

Ordered by the court that Richmond Archer be overseer of the road instead of John Thomas from Clouds ford on Clinch river to Clouds old place and that Jason Cloud Esquire point out his hands.

Ordered by the court that Paul Harmon be appointed the constable to attend the petit Jury.

195 Ordered by the court that John Brown be appointed overseer of the Grantsbrough road leading to Powells valley from the north bank of Powells river to the top of the dividing ridge to where Reuben Morris ends and that Lewis Grant Esquire assign him his hands.

A deed from Conard Sharp to Samuel McKay for ninety acres of land was proved in open court by Peter Poor and ordered to be registered.

Ordered by the court that John McEntire Junior enter into bond who gave Reuben Roberts and Robert Warren securties in the sum of five hundred dollars to indemnify the county of Anderson from the maintainance of a Bastard child begotten by him on the body of Betsy Austin.

A deed of conveyance from Robert Burton to Jashua English for one hundred and six acres of land was proved in open court by John English & ordered to be registered.

A deed of conveyance from Robert Gordon to Joseph Keeny for five hundred and twenty acres of land was proved in open court by Jessee Roysdon and ordered to be registered.

A deed of conveyance from John Underwood Sheriff to Robert C. Gordon for six hundred acres of land was proved in open court by Arthur Crozier and ordered to be registered.

A deed of conveyance from John Unstead by James Grant his attorney in fact to Robert Dunlap for two hundred acres of land was acknowledged in open court and ordered to be registered.

196 Ordered that Henry Russell be overseer of the road from R. C. Cobb fence in the big valley to the ford of Buffaloe Creek at Elijah Whittons and that Soloman Massingale point out the hands to work on said road.

A deed of conveyance from Charles J. Love to Hugh Montgomery for one thousand five hundred acres of land was acknowledged in open court and ordered to be registered.

A deed of conveyance from Charles J. Love to Hugh Montgomery for two thousand seven hundred and fifty four acres of land was acknowledged in open court and ordered to be registered.

Court adjourned till tomorrow morning 9 o'clock.

Tuesday 10th September 1805.
The court met according to adjournment.
Present James Grant, William Underwood, Arthur Crozier & William McKamey Esquires.

197 Robert Burton)
   vs covenant)
Joel Bowling) Present James Grant, William Underwood, James Scarbro, Jason Cloud, Arthur Crozier and Aquella Johnson.

Whereupon came a jury to wit, Robert Macey, John English, John Lamb, Isaac Norman, Joseph Galaher, Seth Johnson, Charles Pruett, William Stone, Churchill Jackson, John Simpson, Nathan Aldridge and John P. Masterson who being duly sworn say they find that the defendant hath not kept and performed his covenant and assess the plaintiffs damage by reason thereof to one hundred and thirty seven dollars and fifteen cents and costs.

John Spencer)
   vs)
Bladley Dalton) In this case William Wyatt who was Bail for the Defendant surrendered him in open court in discharge of himself and Nathan Haile and Joseph Wyatt came into open court and undertook that in case the defendant should be cost in the action he shall pay to the plaintiff his damage or surrender his body in discharge of the same or that they will do it for him.

A deed from Robert Brazle to David Hall for eighty nine acres and one half of land was proved in open court by William Brazle and ordered to be registered.

A deed of conveyance from John Leib to Elizabeth Lucus for Lott No. 1 in the town of Burrville was acknowledged in open court and ordered to be registered.

A deed of conveyance from the commissioners of the town of Burrville to Elizabeth Lucus for the lotts No. 7 and No. 4 in the town of Burrville was proved in open court by John McWhorter and ordered to be registered.

198 Robert McWaly   )
      vs assembls   )
    William Hogshead) Present James Grant, Joseph Hart, William Underwood,
Aquella Johnson, Joseph Sinclair and Jason Cloud, Esq.

      Whereupon came a jury (to wit) Robert Macey, John English, Isaac Norman, Joseph Galaher, Seth Johnson, Charles Pruett, William Stow, Churchill Jackson, Peter Helton, Nathan Aldridge, William Horton and Joseph Rogers who being duly sworn say they find for the defendant.

Nathan Roberts)
    vs   )
Michael Robbins) John Masterson surrendered the defendant in open court
in discharge of himself and Moses McWhorter and Shadrack Tipton came into open court and undertake that in case the defendant shall be cast in this action he shall pay the plaintiff his damages and costs or surrendered his body in discharge of the same or that they will do it for him.

      The amount of sales of the estate of Joseph Cross deceased was returned by the administratrix.

      Ordered by the court that Edmund Vagun be appointed overseer of the road instead of Charles Bookout and that the same hands work under him and that William Underwood point out the hands.

      A deed from John Ashurst to Charles Crabough for six acres of land was acknowledged in open court and ordered to be registered.

Andrew White   )
    vs   )
William Davidson) In this case Edward Hawkins & William Wyatt surrendered the defendant in open court in discharge of themselves and Nathan Hale & Joseph Denham come into open court and under took that if the defendant should be cost in the action he should pay the plaintiff his debt & cost or surrender his body in discharge of the same or that they would do it for him.

199   Ordered by the court that George Sharp be appointed overseer of the road instead of Rowley Duncan on the Grantsborough road from little Buffaloe to Bryans fork. And that the following hands work under him (to wit) John Cole, James Murray, Jesse Helton, Robert Sutton, Felix Gilbert, Richard C. Cobbs hands & Thomas Landrum.

      Ordered by the court that George Grimes be appointed overseer of the Powells Valley road from Conrite Willhites fence to Indian Creek in place of Thomas Campbell and that Richard Lenville point out his hands.

Christopher Haynes)
    vs   )
John Collinsworth) In this case William Hogshead who was bail for the defendant surrendered him in open court in discharge of himself and Janet Harbin and Reuben Roberts came into open court and undertook that if the defendant should be cost in the action he shall pay the plaintiff his debt and costs or surrender his body in discharge of the same or that they would do it for him.

      A deed of conveyance from George Maxwell and Francis Mayberry to Thomas Campbell for five hundred acres of land was proved in open court by William Rains and ordered to be registered.

      A deed of conveyance from John Rains to William Rains for two hundred and twenty acres of land was proved in open court by William Rains and ordered to be registered.

      A deed of conveyance from John Rains to William Rains for two hundred and twenty acres of land was proved in open court by Thomas Campbell and ordered to be registered.

    Ordered by a majority of the acting Justices of Anderson county that Henry Sharp be allowed the sum of nine dollars for having kept William Keeling previous to this term and that he be allowed the sum of four dollars for each month he may support the said William Keeling so long as he may remain with the county or need it.

    Ordered by a majority of the acting Justices that the sum of three dollars be appointed to be paid to James Grant Esquire and the sum of three dollars and fifty cents to be paid to Arthur Crozier Esquire for books furnished by them for the use of the court.

    Ordered by a majority of the acting Justices that Hugh Montgomery Esquire, Sampson David, James Grant Esquire, John English, James Finley and Shadrack Reedy be appointed a jury to view and mark out a road the nearest and last way from the north bank of Powels river at the junction of that river with the Clinch river thence along near to or where the road from Claiborne county between the said rivers passes where Shadrack Reedy now lives thence down thro Henderson & Companys survey so as to intersect the road leading down Powells valley at or near the place where Sampson David is now building a new store and house and that they report to next court.

    Ordered by the court that Isaac Freels be overseer of the road from the cumberland ford to William Wyatts.

    A deed of conveyance from James McCracklin to Samuel Curtis for one hundred and fifty acres of land was proved in open court by Richard Juville and ordered to be registered.

    A deed of conveyance from Richard Lenville to John Vanderpose was acknowledged in open court and ordered to be registered.

    Ordered by a majority of the acting justices the following persons be appointed a jury to view and lay off a road the nearest and best way up Powels Valley from the Cross mountain to the Claiborne line near Robert Glenns passing near to Sampson Davids store (to wit) Hugh Montgomery, John English, Richard Juville, Sampson David, Daniel White, Joseph Sharp and Joshua English and that they report to next court.

    A deed of conveyance from John Day to John McAdoo for one hundred and seventy five acres of land was proved in open court by Thomas H. Payne and ordered to be registered.

    Ordered by a majortty of the acting justices that the following persons be appointed a jury to review the road from the fork of the Knox and Burrville roads at William Standfers Spring Branch to intersect the main road opposite or near Kieths old cabbins (to wit) Douglas Oliver, Jacob Peak, Samuel Galbreath, Alexander Galbreath, Michael Hastler, William Griffith and William Roberson and that they report to next court.

    James Grant Esquire, Joseph Hart Esquire and John McAdoo were elected to attend as Grand jurors at the next Superior court to be holden for the District of Hamilton.

    The court then adjourned till tomorrow morning 9 o'clock.

    Wednesday 11th September 1805.
    The court met according to adjournment.
    Present, James Grant, Arthur Crozier, Joseph Sinclair, Spencer Graham, William Underwood, Aquella Johnson & James Scarbro Esquires.

    Ordered by the court that the hands in the following bounds be observed by Isaac Freels overseer of the road (to wit)

    Beginning at the mouth of Johnsons Mill creek thence across the chesnut ridge thence up the valley including John Terry and Austin Choat thence along the valley to the road leading to Scarbros ferry thence along said road to Reeds Branch thence down said branch to the mouth thence up the river to the beginning.

State)
vs)
Abner Tazele) In this case Robt. Pollock who was bail for George Steele the prosecutor surrendered him in open court in discharge of himself.

State)
vs)
Abner Tazelle) Present James Grant, John Kirby, William Standfer, Arthur Crozier, Soloman Massingale, Spencer Graham, William Underwood, Aquella Johnson, James Scarbro, Joseph Sinclair & Jason Cloud, Esquires.

Whereupon came a jury (to wit) Robert Macey, John English, John ---- Isaac Norman, Joseph Galaher, William Hogshead, James Standfer, Israel Standfer, Henry Lamb, Daneil White, Jacob Butler, & Michael Clardy, who being duly sworn say they find the defendant not guilty. Rule to shew cause why the prosecutor should be taxed with the costs.
Rule made absolute.

203 John Kirby, Samuel Frost, Joseph Grayson, John McWhorter & Isaac Norman who were appointed to view the old Knox road from the Eagle ford on Clinch river to the Knox line report that the road leading from the said ford to Page Portwoods thence by Thomas Wilsons thence by Isaac Normans thence to the extreme height of the copper ridge so as not to injure farms on plantations according to our skill and judgment do deem this public road &---

Ordered by the court that an orphan girl named Polly Carrell now of the age of ten years be bound to Henry Buckerstaff is to teach or cause her to be instructed to read and write and to give her two good new suits of clothes, a good feather bed and furniture and a good milk cow at the experation of her time.

The grand jury were discharged from further amendom.

Lachariah Kee received a draft on the treasure of Anderson County for the sum of nine dollars for supporting Martha Kine from term until the present.

The court then adjourned untill to morrow morning 9 o'clock.

204 Thursday 12th September 1805.
Court met according to adjournment.
Present William Underwood, Arthur Crozier & William Standfer Esquires.

State)
vs)
Charles Pruett) Present James Grant, Arthur Crozier, William Standefer, Joseph Sinclair & Joseph Sinclair Esquires.

Whereupon came a jury (to wit) Robert Macey, John English, John ? Joseph Galaher, Isaac Norman, Henry B. Greenwood, William Wyatt, Robert Warren, William Bishop, Jodiah Wood, Joseph Keeny & John Dwiggins who being duly sworn do say they find the defendant not guilty.

State)
vs)
Charles Pruett)

) Present James Grant, Arthur Crozier, Joseph Sinclair, William Stand-
) fer, Jason Cloud, John Kirby & Joseph Hart Esqrs.

Whereupon came a jury (to wit) Richard Luallen Michael Clardy, Nathan Hale, James Mode, William Seveirs, John Boyd, Henry Lamb, William Hogshead, John Leib, Thomas Mode, Matthew Hawkins & Hugh Barton who being duly sworn say they find the defendant guilty.
 Rule to shew cause why a new trial should not be granted.
 Rule discharge & the defendant is fine twnety five cents.

205 State   )
  vs   )
 Caleb Greenwood) Present James Grant, Spencer Graham, Soloman Massingale, Joseph Sinclair, Alex. Gastin & John Kirby Esq.

 Whereupon came a jury (to wit) Robert Macey, John English, John Landen, Joseph Galaher, Isaac Norman, Thos. Shelly, William Wyatt, Robert Warren, William Bishop, Obadiah Wood, Joseph Keeney, and John Dwiggins who being duly sworn say they find the defendant guilty. Rule for a new trial Rule discharge & the defendant is fined twenty five cents- appeal prayed.
 Ordered by the court that Joseph Hart and Thomas Hart have leave to rebuild their dam on Hinds creek and in line of the present mill to erect a saw and grist mill and a cotton machine.
 A deed of conveyance from Charles McClung to James Standfer for twenty acres of land was proved in open court by Jacob Butler & ordered to be registered.

 State   )
  vs   )
 Shadrack Morris) Present James Grant, Soloman Massingale, Spencer Graham, Joseph Sinclair, Alexander Gastin and William
Underwood Esquires.

 Whereupon came jury (to wit) Richard Luallen, Michael Clardy, Nathan Hale, James Mode, William Seveirs, John Boyd, Henry Lamb, William Hogshead, John Leib, Thomas Mode, Mathew Hawkins, and Hugh Barton.
 Who being duly sworn say they find the defendant not guilty.
 Rule to shew cause why the prosecutor should be taxed within the costs — Rule discharged.

206 The following persons are appointed to attend as jurors at December term 1805 (to wit) Joel Bowling, John Terry, John Mayo, Harris Tudore, William Sharp, John Lay, William King, Enoch Foster, Felix Gilbert, James Hill, Henry B. Greenwood, Joseph Barren, Jonathan Bashaw, Archibald McDonald, James Cunningham, Richard Tilpot, Jacob Queener, Robert Pollock, Thomas Campbell, James Leech, Charles Sinclair, John Ashurst, Craven Johnson, Charles Shinliver, Andrew Braden, Henry Farmer, Jun., William Farmer, Samuel Galbreath, Henry Butler, William Russell, Zacariah Kee, William Davidson, Mathew Hawkins, Henry Russell, John Thomas, Levi Sallar, Joseph Grayson, Page Portwood, Reuben Bagland.
 Ordered by the court that Jacob Lander be appointed overseer of the road from the Eagle Ford to the top of the chesnut ridge and that Thomas Wilson be overseer from the top of the chesnut ridge to the top of the copper ridge .
 William Wood came into open court and made oath that he has attended sixteen days as constable of the grand jury that is to say four days at September term 1804 three days at March term 1805 three days at June term

1805 and three days at September term 1805.

207   Friday 13th September 1805.
Court met according to adjournment.

Present James Grant, William Underwood, Arthur Crozier, Soloman Massengale and Joseph Hart Esquires.

Whereupon came a jury (to wit) John English, John Lamler, Joseph Galaher, Isaac Norman, Richard Luallen, Hugh Barton, William Davidson, John McBridge, Robert Pollock, Joseph Jeffery, John Boyd and Charles Pruett who being duly sworn say they find for the plaintiffs and assess their damage to one hundred and ninety four dollars Sixteen cents and two thirds of a cent.

Patrick Campbell returned five thousand acres of land for taxes for the year 1805.

John Spencer   )
   vs   )
Bradley Dalton)   Present James Grant, Arthur Crozier, William Underwood, John Kirby Esquires.

Whereupon came a jury (to wit) John English, John Lamler, Joseph Galaher, Isaac Norman, Richard LuAllen, Hugh Barton, John McBridg, Robert Pollock, Joseph Jeffery, Charles Pruett, Robert Macey, and William Severis who being duly sworn say they find that it is his deed and find for the plaintiff his debt in the claration mentioned to be discharged by the payment of one hundred and ten dollars and costs.

208   Thomas Tavery was excused by the court for non attendance as a juror at the present term.

John Underwood Esquire collector for the county of Anderson reports that the tax remains unpaid on the following tracts of land the property of the heirs of David Hart deceased (to wit) one thousand six hundred and twenty five acres in lott 2 Powells Valley one thousand three hundred and forty three acres in lott 11 Big Valley one thousand three hundred and forty three acres in Lott G. for the years 1804 and 1805.

Ordered by the court that Jesse Boysdan be appointed a commissioner to act with two already appointed to settle with the officers of the county who collect and are liable to pay public monies who gave bond and security as the law requires.

Court adjourned till tomorrow morning.

209   Saturday 14th Sept. 1805.
Court met according to adjournment.

Present James Grant, Arthur Crozier, Joseph Hart and John Kirby Esquires.

John Underwood Esquire Sheriff and collector for the county of Anderson having heretofore returned a number of tracts of land on which the tax remains unpaid for the years 1803 and 1804.

It is therefore ordered by the worshipful court that he have leave to sell the same on which the tax yet remains unpaid or so much thereof as shall be sufficient to satisfy the said tax after having advertised the same as the law requires.

Ordered by the court that an order directing Shadrack Reedy to bring an orphan child to court at the present term be received.

The court then adjourned until court in cause.
                         James Grant, Chairman.

210 At a court begun and held in and for the county of Anderson at the court house in Burrville on the second Monday of December in the year of our lord one thousand eight hundred and five. There were present James Grant, William McKamey, Aquella Johnson and James Scarbro Esquires.

John Underwood Sheriff then returned the Venire facias executed on all except William Davidson & Mathew Hawkins of whom the following were drawn as grand jurors (to wit) Page Portwood foreman, William Farmer, Archibald McDonald, Craven Johnson, Charles Sinclair, William King, Zacariah Kee, John Terry, Henry Farmer Junor, John Thomas, Robert Pollock, John Ashurst, Andrew Braden, Henry B. Greenwood & James Leach who being sworn retired to enquire.

The following are Traverse jurors Richard, Filpot, Joseph Grayson, Henry Russell, James Cunningham, James Hill, Reuben Ragland, William Russell, Jonathan Boshaw, Enoch Foster, Charles Shinliver, Harris Tudor, Felix Gilbert, Thomas Campbell and Lee Lanier.

Ordered by the court that Lunsford Oliver be overseer of the road instead of William Wyatt from William Wyatt to the head of Reuben Williams Spring Branch.

211 A commission from his Excellency John Seveir with the great seal of the State annexed was produced in open court appointing Sampson David, Robert Dew, Douglas Oliver, Samuel Galbreath, Hutchins Burton and Benjamin C. Parker Justices of the peace in & for the county of Anderson of whom Sampson David, Robert Dew, Samuel Galbreath, Hutchins Burton, and Benjamin C. Parker, Esquires were qualified as the law requires and took their seats.

The following persons are appointed to view and lay off a road from the fork of the road between Jesse Hoskins and Oliver Dotsons on Cave creek to Constantine Claxons (to wit) Constantine Claxon, Charles Shinliver, John Sheppard, Oliver Dotson, Jacob Linard, George Hoskins and Craven Johnson & that they report to next court.

William Johnson, William Griffith, Jacob Peak, Michel Hostler, Samuel Galbreath & Alexander Galbreath who were appointed to review the road from the fork of the Knoxville & Burrville roads at Standfers Branch to Keaths old Cabbins report that they have viewed the same and are of opinion that it is nighest and best to take off at said branch and intersect the old road at Jacob Butlers house and Jacob Butler is appointed overseer of the same.

212 A deed of conveyance from Robert Burton to Jason Cloud for five hundred acres of land was proved in open court by Conrad Sharp and ordered to be registered.

John Howard brought into court and orphan boy named John Austin who had been formerly bound to him by this court and was discharged from the obligation of his indenture said Howard being about to release.

Ordered by the court that Aquilla Johnson Esquire have leave to sell any perisable property in his possession belonging to an orphan boy named William Smith to whom he is appointed guardian & put out the money arising therefrom on interest for the benefit of said boy.

A deed from Robert Burton to Conard Sharp for five hundred acres of land was proved in open court by Jason Cloud and ordered to be registered.

Ordered by the court that Jacob Weaver be overseer of the road instead of James McNutt from Millers ford on the couth side of Clinch river to Big Buffaloe.

The court then excused Aron Sharp for non attendance as a juror at September session 1805.

A deed from Jesse Burris to Martin Ridenour for thirty three acres & one third of land was proved in open court by John Parks & ordered to be registered.

213   A deed from Caleb Friley to David Harley for one hundred acres of land was proved in open court by Harris Ryan and ordered to be registered.

A deed from Robert Houston to Robert E. Warren for one hundred acres of land was proved in open court by Robert Warren & ordered to be registered.

A deed from Stockley Donelson by his attorney John Adair for sixty acres of land was proved in open court by Conrad Sharp and ordered to be registered.

Ordered by the court that an orphan boy named John Austin be bound as apprentice unto William Underwood Esquire until he shall attain to the age of twenty one years who entered into indentures as the law requires.

Ordered by the court that William Sharp be excused from attending as a juror at the present term.

Ordered by the court that William Sharp be allowed the sum of four dollars for each month he shall keep William Keeling an infirm man so long as he shall stay in the county or need it instead of Henry Sharp who has ?--

Ordered by the court that John Tunnell be overseer of road in place of Joseph Jeffery.

214   Ordered by the court that Daniel White be appointed a constable in Captain Huffakers company who gave bond & security and was qualified as the law directs.

Ordered by the court that Joel Bowling be excused from attending as a juror at the present term on affidavit.

Court then adjourned till to-morrow morning 9 o'clock.

Friday 10 December 1805.
The court met according to adjournment.
Present, James Grant, Sampson David, Jason Cloud, William Underwood, William McKamey, Aquella Johnson, Spencer Graham, & Joseph Sinclair, Esquires.

John W. Clay   )
   vs   )
Richard C. Cobb   ) Present, James Grant, Sampson David, Richard Linville, James Scarbro, Arthur Crozier, Joseph Sinclair, William Underwood, Alexander Gastin, Spencer Graham, Joseph Hart, William McKamey & Jason Cloud Esquires.

Whereupon came a jury (to wit) Richard Philpot, Enoch Foster, William Russell, Harris Tudor, Jonathan Bashaw, Jacob Butler, Thomas Campbell, Levi Lamler, Hugh Barton, Reuben Ragland, Felix Gilbert, & Henry Russell, who being duly sworn say they find for the plaintiff.

215   And assess his damage to twenty seven dollars and fifty cents. Rule to shew cause why a non suit should be entered- Rule discharged.

A deed from John McWhorter to the commissioners of the town of Burrville for one acres of land was proved in open court by John Underwood & ordered to be registered.

A deed from John Hackett to William Russell for one hundred and thirty three acres of land was proved in open court by Alexander Galbreath and ordered to be registered.

A deed from Caleb Friley to James Mode for two hundred and twenty five acres of land was proved in open court by Henry B. Greenwood.

Jacob Butler   )
   vs   )
Edward Freels   ) In this case William Gamble, William Evans, William Dav-

idson, William Wyatt, James Worthington, Samuel Worthington, Reuben Brown, William Scarbro, John Nail, Nicholas Nail and Henry Peters, who were appointed arbitrators returned their award saying they find for the defendant.

In an election opened and held for a sheriff for the county of Anderson for the next succeeding two years it appeared on counting out the votes that John Underwood was duly constitutionally and in*amiously* elected.

216   At an election opened and held for coroner for the county of Anderson appointed on counting out the votes that Robert Dew Esquire was duly and unanimously elected.

Ordered by the court that John McCracken be appointed a constable in Captain Huffakers company who gave bond & security and was qualified as the law directs.

A deed from John Underwood Sheriff of Anderson county to Robert Macey for three eighth parts of lott C. no. 2, Henderson & Companys survey was acknowledged in open court 7 ordered to be registered.

A letter of attorney from William Murphy to Samuel Worthington was proved in open court by John Murphy and ordered to be recorded.

John Southerland, William Brazle, John Hanna, Nathanal Davis, John Garner, David Hall, & Thomas Benson, who were appointed a jury to view the road from the fork of the road in the Raccoon Valley to Aldridges ford on Clinch river report that they have viewed the same and are of opinion that the road now runs in the best direction that can be had.

217   Ordered by the court that the following persons be appointed a jury to view a road from the town of Burrville to Henry farmers mill the only place to be renewed is round Reuben Roberts farm (to wit) John Leib, William Horton, Obidah Wood, Edward Frost, Richard Forrest, William Ashlock and Joseph Jeffery & that they report to next court.

Ordered by the court that the following persons be appointed a jury to review the road from poplar creek which leads thro the lands of Roberton Asher & Thomas Adair (to wit) George Hoskins, Craven Johnson, Constantine Claxon, Charles Shinliver, & Jesse Hoskins & that they report to next court.

A deed from Benjamin C. Parker to George Baningertur for three hundred acres of land was acknowledged in open court & ordered to be registered.

A deed from Robert Huston to John Scruggs for fifty acres of land was proved by Robert Dew and ordered to be registered.

John Siler, Enoch Foster, & William Derrick, entered into bond in the sum of five hundred dollars to keep the county indemnified from the maintainance of an ille*gima*te child begotten by said Siler on the body of Judah Brumley.

Ordered by the court that Enoch Foster be appointed a constable in Captain Underwoods Company who gave bond & security and was qualified as the law directs.

The court then adjourned ill 9 o'clock to-morrow.

218   Wednesday 11th December 1805.
Court met according to adjournment.
Present James Grant, William Underwood, Sampson David, Alexander Gastin, William McKamey & Joseph Sinclair Esquires.

Ordered by the court that Thomas Hart be appointed a constable in Captain Sinclairs company who gave bond and security and was qualified according to law.

James Tumble)
    vs   )
Robert Ross)   In this case John Shepard surrendered the defendant in dis-

charge of himself & Joseph Denham and William Davidson come into open court and undertook that the defendant should pay to the plaintiff his deft or surrender his body in discharge of the same or that they would do it for him.

Ordered by the court that Joseph Ridenour be overseer of the road in place of Abreham Jones from the ferry at the south bank of clinch to Little Buffaloe.

Ordered by the court that Robert Dew Esquire make an equitable destitution of the hands between Amos Elliott & Geo. Sharp.

Ordered by the court that John Sutherland have leave to keep a public Ferry on clinch river & they approved of Joseph Hart & Stephen Heard surties for the same who gave bond in the sum of one thousand dollars also ordered that the following rates of ferrage be observed (to wit) for a foreman six and one fourth cents led horse six and one fourth cents man and horse eight and one third cents a cart and two horses fifty cents. Waggon & team seventy five cents- cattle hogs & sheep three cents. Two wheeled pleasure carriage fifty cents--- four wheeled pleasure carriage one dollar.

Andrew White Assess)
vs)
Willliam Davidson) Present James Grant, Robert Dew, Jason Cloud, Arthur Crozier, William McKamey, Wm. Underwood, Alex. Gastin, Benj. C. Parker, Jas. Scarbro, John Kirby & Saml. McKoy, Esquires.

Whereupon came a jury (to wit) Richard Philpot, Jas. Grayson, Henry Russell, James Cunningham, James Hill, Wm. Russell, Jonathan Boshaw, Charles Shinliver, Harris Tudor, Felix Gilbert, Thomas Campbell, Levi Lamler, who being duly sworn say they find the defendant hath not paid the debts in the debt in the declaration mentioned except two hundred dollars and that a ballance of four hundred and forty nine dollars and sixty cents yet remain unpaid and assess the plaintiffs damage by reason of the detention of that sum to two hundred and thirty one dollars & seventeen cents.

Rule for new trial- Rule made absolute.

Paul Harmon came into open court and made oath that he attended the traverse jury five days as a constable at September Session 1805.

Ordered by the court that Allen Brock be overseer of the road instead of Robert Furl from the top of the black oak ridge to the county line.

Ordered by the court that Jason Cloud Jun. entered into bond with security in the sum of five hundred dollars to keep the county idenified from the maintainance of a bastard child begotten on the body of Margaret Reynolds. Also in one other bond in the same sum to keep the county idenified from the maintainance of one other bastard child begotten on the body of Mary Masons which was done accordingly.

Manpage Vowell)
vs)
John Dwiggins) Present James Grant, William Underwood, John Kirby, Sampson David and Robert Dew Esquires.

Whereupon came a jury (to wit) Richard Philpot, Joseph Grayson, Henry Russell, James Cunningham, James Hill, William Russell, Jonathan Basleaw, Charles Shinliver, Harris Tudor, Felix Gilbert, Thomas Campbell & Levi Lamler who being duly sworn say they find for the plaintiff and assess his damage to one hundred dollars   appeal prayed- and reason filed.

A deed from Shadrack Morris to Micajah Cross for two hundred and fifty acres of land was acknowledged in open court and ordered to be registered.

221   Ordered by a majority of the presiding Justices of Anderson that Soloman Massengale, Samuel McCoy, James Grant Esquire.

John Ridenour, Hardy Medlin and Shadrack Reedy be appointed a jury to view and lay out a road the nearest and best way from the south bank of Clinch river at the junction of Clinch and Powels river to Samuel McKays and that they report to next court.

James Grant, Esqr. Hugh Montgomery, Sampson David, John English and Shadrack Reedy, being duly qualified as the law directs in conformity to an order of the court of Pleas and Quarter sessions for Anderson county viewed and marked a way for a road from the bank of Powels river at the Junction with Clinch thro the fields where Nicholas Reedy & Shadrack Reedy now live leaving the house unmediately on the right hand, thence to the point of the ridge next to clinch river thence along said ridge thro Henderson and Companys Survey to the point of an hill marked & designated round the point of said hill to a long leading ridge thence on said ridge to an hollow, thence up that to a Spur that leads to the deviding ridge between Clinch river and Jordian or Big creek thence on said ridge as marked to a Spur that leads down to the dividing ridge between Clinch river and Jordian Big Creek thence on said ridge as marked to a Spur that leads down to the long Sugar hollow a little above where John Whitman lives thence down said sugar hollow to said Big creek at the mouth of Spring Branch just by said Whitmans, leaving his house on the right hand crossing said creek where the old pathway did, thence thro a small field of said Whitmans as marked and up a large ridge the old

222   pathway. Winding round some steep places so as to gain the top of the same thence along said ridge and crossing an hollow & thro a field now occupied by John Duckworth and thence on said marks until it strikes the field where Conrite Wilhite lives thence thro said field leaving the house of said Wilhite on the right or north west and thence down an hollow until the same strikes the Powels Valley road near the store of Sampson David Esquire and that Sampson David be overseer of the same from his store to the waters of Big creek on the west side and Shadrack Reedy from the north bank of Powels River to the south or east bank of Indian creek so as to meet Sampson Davids road and all the hands from the cross mountain up to the Claborne line south of Cumberland mountain & north of Clinch river be equally distributed between the said two overseers until the said road as viewed is opened according to law and that James Grant Esquire distribute said hands.

Ordered that Nancy Crouch have leave to administer on the estate of Solomon Crouch deceased who entered into bond in the sum of five hundred dollars and gave John Ridenour and Nicholas Reedy securities.

The court adjourned till tomorrow morning 9 o'clock.

Thursday 12th December 1805.

The court met according to adjournment present, James Grant, Sampson David, William Underwood, William McKamey & Jason Cloud Esquires.

223   The Petition of Mary W. Burk, Francis Doherty & Helen Doherty, praying a division of a certain tract of land lying in Anderson county near the Pilot Knob on the north west side of Clinch river beginning at Spanish oak and white oak thence due east three hundred and eight poles across a creek to a stake, thence due south five hundred poles to a stake thence due west three hundred and eight poles to a stake thence due north five hundred poles to the beginning was filed and together with a notice and Jesse Roysdon, Arthur Crozier, Joseph Sinclair, James Scarbro, Wm. McKamey, William Standefer & John Sutherland were appointed commissioners to devide the same agreeable to the act of assembly in such case made and provided & that they report to next court.

Ordered by the court that Richard Bullock be released from the payment of the tax on eleven hundred and twenty five acres of land for the year 1805 being overchargedon the tax list.

The following persons are jurors to attend at March Session 1806 (to wit) John Hancock, Jacob Strader, Joel Bowling, Littleberry Crowley, Nicholas Moses, John Lamler, Jacob Weaver, Constant Claxon, Joseph Lea, Andrew Farmer, Thomas Adair, Aron Slover, Joseph Sharp, Joseph Barron, Samuel Curtis, James McCracklin, Jacob Peak, John McKamey, Andrew McKamey, William Standford, William Tunnell Sen., Thomas Worthington, John Cooper, - Samuel Frost, John Lynch, Patrick Cormick, Arnole Sharp, Amos Elliott, John Scruggs, William Sharp, William Scarbro, John England, Thomas Menefee, Robert Macey, William Thompson, William Lamor, John McAdoo.

A deed from Charles J. Leave by his agent Benjamin Wheeler to John English for three hundred and fifty seven acres of land was proved in open court by Hugh Montgomery & ordered to be registered.

The Grand Jury were then discharged by James Grant, Esquire chairman of the court.

Richard Forrest made oath in open court that he had attended on the Grand Jury as constable at the present term four days.

The court then adjourned until tomorrow morning 9 o'clock.

Friday 13th December 1805.
Court met according to adjournment.
Present James Grant, Joseph Sinclair, and Arthur Crozier Esqrs.

Ordered by the court that Edmund Mayson an orphan boy be put apprentice to Jeremiah Cloud until he attains to the age of twenty one years said Cloud is to teach or cause him to be taught to read and write and arithmetic for as the rules of three, and learn him the black smiths trade & give him two new suits of clothes at the expiration of his time.

Robert Dew who was elected coroner then entered into bond with security and was qualified as the law requires.

John Underwood who was elected Sheriff having failed to give bond & security the court considered the office vacant and immediately proceeded to the election of another Sheriff when it appeared on counting out the votes that Hugh Montgomery was duly and constitutionally elected who entered into bond with security and took the oaths prescribed by law.

Hugh Montgomery then entered into bond with security for the collection of the public and county tax and was qualified as the law requires.

Ordered by the court that Jesse Roysdon be appointed a constable in Captain Adairs company who gave bond and security and was qualified as the law directs.

A deed from the commissioners of the town of Burrville to William Standfer for lott No. 2 in said town was acknowledged in open court to be registered.

Ordered by the court that Jerimah Cloud have his mark recorded which is a swallow fork in each ear.

John Silor made oath that he attended four days as a constable on the traverse jury at the present term.

The commissioners of the town of Burrville produced their accounts before a committee appointed by the court to examine the same who reported they were regular. The court then proceeded to make an allowance to the commissioners for their services as follows (to wit)

To Joseph Grayson, sixty dollars and twenty five cents.
To Hugh Montgomery, fourteen dollars.
To William Standfer thirty eight dollars.
To Kinza Johnson, forty eight dollars and fifty cents.
To Wm. Roberson, thirty nine dollars seventy five cents.

The court then adjourned until tomorrow 9 o'clock.

The court met according to adjournment.

Present James Grant Esquire, Arthur Crozier, Solomon Massengale, Sampson David, John Kirby, William McKamey Esquires.

Ordered by the court that the Sheriff have leave to expose to sale the reported lands of the heirs of David Hart deceased.

Ordered by the court that Joseph Jeffery be appointed a constable in Captain McKameys company who gave bond & security and was qualified as the requires.

227 Ordered by a majority of the acting justices that George Steele who was fined twenty five dollars at last term have a remission-- of twenty four dollars and fifty cents.

Alfred Massengale was qualified as Deputy Sheriff of Anderson county.

Ordered by the court that Richard Forrest be allowed the sum of one dollar for each day he has attended the Grand Jury as constable at the present term.

Ordered by the court that Francis Mayberry be released from payment of tax on six hundred acres of land for the years 1804 & 1805.
As lying in the Indain Boundary being part of a thousand acre tract.

Ordered by the court that the present commissioners appointed to settle with the holders and collectors of public monies in said county take up the business from the organization thereof and make report to next court.

Ordered by the court that John Silor be allowed the sum of one dollar for each day he has attended the traverse Jury as constable at the present term.

The court then adjourned till court in cause.

James Grant Chairman.

228 At a court began and held in and for the county of Anderson at the court house in Burrville on the second Monday of March in the year of our lord one thousand eight hundred and six.

Present, James Grant, Arthur Crozier, William Underwood, Joseph SinClair, and William McKamey Esquires.

Hugh Montgomery Esquire, Sheriff, returned the Venire facias executed of whom the following persons were appointed Grand Jurors (to wit) Thomas Adair foreman, Samuel Frost, Andrew Farmer, Aron Slover, Constand Claxon, Nicholas Moses, John Hancock, Samuel Curtis, Andrew McKamey, Thomas Worthington, Joel Bowling, John Scruggs, Joseph Sharp, Littleberry Crowley and Jacob Weaver, who being sworn retired to Esquire.

The following are traverse Jurors (to wit) Aron Sharp, John Lamler, Amos Elliott, William Thompson, Joseph Barron, Jacob Strader, William Lamar, John McAdoo, William Sharp, James McCrackin, William Standefer, William Scarbro, John Cooper, John Lynch, John McKamey, John England, William Tunnell Senior, Thomas Menefee, Jacob Peak & Patrick Cormick.

John M. Campbell Esquire produced his Lincense in open court authorising him to practise law took the oaths required by law & was admitted an attorney of the court.

229 The last will and testament of Conrite Wilhite deceased was proved in open court by Hugh Montgomery Esquire and Elizabeth Wilhite Executrix and Henry McKenney & Simon Wilhite Executors therein were qualified as the law directs.

Douglas Oliver who was appointed a justice of the peace for Anderson county by a commission from the Governor was qulaified in open court as the law requires.

A conveyance from William Ragland to John Parks for one hundred acres of land was acknowledged in open court and ordered to be registered.

Richard Forrest, William Ashlock, Obdiah Wood, Joseph Jeffery & William Horton who were appointed jurors to review the road round Reuben Roberts farm, report that they have proceeded to review the same and are of opinion that where said Roberts has turned said road it is as good as the other and nearer.

A conveyance from Henry Farmer Senior to John Farmer for two hundred and forty acres of land was acknowledged in open court and ordered to be registered.

A conveyance from Henry Farmer Senior to Abner Farmer for one hundred and sixty eight acres of land was acknowledged in open court and ordered to be registered.

A conveyance from Thomas Bateler? to Reuben Williams for four hundred acres of land was proved in open court by Ansel Manley & ordered to be registered.

230 Ordered by the court that Mattheas Williams be appointed a constable in Captains Tunnells company he having given bond and security and took the oaths required by law.

Ordered by the court that George Shetter have leave to keep up his mills on Hinds creek in subjection to the laws in such case made and proceeded.

A deed from John Ferry to William Cooper for two hundred acres of land was proved in open court by Jerimah Cloud and ordered to be registered.

A deed from Hugh Montgomery to William King & Sampson David under the firm of King and David for one hundred and sixteen acres of land was acknowledged in open court and ordered to be registered.

A deed from Spencer Graham to Aron Lenville for one hundred and fifty six acres and one half of land was acknowledged in open court and ordered to be registered.

Craven Johnson, George Hoskins, Constant Claxon, John Sheppard, Charles Shinliver, Jacob Linard, Oliver Dotson who were appointed to view and lay off the road from the fork between Jesse Hoskins and Oliver Dotsons do report that we have viewed and laid off the same and do recommend the right hand was and John Sheppard is overseer from Ross's to the top of the hill below Charles Shinliver field and Craven Johnson overseer in Joseph Leas place.

The court then adjourned till tomorrow morning 9 o'clock.

231 Thursday 11th March 1806.
Court met according to adjournment.
Present William Underwood, Joseph Sinclair, and William McKamey, Esquires.

John H. Madeson)
    vs.)
John King) Robert Blair being sworn as a garnishee in this cause deposed that at the time he was summoned he had in his possession a note given by John H. Madison to Barnard McMahen for twenty pounds current money of Virginia. That said note was assigned by said McMahan to Wigton King previous to the time it came into his possession and further believes that the interest of said note was in John King from a letter he received from him. That since he has been summoned said note has been assigned by Wigton King to Francis Mayberry at the instance of him the said Robert Blair who acted as agent for said Frances Mayberry and that Francis Mayberry is responsible for the value of said note to said John King.

That he the deponent get said note from Hugh L. White by virtue of an order from Benard McMahan and sent to him by John King to deliver said note to said John King.

That said order was dated subsequent to the time said note was assigned to Wigton King.

That at the time Wigton King assigned said note he Robt. Blair took it to him & Wigton King did not state that he had or not any interest in the same.

The note was dated the 26th of October 1802. Ordered by the court that said note be condemed as the property of John King to answer the debt mentioned in the attachment.

232   Jesse Hoskin, Constant Claxon, Charles Shinliver, Craven Johnson and George Hoskins who were appointed a jury to view and lay off a road thro the lands of Robertson Asher and Thomas Adair report that they have layed off and marked a new way agreeable to their order.

James Pepper)
vs.)
John H. Madison) Present James Grant, William Underwood, Douglas Oliver, Sampson David, Alexander Gastin & Samuel Galbreath, Esquires.

Whereupon came a jury (to wit) Aron Sharp, John Lamler, Amos Elliott, William Thompson, Joseph Barren, Jacob Strader, William Lamor, John McAdoo, William Sharp, James McCrackin, William Scarbro and John Cooper who being duly empanelled tried and sworn say they find that the defendant did assume and that within three years and do assess the plaintiffs damage by reason of his non performance to two hundred and ninety five dollars and eighty one cents. Rule to shew cause why a new trial should not be granted.
Rule made absolute.

A deed from John Menefee to Thomas Menefee for four hundred and eight acres of land was acknowledged in open court and ordered to be registered.

A deed from Israel Standefer to Simon Derrick for one hundred acres of land was proved in open court by Kinza Johnson and ordered to be registered.

233   A deed from Thomas Benson to John Sutherland for one hundred acres of land was acknowledged in open court and ordered to be registered.

Daniel White paid into office five dollars the amount of a fine imposed on Druery Puckett for trading with a negro.

A bill of sale from Quin Marton to James Worthington for a negro girl named Patty was proved in open court and ordered to be recorded.

A bill of sale from John McIntire to Archibald McDonald for a negro man named Jim was acknowledged in open court and ordered to be recorded.

Ordered by the court that William Hoskins be overseer of the road instead of William Hancock Sen. from the point between Powells & Clinch Rivers thro Grantsbro-----. between the aforesaid rivers to the county line of Anderson -- and that Samuel McKay & Jason Cloud or either of them point out his hands.

Heunella Sartain and Garland Stanley had leave to administer on the estate of David Sartain deceased entered into bond in the sum of two thousand dollars gave Moses McWhorter and Joseph Hart security and were qualified as the law requires.

Nancy Leath had leave to administer on the estate of her husband Epram Leath deceased gave bond with John McKamey security in the sum of one thousand dollars and was qualified as the law requires.

234   James George paid into office six dollars and twenty five cents for Crota George who refused to swear a Bastard child begotten on her body and gave bond with Samuel Wilson & Felix Gilbert security in the sum of five hundred dollars to keep the county undenified from the maintainance of said child.

Nathan Haile who was bail for Bradley Dalton surrendered him in discharge of himself in open court.

Daniel White who was bail for Absolam Morris surrendered him in open court in discharge of himself.

The court then proceeded to elect a county trustee for the two years ensuing when it appeared on counting the votes that Arthur Crozier Esquire was duly and unanimously elected who gave bond and security as the law directs.

Ordered by a majority of the court that Stephen Heard clerk and John Underwood sheriff be allowed the sum of fifty dollars each for their ex-office services for the year 1805.

The court then adjourned till tomorrow morning 9 no'clock.

Wednesday March 12th 1806.
The court met according to adjournment.
Present James Grant, Sampson David, William Underwood, Douglas Oliver and James Scarbro Esquires.

235   Ordered by the court that Page Portwood be appointed constable in Captain Chapmons Company who gave bond and security and was qualified as the law requires.

Solomon Massengale who was bail for John Couce Senior - surrendered him in discharge of himself.

Ordered by the court that Henry Harless have his marks and brand recorded which is on hogs a smooth cross and slit in the left ear and a slit in the right on cattle a slit in the ear horses branded thus H on the off shoulder and buttock.

A deed from Alexander Kirkpatrick to John Kirkpatrick for eighty acres of land was proved in open court by Wm. Hogshead and ordered to be registered.

John H. Madison)
    vs   )
James Pepper   )   Present James Grant, Joseph Sinclair, Alexander Gastis,
                    William Underwood, Ben C. Parker, Samuel Galbreath &
Douglas Oliver Esquire.

Whereupon came a jury (to wit) Aron Sharp, John Lamler, Amos Elliott, William Thompson, Jacob Strader, John McAdoo, William Standfer, William Scarbro, John Cooper, and John Lynche who being duly empanelled tryed and sworn say they find for the defendant.

Rule to shew cause why a new trial should not be grant.
Rule discharged.

A deed from Alexander Kirkpatrick to John and James Kirkpatrick for one hundred acres of land was proved in open court by William Hogshead and ordered to be registered.

236   A deed from Joseph Lea to George Baumgertner for one hundred acres of land was proved in open court by John Ashurst and ordered to be registered.

Ordered by the court that Charles Weeks be overseer of the road from Aldridges ford to William Standfers and that Douglas Oliver assign to him his hands.

Ordered by the court that Ansel Manley be overseer of the road from Reuben Williams to Moses Wenters and that Samuel Galbreath Esqr. point out his hands.

Ordered by the court that David Hall be overseer of the road from the fork of the road in the Racoon valley to Aldridges ford.

Ordered by the court that Douglas Oliver and Samuel Galbreath assign the hands to Jacob Butler overseer.

Nancy Crouch returned an inventory of the estate of her late husband deceased.

Stephen Haynes for the use of Edward Scott)

vs)
John McIntire) Present James Grant, William Underwood, James Scarbro, A. Gastin, Jos. Sinclair, Wm. McKamey and Richard C. Cobb, Esquires.

Whereupon came a jury (to wit) Aron Sharp, John Lamler, Amos Elliott, William Thompson, Jacob Strader, William Lamler, John McAdoo, Wm. Sharp, James McCrackin, Wm. Scarbro, John McKamey and John England who being empanelled tryed and sworn say they find for the plaintiff and assess his damage by reason of the non payment of the sum in the declaration mentioned to forty two dollars and forty cents.

237   James Grant, William McKamey and James Scarbro was appointed Jurors to the next superior court to be holden for the District of Hamilton.

Ordered by the court that Simon Derrick be overseer of the road instead of Alexander Cole.

John Anderson & Wife)
vs)
Absolom Norris) In this case Joseph Barron and Littleberry Cromley came into court and undertook that the defendant should pay to the plaintiff his debt he were cost in the suit or surrender his body in discharge of the same or that they would do it for him.

The court then adjourned till to-morrow morning 9 o(clock.

Thursday 13th March 1806.
The court met according to adjournment.
Present James Grant, William Underwood, Jason Cloud, Wm. McKamey & Aquella Johnson Esquires.

State)
vs)
James Adkins) Present James Grant, William Underwood, Jason Cloud, Wm. McKamey & Aqulla Johnson Esquires.

Whereupon came a jury (to wit) John McKamey, Aron Sharp, John Lamler, William Thompson, Jacob Strader, William Lamar, William Sharp, John England, James McCracken, William Standefer, William Tunnell Sen. and Joseph Barron, who being duly elected tried and sworn say they find the Defendant guilty. Whereupon it is considered by the court that the Defendant, James Adkins do receive ten lashes on his bare --- -
238 back at the public whipping post in Burrville at the hour of five o'clock P. M. of this day to be laid on by the sheriff of the county.
From which judgment the defendant prays an appeal filed his reasons entered into recognizance with security appeal granted.

Thomas H. Payne was appointed commissioner to act with those already appointed to settle with the receivers & holders of county monies who entered into bond with security as the law requires.

Ordered that Jonas Scroggins be overseer instead of Austin Hackworth.

Moseley Webb)
vs)
James Worthington) In this case Mosley Webb prefered a petition to the court praying writs of Suspersedeas and certiorari which were granted.

William Hogshead who was bail for William Markham surrendered him in open court in discharge of himself.

Richard Forrest made oath that he atended three days at the present term as constable of the grand jury.

John Underwood on the oath of Alfred Massengale his deputy returned the following persons as delinquents who have not paid their poll tax for the year 1805 (to wit) Hutchenson Reuben, Hunley William, Lay Juel, Lay John, McFarland James, McFarland George, Okes Isaac, Robertson Cornelius, Roberts James, Teague Williams, John---- Woods Matthew, Cox Joab, Doherty Andrew, English Richard, Triley Reuben, McAnelly Littleberry, Pollock ----- Parmer, John --Ruckman, Josiah-- Sweeton, Robert-- Boyd, Jordan--- Bennett, Willson-- Crumpton, Johnson-- Aldredge, William-- Owens, William--- Reynolds, Furney-- Thomas, Christopher, whose county tax 12 1/2 cents each also Grancis Mayberry for 220 acres of land the tax on which is 45 cents.

239 Solomon Massengale, Samuel McKay, John Ridenour and Shadrack Reedy who were appointed a jury to view and lay off a road the nearest and best way from the south bank of Clinch river at the junction of Powells and Clinch river to Samuel McKoys.

Report that they have viewed and lay off the same from the junction of said rivers along the old road that leads from the ford to the big valley until it comes to the place where Joseph Ridenour formerly lived thence thro said plantation and into the old road again thence along old road along the leading ridge to the indian grave gap thence to Hardy Medlins thence to Nicholas Mosers thence to the cross roads on the bank of Big Buffaloe thence up the orad that leads to Samuel McCoys.

N 5 The order for this jury continued-

Ordered by the court that the following tax be laid in the county of Anderson for the year 1806. (to wit)

	cents-
on each white poll	16 2/3
on each black poll	33 1/3
on each hundred acres of land	16 2/3
on each townLott	16 2/3
Stud horses the season of one mare-	
Merchants, pedlars and hawkers	$5.00

And the State tax as the law directs.

Ordered by the court that John Leib be allowed the sum of fifteen dollars for taking care of the publick buildings furnishing wood, window glass and up to the present term being one year.

240 Ordered by the court that the following persons be appointed to take the lists of taxable property & polls for the year 1806- to wit-

Captain Clouds Company-	James Grant Esqr.
Captain Loys Company	Saml. McKoy Esquire
Captain Huffakers Compy.	Spencer Graham Esquire
Captain Underwood Compy	Richard C. Cobb Esqr.
Captain Sinclairs Compy.	Joseph Hart Esqr.
Captain McQuines Compy.	Sampson David Esqr.
Captain Adairs Compy.	Benj. C. Parkes Esqr.
Captain Olivers Compy.	James Scarbro Esqr.
Captain Tunnells Compy.	Douglas Oliver Esqr.
Capt. Chafmans Compy.	John Kirby Esqr.

The following persons are appointed as Jurors to attend at June term 1806, (to wit)

Robert Ross, John Frost, Joseph Keeny, Wm. Seveirs, John Bounds, James Bounds, Abraham Jones, Edward Williams, James McGehee, Nicholas Reedy,

John Scarbro, John Galston, Arch. McDonald, Rhodes Stanley, Alexander Cole, John Wallace, James Hill, Marmaduke Bookout, Charles Sinclair, William Derrick, Sam'l. Davis, Hardy Medlin, David Bullock, Jacob Linder, William Ragland, John P. Masterson, Isaac Norman, John Hanna, Aron Jenkins, Rawley Duncan, George Shetter, John Hickman, Henry Harless, Sen., John Lamb, Joshus English, Michael Halfacre, Thomas Tonery, William Mcguire, Thos. Hill and Saml. Wilson.

The court then adjourned till tomorrow morning 9 o'clock.

Friday 14th 1806.
The court met according to adjournment.
Present James Grant, William Underwood, William McKamey, James Scarbro, & Jas. Sinclair Esquires.

John Howard)
vs)
John Thomas) Present James Grant, Benjamin C. Parkes, Joseph Sinclair, Alexander Gastin, James Scarbro, William McKamey, William Underwood & Arthur Crozier- Esqr.

Whereupon came a jurty (to wit) Aron Sharp, Jacob Peak, John Lamler, Amos Elliott, William Thompson, Joseph Barron, Jacob Strader, William Lamar, William Sharp, James McCrackin, William Standfer & William Scarbro, who being duly empannelled and sworn say they find the defendant hath not paid the debt in the Declaration mentioned as by pleading he hath alledged and assess the plaintiffs damage by reason of the detention thereof to two dollars and thirty five cents.

241 Whereupon it is considered by the court that the said John Howard recover of the said John Thomas the debt in the decleration mentioned and the sum of two dollars and thirty five cents for the damage he hath sustained by reason of the detention thereof also the further sum of------- for costs and charges about said suit in that behalf expended and be the said Defendant in mercy and so forth.

Robert Macey)
vs)
Jesse Wilson)
Joel Hancock) The same court & the same jury as above who being duly empannelled tried and sworn do say they find the defendant hath not paid the debt in the ---------

242 for costs and charges about said suit in the behalf expended --- and be the said defendant in mercy and so forth.

Moses White for the use of John Kean)
vs)
Joseph Denham) The same court and jury as above who being duly empannelled tried & sworn say they find the defendant hath not paid the debt in the Declaration mentioned and assess his damage by reason of the detention thereof to eight dollars and fifty cents wherefore it is considered by the court that the plaintiff do recover his debt in the declaration mentioned and the sum of eight dollars and fifty dents also the further sum of ---
for costs and charges about said suit in that behalf expended- and be the said defendant in mercy and so forth-

Hugh M. Alexander)

vs)
Hugh Montgomery) Same court and jury as above.

Who being empannelled tried and sworn do say they find that defendant hath not paid the debt in the declaration mentioned as by pleading he hath alledged and assess the plaintiffs damage by reason of the detention thereof to one dollar and security— wherefore it is considered by the court that the plaintiff do recover his debt and the sum of one dollar and seventy cents for his damage sustained by reason of the detention thereof also the further sum of------- for his cost about said suit---- in that behalf expended- and be the said defendant in mercy and so fourth.

243   At a court of pleas and quarter Session opened and held for the county of Anderson at the court house in Burrville on the second Monday of September in the year of our lord one thousand eight hundred and seven.

Present Arthur Crozier, Joseph Sinclair, William McKamey and James Scarbro, Esquires.

On application to the court Daniel Martin was excused for non attendance as a juror at last term.

John Underwood, Sheriff then returned the Venire facias of whom the following are Grand Jurors (to wit)
Samuel Standefer, Aron Sharp, Joseph Moore, Obidah Wood, Thomas Lytle, Edward Hawkins, John Ashurst, John P. Masterron, Hugh Lakey, Jacob Lindey, John Gamble, Charles Sinclair, James Underwood, Constant Claxon & Thomas Galbreath who being sworn retired to enquire.

The following are traverse jurors (to wit) John J. Deurrat, John Hibbs, Daniel Martin, John Scruggs, Lewis Richards & George Baumgertner.

244   A deed from Robert Macey to John Kirk for two hundred acres of land was proved in open court by Robert Dew and Elijah Kirk and ordered to be registered.

A deed from Tobias Tilmon to Jacob Weaver for one hundred and eighty five acres of land was proved in open court by John Lay & Lewis Clapp and ordered to be registered.

A deed from Tobias Tilmon to Jacob Weaver for forty acres of land was proved in open court by John Lay & Lewis Clapp and ordered to be registered.

A deed from Robert Scarbro to James Smith for one hundred and twenty acres was acknowledged in open court and ordered to be registered.

A deed from John Frost to Richard Kirby for two hundred acres of land was acknowledged in open court and ordered to be registered.

The court then adjourned till to-morrow morning 9 o'clock.

245

Thursday 15th September 1807.
The court met according to adjournment.
Present Arthur Crozier, William McKamey and Robert Dew, Esquires.

Received from the administrators the amount of sales of the estate of Thomas Tonera deceased.

Crozier, Johnson & Crozier)
    vs)
Richard C. Cobb) Present William Underwood, William McKamey,
                                        Alexander Gastin & James Scarbro Esquires.

Whereupon came a jury (to wit) John J. Durratt, John Fibbs, Daniel Martin, John Lynch, John Ridenour, William Thompson, William Green, Polly Duncan, John McBride, Thomas Hill, Peter Clare and Martin Ridenour-who being duly sworn say they find for the plaintiffs and assess their damage to one hundred and eighteen dollars, twelve and one half cents and also the further sum of ---

245 for cost and charges about said suit expended.

Whereupon it is considered by the court that the said Crozier Johnson & Crozier do recover of the said Richard C. Cobb -----

246 the aforesaid sum of one hundred and eighteen dollars twelve and one half cents & also the further sum of for cost and charge -

About said suit expended & be the said Richard C. Cobb in mercy & ca----

Ordered by the court that Thomas Wheeler be overseer of the road from the Campbell County line to Samuel Wilson's at the cross mountain & that Sampson David point out his hands.

Ordered by the court that Stephen McCommins be overseer of the road from Samuel Wilson's, at the Cross mountain to the fork of the Island ford road and that Sampson David point out his hands.

James Bruton)
   vs)
H. Montgomery) The same court and same jury who being duly sworn say they find the defendant hath not kept and performed his covenant as by pleading he hath alledged and assess the plaintiffs damage by reason thereof to one hundred and ninteen dollars- wherefore it is considered by the court that the plaintiff do recover the said sum and the further sum of ---- for cost and charge.

About said suit expended & ---? A Rule was then entered to shew cause why a new trial should be granted.

247 John English, Sampson David, Robert Sinclair, Stephen McCommins, Thomas Wheeler & Daniel Martin, who were appointed a jury to review the road from the Campbell county line, near the widow Wilsons to Burrville report that they have received the same and pursue the old road as it now runs from Campbell county line without any alterations as it now runs to near John Sampsons Tan Yard thence leave the old road on the left going down the branch by the Cabbins where Abner Dazell lives then into the old road and down the same until below John English then leave the old road on the left going thro a small piece of enclosed ground belonging to Thomas Wheeler falling into the old way near the house of Thomas Hill on the left crossing cove creek at the farmer place thence continue the old way below where John McBride formerly lived to near the head of a branch-- known by the name of Leaves Branch then leave the old way on the left taking the point of a ridge and fall into the old road a few poles below a place called Poage's encampment then continue the old way thro a piece of enclosed ground at the place where Green lived the same way the road formerly run- then continue the old way as it now runs to the Hill at Taylors at which place turn out a little before raising the steepest part of said hill near some large rocks leaving the road on the right falling below the rocks winding round the point of the hill and falling into the old way round the point of said hill the old way to Burrville.

248 A bill of sale from John McEntire Senior to John McEntire Jun. was acknowledged in open court and ordered to be registered.

A deed from the administrators of Thomas Tonera deceased to Henry Farmer for one hundred and fifty acres of land was proved in open court by Isaac Brazleton and John Hoskins & ordered to be registered.

David Ayers & Chastely Ayers)
   vs)
William Boyd)

)
) Present William Underwood, Robert Dew, Alexander Gastin & James
Scarbro Esquires.

Whereupon came a jury (to wit) John Scruggs, Lewis Richards, George Bumgertner, Andrew Breden, Charles Crabough, John Bickerstaff, Aron Jenkins, Joel Bowling, James Wirdon, John Beery, Briton Ragsdale & Joseph Robinson who being duly sworn say they find the defendant hath not paid the debt -- in the declaration mentioned & assess the plaintiffs damage by reason of the detention thereof to ten dollars-

Wherefore it is considered by the court that the plaintiffs do recover the debt and damages aforesaid & also the further sum of- for costs and charges about said suit expended and be the said defendant in mercy and so fourth.

249 King & Crozier)
vs)
Richard C. Cobb) Present William Underwood, Robert Dew, Benjamin C. Parker, Alexander Gastin, William McKamey Esquire.

Whereupon came a jury to (wit) John J. Durratt, John Hibbs, Daniel Martin, John Ridenour, William Thompson, William Green, Polly Duncan, Thomas Hill, Peter Clare, Martin, Ridenour, Aron Slover and Samuel Dunn who being duly sworn say they find for the plaintiffs and assess their damages thirty four dollars & forty eight cents.

Whereupon it is considered by the court that the plaintiffs do recover their damages aforesaid & also the further sum of - for costs and charges about said suit expended and be the said defendant in mercy and so forth.

A deed from Jacob Cheney to Elijah Henden for one hundred acres was proved in open court & ordered to be registered.

A deed from Jacob Cheney to Elijah Hardon for a place called the fish Trap Island was proved in open court by Richard Hall & John Bickerstaff and ordered to be registered.

250 A deed from Gibson Hardin to Amos Hardin for one hundred acres of land was acknowledged in open court and ordered to be registered.

A deed from Gibson Hardin to John Galaher for one hundred acres of land was acknowledged in open court and ordered to be registered.

In conformity to an order of last court directing James Bruton to take charge of two orphan children & bring them to the present term he acted accordingly & was allowed the sum of sixteen dollars for having kept them from the last term until the present.

It was then ordered that William Noble have charge of them until the next term & that he then bring them to court for which he is to be allowed a compensation.

A power of attorney from Thomas Hill to William Hogshead was acknowledged in open court and ordered to be recorded.

Ordered by the court that Henritta Sartain and Garland Stanley be appointed guardian of four children (to wit) Right Sartain, David Sartain, Nancy Sartain and Rosey Sartain they having given bond and security in the sum of one thousand dollars as the law requires.

251 Ordered by the court that Isaac Lowe be appointed overseer of the road instead of William Davidson.

A petition to vacate and another to support the ferry of Joseph Robertson and the road that passes at the same were prefered to the court and filed and t e road and ferry continued.

Joshua Adkins who was bound in Recognizance to answer a charge of the government exhibited against him was discharged from the same on proclamation.

The court then adjourned till tomorrow morning 9 o'clock.

Wednesday 16th September 1807.
The court met according to adjournment.
Present Arthur Crozier, Joseph Sinclair, Benjamin C. Parker and William Underwood Esquires.

252 Ordered by the court that Jacob Queener have leave to erect a set of mills on cove creek and that he be entitled to the profits and ---? arising therefrom in conformity to an act of assembly in such case made and provided.

Ordered by the court that John Scruggs be overseer of the road from Days ford to his own house and that Robert Dew Esquire point out his hands.

State   )
 vs   )
Jesse Roysdon) Present Arthur Crozier, Robert Dew, Samuel Galbreath, Joseph Sinclair, William Underwood, James Scarbro, Douglas Oliver and Alexander Gastin Esquire.

Whereupon came a jury (to wit) John J. Durratt, John Hibbs, Daniel Martin, James Cunningham, Jeremiah Jeffery, William Horton, Robertson Asher, John Malaby, William Robbins, John Silor, Martin Ridenour & Thomas Adair who being duly sworn say they find the defendant not **guilty**.

Whereupon it is considered by the court that the defendant go without day & ca----

A rule was entered to shew cause why the Dec. term 1807 Rule discharged.

253 Benjamin C. Parker Esquire and Hugh Barton entered into bond with security and were qualified as the law directs as inspectors of cotton.

Ordered by the court that James Galaher and Amos Harden have leave to administer on the estate of John Galaher deceased who gave bond and security in the sum of one thousand dollars and were qualified as the law requires. They then produced an inventory and an order of sale was granted of the property specified therein.

John P. Martin retired one hundred acres of land the property of Elliott Grills subject to tax for the year 1807.

White & Lynch)
 vs   )
James Davidson) In this case John Kirby who was bail surrendered the defendant in discharge of himself and John P. Masterson and John Fry came into open court and undertook that the defendant should pay the plaintiff his debt if cost in the action or surrender his body in discharge of the same or that they will do it for him.

254 James Scarbrough, Samuel Galbreath, and Joseph Sinclair, Esquires were appointed grand jurors to the next superior court for Hamilton District.

State   )
 vs   )
John Silor) Present Arthur Crozier, Robert Dew & James Scarbro Esquires.

Whereupon came a jury (to wit) John Scruggs, Lewis Richards, Manpage Vowell, James Bruton, John Davidson, John H. Clapman, Joseph Keeny, William Hogshead, Jacob Peak who being duly sworn say they find the defendant stand acquitted and go thereof without day.

Rule to shew cause why the prosecutor should be taxed with the costs

Dec. term 1307 Rule discharged.
    Ordered by the court that James Drake be appointed overseer of the road instead of Alexander Williams.
    The court then adjourned till to morrow morning 9 o'clock.

255   Thursday 17th September 1807.
    The court met according to adjournment.
    Present Arthur Crozier, Benjamin C. Parker, James Scarbro & William McKamey Esquires.
    A deed from John Underwood Sheriff to Micajah Cross for three thousand eight hundred and sixty three acres of land was acknowledged in open court and ordered to be registered.

M. Armstrong)
  vs)
James Worthington) Present William Underwood, Robert Dew & William McKamey Esquires.

    Whereupon came a jury (to wit) John J. Durratt, John Hubbs, Daniel Martin, John Lynch, James Hanna, John Kirkpatrick, John McEntire, John Strong, Charles Crabough, Reuben Roberts, Larkin Bowling, Joel Hancock who being duly sworn say they find the defendant guilty.
    Whereupon it is considered by the court that the plaintiff do recover his term yet- unexpired and also the sum of--- for costs and charges about said suit expended & be the said defendant in mercy & ca------.

256   A deed from Squire Hendrix to James Porter, for one hundred acres of land was proved in open court by abraham Standefer & Richard Forrest and ordered to be registered.
    Ordered by the court that Thomas Frost have two boys bound to him (to wit) John Guthory & William Guthry to stay until John attains to the age of twenty years & William to the age of eighteen years. And the said Thomas Frost is to teach or cause them to be taught to read, write and arthmetic as for as the rule of three & when free to give each of them two suits of home spun clothes and a horse saddle & bridle worth eighty dollars.
    Ordered by the court that Solomon Alred be overseer of the road instead of Charles Weeks & have the same hands & bounds.

John Frost)
  vs)
Menon Langford) In this case Clabiorne Brown surrendered the defendant in discharge of himself and William Wyatt and James Davidson come into open court and undertook that defendant should pay the damages to the plaintiff if cost in the action-------
257 or surrender his body in discharge of the same or that they would do it for him.

Micajah Cross)
  vs)
Thomas Walker) Present William Underwood, Robert Dew and William McKamey Esquires.

    Whereupon came a jury (towit) John Scruggs, Lewis Richards, George Baumgertner, Page Portwood, Boyce Guthery, Charles Weeks, Joseph Horton, Jacob Butler, James Bruton, John Stone, James Davidson and Greenberry Jacobs who being duly sworn say they find for the plaintiff the sum of fifty dollars. Whereupon it is considered by the court that the plaintiff do re-

cover the sum aforesaid and also the further sum of----
for cost and charge about said suit expended and be the said defendant in mercy & ca-----

A Rule was then entered to shew cause why a new trial should be granted---

Dec. term 1807 Rule made----- absolute-----

Ordered by the court that the hands in the following bounds work under Elijah Kirk overseer (to wit) up Bryans fork and the waters thereof from where the Grantsborough road crosses said creek to the line of Campbell county thence with said line to the chesnut Ridge thence with the Knox line opposite Marmaduke Bookouts leaving said Bookout out of said bounds thence along the Grantsborough Road to Byrans fork as mentioned at the beginning.

258   Ordered by the court that Marmaduke Bookout and his hands and the --- of William Underwood work under John Kirk overseer Grantsborough road.

Richard Forrest made oath that he has attended three days as constable of the grand jury at the present term.

John Sutherland, Samuel Calbreath, Reuben Williams, Alexander Galbreath and Samuel Worthington who were appointed a jury to view the road from near Thomas to near the house of Charles Oliver & from the bridge near John McKameys to the head of William Standefers lane. Report that they have view the same and that Lumford Oliver open the road from near the house of Thomas Jones to near the house of Charles Oliver and that Charles Weeks open the road from the bridge near John McKameys to the head of William Standfers lane.

259 David Owens)
    vs)
    R. C. Cobb) Present Arthur Crozier, Benjamin C. Parker and John Kirby Esquires.

Whereupon came a jury (to wit) William Derrick, John J. Durratt, John Hibbs, Daniel Martin, John Strong, Reuben Roberts, Joel Hancock, Larkin Bowling, John Lynch, James Kirkpatrick, Ephraim Brunhaw & James Bruton, who being duly sworn say they find for the defendant.

Wm. Mankins)
   vs.)
Palaitah Shelton) This suit --?-- by the death of the defendant.

The following persons are appointed jurors to attend at December term 1807 (to wit) Henry Butler, Andrew McKamey, Zacariah Key, Samuel Davidson, Zacariah Peak, Samuel Wyatt, John Terry, Aron Jenkins, Isaac Norman, Thomas Ketcherside, John Park s, Henry Hill, James Hill, Paul Harmon, Alexander Graham, John McAdoo, Shadrack Tipton, James Kirkpatrick, Layton Smith, James Worthington, Jacob Peak, John McKamey, Jesse Hoskins, Charles Shinliver, John Tunnell, Craven Johnson, James Beasley, James Hicks, Rowley Duncan, John English, Peter Helton, William Johnson, William Ashlock, James Cunningham----

260 John Tylor, William Thompson, Edward Williams, Simon Derrick, James Leach.

The court then adjourned till tomorrow morning eight o'clock.

Friday 10th September 1807.
The court met according to adjournment.
Present Arthur Crozier, Benjamin C. Parker, Robert Dew and William McKamey Esquires.

White and Lynch)

vs)
James Davidson) Present Arthur Crozier, John Kirby, Robert Dew, Benjamin C. Parker & Wm. McKamey Esquire.

Whereupon came a jury (to wit) John Scruggs, Lewis Richards, George Baumgertner, Hugh Barton, Joseph Day, Abraham Jones, George Sutherland, William Seward, John Silor, James Hanna, Edward Freels & John H. Chapman who being duly sworn say the defendant hath not paid the debt in the declaration mentioned and assess the plaintiffs damage by ---

261 reason of the detention thereof to two dollars and forty cents.
Whereupon it is considered by the court that the plaintiff do recover their debt and damages aforesaid and also the further sum of-
for costs and charges about said suit expended and be the said defendant in mercy & ca.-----

Samuel P. Montgomery)
by his next friend)
vs)
Joel Hancock) Present Arthur Crozier, Douglas Oliver, John Kirby & William McKamey Esquire.

Whereupon came a jury (to wit) Lewis Richards, George Bumgertiner, Hugh Barton, Joseph Day, Abraham Jones, George Sutherland, William Seward, Edward Freels, John H. Chapman, John Kirkpatrick, John Bruton & William Cooper- who being duly sworn say they find for the defendant.-----
Whereupon it is considered by the court that the plaintiff do recover the sum of-----
for costs and charges about said suit expended and be the said defendant in mercy & ca-----
A Rule was then entered to shew cause why a new trial should be granted.
Dec. term 1807 an appeal prayed- Reasons filed Bond given & appeal granted.

262 Saturday 10th September 1807.
The court met according to adjournment.
Present Arthur Crozier, Esquire.
Thomas Hart made oath that he has attended five at the present term as constable of the traverse jury.
The court then adjourned until court in cause.
       Arthur Crozier, Chariman
       A- C-

263   At a court of pleas and quarter sessions opened and held for the county of Anderson at the court house in Burrville on the second Monday of December in the year of our Lord one thousand eight hundred and seven.
Present William Underwood, Joseph Hart, Joseph Sinclair, James Scarbro, Alexander Gastin, Douglas Oliver, Robert Dew & John Kirby Esquires.
John Underwood Esquire sheriff returned the Venire Facias of whom the following are grand jurors (to wit) Aron Jenkins, foreman, Charles Shinliver, Zacariah Kee, Samuel Wyatt, William Ashlock, James Kirkpatrick, Paul Harmon, Alexander Graham, James Hicks, William Johnson, William Thompson, Layton Smith, Edward Williams, Isaac Norman, & Craven Johnson, who being sworn retired to enquire.
Ordered by the court that Thomas Hart be appointed a constable who gave bond and security as the law requires & was qualified.
Ordered by the court that William Keeling be allowed-----

264 The sum of four dollars per month for his support so long as he shall remain in Anderson county and that the money be paid to William Underwood.

A commission appointing John McAdoo, Isaac Lane, Samuel McKay, Johnston Heath & Joseph Keeny, Justices of the peace for Anderson county was produced in open court & they were qualified and took their seats accordingly.

John F. Jack Esquire resigned his scholarship and John M. Campbell Esquire was by the court appointed in his place.

William Underwood Esquire was then appointed chairman of the court pro Tempore in place of Arthur Crozier Esquire.

James Cunningham was excused from attending as a juror at the present term on account of the undisfaction of one of his children.

The following are traverse jorors (to wit) Henry Butler, John Terry, James Worthington, Peter Hilton, Thos. Keterchide, James Beasley, Shadrack Tipton, Andrew McKamey, Simon Derrick & John Parks were appointed Traverse Jurors.

265 Michael Clardy who was appointed a juror for last term was excused for non attendance.

Ordered by the court that Robertson Asher have his mark recorded which is a smoothe cross in the right ear.

The last will and testament of Thos. Frost deceased was proved in open court and ordered to be recorded and Page Portwood, Elijah Frost and Rowland Chiles were qualified as execution returned and inventory of the estate & an order of Sale was granted.

Ordered by the court that William Williams be appointed overseer of the road instead of Ansill Manley from Reuben Williams to Moses Winters.

A deed from Chrisley Steekley and Daniel Steekley to George Galaher for four hundred acres of land was proved in open court by Sylvanus Brewer and Thomas Vance and ordered to be registered.

A Bill of Sale from Bradley Daleon to George Galaher was proved in open court by Sylvanus Brewer & Daniel Mattox and ordered to be recorded.

Ordered by the court that Saml. Johnson be overseer of the road instead of Andrew Braden.

266 A deed from John Sartain & Elizabeth Lucas to John Underwood for Lotts No. 7 & 4 in the town of Burrville was acknowledged in open court & ordered to be registered.

Ordered by the court that Matthew Heath be appointed a constable in Captain Martins company who gave bond & security & was qualified as the law requires.

Ordered by the court that Reuben Ragland be allowed the sum of fifteen dollars for services as a commissioner to settle with those holding public monies in Anderson county.

John Cole who was appointed a constable resigned.

Robert Macey was excused for his non attendance at last term as a juror.

Ordered that Thomas Hart be appointed a commissioner to settle with the Treasurer of Anderson county.

Ordered by the court that Elijah Whitton be appointed constable who gave bond & security and was qualified as the law requires.

The court then adjourned till tomorrow 9 o'clock.

267 Tuesday 15 December 1807.

The court met according to adjournment.

Present William Underwood, Joseph Keeney, Johnson Heath, Samuel McKoy, Douglas Oliver, William McKamey, James Scarbro & Isaac Low Esquires.

Ordered by the court that Jesse Royson be appointed a constable who gave bond and security and was qualified as the law requires.

An election then ensued for a Sheriff for Anderson county for the succeeding two years- when it appeared on counting out the votes that John Underwood was duly & constitutionally elected who gave bond & security & was qualified as the law requires.

A deed from Stephen Duncan to George Gordon for two thousand acres of land was proved in open court and ordered to be registered.

Ordered by the court that John Terry have his mark recorded which is a cross off each ear and a slit in the right.

Robert Dew Esquire was appointed coroner of Anderson county who gave bond and security and was qualified as the law requires.

The court then adjourned till tomorrow 9 o'clock.

268 Wednesday 16th December 1807.
Court met according to adjournment.

Present William Underwood, Joseph Keeney, William McKamey and Joseph Sinclair Esquires.

A deed from John Unstead to William Underwood for four hundred and forty eight acres of land was proved in open court by James Grant & Marmaduke Bookout & ordered to be registered.

A deed from William Underwood to Marmaduke Bookout for three hundred acres of land was acknowledged in open court & ordered to be registered.

John Leib entered into bond with security and was qualified as an Inspector of Cotton.

State)
vs)
Jesse Roysdon) Present William Underwood, Robert Dew, Johnson Heath, William McKamey & Joseph Keeney Esquires.

Whereupon came a jury (to wit) Thomas Keterchside, James Beasly, Henry Butler, James Worthington, John Hoskins, Felix Gilbert, Obidah Wood, Charles Sinclair, John Fry, John Chapman, Elijah Frost & Samuel Winson, who being duly sworn say they find the defendant is five dollars and costs & S. Heard security.

269 State)
vs)
John Thomas) In this case John P. Masterson who was bail for the defendant surrendered in discharge of himself.

State)
vs)
John Thomas) Present Joseph Sinclair, Joseph Keeny, Johnson Heath, Samuel McKoy & John Kirby Esquires.

Whereupon came a jury (to wit) John Bickerstaff, Samuel Dunn, John Tunnell, Thomas Ketcherside, James Beasley, Henry Butler, James Worthington, Obediah Wood, Charles Sinclair, John Chapman, Elijah Frost and Samuel Johnson-

Who being duly sworn say they find the defendant guilty in manner and form as charged in the bill of indictment.

Whereupon it is considered by the court that the said John Thomas be committed to the good of Anderson county paid that the sheriff be authorised to summon a sufficient guard to be paid at the expense of the county and that he be taken from thence tomorrow morning to the public whipping post in the town of Burrville and that he the said John Thomas then and there receive ten lashes on his bare back.

A deed from John Stone to John Underwood for five hundred acres of land was proved in open court by Quin Marton & Benjamin C. Parker & ordered to be registered.

270 A Bill of Sale from Isaac Brazleton to James Worthington for a negro woman named Seen was proved in open court by Samuel Worthington Senior and ordered to be recorded.

Ordered by the court that Edward Williams be overseer of the road leading to Grantsborough from Buffaloe to Clinch river at the mouth of Powels river and that Richard C. Cobb Esquire point out the hands to work on said road.

Ordered by the court that Isaac Rains be overseer of the road from the top of the Black Oak Ridge to Samuel McCoys Esquire, and that Samuel McCoys Esquire point out the hands to work on said road.

Ordered by the court that John Thomas be overseer of the road from Saml. McKoys Esqr. to Clouds ford on Clinch river and that Samuel McKoy Esquire point out his hands.

Ordered by the court that Jesse Martin be overseer of the road from his house to Warwicks meeting house and that all the hands between the pine and chesnut ridge from said overseers house to said meeting house work under said Jesse Martin.

The court then adjourned till to-morrow morning 9 o'clock.

271 Thursday 17th December 1807.
The court met according to adjournment.
Present William Underwood, Samuel McKoy, John Kirby, Joseph Keeney, Benjamin C. Parker & William McKamey, Esquires.

Ordered by the court that Jesse Roysdon be overseer of the road instead of Jonas Scroggins.

Ordered by the court that Edward Williams be overseer of the road from Buffaloe Creek to Clinch river.

Ordered by the court that James Worthington be overseer of the road instead of Jeremiah Jeffery.

Ordered by the court that John Parks be overseer of the road instead of Edward Frost.

State)
  vs)
Richard C. Cobb) Prese nt William Underwood, Samuel McKoy, John Kirby, Benjamin C. Parker & Joseph Keeney.

Whereupon came a jury (towit) Henry Butler, Peter Helton, Thomas Keterchisside, James Beasly, Samuel Dunn, Samuel Standfer, John F. McEntire John Buckerstaff, Moses Roberts, Charles Crobough, John Spessard & John Wallace who being duly sworn say they find the defendant guilty.

272 Whereupon it is considered by the court that the said defendant be fined in the sum of five dollars and also the further sum of ---for costs and charges.

About said suit expended and be the said defendant in mercy and so forth.

Ordered by the court that Isaac Mayberry be overseer of the road leading from Burrville to the Eagle ford & that Joseph Moore, Alexander Graham, Moses McWhorter & the hands that live on the plantation of Benjamin C. Parker work on said road.

Ordered by the court that Felix Gilbert be overseer of the Grantsborough Road from Bryans fork of Hinds Creek to Buffaloe creek.

Ordered by the court that William Ashlock, Robert Tunnell, Joseph Jeffery, Samuel Johnson, Thomas Adair, Reuben Roberts and John Leib be appointed to review the road leading from Burrville down the Buckham Valley near the plantation of Andrew Breden and that they report to next court.

Ordered by the court that the following persons be appointed a Jury to view and mark a way for a public road from George Shetters mill down the valley to the head of Mosers mill pond thence up a gap to the Knox line that they report to next court (to wit)

273 Samuel McKoy, John Carmile, Johnson Heath, Pleasant McBride, Jacob Moses, Christopher Baker, & George Shetter and that they report to next court.

The grand jury were then discharged.

State)
vs)
Ann Hogshead) Present John Kirby, Douglas Oliver, Joseph Keeney & Benjamin C. Parker Esquires.

Whereupon came a jury (to wit) Henry Butler, Peter Helton, Thomas Ketcherside, James Beasley, Samuel Dunn, Samuel Standefer, John F. McEntire, John Bickerstaff, Moses Roberts, Charles Crabough, John Spessard & John Wallace, who being duly sworn say they find the defendant guilty.

Whereupon it is considered by the court that the defendant be fined in the sum of twelve and one half cents. William Hogshead became security for the same.

Ordered by the court that Daniel Day be appointed a constable in Captain Tunnells company who gave bond & security and was qualified as the law directs.

The court then adjourned till tomorrow morning 9 o'clock.

274 Friday 18th December 1807.
The court met according to adjournment.
Present William Underwood, Robert Dew & William McKamey, Esquires.

Daniel Martin)
vs)
John Cox) In this case it appearing that Abner Lazell a constable had failed to render the money by him collected on an execution put into his hands within the time required by law and on motion of said Daniel Martin by James Trumble his attorney it is ordered that judgment be entered against said Abner Lazell and his securties for the sum of ten dollars forty seven cents the debt and costs and also the costs of this motion and that Execution issue for the same.

Ordered by the court that an orphan girl named Elizabeth Myraw, eight years of age be bound unto Samuel Standfer until she attain to the age of eighteen years.

Crosses Lessee)
vs)
Dunn & others) In this case it is ordered that Jesse Roysdon be appointed to survey the land in dispute and make out two fair platts.

And Charles Crabough and Larkin Bowlin became securties for the prosecution of said suits.

275 Sampson David Esquire assigned his office of justice of the peace for Anderson county.

Richard C. Cobb)

vs)
John Underwood) Present Douglas Oliver, William McKamey, Joseph Keeny Esquires.

Whereupon came a jury (to wit) Peter Helton, Thomas Ketcherside, James Worthington, Henry Butler, James Beasley, Shadrack Tipton, Manpage Vowel, James Stuart, Thomas Adair, Jesse Roysdon, Moses McWhorter & John Stuart who being duly sworn say they find the defendant not guilty.

Whereupon it is considered by the court that defendant go without day & the plaintiff be answered for his false clamour- from which judgment there was an appeal prayed & reasons filed.

Ordered by the court that Matthew Hawkins, James Scarbro, Isaac Lowe, William Scarbro, Nathan Hale, William Durrett and Alexander Galbreath be appointed a jury to view and assess the damage sustained by Thomas Jones by a road.

Ordered to be cut and opened this his land leading from Scarbros ferry to William Standefers & that the Sheriff summonsaid jury to view the same and that they report to next court.

Ordered by the court that John Leatch be appointed a constable who gave bond and security & was qualified as the law requires.

276 Ordered by the court that the following persons be appointed Jurors to March Term 1808 (to wit) John Hoskins, Thomas Adair, Hugh Barton, John Hickman, Pleasant McBride, John Warwick, Christopher Baker, James Hill, Marmaduke Bookout, David Nobles, James Leatch, Andrew Farmer, Roads Stanley, Jacob Peak, John McKamey, John Tanera, Ansel Manley, Tobias Peters, Nathan Hale, Edward Freels, Michael Clardy, Elijah Frost, John Cooper, Quin Morton, Thomas Menefee, Samuel Frost, John Lamler, Hardy Medlin, William Sharp Junior, Samuel Davidson, Reuben Gaston, John England, Joseph Gallaher, Nicholas Moser, John King, Rowley Duncan, Robert Tunnell, Aron Norman, William Seveirs.

Ordered by the court that the old road leading from near the house of Thomas Jones to William Standefers lane be disannulled and the new one leading to McKameys bridge be established.

Thomas Hart made oath that he has attended five days as constable of the traverse jury.

Ordered by the court that John Frost machine & one acre of land be exposed to sale at the suit of Scruggs.

Joseph Jeffery made oath that he has attended four days constable of the grand jury.

277 Ordered by the court that Wiley Warwick be overseer of the road from the top of the Black Oak Ridge to the county line on the top of Chestnut ridge and that Samuel McCoy Esquire point out the hands.

Ordered by the court that Barnabas Butcher be overseer of the road from the upper corner of Cobbs fence to dry Buffaloe & William Sharp from there to the county line at McNutts ford and that Samuel McKoy Esquire point out their hands.

The court then adjourned till tomorrow morning 9 o'clock.

Thursday 19th December 1808.
The court met according to adjournment.
Present William Underwood, John Kirby, & Joseph Keeny Esquires.
A deed from Joseph Robertson to Patrick Campbell for five thousand acres of land was proved in open court by James Trimble & Thomas Dardis and ordered to be registered.
Ordered by the court that Enoch Foster be appointed a constable who gave bond & security & was qualified as the law requires.

278 Ordered by the court that William Noble be overseer of the road from the old fork of the island ford road to James Taylors and John Taylor from there to Burrville agreeable to the old bounds.
   The court then adjourned until court in cause.
   Wm. Underwood
   Chairman Pro. Tem.

279   At a court of pleas and quarter Session opened and held for the county of Anderson at the court house in Burrville on the second Monday of March in the year of our Lord one thousand eight hundred and eight.
   Present Arthur Crozier, Joseph Sinclair, John McAdoo, and Isaac Lowe Esquires.
   John Underwood Sheriff returned the Venire Facias executed on all except Joseph Galaher & Aron Norman of whom the following are grand jurors (to wit) Quin Morton foreman, Jacob Peak, Rowley Duncan, Marmaduke Bookout, Thomas Menefee, John Tonera, Samuel Frost, John King, Rhodes Stanley, James Hill, James Leach, Ansel Manley, Elijah Frost, Andrew Farmer & Michael Clardy who being sworn retired to enquire.
   The following are traverse jurors (to wit) John Hoskins, John Hickman, John Warwick, Reuben Golston, William Seveirs, Tobias Peters, Thomas Adair, Hugh Barton, John Lamler, John McKamey, Hardy Medlin, David Noble, Christopher Baker & Pleasant McBride.
   A deed from Benjamin C. Parker to Frederick Sadler for sixty acres of land was acknowledged in open court and ordered to be registered.
   A deed from George Baumgertner to Charles Shinliver for three hundred acres of land was acknowledged in open court and ordered to be registered.
280   A deed from Lewis Stephens to George Shetters for fifty five acres of land was proved in open court by John Hackman and Matthrw Heath and ordered to be registered.

John & Arthur Crozier)
   vs)
John Frost) This being a judgment before a justice of the peace and an execution having bee levied on land. It is ordered by the court that the same be exposed to sale to satisfy said judgement & costs.

John Sartin)
   vs)
John Frost) This being a judgment obtained before a justice of the peace and an execution having been levied on land it is ordered by the court that the same be exposed to sale to satisfy said judgment.

John & William Allen)
   vs)
John Frost) This being a judgment had before a justice of the peace and execution having been levied on land it is ordered to by the court that the same be exposed to sale to satisfy said judgment.

Lewis Harmon)
   vs)
John Frost) In this case Aron Jenkins surrendered the defendant in open court in discharge of himself as bail and Elijah Frost and Samuel Frost came into open court and undertook that the defendant

should pay the plaintiff his debt if cost in the action or surrender his body in discharge of the same or that they would do it for him.

281 Lewis Harmon)
vs)
John Frost) In this case Aron Jenkins surrendered the defendant in open court in discharge of himself as bail and Elijah Frost and Samuel Frost came into open court and undertook that the defendant should pay the plaintiff his debt and damages if cost in the action or surrender his body in discharge of the same or that they would do it for him.

White & Lynch)
vs)
John Frost) In this case Aron Jenkins surrendered the defendant in open court in discharge of himself as bail.

And Elijah Frost and Samuel Frost came into open court and undertook that the defendant should pay to the plaintiff his debt if cost in the action or surrender his body in discharge of the same or that they would do it for him.

Ordered by the court that squire Hendrix be appointed overseer of the road in place of Lunsford Oliver from William Wyatts to Reuben Williams spring.

A deed from Patrick Campbell to William Horton for fifty acres of land was proved in open court by John McAdoo & Edward Freel Sen. & ordered to be registered.

Henry Hill was then excused for his non attendance as a juror at last term.

A bond from William Cobb deceased to Rowley Duncan to make a title to one hundred acres of land was proved in open court by Thomas Davis.

The court then adjourned till tomorrow 9 o'clock.

282 Tuesday 15th March 1808.
The court met according to adjournment.
Present Arthur Crozier, Benjamin C. Parker & William McKamey Esquires.

Micajah Cross)
vs)
Thomas Walker) In this case Abner Lazell, Lucretia Lazell, Mary Baker, Squire ? and William Markham being solemnly came not wherefore it is considered by the court that they perfect according to act of assembly.

Robertson Asher)
vs)
Charles Crabough & others) In this case Craven Johnson being solemnly called came not wherefore it is considered by the court that he forfeit according to act of assembly.

Ordered by the court that Samuel Dunn be overseer of the road in place of Charles Crabough.

Robertson Asher)
vs)
Charles Crabough & others) Present Arthur Crozier, Benjamin C. Parker & William McKamey Esquires.

Whereupon came a jury (to wit) John Hoskins, John Hickman, John Warrich, Reuben Goldstone, William Seveirs, Tobias Peters, Hugh Barton, John Lamler, Hardy Medlin, David Noble, George Bamgertner, and Malon Hibbs who ---

283 being duly sworn say they find the defendants not guilty.

A deed from Robert Burton to Marmaduke Bookout for one thousand three hundred acres was proved in open court by James Hill and Jesse Bookout & ordered to be registered.

A deed from Edward Frost to John Frost for one hundred and seventy five acres of land was proved in open court by Obadiah Wood & Stephen Heard & ordered to be registered.

A deed from Stephen Heard to John Frost for one acres of land was acknowledged in open court & ordered to be registered.

State)
vs)
John Stuart) In this case John Parks surrendered the defendant in discharge of himself as bail and Reuben Roberts and Charles Crabough came into court and undertook that the defendant should Obedely and perform the judgment or decree of the court surrender his body in discharge thereof or that they would do it for him.

Ordered by the court that John Leib Jun., Hugh Barton, John Sartain, William Hogshead, Richard Luallen, Benjamin C. Parker, John McWhorter be appointed a jury to review the roads around the farm of Quin Morton to days and the Eagle ford and that they report to next court.

284 William McKamey, John Kirby & John Lamler were appointed Jurors to attend at the next superior court to be holden for Hamilton District.

Arthur Crozier was elected Trustee for Anderson County who gave bond and security as the law directs.

Den on demise of cross)
vs)
Robertson Asher) In this case R. Thornberry surrendered the defendant in discharge of himself as bail and Reuben Roberts came into open court and undertook that the defendant should pay the plaintiff his damages if cast in the action or surrender his body in discharge if cost in the action or surrender his body in discharge of the same or that he would do it for him.

Arthur Crozier)
vs.)
Thomas H. Paine) Thomas H. Paine on motion of John McCampbell his attorney to plead to issue in this cause on his young special bail and replevying the property attached whereupon John Sutherland and Thom. Manefee came into open court and acknowledged themselves indebted to Arthur Crozier in the sum of one hundred and eight dollars to be levied of their respective goods and cattels lands and tenements but to be void on condition that the said Thomas H. Paine do make his personal appearance from court to court and do abide by stand to and perform whatever judgement said court shall make in said cause or that he shall render his body in discharge of said judgment or if he fail that they will do it for him.

285 Crozier Johnson & Crozier)
vs)
Thomas H. Paine) Thomas H. Paine on motion of John McCampbell his attorney is allowed to plead to issue on his giving special bail and replevying the property. Whereupon John South-

erland and Thomas Manefee came into open court and acknowledged themselves indebted to said Crozier Johnson & Crozier in the sum of one hundred and twenty seven dollars sixty two cents to be levied of their respective goods and chattels lands, and tenaments but, to be void on condition said Thomas H. Paine do make his personal appearance from court to court to answer said complaint and do abide by stand to and perform whatever judgment said court shall make in said cause or render his body in discharge of the same or if he fail that they will do so for him.

A deed from William Johnson to Samuel Dunn for fifty seven acres of land was proved in open court by Charles Crabough and Constantine Claxon and ordered to be registered.

Ordered by the court that the following tax be laid in Anderson County for the present year (to wit)

	cents
on each white poll	33 1/3
on each black poll	66 2/3
on each hundred acres of land	33 1/3
on each town lott	33 1/3
on each stud horse the season of two mares.	

A deed from joseph Keeny to John Weldon for fifty acres of land was acknowledged in open court and ordered to be registered.

Ordered by the court that the road leading from Burrville by Joseph Jeffery's to Henry Farmer be discontinued.

Ordered by the court that John Mattox be allowed the sum of two dollars per month until September Term next.

Ordered by the court that Isaac Mayberry, Alexander Graham, Moses McWhorter, Benjamin C. Parker, William Lamor and John McAdoo be appointed a jury to view and mark a road from Burrville to Benjamin C. Parkers crossing Clinch river below the plantation of Isaac Mayberry from thence to the plantation of James Underwood & from thence to the line of Knox county on the direction the old road formerly went and that they report to next court.

Daniel Martin)
vs)
Abner Lazall) Present Arthur Crozier, Douglas Oliver, Benjamin C, Parker, Robert Dew, William Underwood, Joseph Keeny, Joseph Sinclair, John McAdoo and Samuel Galbreath.

Same jury as the foregoing except James Firley, & Charles Crabaugh who are in the place of George Baumgertner & John Warrick who being duly sworn say they find for the plaintiff and assess his damage to sixteen dollars and ten cents.

Whereupon it is considered by the court that the plaintiff do recover the aforesaid sum of sixteen dollars and ten cents also the further sum of for costs and charges.
About said suit expended and be the said defendant in mercy & C. A. --

Abraham Denton)
vs)
Abner Lazell) Same court & Jury as above-
Who being duly sworn say they find for the plaintiff and assess his damage to one dollar & fifty cents.
Whereupon it is considered by the court that the plaintiff recover the aforesaid sum & also for coste & charges about said suit expended and be the Def. in mercy & ca.

The court adjourned till to-morrow 9 o'clock.

Wednesday 16th March 1808.
The court met according to adjournment.
Present William Underwood, Joseph Sinclair & William McKamey Esquires.

State)
vs)
John Stewart) In this case Reuben Roberts surrendered the defendant in discharge of himself.

A deed from Walter Alves to James Hill was proved in open court by John McCampbell and William Underwood for four hundred and seventy acres of land and ordered to be registered.

John McKamey was excused for non attendance as a Juror at last term.

State)
vs)
John Stewart) Present William Underwood, Isaac Low, Samuel Galbreath, Joseph Sinclair & William McKamey Esquires.

Whereupon came a jury (to wit) John Hoskins, John Hickman, John Warrick, Reuben Galson, William Seveirs, Tobias Peters, Hugh Barton, John Lamler, John McKamey, John Leib, Joel Hancock, & Robert Masey, who being duly sworn say they find the defendant guilty-- whereupon it is considered by the court that he be fined in the sum of five dollars and also the further sum of-------- for costs and charges about said- --------- - suit expended in mercy & ca.
Elijah Frost, Then entered himself security for the fine & costs.

Ordered by the court that Jacob Peak be excused for non attendance as a juror at last term.

Ordered by the court that the order respecting the damage done to Jones land be continued----- Pleasant McBride, JohnsonHeath, George Shetter, Jacob Moser, Christopher Baker & John Carvile who were appointed a jury to view a road from Knox to Grainger line report that they have viewed and marked the same and John Warwick is appointed overseer from the cross road to the Knox line and David Wilson from the cross road to the Grainger line.

Ordered by the court that the following persons be appointed a jury to review the road leading from Brays fork of Hinds creek to the Knox county line commonly called The Grantsbonough road (to wit) Robert Dew, John Gibbs, Enoch Foster, John Kirk Sen., James Hill, William Underwood & John Scruggs and that they report to next court.

Hugh Montgomery)
vs)
James Bruton) Present William Underwood, Douglas Oliver, Alexander Gastin, Joseph Sinclair, & Saml. Galbreath Esquires.

Whereupon came a jury (to wit) Hardy Medlin, Christopher Baker, Pleasant McBride, David Nobles, Andrew Braden, James Stewart, Matthew Hawkins, Malon Hibbs, John Hickman, John Warrick, Reuben Galston & Tobias Peters who being duly sworn say they find for the defendant--
Whereupon it is considered by the court that the plaintiff be <u>Amered</u> for his false clamour & that the defendant go there without day.

The following persons are appointed to attend as jurors at June Term

1808--
Andrew McKamey, William Butler, Jun., Alexander Galbreath, Jun., Charles Oliver, William Griffith, Michael Hostler, William Scarbrough, David Scarbrough & Abraham Hagler, Thomas Kinkaid Sen., Joseph Gallaher, William Gamble, George Hoskins, Andrew Braden, Jacob Linert, William Horton, James Stewart, John Leib, John Garner, Aron Norman, Aron Jenkins, Henry Norman, Sampson Wood, John Farmer, Jun., William Royland, Moses McWhorter, Isaac Mayberry, Alexander Graham, John Warren, William Lamor, Paul Harmon, Joel Hancock, John Lay, Jacob Moser, Abraham Jones, Jacob Weaver, Alexander Williams, Robert Tunnell, & William Ashlock.

Ordered by the court that Jesse Roysdon be allowed the sum of twenty one dollars being one half of his allowance by law for running the line between this county and Roane, also John McKamey nine dollars being one half of the amount of his services as a marker in running the line between this county and Roane.

290   Joel Hancock   )
        vs   )
    Hugh Montgomery)   Present Douglas Oliver, Saml. Galbreath, & John Kinby Esquires.

The same jury as the proceding who being duly sworn say they find for the plaintiff and assess his damage to thirty five dollars- Whereupon it is considered by the court that the plaintiff do recover the sum of thirty five dollars and also the further sum of------------ for costs and damages about said suit expended and be the said defendant in mercy & ca.--- Appeal prayed reasons filed appeal granted.

Ordered by the court that Matthias Williams be appointed a constable in Capt. Tunnells company he having given bond & security and qualified as the law requires.

Ordered by the court that Rhodes Stanley be appointed overseer of the road leading from Burrville to the Walnut Cove from where the island ford road intersects to the county line & that Joseph Keeny, point out his hands.

George Peery   )
    vs   )
John McEntire   )   In this case William Cotter being solemly called came not- whereupon it is considered by the court that he forfeit according to the act of assembly in such case made and provided.

291   Wednesday 11th March 1807.
The court met according to adjournment.
Present-- Arthur Crozier, Joseph Sinclair, James Sacrbro, William McKamey, William Underwood & Dauglas Oliver Esquires.

Ordered by the court that the following persons be appointed jury to review that part of the orad which Andrew Braden is overseer of that is to view round the hill be the river from Hortons to Johnson and that they report to next court (to wit) Samuel Johnson, John Leib, Joseph Sinclair, William Horton, William Ashlock, Hugh Barton and Richard Forrest.

State   )
    vs   )
Anderson Freels   )   Arthur Crozier, William Underwood, Douglas Oliver, Joseph Sinclair, James Scarbro, Sampson David and William McKamey Esquires.

Whereupon came a jury (to wit) Henry McKinney, Joseph Keeny, Paul

Paul Harmon, Thomas Menefee, James Leatch, Austin Hackworth, Charles Sinclair, Reuben Williams, James Cunningham, Thomas Wheeler, Francis Hatmaker, and Daniel Martin. Who being duly sworn say they find the defendant not guilty- A rule was then entered to shew cause why the prosecutor should not be taxed with the cost which rule after solemn argument was ordered by the court to be discharged.

Ordered by the court that John Leib be allowed the sum of seven dollars twelve and one half cents for repairs done to court house wood candles & ca.

292   A deed from Thomas Bateler to Ansell Manley for two hundred acres of land was proved in open court by Caleb Manley and William Bateler and ordered to be registered.

Richard Forrest made oath in open court he has attended three days as constable of the grand jury - at the present term.

A deed from Thomas Forst to Boyce Guthery was proved in open court by Auther Crozier and Benjamin C. Parker in open court and ordered to be registered.

A deed from Hugh Montgomery to Daniel Martin for one hundred and sixty four acres of land was acknowledged in open court and ordered to be registered.

A deed from James Finley to Thomas Wheeler for one hundred and eighty two acres of land was proved in open court by Hugh Montgomery and Daniel Martin and ordered to be registered.

A receipt from Jacob Peak to William Robertson was acknowledged in open court and ordered to be recorded.

A deed from William Roberson to Jacob Peak for two hundred and thirty acres of land was acknowledged in open court and ordered to be registered.

John Wildon returned one poll for taxes for the year 1807.

Court adjourned till tomorrow 9 o'clock.

293   Thursday 12th day of March 1807.
The court met according to adjournment.
Present William Underwood, Joseph Sinclair, Samuel Galbreath and Benjamin C. Parker, Esquires.

William Cotter prefered a petition pray writs of certiorari and supersedeos which was granted provided he enter into bond with security for the prosecution thereof.

State   )
  vs   )
John Leatch   )   Present Arthur Crozier, Benjamin C. Parker, Richard C.
              Cobb, William Underwood, Joseph Sinclair, Samuel Galbreath and William McKamey Esquires.

Whereupon came a jury (to wit) Michael Clardy, Paul Harmon, Thomas Menefee, John Scarbro, Austin Hackworth, Charles Sinclair, Edward Williams, Thomas Wheeler, Francis Hatmaker, Joseph Keeney, Jacob Derrick and Joseph Jeffery, who being duly sworn say they find the defendant not guilty.

Ordered by the court that John Kirk be overseer of the road leading from Grantsborough to Knoxville to begin at Byrans fork to Hinclss creek where the road crosses the same to the line of Knox county and that William Underwood Esquire point out his hands.

Ordered by the court that Elijah Kirk be overseer of the Hinds creek road from the fork of said road to the line of Campbell county and that William Underwood Esquire point out his hands.

294   Ordered by the court that the following tax be laid for the county

of Anderson for the year 1807 (to wit)

on each white poll	16 2/3
on each black poll	33 2/3
on each hundred acres of land	16 2/3
on each town lott	16 2/3
on stud horses the season of one mare	
on merchants, pedlars & hawkers	- 5 -

Ordered by the court that Abner Lazell be appointed a constable in Captain McQuire's company he having given bond & security and qualified as the law requires.

Ordered by a majority of the acting justices that John Parks be allowed the sum of five dollars in addition to the sum heretofore allowed him as a commissioner.

Ordered by a majority of the acting justices that the Sohetion Sheriff and clerk shall be entitled to receive their respective fees which have already arisen or may hereafter arise on bills of indictment which are not found true and in cases where a noble prosequi is ordered or entered from the Treasurer of the county.

Ordered by a majority of the court that John Underwood Sheriff and Stephen Heard Clerk be entitled to receive the sum of fifty dollars each for their ex office services for the year 1806- and that John F. Jack Esquire be allowed at the rate of fifty dollars for annum for his services in future as   ?—

295 State   )
    vs   )
    Thomas Adair)   Present Arthur Crozier, Sampson David, William McKamey, Robert Dew, William Underwood, Joseph Sinclair & John Kirby Esquires.

Whereupon came a jury (to wit) Henry McKamey, John Leatch, James Leatch, William Tunnell Jun., Willaim Horton, John Silor, Jesse Helton, James Cunningham, Jacob Jackson, Joab Dodd, Joel Hancock & William Seward who being duly sworn say they find the defendant guilty-

Whereupon it was considered by the court that the defendant be fined the sum of twenty five cents and be the defendant in mercy & ca.

Ordered by the court that the following persons be appointed as Jurors to attend June Term 1807. (to wit) Henry Peters, Carter Hendrix, Lumford Oliver, Joseph Gallaher, Thos. Hill, Daniel Martin, John McWhorter, Robert Galbreath, Saml. Johnson, Wm. Ashlock, John Rector, William Russell, James Hill, Wm. Thompson, John Wallace, Joshua Frost, Henry Norman, Thomas Carnal, James Bruton, James ? - Elijah Frost, John Sutherland, Hugh Barton, John Kirkpatrick, Daniel Jennings, Jesse Hoskins, Marmaduke Bookout, Jacob Linder, John McAdoo, Wm. Lamar, John P. Masterson, Isaac Mayberry, Joseph Overton, Wm. Derrick & James Cunningham.

State   )
  vs   )
H. Montgomery) Present Arthur Crozier, Benjamin C. Parker, Joseph Sinclair, Robert Dew, & William Underwood Esquires.

The same jury as above except Reuben Williams in this case there was a plea to the jurisdiction of the court stating that the house of Sampson David where the office-----

296 committed was in Campbell county and not in the county of Anderson.
When the jury on hearing the evidence were of opinion that the house of Sampson David is in Anderson County.
James Hanna returned 300 acres of land & one white poll subject to taxation for the year 1807.
The court then adjourned till tomorrow 9 o'clock.

Friday 13th March 1807.
The court met according to adjournment.
Present William Underwood, Benjamin C. Parker, Sampson David and Robert Dew Esquires.

Jacob Sharp)
vs)
Philip Fry) Present Arthur Crozier, Robert Dew, Sampson David, Benjamin C. Parker & Wm. Underwood Esq.

Whereupon came a jury (to wit) Henry McKinney, Joseph Keeny, Thomas Menefee, John Scarbro, James Leatch, Austin Hackworth, Charles Sinclair, William Horton, Reuben Williams, Thomas Wheeler, Edward Williams, Thomas Hill.
Who being duly sworn say they find the defendant hath not paid the debt in the decleration mentioned and assess the plaintiffs damage to six dollars & thirty cents.
Whereupon it considered by the court that the plaintiff do recover of the defendant the debt and damages aforesaid.
297 And also the further sum of for costs, and charges about said suit in that behalf expended and be the said defendant in mercy and so fourth.

Jesse Helton)
vs)
Jesse Wilson) The same court.

Same jury as above- who being duly sworn say they find for the plaintiff and assess his damage to two dollars.
Micajah cross returned two hundred and nine acres of land one black poll & one white poll subject to taxes in Anderson County for the year 1807.

William Hogshead)
vs.)
John Ferguson) Present William Underwood, Douglas Oliver, Alexander Gastin, Joseph Sinclair, Sampson David, & John Kirby Esquires.

Whereupon came a jury (to wit) Michael Clardy, Paul Harmon, John Leach, Francis Hatmaker, William Tunnell Jun., Benjamin T. Warren, Garland Stanley, James Worthington, Thomas Adair, Andrew Stuart, Richard Luallen, & James Underwood who being duly sworn say they find for the defendant.
Whereupon it is considered by the court that the plaintiff take nothing by his claim and that the plaintiff recover the sum of- for costs and charges about said suit in that behalf expended an appeal was then prayed by the plaintiff reasons filed Bond given & appeal granted.

298 Richard C. Cobb)
vs)
John Underwood) Present Joseph Sinclair, Sampson David & Alexander

Gastin Esquires.

Whereupon came a jury (to wit) Paul Harmon, John Scarbro, James Leatch, William Tunnell, Jun., Austin Hackworth, Joseph Keeny, Henry McKamey, Charles Sinclair, Reuben Williams, Thomas Menefee, Edward Williams, & John Leatch who being duly sworn say they find for the defendant.

Joel Hancock)
vs)
H. Montgomery) Hugh Montgomery prefered a petition praying writs of certiorari and Superseades, which was granted, he having given Security as the law requires.

John Frost entered bond with security as the law requires and was qualified as inspection of cotton.
The court then adjourned till tomorrow 9 o'clock.

Saturday 14th March 1807.
The court met according to adjournment.
Present, William Underwood, John Kirby and Robert Dew Esquires.

299 David Henley agent for Lewis Clapier returns twelve thousand acres of land subject to taxes in Anderson county for 1807.
Ordered by the following persons be appointed a jury to review the road from Burrville to the line of Campbell county leading through the Walnut cove (to wit) William Hogshead, John Kirkpatrick, Hugh Barton, Samuel McWhorter, Jesse Roysdon, Robert Sinclair & Stephen Heard and that they or five of them report to next court.
Ordered by the court that Stephen Heard take charge of the court house in future instead of John Leib.
Ordered by the court that Richard Forrest be appointed a constable in Captian Adairs company he having given bond and security and qualified as the law requires.
Whereas Hugh Montgomery name was returned on the tax list without the amount of property and polls being annexed for the year 1805.
It is ordered by the court that he have leave to add the amount of property and polls & pay the tax and that the collector pay the same to the different Treasurer the amount is 1500 acres of land seven black polls and one white.
John Underwood entered into bond with Thomas Menefee and Robert Dew his securties for the public and county tax for the year 1807 - two thousand dollars.
The court then adjourned until court in cause.

Arthur Crozier C. A. C.

300 At a court of pleas and quarter Sessions opened and held for the county of Anderson at the court house in Burrville on the second Monday of June in the year of our Lord one thousand eight hundred and seven
Present Arthur Crozier, Douglas Oliver & Samuel Galbreath Esquires.
John Underwood Sheriff returned the Venire facias executed on all except Daniel Jennins of whom the following are Grand Jurors (to wit) Joseph Galaher, foreman, Samuel Johnson, Henry Peters, Marmaduke Bookout, James Bruton, William Thompson, William Derrick, Henry Norman, William Gamble, Thomas Worthington, Carter Hendrix, Joseph Overton, Robert Galbreath, Thomas Carnall and Elijah Frost who being sworn retired to enquire.
The following are traverse Jurors (to wit) James Hill, William Ashlock, Joshua Frost, Hugh Barton, John Riector, Isaac Mayberry, John Mc-

Adoo, James Cunningham, William Lamar, John Wallace, Thomas Hill & William Russell.

Joseph McKinley returned one hundred acres of land and one pole for taxes for the year 1807.

A deed from James Russell to William Wyatt for two hundred acres of land was proved in open court by Bryce Russell & ordered to be registered.

301 A deed from Isaac Norman to Samuel Marshall for fifty acres of land was acknowledged in open court & ordered to be registered.

Edward Scott)
   vs)
William Patterson) Present, Arthur Crozier, Sampson David, James Scarbro, Samuel Galbreath, and Alexander Gastin Esquires.

Whereupon came a jury (to wit) James Hill, William Ashlock, Joshua Frost, Hugh Barton, John Rector, Isaac Mayberry, John McAdoo, James Cunningham, William Lamar, John Wallace, Thomas Hill and John Peery, who being duly sworn say they find the defendant hath not paid the debt in the decleration mentioned and assess the plaintiffs damage by reason of the detention thereof to three dollars and seventy five cents— Wherefore it is considered by the court that the plaintiff do recover his debt and damages aforesaid and also the further sum of — for costs and charges about said suit expended— and be the said defendant in mercy & ca.

John Wallan returned six hundred acres of land for taxes for the year 1807.

John Ridenour returned four hundred and ten acres of land subject to taxes for the year 1807.

Ordered by the court that James Scarbro be released from the payment of one dollar in the tax of his stud horse for the present year.

302 Ordered by the court that John English, Daniel Martin, Thomas Wheeler, Henry McKenney, Stephen McOmnis, Sampson David and Robert Sinclair be appointed to view and lay off the road from the line of Campbell County, near the widow Wilsons to Burrville and that they report to next court.

A deed from Aqulla Johnson to James Scarbro for one hundred acres of land was proved in open court by Austin Chat & Isaac Freel & ordered to be registered.

James Wisdom returned one white poll for taxes for 1807.

Ordered by the court that Dorcas Tonera, John Tonera, Jane Tonera & Robert Tonera have leave to Administer on the estate of Thomas Tonera deceased who entered into bond in the sum of two thousand dollars with Thomas Menefee & Quin Morton securties & were qualified as the law directs.

The court then adjourned till tomorrow morning 9 o'clock.

303 Tuesday 9th June 1807.
The court met according to adjournment.
Present Arthur Crozier, William McKamey & Sampson David, Esquires.

James Adkins)
   vs)
John Dwiggins) Present Arthur Crozier, William Underwood, Sampson David, & William McKamey Esquires.

Whereupon came a jury (to wit) James Hill, Hugh Barton, John Wallace, Thomas Hill, William Ashlock, Page Portwood, Benjamin T. Warren, James Hanna, Quin Marton, Thomas Menefee, James Underwood, and John Peery who being duly sworn say they find for the plaintiff and assess his damage to one hundred and eighty dollars and fifty cents.

Wherefore it is considered by the court that the plaintiff do recover his damages aforesaid and also the further sum- for costs and charges about said suit expended and be the- said defendant in mercy & ca.

The plaintiff directs a credit on the above judgment paid by James Trimble of thirty dollars.

John Leib, William Ashlock, William Horton, Saml. Johnson, Joseph Sinclair, & Hugh Barton who were appointed a jury (to wit) to view that part of the road which Andrew Braden is overseer of (that is) round the hill by the river from Hortons to Johnsons report that the way round the hill with considerable work is the best but think it too much for the hands upon said road to make it without assistance.

304 Robert Macey)
       vs   )
     John Peery)   Present William Underwood, Joseph Sinclair, Samuel Galbreath, Sampson David & Douglas Oliver Esquires.

Whereupon came a jury (to wit) Joshua Frost, Isaac Mayberry, John McAdoo, William Lamar, William Russell, James Cunningham, John Rector, Dharles Oliver, Robertson Asher, Isaac Brazleton, Jacob Butler & William Standefer who being duly sworn say they find the defendant has paid the debt in the declaration mentioned except fifty four dollars & assess the plaintiffs damage by reason of the detention of that sum to three dollars and twenty four cents.

Wherefore it is considered by the court that the plaintiff do recover his debt and damages aforesaid and also the sum of —   for costs and charges about said suit expended & be the said defendant in mercy & Ca——— Rule to shew cause.

King & Crozier)
     vs   )   as above
H. Montgomery)   Same court & jury/who being duly sworn say they find the defendant hath not paid the debt in the decleration mentioned & assess the plaintiffs damage by reason the detention thereof to seventeen dollars and twenty seven cents.
Wherefore it is considered by the court that the plaintiffs do recover their debt and damages & also the further sum of ---   and be the said defendant in mercy & Ca.

305   Samuel Worthington Sen. returned two hundred acres of land for taxes for the year 1807.

Thomas Freel)
     vs   )
John Peery   )   Present William Underwood, Douglas Oliver, Sampson David & Saml. Galbreath Esquires.

Same jury as above who being duly sworn say they find for the defendant- Wherefore it is considered by the court that the plaintiff be <u>amered</u> for his false clamour & he in mercy & Ca.

A rule was then entered to shew cause why a new trial should be granted.

Rule discharged.

John Peery surrendered himself in open court in discharge of his bail.

The last will and testament of Joseph Adkins deceased was proved in open court by Felix Gilbert, and George Drake and ordered to be recorded.

John Wallace was then excused for non attendance as a juror at last term.

Ordered by the court that judgment be entered up against Austin Choat for one hundred and nine dollars and three cents in favor of James Gordon & Charles Robertson executors of the last will and testament of Charles Robertson deceased.

Ordered by the court that Joseph Galaher be excused for his non attendance at last term.

Ordered by the court that Lumford Oliver be excused for his non-attendance at the present term.

The court then adjourned till tomorrow morning 9 o'clock.

306

Wednesday 10th June 1807.
The court met according to adjournment.
Present Arthur Crozier, Sampson David & William McKamey Esquires.

A deed from John Underwood Sheriff to Joseph Greer for six hundred and forty acres of land was acknowledged in open court and ordered to be registered.

Joseph Greer returned six hundred and forty acres of land for taxes for 1807.

Ordered by the court that John Underwood be released from the payment of John Hanna's poll tax.

Ordered by the court that Sampson David, William Underwood & Benj. C. Parker be appointed to settle with the administrators of the estate of William Havens deceased.

State)
vs)
William Hogshead)   Present Arthur Crozier, William McKamey, Douglas Oliver & Joseph Sinclair Esquire.

Whereupon came a jury (towit) William Ashlock, Joshua Frost, Hugh Barton, John Rector, John McAdoo, James Cunningham, William Lamor, James Harbson, Robertson Asher, Garland Stanley, John Leib, Sen., & Malon Hibbs who being duly sworn say they find the defendant quilty.

Whereupon it is considered by the court that the defendant be fined in the sum of six and one fourth cents, and also the further sum of -------- for costs and charges about said suit expended and be the said defendant in mercy & Ca.

307   John Tonera one of the administrators returned an inventory of the estate of Thomas Tonera deceased.

Micajah Cross)
vs)
Thomas Walker)   Present Alexander Gastin, Douglas Oliver and Joseph Sinclair Esquires.

The same jury as in the proceding cause except James Hanna who was instead of Hugh Barton who being duly sworn say they find for the plaintiff and assess his damage to fifty dollars.

Wherefore it is considered by the court that the plaintiff do recover his damages aforesaid and also the further sum of----------
for costs and charges about said suit expended and be the said defendant in mery & Co.

Rule to shew cause why a new trial should be granted- Rule made absolute.

A deed from William Brazle to John Sutherland for one hundred acres of land was proved by Robert Warren & Richard Hall and ordered to be registered.

Ordered by the court that Thomas Menefee be overseer of the road instead of Samuel Frost.

State)
vs)
William Seward &)
Larking Bowling) Present Arthur Crozier, William McKamey & Sampson David Esquires.

Whereupon came a jury (to wit) James Hall, Thomas Hill, Isaac Mayberry, William Russell, James McGee, Samuel Frost, Joseph Robertson, Moses McWhorter, Jeremiah Jeffery, Robert Smith, John Peery, and William Hogshead who being duly sworn say they find William Seward not guilty and Larking Bowling --------

308 guilty wherefore it is considered by the court that Larking Bowling be fined in the sum of one dollar & costs and be the said defendant in mercy & Ca. A Rule was then entered to shew cause why the prosecutor should be taxed with the costs so far as respects William Seward-   And on Solemn argument the rule was discharged.

Robert Houston returned for Charles Mcling ? Six thousand seven hundred eighteen and three fourth acres of land for taxes for 1807 being land heretofore purchased in Henderson & cas_ Grant.

The court then adjourned till to-morrow 9 o'clock.

Thursday 11th June 1807.
The court met according to adjournment.
Present William Underwood, William McKamey & Samuel Galbreath Esquires.

Robert Burton returned eight thousand one hundred and twenty four acres of land for taxes for 1807.

John Brown returned two thousand acres of land for taxes for 1807.

Ordered by the court that John English, Daneil Martin, Thomas Wheeler, Henry McKinney, Sampson David, Daniel Queener & Jacob Queener be appointed to view and lay off a road from the store of King & David in the Walnut Cove to the Kentucky State line near Shitwoods & report to next court.-----

issued-------

Begun--------

309   John Lynch, William Horton, Andrew Braden, Samuel Johnson, William Ashlock who were appointed to view the road from Burrville to Leibs mill report that the same is to go as they have marked it.

State)
vs)
H. Barton) Sampson David, William McKamey, Saml. Galbreath, Alexander Gastin & William Underwood Esquires.

Whereupon came a jury (to wit) James Hill, William Ashlock, John McAdoo, William Lamar, John Wallace, Joshua Frost, George Baumgertner, George

Sutherland, Charles Crabough, Reuben Roberts, Joel Hancock, James Worthington who being duly sworn say they find the defendant guilty.

Wherefore it is considered by the court that William Hogshead, Thomas Walker & John Leach be fined in the sum of fifteen dollars each and Hugh Barton in the sum of five dollars- on application to the court they mitigated the fines of William Hogshead & John Leach to two dollars and fifty cents each & that of Hugh Barton Twenty five cents- and Thomas Walkers fine be mitigated to two dollars and fifty cents.

A deed from Jesse Roysdon to Arthur Crozier for lott No. 23 in the town of Burrville was proved in open court by John Sartain & James S. McWhorter & ordered to be registered.

Ordered by the court that Thomas Walker be fined in the sum of fifty dollars and be imprisoned for the space of one month for an outrageous contempt committed in open court,------ from which judgment be prayed an appeal filed reasons and entered into bond with security as the law requires.

310   Richard Forrest made oath that he has attended three days as constable of the Grand jury at the present term.

Jacob Sharp)
  vs)
John Underwood)   John Underwood in open court confessed judgment to the said Jacob Sharp for one hundred and twelve dollars & eighty cents.

Wherefore it is considered by the court that the plaintiff recover the sum aforesaid and be the said defendant in mercy & ca.

The above judgment is satisfied.

Ordered by the court that John Lamler, John McAdoo, Samuel Galbreath, Alexander Gastin & Wm. McKamey & Sampson David, appointed inspectors of the ensuing election in Anderson county for Governor, members to Congress & members to the State Legislature.

The following persons are appointed as Jurors to attend at September Term 1807- Daniel Martin, Robert Macey, Lewis Richards, Aron Sharp, Stephen McOmmins, James Underwood, William Williams, Henry Butler, Andrew McKamey, Thomas Galbreath, John J. Durratt, William Tunell, Jur., Zacariah Peek, Joseph Gardner, Isaac Low, Hugh Lackey, Edward Hawkins, John Gamble, Alexander Greyham, Joseph Moore, John P. Masterson, John Hibbs, Joel Hancock, John Scruggs, Henry Ganson, George Hoskins, Constant Claxon, John Ashurst, George Bamgertner, Jacob Linder, Saml. Standefer, John Cooper, Elijah Hendon, Michael Clardy, Obediah Wood, Lewis Harmon, John Lynch, Charles Sinclair, Thomas Lytle.

311 Davie Owens)
  vs)
Richard Cobb)   Present Arthur Crozier, Saml. Galbreath, Alexander Gastin, William McKamey, & William Underwood, Esquires.

Whereupon came a jury (to wit) John Rector, Thomas Hill, William Russell, James Cunningham, James Wisdow, John Kirkpatrick, William Horton, John Ashurst, John McEntire, Andrew Braden, Robertson Asher, & James Hanna who being duly sworn say they find for the defendant.

Wherefore it is considered by the court that the plaintiff be amered for his false clamour.

A rule was then entered to shew cause why a new trial should be granted. Rule made absolute.

Ordered by the court that a Dedimus Postatem issue to take the depositions of Thomas Willing & George Sampson with thirty days notice.

The court then adjourned till tomorrow morning 9 o'clock.

Friday 12th June 1807.
Court met according to adjournment.
Present Arthur Crozier, William Underwood, Benjamin C. Parker & Sampson David Esquires.

Ordered by the court that Hugh Montgomery be allowed the sum of twenty five dollars for his ex office services as sheriff six months in Anderson county.

Ordered by the court that James Bruton take care of two children by the name of Chambers until next term & being then to our next court to be disposed for the justices may direct.

312   A bill of sale from James Baker to Christean Isley for a negro girl named Ester was proved in open court by Thomas Hill and ordered to be recorded.

Francis Mayberry by John F. Jack returned four hundred and twenty five acres of land for taxes for 1807- Beginning on the water white oak.

Archibald Roberts had leave to return a lott in the town of Burrville for taxes for the year's 1806 - 1807.

Ordered by the court that John Southerland, Samuel Galbreath, Samuel Worthington, Reuben Williams, Alexander Galbreath, William Butler and William Griffeth be appointed to view and lay off a road from near the house of Thomas Jones to near the house of Charles Oliver, also the road from John McKameys Bridge to the upper end of Standfers Leave and that they report to next court.

Thomas Hart made oath that he has attended five days as constable of the traverse jury at the present term.

A deed from the commissioners of the town of Burrville to Archibald Roberts for seventy three poles of land in said town was proved in open court by Arthur Crozier Esquire & ordered to be registered.
                                               Arthur Crozier C. A. C.

313   A deed from Lewis Stephens to John Hickman for fifty acres of land was acknowledged in open court and ordered to be registered.

James Worthington)
    vs   )
Jermiah Jeffery   )   Edward Freels Sen. surrendered the defendant in discharge of himself as bail and Joseph Jeffery, Joseph Keeny and came into open court and undertook that the defendant should pay the plaintiff his damages if cost in the action of a surrender his body in discharge of the same or that they would do it for him.

A deed from Lewis Stephens to John Warrick for one hundred acres of land was acknowledged in open court & ordered to be registered.

A deed from Lewis Stephens to Jacob Moser for two hundred and fifty acres of land was acknowledged in open court & ordered to be registered.

A deed from Lewis Stephens to Travis George for three hundred acres of land was acknowledged in open court & ordered to be registered.

Ordered by the court that Joseph Overton be overseer of the road instead of John Kirk & that Marmaduke Bookout & his hands the hands of William Underwood & William Thompson & his hands work under him.

State   )
   vs   )
Andrew Stuart   )   Bastardy----

Ordered by the court that Andrew Stewart enter into bond with security in the sum of five hundred dollars to keep the county of Anderson idennified from the support & maintaince of a Bastard child begotten by him on the bocy of Polly Walker which he did and that he pay into the hands of William McKamey Esq. the sum of three dollars quarter yearly for its support & maintaince for six years.

314

James Trimble)
vs)
John F. McEntire & others) In this case Quin Marton and John Sutherland surrendered the defendant in discharge of themselves as bail and Larkin Bowling, David Noble & James Steward came into court and undertook that the defendant should pay to the plaintiff his debt and damages if cost in the action or surrender his body in discharge of the same or that they would do it for him.

Ordered by the court that Benjamin Bowling be overseer of the road from James Taylors to the fork of the Powels Valley round on this side Joseph Keenys in place of Simon Derrick & have the same bound.

Ordered by the court that the road leading from the Old Tan Vats in the Racoon Valley be discontinued and that the hands living below the same work under Jesse Roysdon & those above work under Thomas Wilson.

Ordered by the court Walter Taylor be overseer of the road from James Taylors to Burrville in place of John Taylor & that he have the same bound & hands.

Ordered by the court that Enoch Foster, Robert Peery, John Wallace Sen., & James Leach work under James Drake overseer.

Ordered by the court that John Lynn be overseer of the road instead of Elijah Kirk & that the same hands work under him except those of William Thompson.

315 Ordered by the court that the hands in the following bounds work under Felix Gilbert overseer (to wit) from the valley road including said Gilbert to the lowe mountain, thence along the same to Richard C. Cobbs thence to the valley road & down the same to the beginning.

Ordered by the court that the hands betwwen Clinch river and the valley road from Days ford to John Scruggs work under him as overseer.

The court then adjourned till tomorrow 9 o'clock.

Thursday 17th March 1808.
The court met according to adjournment.
Present William Underwood, Benjamin C. Parker & John Kirby, Esquires.

James Worthington)
vs)
Jermiah Jeffery) Present Arthur Crozier, William Underwood, Benjamin C. Parker & John Kirby Esquires.

Whereupon came a jury (to wit) John Hickman, John Warrick, Reuben Galston, William Seveirs, Tobias Peters, Hugh Barton, John Lamler, John McKamey, Thomas Adair, Robert Masey, William Lenard and James Underwood who being duly sworn say they find for the plaintiff and assess his damage to seven hundred and seventy one dollars.

Whereupon it is considered by the court that the plaintiff recover the sum aforesaid & also the further sum of ---- for cost and charges about said suit expended-- and be the said defendant in mercy & Ca.

316 A deed from John Leib to John McWhorter for one acre of land was acknowledged in open court & ordered to be registered.

A deed from George Baumgertner to John Sartain for lott No. 400 in the town of Burrville was acknowledged in open court and ordered to be registered.

A bill of sale from Robert Lampkins to John Sartain for a negro man named Jess was proved in open court by William Seveirs and ordered to be recorded.

A bill of sale from John Underwood to John Sartain for a negro girl named Seal about eighteen years old was acknowledged in open court & ordered to be recorded.

John McWhorter entered into bond & security relative to his ferry near Burrville and it was ordered by the court that John Leib be relieved from the obligation of his bond given jointly with John McWhorter.

Ordered by the court that Jane Cunningham & John McWhorter have leave to administration of all and singular the goods and chattels, rights and credits of James Cunningham have deceased who gave bond and security as the law directs and were qualified.

A bill of sale from John Scruggs to Elizabeth Lucas for a negro woman named Winn & her child was proved in open court by John Underwood & ordered to be recorded.

317   Ordered by the court that the following rates be observed by ordinary keepers in Anderson county (to wit) —

The Breakfast, dinner or supper	.25
Half pint whiskey	.08 1/3
Half Pint Brandy	.12 1/2
Half pint Rum or wine	.25
Quart Beer, Cyder or ?	.12 1/2
gallon of oats or corn	.12 1/2
Horse at hay & corn or oats per day & night	.25
Lodging	.06 1/4

Ordered by the court that the following justices be appointed to take lists of taxable property for the year 1808.

For Captain Martins old company Saml. McKoy Esquire.
James Underwood Company—   John McAdoo
Larkin Bowling Company   Arther Crozier
John Chapmans Company   John Kirby
William Tunnells Company   Sam. Galbreath
Lunsford Olivers Company   Isaac Lowe

John Leatch made oath he has attended four days as constable of the grand jury.

James Adkins)
  vs)
John Dwiggins) Ordered by the court that judgment be entered against
Peter Looney Sheriff & his securties for the sum of an execution having issued & not returned.

A bill of sale from John H. Madison to James Trimble for a negro man named Jacob was proved in open court by Laurel P. Montgomery & ordered to be recorded.

318 Hugh Alexander)
       vs)
     Joseph & Thomas Harts) Present Arthur Crozier, William Underwood & Benjamin C. Parker Esq.

Whereupon came a jury (to wit) John Hickman, John Warrick, William Seveirs, Hugh Barton, John Lamler, Thomas Adair, Robert Macey, John McKamey, William Lenard, Hardy Medlin, Christopher Baker, & Pleasant McBride who being duly sworn says they find the defendant has not paid the debt in the decleration mentioned and assess his damage to eighteen dollars- whereupon-

Ordered by the court that John Leib who was overseer of the road from Burrville to the head of John McWhorters Lane be released from the same.

John Steward)
vs)
Jerimah Jeffery) In this case William Tunnell and William Ashlock being solmnly called came not- whereupon it is considered by the court that they forfeit according to act of assembly.

319 Friday 18th March 1808.
The court met according to adjournment.
Present Arthur Crozier, William Underwood, Benjamin C. Parker & William McKamey Esquires.

Arthur Crozier)
vs)
Thos. H. Paine) Present William Underwood, Benjamin C. Parker & William McKamey Esquires.

Whereupon came a jury (to wit) John Hoskins, John Hickman, Reuben Galston, William Seveirs, Tobias Peters, Thomas Adair, Hardy Medlin, David Noble, Christopher Baker, Robert Macey, George Baumgertner & Samuel Dunn, who being duly sworn say they find for the plaintiff and assess his damage to fifty four dollars- Whereupon it is considered by the court that the plaintiff do recover the sum aforesaid and also the further sum of——— for costs and charges about said suit expended and be the said defendant in mercy & Ca.

A rule was then entered to shew cause why a new trial should be granted- and it was ordered by the court that the rule be discharged.

Crozier Johnson & Crozier)
vs)
Thos. H. Paine) Present William Underwood, William McKamey & Alexander Gastin Esquires.

Whereupon came a jury (to wit) Pleasant McBride, John Warrick, Simon Derrick, Enoch Foster, James S. McWhorter, John F. McEntire, Isaac Mayberry, Robert Smith, James Taylor, James Worthington & John P. Masterson- A mistrial was then- consented to----

320 Ordered by the court that the land of John Frost be exposed to sale for a judgment obtained by Andrew Braden against him.

100) Charles J. Levi 8150 acres for 1805 amount to $20.37
Charles J. Levi for 1806 & 1807- 3150 acres 18.46
Both those tracts in the Walnut Cove

Patrick Campbell for 1806 & 7 - 5000 acres Poplar Creek $20.32

Heirs of David Hart for 1806 & 7 - 5375 H & Co. Survey $31.52

John McEntire Jun. for 1806 & 7 -3733 Anderson County $21.88

Micajah Cross for 1804 & 7 for 3683-- Poplar Creek $29.26

William Henry for 1802, 3, 4, 5, & 7 Poplar Creek $27.33 1/3

 Ordered by the court that Stephen Heard & John Underwood be allowed the sum of fifty dollars each for their ex office services for the year 1807.
 Ordered by the court that the county business be done on Monday at next term & that the State business commence on Thursday.
 Thomas Hart made oath that he attended five days as constable of the traverse jury.
 Ordered by the court that ferriage to be paid at John McWhorters ferry be six pence.
 The court then adjourned till tomorrow 9 o'clock.

321 Saturday 19th March 1808.
 The court met according to adjournment.
 Present Arthur Crozier, William Underwood & John Kirby Esquire.
 The court then adjourned until court in cause.
        Arthur Crozier, C. A. C.

322 At a court of pleas and quarter Sessions opened and held for the county of Anderson at the court house in Burrville on the second Monday of June in the year of our lord one thousand eight hundred and eight.
 Present, Arthur Crozier, William Underwood and Robert Dew Esquires.
 John Underwood returned the Venire facias executed on all of whom the following are grand jurors (to wit) John Leib, foreman, Aron Jenkins, Charles Oliver, James Stewart, William Gamble, Michael Hostler & Alexander Graham, Abraham Jones, Robert Tunnell, Andrew McKamey, Isaac Mayberry, Jacob Linert, Joseph Golaher, William Ashlock & Moses McWhorter.
 The following are traverse Jurors (to wit) Jacob Moser, David Scarbro, John Farmer, Jun., John Garner, Alexander Galbreath, William Rayland, John Warren, William Butler Jun., William Scarbro, George Hoskins, William Griffith, Henry Norman, William Lamar, Abraham Hazler, Sampson Wood, Thomas Kinkaid, Aron Norman, Jacob Weaver, Alexander Williams, Paul Norman, William Horton & Andrew Braden.

323
John & A. Crozier)
  vs   )
Joel Hancock) In this case the defendant comes into court and confesses judgment for the sum of one hundred and one dollars and forty cents and costs. Wherefore it is considered by the court that the plaintiffs recover from said defendant the debt aforesaid & costs & be the said defendant in mercy & Ca.
 Ordered by the court that Nicholas Moser, William Sharp & Edward Freels Jun. be excused for non attendance as jurors at the last term of this court.
 A deed from Joseph Grayson to William Wright for three hundred acres of land was proved in open court by Thomas Wright & Samuel Frost and ordered to be registered.
 A deed from Joseph Keeny Sen. to Joseph Keeny Jun. for five hundred acres of land was acknowledged in open court and ordered to be registered.
 A bill of sale from Joseph Keeny Sen. to Joseph Keeny Jr. for divers kinds of property was acknowledged in open court and ordered to be recorded.
 A deed from Aron Jenkins to Nancy Jenkins for two hundred and thirty

five acres of land was acknowledged in open court and ordered to be registered.

A bill of sale from Aron Jenkins to Nancy Jenkins for sundry kinds of property was acknowledged in open court & ordered to be recorded.

324 A deed from John Frost Sen. to Stephen Heard for eighty one acres and sixty five poles of land was proved in open court by Samuel Frost and Solomon W. Jones and ordered to be registered.

A deed from William to John Sutherland for thirty one acres of land was proved in open court by Quin Morton and Stephen Heard and ordered to be registered.

A deed from George Baumgertner to Arthur Crozier for lott No. thirty in the town of Burrville was acknowledged in open court and ordered to be registered.

John McWhorter one of the administrators returned an inventory of the estate of James Cunningham deceased.

Lewis Hariman)
   vs)
George Baumgertner) In this case John McCampbell moved to amend the writ by adding the words James Horton for the use of which after solemn argument was granted from which decision an appeal was prayed by the defendant.

325 White & Lynch)
   vs)
John Frost) In this case Samuel Frost surrendered the defendant in discharge of himself as bail- and Elijah Frost and Stephen Heard came into open court and undertook that the defendant should pay the plaintiff their debt if cast in the action or surrender his body in discharge of the same or that they would do it for him.

Lewis Harmon)
   vs)
Manpage Vowell) In this case William Wyatt surrendered the defendant in discharge of himself as bail and Alexander Graham and Moses McWhorter came into open court and undertook that the defendant should pay the plaintiff his debt if cost in the action are surrender his body in discharge of the same or that they would do it for him.

Lewis Harmon)
   vs)
John Frost) In this case Samuel Frost surrendered the defendant in discharge of himself as bail and Elijah Frost and Stephen Heard came into open court and undertook that the defendant should pay the plaintiff his debt if cost in the action or surrender his body in discharge of the same or that they would do it for him.

326 Ordered by the court that Joseph Hart be appointed an additional commissioner to settle with the administrators of the estate of William Havens deceased.

Samuel Galbreath Esquire returned a list of the taxable property and polls in Captain Tunnells company for the year 1808.

A deed from John Underwood Sheriff to John Sutherland for eighty acres and sixty five poles of land was acknowledged in open court & ordered to be registered.

A deed from Stephen Heard to Thomas H. Paine for eighty acres and sixty five poles of land was acknowledged in open court and ordered to be registered.

Ordered by the court that John Spessard overseer have the hands in the following bounds (to wit) from Charles Shinlivers lower field to where the Powels valley road goes into the cove road, thence from the fork of the road to Cumberland mountain and down the same to opposite Charles Shinliver thence including said Shinliver across to the pine ridge including Kinza Johnson thence up the pine ridge to the cove road thence up the north side of the cove road to the beginning.

Ordered by the court that William Underwood have leave to build a mill on Hinds Creek on his own land.

327 Ordered by the court that James Hart be appointed the guardian of Cynthia Cross a minor, who entered into bond with security in the sum of four hundred dollars.

Dev. on demise)
M. Cross)
vs)
Robertson Asher) In this case Reuben Roberts surrendered the defendant in discharge of himself as bail and Andrew Braden & Larkin Bowling came into open court and undertook that the defendant should pay the plaintiff his damages if cost in the action or surrender his body in discharge of the same or that they would do it for him.

Ordered by the court that Jesse Roysdon be allowed the sum of twelve dollars for his services in summing the line between this county and Campbell and Luke Hall the sum of five dollars and fifty cents for his services as marked.

Ordered by the court that Thomas Hart be released from farther responsibility as a security for Robert Dew coroner said Dew then gave bond & other securties.

Ordered by the court that Robert Dew be released from further responsibility as a security for Thomas Hart as constable. The said Thomas Hart then entered into bond with other security.

William Lamar made oath that two steers taken up by Jesse Hoskins deceased were the property of him the said William Lamar & William Derrick it was then ordered by the court that the Treasurer of this county be released from the payment of the value of said cattle as stated on his book.

328 Ordered by the court that John Parks be allowed the sum of five dollars for his services as a commissioner to settle with the holders of county monies-- up to this time---

John H. Norton was admitted and qualified as an attorney of this court.

Ordered by the court that Squire Hendrix be overseer of the road from the forks of the road near Isaac Lowes field to the fork near Charles Oliver & that Douglas Oliver & Samuel Galbreath Esquires lay off his bounds and hands.

The court then adjourned till tomorrow 9 o'clock.

Tuesday 14th June 1808.
The court met according to adjournment.
Present William Underwood, William McKamey & Joseph Sinclair Esquires.

Ordered by the court that Jacob Peak be overseer of a road from the forks of the road near William Standefers land to the head of Reuben Williams spring & that Douglass Oliver & Samuel Galbreath esquire point out his hands.

329 Ordered by the court that John England be excused for non attendance as a juror at last term.

Hugh Barton, John Sartain, Richard Lewallen, John Leib Sen. and John McWhorter who were appointed a jury to view the road round Quin Mortons farm report that said road is leave the cove road immediately at the upper corner of said Mortons field and to run close to the fence of said Mortons until it intersects said Eagle ford road, thence with said road to the ford. The road from Days ford to be extended until it intersects the from the Eagle ford at or near the upper coroner of said Mortons field next the river.

Micajah Cross)
vs)
Thomas Walker) Present Samuel Galbreath, Alexander Gastin and Samuel McCoy Esquires.

Whereupon came a jury (to wit) Jacob Moser, John Garner, Alexander Galbreath, David Scarbro, William Butler, William Scarbro, George Hoskins, William Griffith, Henry Norman, Abraham Hagler, Sampson Wood & Thomas Kinkaid who being elected tried and sworn say they find for the plaintiff and assess his damage to fifty dollars bounds his costs.

Whereupon it is considered by the court that the plaintiff do recover of the defendant the sum of fifty dollars as aforesaid and also the further sum of ---- for costs and charges about said suit expended- and be the said defendant in mercy & Ca.

A deed from John Galston to William Scarbro for one hundred and fifty one acres & one fourth of land was proved in open court by Carter Hendrix & Douglas Oliver & ordered to be registered.

330 Ordered by the court that the trustee of Anderson county be released from the payment valuation of a stray heifer taken up by John Tunnell- it being proved away but the probate not returned.

James Scarbro Esquire returned one black poll three hundred and eighty acres of land and one stud horse the season three dollars for taxes for the year 1808.

John & Arthur Crozier)
vs)
Joel Hancock) Robert Dew surrendered the defendant in discharge of himself as bail.

White & Lynch)
vs)
Joel Hancock) In this case the defendant was surrendered by his bail Elijah Frost, Rhodes Stanby, & John King into open court & undertook that the defendant should pay the plaintiff his debt if cost in the action or surrender his body in discharge of the same or that they would do it for him.

David Owens)
vs)
Richard C. Cobb) Present Alexander Gastin, John Kirby & Joseph Keeny, Esquires.

Whereupon came a jury (to wit) John Farmer, William Rayland, Aron Norman, Alexander Williams, Paul Harmon, John Warren, William Lamar, Alexander Galbreath, Abraham Hagler, George Hoskins, Jacob Moser, & David Scarbro who being duly sworn say they find for the defendant.

Wherefore it is considered by the court that the plaintiff be amered for his false clamour & the defendant go without day.
Court then adjourned till tomorrow 9 o'clock.

331   Wednesday 15th June 1808.
The Court met according to adjournment.
Present Arthur Crozier, Douglas Oliver, William Underwood and Joseph Keeny Esquires.
Ordered by the court that John Spessard, Jacob Clodfelter, Jacob Lenert, William McKamey, Arthur Crozier, Simon Derrick and Charles Shinliver be appointed a jury to view and lay off a road from Burrville Campbell County line the nearest and best way so as to void the hill on this side of James Taylor and that they report to next court.

George Peery)
vs)
John McEntere) In this cause came a jury to wit, David Scarbro, Garner, Alexander Butler, William Scarbro, George Hoskins, William Griffith, Henry Norman, Abraham Hagler, Sampson Wood, Thomas Kinkaid who being duly sworn say they fine for the plaintiff and assess his damage to thirteen dollars & sixty two cents whereupon it is considered by the court that the plaintiff do recover of the sum aforesaid and also the further sum of- for cost and charges about said suit expended and be the said defendant in mercy & Ca.

George Peery)
vs)
John McEntire) In this case William Cotter who was summoned as a witness- being Solomnly called came not where upon it is considered that he forfeit according to act Assembly.

332   Ordered by the court that John Sharp, Philip Harless, Henry Harless, John Ridenour, John Gibbs, Samuel McCoy, William Thompson, Abraham Jones & William Underwood be appointed a jury to view a road the nearest and best way from the Knox Road leading to Grantsborough to intersect a road from Jacksbro to Lawlers Old place on Clinch river Campbell county line & that they report to next court.
John McAdoo, Alexander Graham, Isaac Mayberry, Moses McWhorter & William Lamar who were appointed a jury to view the road leading from Burrville to Benjamin C. Parkers from thence corssing to river Clinch below Isaac Mayberry Plantation thence to the chesnut ridge to where it intersects the Beaver Creek road report that they viewed the same & that a good road can be made.
Robert Dew, William Underwood, Enoch Foster, John Gibbs, John Scruggs & John Kirk who were appointed a jury to review the road leading from Byrams fork of Hinds Creek to the Knox County line commonly called the Grantsborough road report that they have marked the same & that the new way as marked by them is the best & as near as the old one.
Ordered by the court that Charles Asher and Milly Asher be allowed the sum of twelve dollars quarterly for their support so long as they may live in this county to be paid to Reuben Roberts.

333   Ordered by the court that Jacob Mattox be allowed the same formerly for keeping John Mattox until next court and that Jacob Peak furnish him to that amount.

William Coward

vs....

Robert Ross) in this cause came a jury (to wit) Isaac Norman, Alexander Williams, Paul Harmon, William Horton, Andrew Braden, Jacob Moses, John Farmer, William Ragland, William Lamar, Hezekiah Love, Malon Hibbs & Simon Derrick who being duly sworn say the defendant is guilty in manner and form as charged in the plaintiffs declaration & not justified as in pleading he hath alledged & assess his damage to one cent besides his costs whereupon it is considered by the court that the plaintiff do recover his damages aforesaid & also the further sum of--for cost and charges about said suit expended and be the said defendant in mercy & co.

John Frost)
vs)
Menon Langford) In this cause came a jury to wit, David Scarbro, John Garner, John P. Marterion, John Warren, William Butler, William Scarbro, George Hoskins, William Griffith, Henry Norman, Abraham Hagler, Sampson Wood, & Thomas Kinkaid who being duly sworn say the find the defendant did not assin---? and undertake as the plaintiff hath alledged against him, whereupon it is considered by the court that the plaintiff be armed for his false blamous and the defendant go thereof with out day a rule was ? to show cause why a new trial should be grant & the rule made absolute.

334   Ordered by the court that Richard C. Cobb, heretofore bound by bond as security for Hugh Barton inspector of cotton, be released from the said bond the Hugh Barton agreeing to give other sufficient securities for his performents of the duties of inspector as afore said.

    A bill of sale of a female negro slave named Seal from John Sarton to John Kirby was acknowledged in open court and ordered to be registered.

    Ordered by the court that Writs of Certiorari & Supenedeas do issue on behalf of David Noble agreeable to the prayer of his Petition.

    The court adjourned till tomorrow 9 o'clock.

    Thursday 16th June 1808
    The court met according to adjournment
    Present, Arthur Crozier, William Underwood and Samuel McCoy, Esquires.

    Ordered by the court that Isaac Lowe Esquire have a farther time of three months to take the list of Taxable property and polls in Captain Olivers Company for the year 1808.

335 State)
vs)
Andrew Shannon) in this the defendant pleaded guilty & was fined in the sum of fifty cents & ordered into custody until the fine and cost are paid it was there ordered that he have leave to give security for payment of the same: and David Scarbro & the Defendant acknowledged Judgment for it the court then ordered judgment entered up accordingly.

    William Scarbro was then excused from farther attendance as a juror at the present time.

    Ordered by the court that Joseph Overton be overseer of the road from Byrams fork of Hinds Creek to the Knox County line and that he clear out the new way lately viewed and marked by a jury of view and that the following hands work under him (to wit) William Thompson hands, Martin Ridenour, Thomas Johnson and all within there bounds, copy issued.

    Ordered by the court that Carter Hendrix by overseer of the road leading from the Cumberland ford on Clinch to the house of Reuben Galston and that Isaac Lowe and James Scarbro assign him his hands.

Ordered by the court that Joseph Golaher be overseer of the road from the corner of Isaac Lowes fence to the Roane County line & that Isaac Lowe & James Scarbro assign him his hands.

336 Abraham Jones)
    vs)
William Derrick &)
Moses McWhorter) in this cause a jury towit, David Scarbro, John Garner, Alexander Galbreath, John Warren, William Butler, William Scarbro, George Hoskins, William Griffith, Henry Norman, Abraham Hagler, Sampson Wood, & Thomas Kinkaid who being duly say they fine that the defendant have paid the debt in the declaration mentioned except the sum of ninety nine dollars and fifty cents which they have not- and assess the plaintiff damage by reason of the detention there of to nine dollars and ninety six cents whereof it is considered by the court that plaintiff do recover the sums aforesaid and also the further sum of for cost and charges.

    About said suit expended and be the said defendant in mercy & Co.
    The Grand Jury were then discharged.
    Ordered by the court that John Walls be overseer of the road instead of James Drake & work on the road and have the same hands which were allotted to said Drake.

Lewis Harmon)
    vs)
Manpage Vowell) Same Jury as above who being duly sworn say they fine the Defendant hath not paid the debt in the declaration mentioned and assess the plaintiffs damage by reason of the detention thereof to two dollars and sixty two cents whereupon it is considered by the court that the Plaintiff do recover his debt and damages and also the further sum of for cost and charges about said suit expended and be the said defendant in mercy & Co.

337 White & Lynch)
    vs)
Charles Crabaugh) in this cause came a jury towit, Aron Norman, Alexander Williams, Paul Harmon, William Horton, Andrew Braden, Jacob Moser, John Farmer, Wm. Ragland, William Lamar, Hugh Barton Christian Isely & Malon Hibbs who being duly sworn say they fine the Defendant hath not paid the debt in the declaration mentioned and assess the Plaintiff damage by of the detention thereof to one dollar and forty four cents whereupon it is considered by the court that the Plaintiff do recover their debts and damages and also the further sum of--
for cost and charges about said suit- expended and be the same defendant in mercy & Ca.

    John Leach proved five days attendance at the present term as constable of the grand jury.
    Ordered by the court that Charles Oliver be appointed Commissioner to settle with holders & collectors of county monies instead of Jesse Roysdon for the term of four years next ensuing who gave bond & Saml. Galbreath Security.

James Trimble)
    vs)
John F. McEntire)
& others) in this cause came a jury to wit) David Scarbro, John Jarner, Alex. Galbreath, John Warrner, William Butler

William Scarbro, George Hoskins, William Griffith, Henry Norman, Abraham Hagler, Sampson Wood & Thomas Kink aid, who being duly sworn say they fine the Defendant have not paid the debt in the declaration mentioned as by Pleading they have alledged and assess the plaintiff damage by reason of the detention thereof twelve dollars and twenty one cents where upon it is considered by the court that the plaintiff do recover his debt and damages aforesaid & also the further sum of -   for cost and charges about said suit expended and be the said defendant in mercy & ca.

338   Ordered by the court that John Rhea be overseer of the road from Burrville to the Eagle ford to Mayberry ferry, from thence to the Knox County line as reported by the late Jury of view and that he have the following hands (to wit) John Kirkpatrick, James Kirkpatrick, William Hogshead, Moses McWherter, William Lamar, Philip Fry, John Fry, Alexander Granham, Joseph Moore, Joseph Sinclair, Thomas Hart, Wm. Murrays, Joseph Oldenough, Henry Hankle & James Underwood.

Lewis Harmon)
    vs   )
John Frost   )   The same Jury as the preceding who being duly sworn say the defendant hath paid the debt in the declaration mentioned as by pleading he hath alledged one assess the plaintiff damages by reason of the detention thereof to two dollars and twenty eight cents, whereupon it is considered by the court that the plaintiff do recover his debt and damages aforesaid and also the further sum of- for cost and charges about said suit expended and be the said defendant in mercy & ca.

Lewis Harmon)
    vs   )
John Frost   )   The same Jury who being duly sworn say they find the defendant has not paid the debt in the declaration mentioned except the sum of one hundred dollars which he has paid and assess the plaintiff damages by reason of the detention of said debt to ten dollars and fifty cents besides his cost whereupon it is considered by the court that the plaintiff do recover the Ballance of his debt & damages and also the further sum of--   for cost and charges about said suit expended and be the said defendant in mercy & ca.

339 White & Lynch)
       vs   )
    John Frost   )   The same Jury as before who being duly sworn say they find the defendant hath not paid the debt the declaration mentioned and assessed the plaintiff damage by reason of the detention thereof two dollars besides his cost whereupon it is considered by the court that the plaintiff do recover his debt and damages aforesaid and also the further sum of--   for cost and damages about said suit expended and be the defendant in mercy & Ca.

White & Lynch)
    vs   )
John Frost   )   The same jury as before who being duly sworn say they find the defendant hath not paid the plaintiff damage by reason of the detention thereof two dollars besides his costs where upon it is considered by the court that the plaintiff do recover his debt and damage as fore said and also the further sum for cost & charges about said suit expended and be the defendant in mercy & Ca.

White & Lynch)
vs)
Christopher Bailey) The same jury who being duly sworn say they fine the
Defendant has not paid the debt in the declaration
mentioned except the sum of five dollars & fifty cents which he has paid that
there remains due of said debt fifty six dollars and twenty one cents and assess the Plaintiff damage by reason of the detention thereof to ninty one
cents besides his cost. Whereupon it is considered by the court that the
Plaintiff do recover his debt & damages and also the further sum of ---
for cost and charges about said suit expended and be the Defendant in Mercy
& Ca.

White & Lunch)
vs)
Joel Hancock) Same Jury who being duly sworn say the Defendant hath
not paid the Declaration mentioned as in Pleading he
hath alledged an assess the Plaintiff damage by reason of the detention there
of to one dollar fifty two & two thirds cents, whereupon it is considered by
the court that the Plaintiff do recover their debt and damages aforesaid and
also the further sum of- for cost and charges about said suit expended and
be the said Defendant in Mercy & Ca.

340 John P. Masterson)
vs)
Malon Hibbs) Same Jury who being duly sworn say they fine for the
Plaintiff and assess his damage to ten dollars thirty
three cents & one third of a cent whereupon it is considered by the court
that the Plaintiff do recover his damages aforesaid and also the further
sum of-- for cost and charges about said suit expended and be the defendant in Mercy & Ca.

Ordered by the court that the following persons be appointed Jurors
to September term 1808 (to wit)
William Standefer, James Still, Freeman Still, James Leatch, Mathew Hawkins,
John Peery, Raleigh Duncan, William Sharp, Richard Medlin, Nicholas Moses,
William Davidson, Lumford Oliver, John England, Lewis Campbell, John Ferry,
Jacob Clodfelter, Kinze Johnson, John Ashurst, John Cooper, Hugh Barton,
Moses Roberts, William Seveirs, Hardy Medlin, Thomas Hancock, Marmaduke
Bookout, James Hill, Isaac Norman, Amos Dowlen, John Cooper, Joshua Frost,
Jacob Linder, Robert Roysdon, John Tunnell, J. C. Durratt, Thomas Carnal,
Samuel Worthington, Robert Peery, John King, Joab Dood & John Gibbs.

341 James Pepper)
& Chas. Sinclair)
vs)
Jesse Roysdon &) James Pepper & Charles Sinclair Administrator of Wil-
his Securities) liam Havens deceased by John McCampbell Esquires
their Attorney, moved the court to enter a Judgment
against Jesse Roysdon & his securities for failing to render the amount of
an execution put into his hands at the suit of said Plaintiff against Jesse
Wilson & Joel Hancock and it appearing to the Satisfaction of the Court that
said Jesse Roysdon did levy on property and collect the money, and failed to
pay said sum or return said execution it is therefore ordered by the court
that the said James & Charles recover against the said Defendant four dollars
togather with the lawful cost.

James Peppers)
vs)
Jesse Roysdon &)
his Securities) On motion of said Plaintiff by John McCampbell Esquire his Attorney it appearing to the satisfaction of the Court that said Jesse Roysdon hath failed to make return for an Execution for twenty nine dollars and sixty eight cents put into his hands at the suit of said Plaintiff against Jesse Wilson and Joel Hancock or to pay over said sum it is therefore ordered by the court that the said Plaintiff recover against said Jesse Roysdon and his Securities. The aforesaid sum of twenty nine dollars and sixty eight cents and his lawful costs.

Ordered by the court that Elijah Brummett an infant by & with the consent of his mother be bound as an endented servant unto Benjamin C. Parker Esquire until he attain to the age of twenty one years.
The court then adjourned until tomorrow morning 9 o'clock.

342 Friday 17th June 1808.
The court met according to adjournment, present Arthur Crozier, William Underwood & Joseph Underwood Esqrs.

Robert Macey)
vs)
William Hogshead) Present Arthur Crozier, William Underwood & Joseph Keeny Esquires whereupon come a Jurty (to wit)

1 Aron Norman   5 And w Braden   9 George Hoskins
2 A. Williams   6 John Garner   10 Henry Norman
3 Paul Harmon   7 John Farmer   11 Abrm. Hagler
4 Wm. Horton   8 David Scarbro   12 Sampson Wood

who being duly sworn the truth to Speak on the issue Joined do Say the Defendant has not kept and performed his covenant as in pleading he hath alledged and assess the plaintiff damage to fifty five dollars besides his costs. A rule then entered to shew cause why a new trial should be had and the rule was made absolute.

Ordered by the court that Jacob Weaver be overseer of the Valley road from the Cross roads at the ford of Buffaloe Creek to the county line, and that the hands within the Bounds laid off for --- Weaver former Overseer work under said Jacob Weaver.

Ordered by the court that the following hands work under John Warrick (viz.) George Shilters & his hands Thomas Chatman, Richard Parker, George Bazor, Peter Poore, John Brummitt & that Poore and Brummett be excused from working under Jesse Martin & that all persons in Bounds work under said Warrick.

343 John & Arthur Crozier)
vs)
John Weldon) In this case the Defendant comes into open court and confesses Judgment for forty two dollars and eighty cents & Costs where upon it is considered by the court that the Plaintiff do recover for the Defendant the aforesaid Sum of forty two dollars & eighty cents and also the further sum of- - - for cost & charges about said suit expended and be the said defendant in Mercy & Ca.

John Sutherland)

vs)
John Lynch) In this case on Motion of John Sutherland by his Attorney
it is ordered by the court that the Plaintiff have Judgment against the Defendant for fifteen dollars eighty seven & one half cents being a moiety of two Judgments for which the Plaintiff & Defendant were joint securities for Jeremich Cloud the whole amount of which Judgment were made by the Plaintiff and also for his costs.

Crozier Johnson & Crozier)
vs)
Thomas H. Paine) Same Jury as the preceding who being duly sworn
say the defendant did assume in manner an form as stated in the Plaintiff declaration and assess the plaintiff damages to sixty eight dollars eighty one cents and one fourth of a cent whereupon it is considered by the court that the plaintiff do recover their damages aforesaid and also the further sum of- - - for cost & charges about said suit expended and be the said Deft. in Mercy & Ca.

Ordered by the court that Michael McGran by the consent of his Mother, a boy of six years old be bound to Alexander Gastin until he attains to the age of twenty one years who received and Indenture for the same.

The court then adjourned until tomorrow morning 9 o'clock.

344   Saturday 18th June 1808.
The Court met according to Adjournment.
Present Arthur Crozier, William Underwood, John Kerby Esqrs.
Ordered by the court that the Sheriff have leave to take Security of John F. McEntere for the prison Bounds in the Suit James Trimble v. c. him and others if he offers sufficient security for that purpose.

A deed from James Trimble to John & James Kirkpatrick for seventy five acres of land was acknowledged in open court and ordered to be registered.

Geroge Bumgertner)
vs)
James Sears) In this case John Underwood Sheriff returned Excution
issued for the sum of four dollars & one dollar & twenty five cents costs & that there was no personal property to be found & that he had lived the same on a town lott in Burrville it is therefore ordered by the court that Judgment be entered for said debt and costs and that Execution issue for the same.

A deed from Robert Macey to Quin Morton for six town lotts in Burrville was proved in open court by James S. McWhorter & Geroge Sutherland & ordered to be registered.

William Hogshead)
vs)
Charles Crabaugh) In this case John Underwood having returned the precept levied on one hundred and fifty acres of land lying on Poplar Creek on a precept issued by Arthur Crozier Esquire and on motion it is ordered that Judgment be entered up for four dollars & cost & that Esecution issue accordingly the above Judgment reseinded & Sit Aside it appearing that no execution e\fer issued.

345   John & Arthur Crozier)
vs)
James Sears) In this case John Underwood having returned on a
writ of five facias issued by William Underwood

Page 141

Esquire at the suit of said Plaintiff against said Defendant that there was no personal property and that he had levied the same on a lott in the town of Burrville it is therefore ordered on motion of said Plaintiff that Judgment be intered against Defendant for the sum of to dollars and fifty cents & also one dollar and fifty five cents costs, with the costs if this Judgment and that execution issue for the same.

Ordered by the court that Hugh Barton be appointed one of the commissioners to settle with Clerk Trustee, Sheriff & Ranger for and during the term of four years next insuring instead of John Parks whose appointment the court have vacated & set aside who entered into bond with Moses McWhorter & James Kirkpatrick his securities.

Court then adjourned until court in course.

346   At a court of please & Quarter Sessions opened and held for the county of Anderson at the court house in Burrville on the second Monday of September being the 12th in the year of Our Lord one thousand eight hundred and eight.

Present Arthur Crozier, Benjamin C. Parker, Samuel McKoy, William McKamey and Robert Dew Esquires.

John Underwood Sheriff returned the Venire facias executed generally of whom the following are grand Jurors (to wit) Kiza Johnson, foreman, Moses Roberts, Joshua Frost, Robert Toysdon, Jacob Linder, John Cooper, John G. Durratt, Amos Dowlen, Thomas Carnal, Robert Peery, Thomas Hancock, John King, Jacob Clodfelter, James Still, and William Standefer who being sworn retired to enquire.

The following are Traverse Jurors towit Hardy Medlin, Richard Medlin, John Cooper, Lewis Campbell, William Davidson, Hugh Barton, Samuel Worthington, William Levoirs, John Peery, John Gibbs, John Ashursh, Mathew Hawkins, Roleigh Duncan, John Ingland, Marmaduke Bookout, John Tunnell & Jacob Dood.

Ordered by the court that Lunsford Oliver be executed from attendance as a Juror at the present term.

Eh. Tolbert, Jacob Peck and James Rogers Esquire were qualbfied as attornies of the court.

A deed from Amos Harden to Geroge Tolaher for one hundred acres of land was this acknowledged in open court and ordered to be registered.

Ordered by the court that James Hill be excused from attendance as a Juror at the present term.

Received from James Golaher and Amos Harden the amount of sales of the estate of John Golaher deceased also the amount of debts against said estate.

347   A deed from Robert Houston to Paul Harmon for one hundred and seventy four acres of land was proved in open court by John Scruggs and Robert Dew and ordered to be registered.

A deed from Paul Harmon to Robert Dew for one hundred and seventy four acres of land was acknowledged in open court and ordered to be registered.

Ordered by the court that Trueman Still be overseer of the road instead of John Scruggs.

A deed from William Standefer to John Underwood for lott No. 2 in the town of Burrville was acknowledged in open court and ordered to be registered.

Ordered by the court that William Boyd be overseer of the road from Aldridges ford to William Standefers instead of Soloman Alred and have the same hands and bounds.

348   Ordered by the court that a child named Polly Wheeler between six &

seven years old be bound to Alexander Williams until she attains to the age eighteen years old, who is to give her decent appearl during her servitude and schooling such as it usual for girls to have and at the expiration of her time to give her a good suit of clothes two good cows and calves and a good feather bed and furniture.

Ordered by the court that Isaac Lowe, Hugh Barton and Robert Tunnell be appointed Jurors to the next Superior court.

A deed from John Lawler to Richard Medlin for two hundred and two acres of land was proven in open court by Solomon Massingale and Samuel McKoy and ordered to be registered.

Ordered by the court that the commissioner of the town of Burrville empowered to alter the Prison Bounds in Said Town in Such a manner as they are a majority of then may deem most expidient & that they report to the next court.

Ordered by the court that John Leib be allowed the sum of twenty three dollars fifty six and one fourth cents as a Ballance for procuring a a Standard of weight and measures for the county including his expences.

The court then adjourned till tomorrow morning 9 o'clock.

349   Tuesday 13th September 1808.
The court met according to adjournment.
Present William Underwood, John Kirby & Rich. C. Cobb esquires.

Lewis Harmon)
vs)
Elijah Frost) In this case John Underwood returned an execution for thirty dollars and sixty two cents principal and ninety three & 3/4 cents levied on three head of horses Beast and two head of cattle & sold the whole for fourteen dollars and seventy five cents no more personal property found therefore levyed thee on one hundred and thirty acres of land more or less lying one Clinch river where Elijah Frost lives it is therefore ordered by the court that Judgment be entered up against the said Elijah Frost for the sum of sixteen dollars eighty and three fourths cents and also the costs of this suit and that executor you accordingly.

John Beterson)
vs)
John Brummett &)
Saml. Clark) In this case John Underwood returned an execution signed by William Underwood esq. for twenty one dollars ninety three and three fourth cents that there was no personal property to be found & that he had therefore levied on an improvement Right the property of John Burmmett on the head of Hinds Creek on ? fifty acres more or less. It is therefore ordered by the court that judgment be entered up against the said John Brummett and Samuel Clark for the sum of twenty one dollars ninety three and three fourth cents also the cost of this suit.

350   Ordered by the court that the administrators of the estate of James Cunningham deceased have leave to expose to sale the property belonging to said estate.

Joseph Green exquire returned six hundred and forty acres of land for himself and five hundred acres for the heirs of Doctor Fournier subject to tax for the present year.

John Frost)
vs)
Menon Langeford) In the case Thomas Reed being solemly called come

not whereupon it is considered that he forfeit accordingly to act of assembly.

Robert Macey)
vs)
W. M. Hogshead) Present Arthur Crozier, William Underwood & Gasten, Esquires.

Whereupon came a jury to wit, Hardy Medlin, Richard Medlin, John Cooper, Lewis Campbell, Samuel Worthington, William Sevoirs, John Peery, John Gibbs, John Ashurst, Mathew Hawkins, Raleigh Duncan & John England, who being duly sworn, say they find for the plaintiff. Do Recover. The sum of fifty dollars and also the durther sum of---- for cost and changes about said suit expended and be the said defendant in mercy & Ca. An appears prayed bond given reason filed and appears granted.

351   A deed from James M. Nutt to William Sharp for two hundred acres of land was proved in open court by John Lynch and Stephen Herd and ordered to be registered.

John Chiles returned eighty acres of lands in one tract and sixty three & one acres in another subject to taxes for the year 1808.

William McKamey, Simon Derick, Jack Lynert, Jack Clodfelter & John Spersard who were appointed a jury to review the road from Burrville to the Campbell county line report that they viewed the same & are of opinion that way as marked in the nearest & best- and Walter Taylor is appointed overseer of the same from Burrville to the Laurel Branch & John Leatch from there to the fork of Powells Vally Road. Thods Standle for in to Campbell county line.

Ordered by the court that the following person be appointed as jurors to attend December Session 1808, Towit, Charles Shinliver, Jack Lynert, Hoskins, Lerkins Bowling, Quin Morton, John Beib, John Taylor, Aaron Sliver, Richard Thormberry, William Horton, Ansel Monley, William Russell, William Tunell Junr., Robert Galbreath, John Rector, Andrew McKamey, Reuben Williams, Moses McWhorter, William Lemar, Alexander Graham, Isac Mayberry, John Scruggs, Isaac Neely, Charles Sinclair, Philip Harless, Abraham Moser, Sugar Jones.   ----------

352   --------Isaac Wharton, James Robertson, John Hickman, Christoper Baker, Saml. Frost, Isaac Norman, Robert Lawson, Nathan Hale, Richard Campbell, Tobias Peters & James Musslewhite.

A deed from William Thomas & Charles Crabaugh to Sam Dun for fifty acres of land was proved in open court by Constantine Claxon and Catharine Bowling and ordered to be registered.

A deed from John Chiloress & Charles Conway to Isaac Mayberry for eight hundred and thirty acres of land was acknowledged in open court and ordered to be registered.

A deed from Richard Forrest to John Hoskins for hundred acres of land was proved in open court by Lewis Harmon & James Beesley & ordered to be registered.

A bill of sales from Thomas Hill to John Underwood for a negro boy named Lige was proved in open court by William Stuard and ordered to be registered.

A deed from Gorge Lucas to Isaac Mayberry for thirty acres of land was proved in open court by Charles Conway and Moses McWhorter & ordered to be registered.

353 John Brown)
        vs   )

Thomas Adair &   )
John Kirby   )   Present Joseph Sinclair, William McKamey & John Kerby
                   Esquire--
Whereupon came a jury towit, William Davidson, Hugh Barton, Norman Duke, Bookout, John Tunnell, Hardy Melin, Richard Medlin, John Cooper, Lewis Campbell, John Dood, John Peer, Jooh Gibbs & Raleigh Duncan, who being duly sworn say they find that defendants have not paid the debt in the declaration mentioned and assess the plaintiffs damage by reason of the detention thereof to three dollars twenty one cents and one half cent. Whereupon it is considered by the court that the plaintiff do recover his debt and damages aforesaid and also the further sum of for cost and charges about said suit expered and be the said defendant in mercy & ca.

John McWhorter   )
use of White & Leynoth   )
       vs   )
Thomas Adair   )   The same court & jury above who being duly elected
                               tryed & sworn the truth to speak in the issue
joined defendants hath not paid the damage by reason of the detention there of to three dollars and fifty nine cents wherefore as considered by the court that the plaintiff do recover his debt & damage aforesaid and also the further sum of for cost & charges above said suit expended and be the said defendant in mercy.

354 Admrs Arther Crozier   )
           vs   )
     Jermeah & Joseph Jeffery)   The same court & Jury who being duly sworn
                                    say the defendants have not paid the debt in
the declaration mentioned and assess the plaintiff damage by reason of the detention there of two dollars and fifty cents. Whereupon it is considered by the court that the plaintiffs do recover their debt and damage aforesaid and also the further sum of for cost and charges. About said suit expended and be the said defendants in mercy & ca.

John & Arthur Crozier)
John Scruggs---   )   Same Court & Jury being duly sworn say the defen-
                            dants has not paid the debt in the Declaration men-
tioned and assess the plaintiff damage by reason of the Detention thereof to one dollar and sixty five cents. Whereupon it is considered by the court that the plaintiff do recover their debt and damage and also the further sum of for cost and charges about said suit expended and be the defendant out in mercy & ca.

Same   )
  vs   )
Same   )   Same court & jury who being sworn say they find the defen-
              dant hath not paid the debt in the Declaration mentioned and
assess the plaintiff damage by reason of the Detnetion thereof to six dollars and twenty two cents. Whereupon it is considered by the court that the plaintiff do recover their debt and damage aforesaid also the for cost the sum of-c/or. costs & charges. About said suit expended about said debt in Mercy & ca.

355 John & Arthur Crozier   )
           vs   )
     James & John Kirkpatrick)   Same Court & Jury who being duly & sworn say

they find the defendants have not paid the debt in the declartion mentioned and assess the plaintiff damage by reason of the Detention of the same to two dollars and seventy five cents.

Whereupon it is considered by the court that the plaintiffs do recover their debt and damages aforesaid and also the further sum of --   -- --- for cost and charges. About said suit expended & be the said defendants in mercy & Ca. filed Bond   ? & appeal. Granted-- Appeal prayed reason.

Crozier Johnson & Crozier)
vs)
John Sutherland) Same court & Jury who being duly sworn say the defendant has paid the debt and damage in the declaration mentioned except four hundred and eighty two dollars thirty five and one half cents which sum he has not paid. Whereupon it is considered by the court that the plaintiffs do recover the sum of fore hundred and eighty two dollars, thirty five & one half cents as foresaid and also the further sum of-- for costand charges. About said suit expanded and be the said defendant in mercy & ca.---appeal prayed. Near ? files and Bond given & appeal granted.

This judgment Sales filed except cost--

John Crozier)
vs)
John Sutherland) Same court & Jury as who being duly sworn say they find the defendant has not paid the debt in the declaration mentioned and assess the plaintiff damage to five dollars & sixty five and one half cents.

Whereupon it is considered by the court that the plaintiffs do recover this debt and damage also the further sum of for cost and charges about said suit expended and the said defendant in mercy & Ca.   appears required reason filed duly bond given & appears granted.

The court then adjourned till tomorrow morning 9 o'clock.

356   Wednesday 14th September 1808.
The court met according to adjournment.
Present William Underwood, Benj. C. Parker, James Scarbro & Johnson Heather Esquire.

A deed from Patrick Campbell to Arthur Crozier for one hundred acres of land was acknowledged in open court. Ordered to be registered.

Denon. Demise of)
Micajah Cross,)
Robertson Asher)
Heath & William) Present Arthur Crozier, Joseph Sinclair, Benjamin C. Parker, Thomas Underwood, Esquire-

Whereupon came a jury (to wit) John Cooper, Lewis Campbell, William Davison, Hugh Barton, William Seviors, John Perry, John Gibbs, Matthew Hawkins, Raligh Duncan, John Ingland, Marmaduke Bookout and Sam. Worthington, who being duly sworn say they find the defendants not gilty in manner and form as charge in the plaintiffs declaration----Whereupon it is considered by the court that the plaintiffs be amecerd for his false clamour and the defendants go there of with day a Rule was then entered to Shew cause why new that should be granted discharge.

A Bill of Sale from John Sutherland to James Worthing, for a negro boy named Sam was proved in open court by William McKamey and ordered to be registered.

357   A Bill of Sales from John Scruggs to James Worthing for a negro boy named David has proved in open court & ordered to be registered.

    A deed from Aqulla Johnson to William Gamble for one hundred and forty six acres of land was proved in open court by William Davedson and Joshua Chistenberry, and ordered to be registered.

    A deed from William Hoghead to Gorge Sutherland for lott No. 21 in Burrville was acknowledged in open court and ordered to be registered.

    Mary Edwards returned fifty acres of land subject to taxes for the present year.

    Thursday 15th September 1808.
    The court met according to adjournment.
    Present Arthur Crozier, William McKamey, Joseph Sinclair, Johnson Heath, William Underwood & James Scarbrough, Esqrs.

    Elizabeth Reed by Jacob Gibbs her guardian for one alteration in a Grants of Six hundred and forty acres No. 318 to William Reed, Abraham Swaggerty against Quin Marton to whom notice was given in this case of said application and who opposed said amendment the case came on to be heard in presence of the worshupful.   Arthur Crozier
                                    William Underwood.

358   James Scarbro, Heath, William, McKamey, and Joseph Sinclair Esquires. The petition being real and heard and evidence adduced by said petitioner in support of the same and by said Quin Morton, in opposition to said alteration. After lengthy and learned arguments on both sides the court were a/c opinion that the prayer of the petition be granted and the second line in survey run south five degrees west hundred five hundred and fifty poles to a post oak, instead of north five degrees west-

    James Scarbrough resigned his appointment as Justice of the peace.

    John Leatch, proved fore days attendance as constable of the grand jury.

Lewis Herman   )
  vs   )
Gol. Baumgerter   )   Arthur Crozier, Joseph Frost, John Macadoo, Alexander
                          Gastin, Joseph Sinclair, Robert Dew & Johnson Heath.
    Whereupon came a jury, to wit, Hardy Medlin, Richard Medlin, Lewis Campbell, William Davedson, Hugh Barton, Samuel Worthing, William Sevoirs, John Perry, John Gibbe, Martha Hawkins, Raleigh Duncan, Marmaduke Bookout, who being duly sworn say they find the defendants hath not paid the debt in the declaration mentioned and assess the plaintiffs damages to dollars and eighty cents-- Whereupon it is considered by the court that the plaintiff do recover his and damage also. The further sum of for cost and prayer. About said defend in mercy and so forth--
                                                 Apperes- Prayed-

359 State   )
  vs.   )
William Thompson)   Present James Heath, Robert Dew, John Mcadoo, Joseph
                        Hart and Richard Cobb- the same Jury as before who being duly sworn say they find the defendant not guilty.
Whereupon it is considered by the court that the defendant stand acquitted.

    A Rule was then entered to Shew cause why the prosecutors should be taxed with the costs and made absolute.

John Kirk Esquire resigned his appointment as a justice of the peace for Anderson County.

Ordered by the court that the same Jury who were appointed a jury to review the road from Burrville to the Campbell county line round the hill at James Taylors at last term be appointed to view the hill at James Taylors and make report to next court.

On motion of James Pepper & Charles Sinclair administrator of the estate of William Havens deceased by John M. Campbell their attorney it appearing to the satisfaction of the court that Jesse Roysdon Constable and failed to return an execution put into his hands by them in proper time it is there fore ordered by the court that judgment be entered up against said Jesse Roysdon and his securities for twenty six dollars with interest from the second day of June 1806 and fifty cents costs also the costs of the suit.

The court adjourned till tomorrow morning 9 o'clock.

Friday 16th September 1808.
The court met according to adjournment.
Present Arthur Crozier, William Underwood and William McKamey esquires.

State)
vs)
William Thompson) Whereupon came a jury towit Hardy Medlin, Richard Medlin, Lewis Campbell, William Davidson, Hugh Barton, Samuel Worthington, John Ashurst, Mathew Hawkins, John Ingland, Normaduke Bookout, John Tunnell, Joab Dodd who being duly sworn say they find the defendant not guilty. Whereupon it is considered by the court that the defendant stand acquitted and go there of without day a rule was then entered to tax prosecutors with the costs & on argument made absolute.

A deed from John McWhorter to Quin Morton for one hundred and seventy four acres of land was acknowledged in open court and ordered to be registered.

State)
vs)
John Thompson) Same court and jury who being duly sworn say they find the defendant not guilty whereupon it is considered by the courts that the defendant stand acquitted and go thereof without day a rule was then entered to show cause why the prosecutor should be taxed with the costs and on argument made absolute.

A bill of sale from John Hickman to Travis George for a negro boy named Frank about two years old and was proved in open court by Johnson Heather and ordered to be registered.

A deed from John Simmons to John Sutherland for one hundred acres of land was proved in open court by Thomas Wilson & John Sutherland Junr. and ordered to be registered.

John Sharp, Phillip Harless, Henry Harless, John Ridenour, John Gibbs, Samuel McKoy, William Thompson, Abraham Jones & William Underwood who were appointed a jury to view and lay off a road the nearest & best way from the Knox road leading to Grantsborough to intersect a road leading from Jacksborough to Lawlers old place on Clinch river, Campbell county line. Report that they have reviewed and laid out the same and George Sharp is appointed overseer of the same and to have the hands on the following bounds towit, beginning at Clinch river at Lollers old place thence down the river so as to include the Widow Harmon thence to include William Sharp thence to

include Austin Brumly & Peter Helton thence to the beginning.
Ordered by the Court the following persons be appointed a jury to designate and lay our a road from Burrville to where it will come to the Knox county line the nearest and best way to where it would intersect the beaver creek road..............

362 at or near as may be to George Peerys on said Beaver Creek road to cross Clinch at the ford at Richard Luallens- to wit- John McAdoo, William Underwood, Robert Dew, John Gibbs, Enoch Foster, John Scruggs & Marmaduke Bookout & that they report to next court.

John Leinart)
vs)
Jeremiah Jeffery) Present William Underwood, Joseph Hart, Robert Dew, Alexander Gastin, & Joseph Sinclair esquires.

Whereupon came the same jury as the proceedings who being duly sworn say they find for the defendant whereupon it is considered by the court that the plaintiff be _amerced_ for his false clamour and that the defendant go thereof without day.

Joseph Sinclair esquires having made oath that he gave John Underwood a certificate from the Clerk of the Superior Court of his attendance as a juror & the said John Underwood having made oath that he has lost or mislaid the same it is therefore ordered by the court that he be allowed for the same when the amount thereof is ascertained from the clerk of the superior court aforesaid.

Ordered by the court that the following hands work on the road under Richard LuAllen. Overseers to wit, John McAdoo hands William Hogshead & LuAllens own hands.

363 John Underwood prefered a petition praying a devision of land between him and the devisee s. Geo. Doherty and the following persons are appointed to divide the same to wit, Arthur Crozier, Douglass, Oliver---Robert Dew, Hugh Barton & Charles Z. Oliver.

Arthur Crozier)
vs)
Jer. & Joseph Jeffery) In this case the defendant confessed judgment according to specialty.

Thomas Hart proved five days attendance at last term and five days at this term as constable of traverse jury

Saturday 17th September 1808.
The court met according to adjournment.
Present Arthur Crozier, William Underwood & John McAdoo esquires.

A deed from John Underwood Sheriff to James S. McWhorter for several tracts of land containing one hundred and seventy six acres was acknowledged in open court and ordered to be registered.

364 On motion it is ordered by the court that judgment be entered up against Jesse Wilson in favor of Phillip Fry for the sum of one hundred and twenty dollars seventeen cents and one half of a cent and costs and that execution issue for the same.

Ordered by the court that John Lartin be appointed a constable in Captain Bowlings Company he having given bond & security and qualified as the law requires.

Ordered by the court that John Underwood procured a sledge hammer & crow bar for Samuel Johnson overseer of the road and that he shall be allow-

ed in his first & settlement for the expence thereof.
The court then adjourned until court in course.
Arthur Crozier C. A. C.

365   At a court of Pleas and Quarter session and held for the county of Anderson on the second Monday of December in the year of our Lord one Thousand eight hundred and eight.
Present, Alexander Galbraith, Joseph Sinclair, and William McKamey esquires. John Underwood returned the Venira facias of who the following were appointed grand jurors (to wit) William Tunnell Jur. foreman, Isaac Norman, Nathan Hale, Moses McWhorter, Isaac Manley, Ruben Williams, Jacob Linert, Charles Shinliver, Wm. Horton, Christopher Baker, George Hoskins, Henry Peters, John Leib jr., John Scruggs, L. James, Murph White who being sworn and charged retired esquires.

The following are said jurors (to wit) William Russell, John Rector, Quin Morton, Saml. Frost, Robert Lawson, Richard Thornberry, James Robertson, Ansil Manley, William Lamar, Sugar Jones, Robert Galbreath, Larkin Bowling and W. McKamey, Charles Lindin, Phillip Harless, John Taylor, Aron Slover.

366   Ordered by the court that John Gibbs be overseer of the road in place of Felix Gilbert.

Ordered by the court that Oliver Farmer be overseer of the road in place of John Parks.

Ordered by the court that John McKamey be overseer of the road in place of Jacob Butler and that Douglass Oliver esq. assign him him hand.

Ordered by the court that Moses Roberts be overseer of the road in place of Samuel Johnston.

A deed from Robert Warner to Joseph Overton was proven in open court by Henry Delilah Hill and ordered to be registered.

Ordered by the court that a judgment obtained by the Admrs. of William Haven against Jesse Rossdon and his securities be set aside it appearing to have been obtained improperly.

A deed from Robert Huston to the heirs of Samuel Edwards, were proven in open court and ordered to be registered.

Court adjourned until tomorrow 9 o'clock.

367   Tuesday Dec. 13th 1808.
Court met according to adjournment, present William McKemmy, Joseph Linda, and Richard C. Cobb, Esqr.

Lawson Davis)
    vs)
Breton Ragsdale,)
Machael Holt)   In this case John Underwood return an ? signed by
                      Arthur Crozier, for forty six dollars and eighty cents debts interest and lost and that there was no personal property to be fore. And that he has there fore levied on one hundred and forty fore acres of land more or less, the property of Breton Ragsdale, being the place whereon Jacob Moser now lives, it is there fore ordered by the court that judgment be against the said Britton Ragsdale, and Michael Holt, for the sum of forty six dollars and eighty cents as fore said also the cost of this suit.

James Adkins)
    vs)
Hugh Montgomery)   Present, Joseph Sinclair, Richard C. Cobb & William
                       McKamey, esquire.

Whereupon came a jury (to wit) William Russell, John Rector, Samuel Frost, Robert Lawson, Richard Thornbery, James Robertson, Samuel Manley, William Lainar, Sugar Jones, Robert Galbreath, Larkin Bowling.

368   John Taylor who being duly sworn say they find for the defendant whereupon it is considered by the court that the defendant go thereof without day and that the plaintiff be amerced for his false clamor.

Order by the court that Smith Parley be released from the payment of poll tax for the year 1808.

```
?    ? of Cross )
        vs      )
Thomas Adair    )   Present, William Underwood, Joseph Sinclair and
                         Douglass Oliver Esquire.
```

Whereupon came a jury (to wit) Andrew McKamey, Charles Sinclair, Philip Harless, Martin Ridenour, John Thompson, James Leath, Tapley Bingham, John Rubin Cross, who being duly sworn say they find for the defendant- Whereupon it is considered by the court that the defendant go there on that and that the plaintiff amerced for his false clamor.

A deed from Sameul Worthington, Thos. Worthington to James Worthington for one hundred and eighty two acres of land was proved in open court by William Worthington, Britton Cross, subscribing witnesses thereto.

369 John Arthur Crozier)
    Andrew Bradon   ) John Parker surrendered the papers. ? hisself
                             bail and Constant Claxton and John Hoskins came in optn court and undertook that the defendant should pay to the plaintiff his debt and damage if cost in the action.

```
Larkin Bowling        )
    vs                )
James Stuart & others )   In this case Robert Hays surrendered and Stuart.
```
Court adjourned till tomorrow morning ten o'clock.

Wednesday 14 Dec. 1808.
Court met according to adjournment.
Present Arthur Crozier, William Underwood & Joseph Sinclair Esqr.
Denor Dimis Cross, present Arthur Crozier, William Underwood, & Joseph Sinclair, Esquire.
Whereupon came a jury (to wit) William Russell, Robert Lawson, Richard Thornburry, James Robertson, Alice Manley, William Linart, Sugar Jones, Robert Galbreath, Andrew McKamey, Phillip Harless, John Taylor, Aaron Slover, who said they find the defendant not guilty.
Whereupon it is considered by the court that the said defendant do receive of John Den, as foresaid the cost and damage awarded.

370   A deed from John F. M. Ester to Molly Mills for six hundred and forty acres of land was acknowledged in open court let it be registered.

```
Lewis Harmon   )
    vs         )
William Wright )   Present William Underwood, Joseph Sinclair & Alexan-
                         der Gaston Esquire----
```
Whereupon came a jury who being duly sworn thats, Quin Morton, Charlies Sinclair, Larkin Bowling, John Thompson, Hezikiah Lowe, Tapley Binham & Elyeh Handson, Who being duly sworn say they find for the plaintiff the sum in declaration mentioned assess his damage to three dollars and forty cents whereupon it is considered that the sum ---- Luser Harmon, do recover of the

said William Wright the sum mentioned and assess his damage to three dollars and forty cents in his note also three dollars and forty cents for interest together with the cost and charges.

Where as Samuel Handefer had a girl bound to him and he having surrendered the same he is now released from his indenture.

371 June Court & Jury
Daved Louare)
) The same court and jury as above except John Jouare, in whose place is Thomas Addie & Paul Herman, in place of John Kirkpatrick.
Whereupon it is considered by the court that the plaintiff do recover the debr aforesaid also the sum of ten dollars, eighty eight cents for cost damage ----- damage for fifty eight cents
I cook for A. Crozier
Lantsford Oliver.

Lewis Harmon)
vs)
William Hogshead) Same court and jury. Damage.

J. Crozier)
vs)
Andrew Bradon) Same court and jury who say he has paid the debt in the declaration mentioned except three dollars.
Whereupon it is considered by the court that the Andrew Bradon do pay the debt aforesaid also three dollars and forty three cents and be the said defendant in money.

372 Lewis Harmon)
vs)
John Kirkpatrick) Same court and jury above. Verdict according to
? damage six dollars and six cents.

A deed from Joseph Jeffers to Arthur Crozier, goes two hundred acres of land was acknowledged in open court. (to wit) Registered.
A bill of sale from Hugh Montgomery to Arthur Crozier for a negro man named Spencer was acknowledged in open court and ? to be received.
A bill of sale from John Scruggs to Arthur Crozier for a negro girl named Hanna, acknowledged in open court.
A deed from Elijah Frost to Joseph Barron, for one hundred and fifty acres of land was proved in open court by John Underwood, and Arthur Crozier. Order by the court that Phillip Severs be ? of Bade instead of Henry Farmer. John Leath made oath that he has attended three days as constable of the grand jury.

Larkin Bowling)
James Stuart & others) In this case the defendant being surrendered,
Tayley Bingham and Richard Thornberry undertook for him. Elizbath Morcon was then ordered to be bound to William Russell.

373 White Lynch)
Douglass Oliver)
Joseph Jeffery) Present Arthur Crozier and Robert Dunn.
Whereupon came a jury (to wit) Samuel Frost, Charles Sinclair, John Thompson, Herbert Lane, was made in Bookout , Thomas Anders, Tapley Bingham on Elijah Bradon, John Farmer, Jail Hencock, James Robinson,

who being duly sworn say they find for the plaintiff and assess his damage for two dollars eighty five cents and one half cent. Whereupon it is considered by the court.

It is ordered by the court that a girl named Betsy Brumett, bound to Samuel Worthington --- which is done accordingly.

J. A. Crozier)
Stephin Heard) In this case Stephens came into court and confessed judgment for three hundred seventeen dollars and thirty eight cents when paid it is considered by the court that the plaintiff recovered of said defendant sum of three dundred seventeen dollars, seventeen eight cents and the cost and the defendant in mercy.

374   The court adjourned till to morrow morning nine o'clock.

Thursday December 15th 1808.
Court met accofding to adjournment.
Present Arthur Crozier, Joseph Sinclair, Samuel McCoy and John Mcadoo.

Denon Demise, Michael Crozier)
vs)
Norton Asher) on motion of James Tremel to ? an execution against Larkin Bowlingconfirmed.

Moss Wintin)
vs)
Tophy Bingham) Writs of Superiai as and Certirape granted.

State)
vs)
Page Portwood) Present Arthur Crozier, A. Gastin, Isaac Law.
Whereupon came a jury (to wit) William Russel, John Norton, Quin Morton, Aaron Slover, Robert Lewis, Richard Thornbury, James Robinson, Ancil Manly, William Linard, Sugar Jones, Robert Galbreath, Philip Harless who say they fine the defendant guilty and he is fined six and one fourth cents. Whereupon it is considered by the court.

375   A deed from Richard Kirby to Purnal Ingram for two hundred acres of land was proven.
John Garner overseer in place of J. Roysdon.

State)
vs)
J. Portwood & others) Micajah Portwood submitted himself and was fined six and one fourth cents.

State)
vs)
Page Portwood) In this case John Underwood, Page Portwood securities for Micajah Portwood.

John Fry entered into bond with security to indemnify the county of Anderson from the maintenance of a bastard child begotten by him on the body of Betsy Austian.

State)

vs)
John Portwood & others) In the case Benj. Wood and Micajah Portwood are
fined in one dollar and fifty cents. Page Portwood, Micajah Portwood security for fine & cost.

Simon Derrick)
vs)
James Stuart) In this case it is ordered that Dedemus Potertatain issue
to take de ? of Isaac Standefer Sen.

376   The court adjourned till tomorrow morning nine o'clock.

Friday 16th December 1808.
Court met according to adjournment.
Present William McKamey, John McAdoo, and Samuel Galbreath, Esquires.

William Hogshead)
vs)
William Cotter) In this case William Hogshead has recovered of William
Cotter the amount of his forfeited ? and cost also
for a Serifaceous against William Hogshead.

Lewis Harmon)
vs)
Boice Gentry) By the court order of Sale awarded in pursance of Judgment before the Justices.

A deed from William Wright to John Underwood for three hundred acres of land and ordered to be registered.

377 J. & A. Crozier)
vs)
A. Bradon)

L. Harmon)
vs)
W. Hogshead)

Lewis Harmon)
vs)
Jno. Kirkpatrick)

The foregoing codus appeals Pray Bond given reason failed and appeals granted.

Amount of Sales of the Estate of James Cunningham & returned by John McWasted Administrator.

Ordered by the court that David Hall, Elijah Hendon, John Garner, William Baid, John Cooper, Aaron Jenkins, Thomas William be appointed to view a small part of a road from the fork leading to Sutherland ferry, thence down the road to a suitable place for a ford.

Ordered by the court that John Southerland be entitled to receive twelve and one half cents for man and horse at his ferry.

378   Ordered by the court that Isaac Mayberry observe the following rates at his ferry he having given bond and security as the law requires.

man & horse   12 1/2 cents
led horse   6 1/4 "
foot man   6 1/4 "
waggon $1.00

White & Lynch
v

vs)
William Davison) Ordered by the court that judgment an execution issue inpursuance to return of the constable for debt and cost.

Ordered by the court that the commissioners appointed to settle with the Treasurer be allowed the sum of twenty four dollars and fifty cents.
Page Portwood resigned his constable Ship.

State)
vs)
George Steal) In this case it is ordered by the court certificate issue in favor of Hugh Montgomery to the Treasurey of this county for the sum of twenty four dollars twenty five cents.

379 State)
vs)
William Cotter) Ordered by the court that judgment be entered against the said William Cotter for his forfeited recognesance and cost.

Court adjourned till tomorrow morning nine o'clock.

Saturday 17th December 1808.
Court met according to adjournment.
Present Arthur Crozier, Richard Childs and Robert Dew.

The Commissioner to divide the land between John Underwood & the Heirs of Doherty viewed the same and returned the same then report.
Ordered by the court that William Lamar be overseer from McAdoo lower ford to Vally Mill & that Robert Dew and John McAdoo assign his hand.
Court then adjourned until court in courrse.
Arthur Crozier, C. A. C.

381 At a court of Pleas and Quarter Sessions opened and held for the county of Anderson at the Court house in Burrville on the second Monday of March in the year of Our Lord one thousand eight hundred and nine.
Present Douglas Oliver, Joseph Sinclair and Alexander Gastin Esquires.
John Underwood Sheriff returned the Venire Facias Executed on all except John Hickman of whom the following are grand jurors (to wit) Hugh Barton foreman, Edward Hawkins, Jacob Linder, Elijah Hendon, Michael Hostler, John Fry, Alexander Cole, Thomas Galbreath, Abraham Moser, Thomas Williams, Rhode Stanley, John Cooper, William Gamble, Henry Butler, Abraham Jones, who being empannelled and sworn retired to inquire.
The following are Traverse Jurors (towit) John Lively, Craven Johnson, Austin Hackworth, Michael Clard, Isaac Horton, John Tonera, Jacob Butler, Samuel Price, Malcolm McEntire, John Hoskins, Andrew Breaden, Henry Peters.

382 William Griffieth, John Parks, Henry Farmer, William Ashlock, Samuel Johnson & Simon Durreck.
Ordered by the court that Richard Campbell be excused for non attendance as a juror at last term.
A deed from Groge Gordon to William Tunnell for fifty acres of land was proved in open court by Charles Pruett and Thomas Shambers and ordered to be registered.
The court then adjourned until to morrow morning nine o'clock.

383 Tuesday 14th March 1809.

The court met according to adjournment.
Present Arthur Crozier, Joseph Sinclair and William McKamey Esquires.
David Hall, William Boyd, Thomas Wilson, John Jarner, Elizah Hendon, and John Cooper, who were appointed to view a part of the road at John Southerlins from the fork of the ferry road to the river. Report that they have viewed the same and that it keep the ferry road until within about four poles of the ferry thence turning so as to leave a large old tree the right hand thence down the river to a point apposite the riffle.

A bill of sale from John Sutherlin to Samuel Worthington Junr. for a negro boy named Peter age eight years was acknowledged in open court and ordered to be registered.

Ordered by the court that Curtus Johnson, Elizah Burris & Isaac Oaks work under David Wilson Overseer.

384 James Grant)
    vs)
Richard C. Cobb) Present William Underwood, Joseph Sinclair & William McKamey, Whereupon came a jury to wit: John Lively, Craven Johnson, Austin Hackworth, Michael Clardy, Isaac Horton, Jacob Butler, Samuel Prior, Malcolm McEntire, Andrew Breaden, Henry Peters, William Griffith and John Tovera, who being empannelled tryed and sworn do say they find for the defendant-- where upon it is considered by the court that the plaintiff be amerced for his false clamour and that the defendant go there of without day.

A Rule was then entered to shew cause why a new trial should be granted June term 1809. Rule made absolute.

James Henderson)
    vs)
Felix Gilbert) In this case it is ordered that a non suit be entered.

John Kirkpatrick)
    vs)
Benjamin C. Parker) Present Samuel Galbreath, Robert Dew & Joseph Sinclair Esquires.

Where upon came a jury to wit, Henry Farmer, William Ashlock & John Hoskins, Simon Durrick, John Parkes.

385   Samuel Johnson, Richard Thornberry, Isaac Thoneper, Britain Cross, Joab Dodd, Samuel Dunn and Austin Hackworth, who being impannelled tryed and sworn the truth to speak on the issue. Joined do say, they find for the Plaintiff and assess his damages to one hundred and twenty seven dollars thirty three & one third cents. Whereupon it is considered by the court that the plaintiff do recover the sum of one hundred and twenty seven dollars thirty three & one third cents also the further sum of--------- for cost and charges about said suit expended and be the said defendant in mercy.

A rule was then entered to shew cause why a new trial should be granted June term 1809. Rule made absolute.

The court then adjourned until tomorrow morning 9 o'clock.

386   Wednesday 15th March 1809.
The court met according to adjournment.
Present Samuel Galbreath, William McKamey and Joseph Keeny Esquires.
Ordered by the court that William McKamey Esq. John P. Masterson & Geroge Sutherlin be appointed Jurors to the next superior court to be holden for Hamelton Districk.

The following persons are appointed jurors to attend as jurors next June term (to wit)
John Leib Junr., Richard Haynes, Quin Morton, Kinza Johnson, Charles Shinliver, Jacob Lynert, Thomas Laxton, Aaron Slover, Paul Harmon, David Noble, James Hill, Marmaduke Bookout, James Leatch, John Scruggs, Thomas Reynolds, Moses, McWhorter, Malon Hibbs, Andrew McKamey, Alexander Galbreath Senr., Charles Oliver, William Butler Senr., John Tunnell, John G. Durrett, William Tunnell Jurn., Edward Williams, Hardy Medlin, William Sharp, John Loy, Christopher Baker, George Shelter, Joab Dodd, Matthew Hawkins, Abraham Hagler, Michel Stonecipher, Hugh Lackey, William Scarbrough, Reuben Golston, Reuben Williams & Isaac Freels.

387   Ordered by the court that the rate of tax in Anderson be the same for the present year. As it was for the year last Passd. and that the same Justices take in the lists of taxable property and polls for this year as did for the last eight.

John Kirby in whose place alexander Gastin appointed.

Ordered by the court that the Sheriff of this county bring to next court the children of Elizabeth Fleener to be dispose of as the court in their wisdom may think proper.

Ordered by the court that the clerk of Sheriff of Anderson county be allowed the sum of fifty dollars each for the year one thousand eight hundred and eight for their exoffice services.

Quinn Morton)
vs)
Aaron Jenkins)   Present Arther Crozier, William McKamey and Joseph Keeney Esqrs.

Where upon came a jury to wit, Craven Johnson, Austin Hackworth, John Lively, Mitchel Clardy, Isaac Horton, John Tovera, Jacob Butler, Samuel Prior, Malcolm McEntire, Henry Peters, William Griffith .

388   John Parks who being duly sworn say they fine for the plaintiff and assess his damages to three hundred and ten dollars. Whereupon it is considered by the court that the plaintiff do recover the sum aforesaid also the further sum of-------for cost and charges about said suit expended and be the said defd. in mercy & C.

On motion of John McCambell Attorney for Aaron Jenkins it is ordered by the court that he have judgment against said John Bradley as, security for him for the damages & cost aforesaid.

Ordered by the court that William Hogshead, Aaron Jenkins, and John Leib be inspectors for the present election for a Seantor in our Electoreal District.

389   John Leatch came into open court and made oath that he had attended three days as constable of the grand jury at this term.

Kinza Johnson)
vs)
Larkin Bowling)   Present William McKamey, Joseph Keeny & Samuel Galbreath Esquires.

The same Jury as above except Craven Johnson in whose place is Richard Sloinberry who being duly sworn say they fine for the plaintiff and assess his damages to six dollars and thirty four cents.

They of Execution three months.

Thomas Hart proved three days attendance as constable the Traverse Jury.

A deed from Geroge Bumgertner to Arthur Crozier for one hundred acres of land was proved in open court by Geroge Sutherlin & John Underwood and ordered to be registered.

A deed of Gift from Bordon Delk to John Delk was acknowledged in open court and ordered to be registered.

390   The court then adjourned until court tomorrow morning 9 o'clock.

Tuesday 16th March 1809.
The court met according to adjournment.
Present Arthur Crozier, William McKamey, and Richard C. Cobb Esquires.

A deed from Richard C. Cobb to Hugh Barton for lotts No. 25 & 28 in the town of Burrville was acknowledged in open court & ordered to be registered.

Ordered by the court that Judgment be entered up against Andrew Stewart for the sum of nine dollars for the support and mantenance of a bastard child by him begotten on the body of Polly Walker.

On motion of Lewis Harmon of John McCambell his attorney it is ordered that Judgment be entered against John Underwood for not returning an execution, Lewis Harmon vs William Wright for fifty three dollars and seventy five cents.

391   Friday 17th March 1809.

Court met according to adjournment, present William Underwood, William McKamey and Caswill Cobb Esquire.

John Underwood collector for taxes for Anderson County reports the following tract of land and lotts on which the tax has not been paid for the year 1808 to wit acres, John McEntire 5,000 on the waters of New river.

Jacob Moser, C. A. Britian	Ragsdale Big Valley	1.44
John Warrner	Clinch river	1.00
Geroge Gordon	Poplar Creek	19.20
Stockley Donelson & Joseph Beard		10.00

South side grant No. 214 dated 27 January 1795--

James Conner   500
South side of Clinch river grant No. 580 dated the 23 of August 1788.

392   Lotts

Robert Hays	1
Robert Macey	6
Edward Long	1

The foregoing tracts of land and on which the tax have not been paid for the year 1808, according to law and which has not been given in for taxes for said year it is there fore ordered by the court that the same or so much thereof as it is sufficient be sold for the taxes on the first Monday of July next. And the succeeding day by the Sheriff at the court house in Burrville.

Joseph Sinclair Esquire, John Lieb, Lewis Harmon, Samuel Johnson, William Horton & William Ashlock who were appointed a jury to view the road from Burrville to Kingston report that they have view and marked the same and it is to go by Leib Mill thence down the Branch until it intersects the old road and that Moses Roberts cut out the same.

393   Simon Durrick   )

vs)
James Stewart) In this case it is ordered that a Dedunm Polestatom issue depoution of Israil Standefer on behalf of the Defendant and that he give Plaintiff twenty days notice.

Ordered by the court that John Underwood be allowed the sum of eight dollars and eight cents sledge hammer and a crow bar which are to be delivered to Moses Roberts overseer of the road.

John Sartain)
vs)
John Kirkpatrick) In this case it is ordered by the court that judgment be entered up against Page Portwood and his securities for forty three dollars and thirty two cents for not returning an execution in due time.

The last will and testament of James Hannah deceased was proved in open court by --------

394
    Lotts Robert Hays   1
    Robert Macey   6
    Edward Long   1

Henry Farmer and John Farmer & ordered to be recorded.

Ordered by the court that the same rates observed by ordinay keepers as was prescribed the last year.

Ordered by the court that Malon Hibbs be overseer in place of Walter Taylor and that he have the same hands and bounds.

Ordered by the court that Thomas Cummins have his mark recorded which is a crop off the right ear and over bit in the left.

395   Ordered by the court that Rhoda Stanley bounds be from the fork of the Powells Valley Road to Campbell County Beginning where Bowlings leaves off thence up the north side of Clinch river to the county line including all the hand on the waters of New river in said county thence adjoining Spessards Bounds to the--

the court then adjourned until court in course.

                            Arthur Crozier, C. A. C.

396   At a court of Pleas and Quarter Sessions opened and held for the county of Anderson at the court house in Burrville on the second Monday of June in the year of our Lord one thousand eight hundred and nine.

Present Douglas Oliver, John McAdoo, William McKamey and Joseph Sinclair Esquire.

John Underwood Sheriff returned the Venire facias executed on all except Reuben Williams of whom the following are grand jurors (to wit) Charles Oliver, Foreman, Paul Harmon, Alexander Galbreath, Junr., William Tunnell Junr., Hardin Medlin, William Sharp, John Low, Reuben Golston, Aaron Slover, Geroge Shelton, Isaac Freels, Thomas Laxton, John Tunnell, Michael Stonecipher and John Leib Junr., who being sworn retired to enquire.

The following persons are Traverse Jurors (to wit) Kinza Johnson, Matthew Hawkins, Moses McWhorter, James Leatch, Charles Shinliver, Richard Haynes, Thomas Reynolds, Andrew McKamey, John Scruggs.

397   William Butler Junr., Joab Dodd, Quin Morton, Christopher Baker, Jacob Lynert, John G. Durrick & James Hill.

A deed from Robertson Asher to Andrew Braden for one hundred acres of land was proved in open court by William and Susannah Asher & ordered to be registered.

Ordered by the court that Young Wood be appointed a Constable in Captain Parks Company who gave bond & Security and was qualified as the law requires.

Ordered by the court that Reuben Golston be overseer of the road instead of Squire Hendrix from the top of Chesnut Ridge to William Standefers and that Douglas Oliver & Isaac Law Esquire divide the hands between Reuben Golston and William Boyd.

A deed from Charles McClung to Matthew Hawkins for one hundred and fifty acres of land was proved in open court by Jacob Peak and Michael Stone - cipher and ordered to be registered.

398 A deed from Charles McClung to Nancy Brazel for eighty acres of land was proved in open court by Jacob Peak & Matthew Hawkins and ordered to be registered.

A commission appointed Jarret Harbin, Michael Clardy, Justices of the peace for Anderson County was produced in open court and they were qualified and took their seats.

Ordered by the court that John Warwick have his ear mark recorded which is a crop & slit in each ear.

A deed from Page Portwood to Micajah Frost for two hundred and thirty nine acres of land was acknowledged in open court & ordered to be registered.

A bill of sale from Page Portwood to Micajah Frost was acknowledged in open court and ordered to be registered.

399 Ordered by the court that the Old Road be discontinued from LuAllens to where it intersects the other road above Harts and that Joseph Hart and Robert Dew Esquires assign to Freeman Still the hands to work on under him on the road from Faulks to where that road intersects the one leading from McAdoo to Wallace Mill.

Ordered by the court that the Old road be discontinued from Leibs Mill Branch to Burrville.

Ordered by the court that Kenzy Johnson be allowed the sum of three dollars sixty to and one half cents for books furnished for the registration of deed.

Ordered by the court that John McAdoo, William McKamey, Joseph Hart, Hugh Barton, Samuel Johnson, Isaac Mayberry & Lewis Harmon be appointed a Jury to review the road from Burrville to days ford & that they report at this term.

Ordered by the court that Thomas and Joseph Hart have leave to build a grist & saw mill on Hynds Creek & that the dam be thirteen feet three inches high.

400 Ordered by the court that Geroge Shelters be overseer of the road instead of John Warwick.

Ordered by the court that the Jurors be paid during the present year.

Ordered by the court that the following hands work under Melon Hibbs overseer (to wit) Walter Taylor, Isaac Robbins, Benjamin Potter, Saml. Tipton, Samuel Hibbs, William Sevoirs, John Stewart & Henry George.

Ordered by the court that the road be discontinued from McWhorters Lane to the Eagle Ford.

The court then adjourned till tomorrow 9 o'clock.

Tuesday 13th 1809.
The court met according to adjournment.
Present, William Underwood, William McKamey & Johnson Heath Esquires.
William Kelly Esquire produced his commission and was qualified as

an attorney of this court.

401 Simon Derrick)
        vs   )
     James Stewart) Present William Underwood, William McKamey, Joseph
                       Keeney, Jarret Harbin & Johnson Heath esquires.
     Whereupon came a jury of (to wit) Matthew Hawkins, James Hill, Charles Shinliver, Richard Haynes, Thomas Reynolds, Andrew McKamey, John Scruggs, William Butler, Joab Dodd, Bhristopher Baker, Jacob Lynert and John G. Durrett who being duly sworn say they find for the defendant. Whereupon it is considered by the court that the plaintiff be ancered for his false clamour & that the defendant go thereof without day.

     A deed from James Porter to Squire Hendrix for one hundred and fourteen acres of land was proved in open court by Israel Standefer & Mitchell Childress ordered to be registered.

     Hugh Barton, William McKamey, John McAdoo, Samuel Johnson, & Lewis Harmon who were appointed a jury to review the road leading from Burrville to Days ford report that they have viewed the same and that the best way is by the house where Baumgertner formerly lived after corssing the-----
402 branch to follow the road as it now runs to where it intersects the old road and that the present overseer cut out the same.

     A transfer from William Lawson to Micajah Cross with a plott and certificate was proved by Craven Johnson, Samuel Dunn.

Conrod Coffroth)
     vs   )
Robert Hays   ) Present William Underwood, Samuel McCoy, Jared Harbin
                       Michael Clardy & Johnson Heaths esquires.

     Whereupon came a jury to wit Moses M. Whorter, Quin Morton, James Leatch, John McEntire, William Lamar, Thomas Adair, James Steward, William Rayland, Jacob Clodfelter, John Rhea, Henry Farmer & Kinza Johnson who being duly sworn say they find for the plaintiff and assess his damage to eighty seven dollars and ninety five cents. Whereupon it is considered by the court the plaintiff do recover his damages aforesaid also the sum of----------- for costs and charges about said suit expended & be the said defendant in mercy & Ca.

403 Robert Lumpkins)
        vs   )
    Page Portwood) Present William Underwood, Johnson Heath, & Samuel
                      McKay, esquires.
     Whereupon came a jury towit, Matthew Hawkins, James Hill, Charles Shinliver, Richard Haynes, Thomas Reynolds, Andrew McKamey, John Scruggs, William Butler, Joab Dodd, Christopher Baker, Jacob Lynert and John G. Durrett who being duly sworn say they find the defendant has not paid the debt in the declaration mentioned except four dollars and fifty cents which he has paid and assessed the plaintiffs damage for the detention to two and eighty eight cents.

     Whereupon it is considered by the court that the plaintiff do recover this debt and damage aforesaid also the further sum of------- for costs and charges about said suit expended and be the said defendant in mercy & c.

     Ordered by the court that John Lay be overseer of the road from Samuel M. Kays to the top of the black oak ridge and have the same bounds as Isaac Rains had.

404   Ordered by the court that Hardy Medlin be overseer of the road from

the ford of Buffaloe Creek to Richard C. Cobbs fence and have the same bounds that Henry Russell had.

Andrew Leinart)
vs)
Quin Morton) This cause is refered to Kinza Johnson, Matthew Hawkins, Charles Shinliver, Richard Haynes and John Scruggs whose award shall be made a judgment of the court.

John Hickman)
vs)
Johnson Heath) In this case defendant confessed judgment for sixty dollars and ninety cents and costs of suit.

Conrad Coffroth)
vs)
Robert Hayes) Hugh Barton and John M. Whorter who were bail for the defendant surrendered him in open court in discharge of themselves.

Simon Derrick)
vs)
Aaron Jenkins &)
William Derrick) Same court and same jury as in preceeding cause who being duly sworn say they find that the defendant have paid the--------

405 debt in the declaration mentioned except three hundred and ninety nine dollars and thirty eight cents and assess the plaintiff damages by reason of the detention of that sum to forty one dollars and ninety three cents.
Whereupon it is considered by the court that plaintiff do recover his debt and damages aforesaid also the further sum of------ for cash and dharges about said suit expended and be the same defendant in mercy & ca.

Richard Luallen)
vs)
Thomas Hart &)
William Lamar.) Same court & same jury who be duly sworn say they fine the defendant have not paid the debt in the debt in the declaration mentioned and assess the plaintiff damage by reason of the declaration thereof to four dollars and twenty eight cents.
Whereupon it is considered by the court that the plaintiff do recover his debt and damages aforesaid also the sum of------- for cost and charges about said suit expended and be the defendant in mercy.
The court then adjourned till tomorrow morning 9 o'clock.

406 Wednesday 14th June 1809.
The court met according to adjournment present.
William Underwood, Michael Clardy and Samuel McKoy esquires.
Ordered by the court that Jesse Bookout be overseer of the road instead of John Lynn and have the same hand.
Ordered by the court that Joseph Bookout be overseer of the road instead of Joseph Overton from Byrams fork of Hynds Creek to the county line and have the same hands.
Ordered by the court that Matthew H. Lett be overseer of the road instead of Willie Warwick from the top of the Chesnut ridge to the top of Hynds ridge & Willis Warwick, Geroge Turner, Joseph Davidson, Sherwood Bowman, ne-

gro fellow & John Warwick are to work under him.

Ordered by the court that John Lane be overseer of the road instead of Rhodes Stanley from the ford of Cole Creek to the county Line and have the same hands.

407   Ordered by the court that Jarret Harbin take a list of the taxable property and polls in Captain Griffith company for the present year & return the same to the next court.

Thomas Dardis Esquire returned four thousand nine hundred and eighty seven and one half acres of land subject to taxes for the present year in the name of Robert Burton.

Samuel Dunn)
   vs pursons)
Robertson Asher) In this case John Underwood returned execution for twenty to dollars and seventy cents that there being no personal property to be found he had lived the same on an occupant Right of said Robertson Asher supported to contain one hundred acres. It is herefore ordered by the court that judgment be entered up against said Asher for said sum & the cost of this suit.

Thomas Hart proved five day attendance on the traverse jury at December last and three day attendance on the grand jury at this term.

408   Ordered by the court that the following pursons be appointed Jurors to attend at September term next (to wit) Jacob Lender, Page Portwood, John Farmer, Elijah Hendon, John Parks, Elijah Frost, Lewis Carney, Isaac Oakes, Adam Moser, Pleasent McBride, William Teague, Barnabas Butcher, John Ridenour, Senr., Releigh Duncan, Marmaduke Bookout, Jail Holbert, Jeremiah Hickson, Isaac Mayberry, David Noble, John Spessard, Thadrick Tipton, Rhodes Stanley, Reuben Williams, William Griffith, William Russell, Hugh Barton, William Ashlock, Thomas Adair, Lewis Harmon, Aaron Jenkins, Henry Norman, John Cooper, John Kirk, Philip Harless, James Taylor, Henry Farmer Senr., Abraham Hagler, John Gambler, Lewis Campbell, & Austin Hackworth-------- the court then adjourned till tomorrow morning 9 o'clock.

Tuesday 15th June 1809.
The court met according to adjournment.
   Present, William Underwood, Joseph Keeny, Michael Clardy & Jarret Harbin Esquire.

409   Ordered by the court that John Miller be overseer of the road from the ford of Cole Creek to James Taylor in stead of Benjamin Bowling and have the same hands.

Ordered by the court that Christopher Baker, John Warwick, James Hill, Jacob Moser, Pleasant McBride & Samuel McKoy be appointed a jury to review the road leading from Underwoods Shop to Mosers Mill Pond & that they report to next court.

State)
   vs)
James Worthington) Present William Underwood, Joseph Keney, Isaac Lowe, Jarret Harbin, Michael Clardy, William McKamey, Joseph Sinclair & Richard C. Cobb, Esquires.

Whereupon came a jury (to wit) James Hill, Thomas Reynolds, Andrew McKamey, Christopher Baker, Jacob Lynert G. Durrett, Joab Dodd, Samuel Dunn, John Spessard, Obadiah Wood, William Noble and Elijah Frost, who being duly sworn say they fine the defendant guilty.

Whereupon it is considered by the court that he be fined in the sum of------- for cost about the same expended and be in mercy.

410 Aron Jenkins)
    vs)
Nathaniel Davis) Same court except Arthur Crozier Esquire in addition the same jury who being duly sworn say they fine for the plaintiff and his damages to four hundred and five dollars also the sum of ----- for cost about said suit expended and be the defendant in mercy & ca.

Ferguson)
    vs)
May) In this case it is ordered that judgment be entered up against Stephen Heard for sixteen dollars and twenty six cents.

    Ordered by the court that Hugh Barton, John Leib, Junr., Michael Clardy, Aaron Jenkins, William Horton, Lewis Hoeman & James Underwood who were appointed a jury to review the road from McWhorters land to the Eagle Ford and from their to Burrville and report that there can be a road the way the old one now goes and from the Ford to Burrville the way the Old one now runs, & that the former overseer & keep in repair an have his former bounds & hands and that Stephen Heard be overseer from the ford to Burrville and have the hands instead of Michael Robbins.

TENNESSEE

RECORDS OF ANDERSON COUNTY

COUNTY COURT MINUTES
1810 - 1814

COPYING HISTORICAL RECORDS PROJECT
Official Project No. 465-44-3-115

COPIED UNDER WORK'S PROGRESS ADMINISTRATION

MRS. JOHN TROTWOOD MOORE
STATE LIBRARIAN & ARCHIVIST, SPONSOR

MRS. ELIZABETH D. COPPEDGE
DIRECTOR OF WOMEN'S & PROFESSIONAL PROJECTS

MRS. PENELOPE JOHNSON ALLEN
STATE SUPERVISOR

MRS. MARGARET HELMS RICHARDSON
PROJECT SUPERVISOR

COPIED BY
MRS. MARY HALL

TYPED BY
MRS. CARRIE B. STUART

Dec. 8, 1938

ANDERSON COUNTY

COURT MINUTES
1810 - 1814

INDEX

Note: Page numbers in this index refer to those of the original volume from which this copy was made. These numbers are carried in the body of the manuscript within parentheses, as (P. 124)

A

Adair, Thomas, 1, 2, 6, 37, 48, 52, 88
Adcock, Thomas, 18, 26, 167
Adams, Robert H., 85, 99, 105, 107, 108, 112, 233
Adkins, George, 63, 64
Adkins, Henry, 45, 47, 51
Aldridge, John, 199, 246
Allbright, Phillip, 189
Allen, John, 206
Allen, William, 206
Alred, Solomon, 128, 139, 247, 255, 260
Alves (Alvies), Walter, 6, 14, 205, 261
Anderson, James, 129
Anderson, Samuel, 8, 42, 85, 132, 133, 150, 167, 168, 171, 173, 187, 227, 229, 233
Argabright, Susanna, 232
Armstrong, John, 48
Arthur, William, 178
Asher, Charles, 166
Asher, Michael, 202
Asher, Milly, 32
Ashley, Francis M., 222
Ashley, Thomas M., 128, 139, 222, 243, 247, 255
Ashley, William, 222
Ashlock, Obadiah, 200, 212, 216
Ashlock, Rebecca, 90, 230
Ashlock, William, 11, 13, 15, 19, 21, 24, 29, 120, 122, 205, 206, 209, 211, 219, 229, 243, 245
Ashurst, John, 29, 51, 104, 132
Aultum, Rachael, 208, 217
Austin, Alexander, 193
Ayres, David, 19

B

Bailey, Christopher, 24, 67, 71, 224, 226
Bailey, Libston, 174
Ball, Valentine, 257
Barton, Hugh, 20, 25, 47, 106, 114, 115, 124, 137, 156, 160, 161, 170, 177, 204, 237, 248, 261
Baumgartner, George, 8, 30, 51, 66, 250
Beach, Elijah, 135, 167, 173, 260
Beaver Creek, 54, 138
Beets, Daniel, 247, 255, 258
Bennett, Silas, 234
Black, Joseph, 128, 139
Blackburn, Delila, (Delia), 187
Blackburn, James, 108, 252
Blagg, William, 135
Bookout, Jesse, 219, 224
Bookout, Marmaduke, 11, 76, 143, 158, 177
Boteler, Thomas, 260
Bounds, Jessee, 208
Bounds, John, 34, 73, 76, 78, 83, 148, 149, 151, 154, 160, 163, 172, 173, 175, 209, 211, 214, 223, 224, 226, 227, 239, 241, 257
Bounds, William, 95, 96, 107, 108, 257
Bowling, Benjamin, 30
Bowling, Joseph, 258
Bowling, Larkin, 2, 4, 11, 20, 30, 128, 144, 197, 203, 216, 217, 220, 236, 258
Boyd, William, 1, 2, 4, 6, 55, 62, 80, 83, 99, 113, 179
Boyter, William, 145, 152
Braden (Breaden-Breden), Andrew, 4, 6, 10, 15, 53, 58, 104, 106, 110, 115, 116, 132, 191, 208, 220, 224, 249, 260
Bradley, John, 41, 42, 69
Branham, Ephraim, 46, 63, 64, 76, 85
Branham, John, 129

Brazleton, Isaac, 34, 92, 98, 99, 167, 241, 242
Breaden, Jane, 203, 249, 263
Brian, William, 230
Brinley, Sarah, 125
Brown, John, 9
Brown, Moses, 127, 139, 145, 149, 151, 154, 247, 255
Brown, Reuben, 234
Brumley, Austin, 131
Brumley, James, 3
Brumley, John, 131, 226
Brummett, George, 23, 32
Brummett, James, 7
Brummitt, J., 7
Bryan (Brian), William H., 198, 230
Buckhorn Valley, 53
Buckingham, Nathaniel B., 61, 83, 89, 199
Burton, Robert, 68, 111
Butcher, Barnabas, 73
Butler, Henry, 34, 127, 139, 151, 243
Butler, Jacob, 49, 67, 72, 76, 77, 90, 153, 179, 187, 216, 243, 245
Butler, Thomas, 119, 153, 216
Butler, William, 119, 130, 142, 226, 234, 236, 241

C

Caldwell, James, 219
Campbell, George M., 149
Campbell, John M., 199
Campbell, Lewis, 32, 46
Campbell, Richard, 18, 34, 172, 173, 174, 206, 219, 229
Carnell, Thomas, 128, 139, 226, 140, 233, 260
Carroll, Drury, 258
Carroll, John, 258
Carrell, Thomas H., 146
Carrell (Carrol), William, 106, 109, 110, 215
Carter, Joseph, 49, 77
Carwile, John, 128
Chapman, John, 187
Chapman, John H., 34, 53, 58, 65, 66, 67, 70, 73, 200
Chapman, Joseph, 40
Chestnut Ridge Meeting House, 141
Childress, James, 103, 108, 179, 227
Childress, Joseph, 190
Childress, William, 109, 226, 227
Childs, John, 235, 257

Childs (Chiles), Paul, 11, 13, 15, 17, 19, 21, 24, 126, 184, 195, 243
Childs (Chiles), Rowland, 56, 57, 41, 195
Clack, Lucy, 26
Clair, Peter, 11, 15, 17, 19, 21, 24, 86, 214
Clardy, M., 65, 206, 208
Clardy, Michael, 11, 34, 40, 63, 69, 100, 105, 113, 187, 210, 235, 248
Clarkson (Clarkston, Claxton), 11, 13, 15, 17, 19, 21, 24, 29, 76, 83, 88, 90, 93, 95, 96, 120, 122, 143, 149, 154, 158, 184, 220, 227, 239, 253 (Constant Clarkson)
Clarkston (Claxton), David, 13, 143, 256
Clarkston (Clarkson), John, 24, 54, 91, 100, 101, 227, 228, 238, 253
Claxon, Aquilla, 239
Clodfelter, Jacob, 15, 92, 98, 101, 104, 106, 110, 116, 243, 245
Cobb, Adam, 50
Cobb, Rebecca, 61, 84
Cobb, Richard C., 14, 21, 24, 41, 44, 45, 47, 61, 83, 188, 190, 203, 212, 253, 259
Cobb, William, 61, 84, 190
Coburn, Isaac, 229
Coburn, Jacob, 216
Coburn, Jonathan, 239
Coffin, Leonard, 86
Coffman, Leonard, 141, 143, 158, 177, 214, 247, 255, 258, 260
Cogbourn, James, 140-142
Cole, Alexander, 241, 260
Condra, Benjamin, 62, 66, 68
Condray, Dennis, 36
Cooper, John, 34, 54, 93, 95, 96, 99, 103, 106, 110, 114, 116, 142, 260
Craig, Thos., 260
Craighead, William, 76, 83, 88, 90, 93, 95, 96, 100, 135, 204, 206, 219, 229
Craven, Richard, 88, 90
Crawford, John, 262
Creswell, James, 119
Cress, John, 201
Crobaugh, Charles, 204
Cross, Britton, 16, 55, 76, 82, 83, 92, 98, 102, 115, 172, 173, 226, 227, 233
Crozier, Arthur, 9 to 13, 19, 21, 23, 26, 30, 31, 36, 42, 44, 47, 51, 54, 55, 58, 62, 66, 72, 74, 80, 86, 88, 97, 98, 100, 104, 113, 114, 117,

Crozier, Arthur, (Cont.), 118, 120,
    121, 122, 128, 129, 133, 138,
    139, 142, 151, 156, 157, 160,
    162, 170, 172, 188, 189, 195,
    199, 200, 201, 204, 206, 208,
    209, 210, 211, 212, 214, 216,
    217, 218, 219, 225, 230, 232,
    248, 249, 250, 252, 259, 260,
    262, 263, 264
Crozier, John, 38, 41, 51
Cunningham, James, 8

D

David, Sampson, 117
Davidson, James, 26, 143, 158, 164,
    172, 173, 177
Davis, John, 160, 163, 175, 214, 218,
    223, 224, 226, 232, 239, 241
Davidson, Samuel, 76, 82, 85, 91,
    100, 101, 124, 133, 170, 219,
    220, 225, 237, 248
Davidson, William, 98, 247, 255
Day, John, 10
Day, Joseph, 10, 162
Deaton, Zadock, 135, 145, 149, 187,
    209, 211
Delk, John, 50
Delk, Jourdan, 8, 37, 50, 63,
Delk, Susanna, 8, 12, 45, 51
Delk, Thomas, 63
Dennison, Joseph, 211
Derrick, Simon, 6, 23, 71, 160,
    240, 253, 260
Dew, Robert, 1, 3, 5, 6, 17, 18,
    23, 48, 51, 56, 57, 62, 140,
    142, 145
Dixon, Harriett, 212
Dixon, Hugh, 120, 122, 125, 126,
    130, 132, 133, 169, 186, 208,
    220, 241, 242, 261
Dixon, Samuel, 34, 41, 56, 61, 64,
    88, 112, 129, 159, 201, 210
Dixon, Thomas, 10, 54, 55, 56, 67,
    108, 113, 140, 142, 149, 164,
    165, 186, 188, 193, 208, 227,
    241, 242, 243, 245, 247, 251
Dizney, Thomas, 154
Dodd, Joab, 25
Doherty, John, 145
Doherty, Joseph, 71, 145, 183
Doherty, William, 41, 47, 66, 67,
    75, 88, 90, 100, 124, 141,
    146, 163, 183, 184, 189, 260
Dossett, Goodlow, 10
Dougherty, White, 36

Dowlin, Amos, 11, 13, 15, 17, 21, 24
Dunn, Samuel, 10, 17, 28, 91, 142,
    187, 220, 243, 260
Dunnivan, John, 159, 167, 226, 233
Durrett, John G., 32, 82, 113, 212
Dyer, Joel, 41, 42, 69

E

Eagle Bent, 55
Eagle Ford, 14, 80
Edmundson, Samuel, 171, 208, 243, 245
Edwrads, Elizabeth, 155
Edwards, William, 135, 188, 189, 227,
    247, 251, 255
Emmerson, Thomas, 8, 42, 44, 144
English, Joshua, 62, 76, 141
Epperson, James, 11, 55, 65, 148, 182
Epperson, Joel, 143, 158
Eskredge, Thomas, 140, 149
Etter (Atter), Henry, 18, 64, 124,
    145, 158, 170, 172, 173, 177,
    214, 233, 226, 233
Evans, Evan, 246
Everett, James, 229

F

Farmer, Abner, 226, 241
Farmer, Henry, 76, 89, 178, 239
Farmer, Henry, Jr., 181, 248
Farmer, John, 76, 121, 122, 123, 130,
    133, 243, 260
Farmer, John Cooper, 260
Farmer, Moses, 121, 179, 181, 184,
    186, 191
Few, Richard, 51
Foster, Enoch, 10, 120, 122, 125, 126,
    130, 132, 133, 201, 224, 225, 247,
    263
Freels (Frields), Anderson, 103,
Freels, Edwrad, 45, 187, 200, 65, 58,
    72, 90, 103, 158, 200, 243, 245
Freels, Edward, Sr., 143
Freels, Isaac, 19, 21, 204, 226
Freels, John, 187, 200
Freels, Wm., 104
Freeman, Lewis, 178, 235
Frost, Elijah, 28, 34, 68, 205, 208,
    219, 236
Frost, Jonas, 47
Frost, Joshua, 76, 83, 88, 90, 93, 95,
    96, 179, 181, 184, 194
Frost, Micajah, 105, 179, 181, 260
Frost, Patty, 131

Frost, Samuel, 54, 67, 76, 122, 184, 187, 225, 244, 253
Fry, John, 23, 32, 53, 58, 62, 66, 68, 70, 73, 92, 98, 101, 108, 115, 116, 120, 122, 142, 173, 193, 207, 208, 214, 222
Fry, Solomon, 67,

G

Galbreath (Gilbreath), Alexr., Jr., 34, 113, 236, 243
Galbreath, Robert, 1, 2, 4, 6, 76, 94, 113, 183, 184, 225, 248, 252
Galbreath, Samuel, 23, 29, 85, 87, 92, 100, 113, 133, 139, 181, 182, 187, 190, 191, 233, 235, 237, 238, 241, 242, 248, 260
Galbreath, Thomas, 34
Gallaher, George, 82, 234
Gallaher, Joseph, 10, 76, 225, 258
Gallion, Thomas, 225
Gamble, John, 1, 81, 82, 159, 179, 225, 246, 258
Gamble, William, 76, 144, 201, 205, 219, 236, 246, 260
Gardenhire, William, 82
Garner, John, 92, 98, 147, 179, 181, 226, 233, 241, 258, 260
Gastin (Gaston), Alexander, 1, 2, 6, 14, 21, 23, 25, 34, 49, 56, 76, 79, 85, 86, 126, 187, 192, 209, 211, 225, 230, 238, 242, 245, 248
Gholson (Goldstone), Reuben, 81, 219, 229
Gibbs, John, 15, 43, 113, 126, 147, 178, 185, 187, 190, 191, 225, 237, 248, 260
Gibbs, Neely, 202
Goodman, Henry, 67
Gordan, George, 127, 179
Gordan, John, 10, 187
Gott, Thomas, 44
Green, John, 21, 37, 46, 48, 52
Griffin, Fielding, 250, 252
Griffith, William, 1, 2, 6, 92, 142, 225
Griffy, James, 35
Griffy, Joseph, 35
Grills, Elliott, 188
Guthrie, James, 59

H

Hackworth, Augustine, 182
Hackworth, Austin, 127, 139, 179, 181, 182, 225
Hackworth, Gabriel, 182, 187
Hackworth, John, 53, 58, 68, 70, 243, 247, 255, 258
Hagler, Abraham W., 34, 99, 113, 127, 139, 187, 200, 212, 225, 226, 243, 258, 260
Hale, Nathen, 34, 127, 139, 140, 187
Hall, David, 3, 27, 34, 43, 92, 98, 115, 143, 147, 158, 171, 177, 179, 184, 225
Hall, Kinchem, 132, 135, 227
Hall, Samuel, 4, 236
Hancock, William, 128, 139, 170
Hannah, James, 179, 213
Hannah, Josiah, 200, 201
Harbin, Jarrot (Jared), 23, 32, 34, 35, 36, 40, 44, 69, 145, 250, 252
Harbison, James, 10, 196
Harless, Henry, 34
Harless, Phillip, 37, 40, 45, 48, 76, 83, 128, 139, 170
Harless, Robert, 46
Harmon, John, 202
Harmon, Lewis, 177, 198, 230
Harmon, Paul, 10
Harper, James, 196
Hart, John D., 167
Hart, Joseph, 31, 57, 92, 95, 97, 120
Hart, Nathaniel, 23
Hart, Thomas, 18, 34, 65, 127, 131, 147, 149, 165, 183, 186, 187, 188, 252
Hatfield, Joseph, 250, 252, 254
Hawkins, Edward, 82, 85, 86, 99, 113, 122, 151, 157, 162, 181, 184, 191, 192, 195, 203, 209, 211, 220, 225, 233, 238, 249, 250, 257
Hawkins, George, 11
Hawkins, Matthew, 99, 148, 154, 179, 190, 248, 252
Hays, Richard, 48,
Hays, Robert, 92, 98, 101, 106, 109, 137
Haynes, Richard, 37, 40, 45, 46,
Heard, Andrew, 117
Heard, Stephen, 4, 5, 14, 29, 30, 51, 55, 62, 74, 79, 83, 86, 95, 120, 126, 134, 137, 156, 173, 208, 227, 238, 252, 257, 261
Heath, Johnson, 10, 14, 16
Heath, Matthew, 14, 16, 143, 162, 164, 170, 172, 173, 177, 263
Heiskell (Haskell), Charles, 160, 205, 209
Henderson, Jesse, 110, 111
Henderson, Joseph R., 59
Hendon, Elijah, 10, 27, 55, 205, 219, 224, 226, 229

Henry, Carter, 122, 220
Hensley, George, 172, 173
Hibbs, Jeremiah, 100, 128, 135, 173
Hibbs, John, 11, 24, 67, 95, 133, 135, 145, 148, 150, 151, 214
Hibbs, Malon, 53, 58, 62, 67, 73, 113, 140, 148, 240
Hibbs, Samuel, 151, 202
Hickey, John, 123
Hicks, David, 76, 83, 253
Hicks, James, 92, 109, 116, 226, 101, 106
Hill, James, 76, 113, 187, 219
Hill, Matthew, 123, 128, 139, 151, 154
Hill, Thomas, 4, 223, 241, 252, 254
Hogshead, Charles, 119
Hogshead, William, 4, 6, 8, 10, 20, 25, 55, 68, 79, 92, 97, 103, 108, 115, 120, 121, 136, 148, 153, 168, 171, 175, 176, 182, 196, 203, 211, 214, 218, 223, 241, 262
Holbert, Joel, 105
Hollin, John, 182
Holt, Michael, 1
Homesley, Joseph, 247, 255, 258
Hope, Thomas, 116, 147, 148, 149, 151, 172, 173, 184
Horton, Fanny, 132, 134
Horton, Isaac, 204, 206, 259
Horton, William, 23, 32, 53, 58, 62, 66, 67, 70, 73, 132, 134
Hoskins, Edward, 219
Hoskins, George, 13, 15, 17, 19, 21, 24, 29, 34, 86, 159, 242, 245, 247
Hoskins, Jesse, 143, 164, 170, 158, 204, 205, 206, 210, 219, 220, 224, 225, 230, 243, 245, 250, 252
Hoskins, John, 2, 6, 13, 14, 16, 23, 32, 36, 47, 50, 81, 90, 101, 104, 125, 126, 159, 165, 174, 175, 182, 186, 191, 204, 216, 217, 222, 243, 245, 252, 256
Hosler (Hostler), Michael, 143, 158, 170, 172, 173, 177, 245
Houston, Robert, 223
Hudson, George, 187, 200, 216, 233
Huffstutler, David, 256
Huffstutler, Jacob, 200, 202, 247, 255, 258
Huffstutler, John, 200, 201
Hutcherson, James, 59
Hutchings, Elizabeth, 189, 207

Hutchings, Priscilla, 261

I

Irwin, Francis, 247

J

Jackson, Jacob, 28, 45, 46, 48, 88, 90, 99, 125, 132
James, William, 188
Jenkins, Aaron, 10, 29, 30, 41, 42, 69, 76, 103, 111, 112, 126, 184, 187, 194, 239, 248, 249
Johnson, Absolom, 228
Johnson, Claiborn,
Johnson, Craven, 2, 14, 23, 27, 28, 29, 90, 93, 76, 83, 88, 95, 96, 205, 210, 219, 220, 229, 260
Johnson, Daniel, 129
Johnson, Elliott, 13
Johnson, Kinza, 32, 76, 146, 165, 188, 210
Johnson, Seth, 13
Johnson, Thomas, 56
Johnson, William, 123
Jones, Abraham, 2, 15
Jones, John, 234, 264

K

Keeling, William, 221
Keeny, John, 202
Keeny, Joseph, 110, 128, 139, 205, 209, 219, 236, 226
Keeny, Joseph, Jr., 123, 128, 144, 239, 241
Keith, Gabriel, 26, 247
Keith, Spencer, 159
Kelly, Thomas, 264
Kenney, Joseph, 106
Kirby, John, 52, 132, 251, 261
Kernall, Thomas, 260
Ketcherside, Thomas, 49, 126
Key, Zachariah, 16, 92, 98, 142, 247, 255, 258, 260
Kincade, Clinging, 187, 200, 203
King, James, 127, 132, 159, 251
King, John, 11
King, Robert, 4, 21
King, William, 42, 95, 118
King, William, 42, 95, 118
Kirby, John, 1, 6, 8, 34, 36, 46, 88, 101, 124, 210, 220, 222
Kirk, Elijah, 126
Kirk, John, 126, 204, 261

Kirk, Thomas, 126
Kirkpatrick, Charles, 55, 101, 106, 110, 184, 186
Kirkpatrick, James, 7, 20, 53, 58, 66, 68, 70, 73, 79, 108, 120, 122, 141, 177, 262
Kirkpatrick, John, 20, 79, 108
Kirkpatrick, Mary, 11, 173
Kitchen, John, 1, 67, 68, 71, 88, 90
Koyl, Samuel, 217

L

Lackey, Hugh, 123
Lamar, William, 18, 34, 92, 98, 111, 128, 139, 147, 165, 204, 206
Landrum, John, 127, 139, 145, 148, 151, 154, 226, 233, 241
Landrum, Thomas, 11, 13, 128, 139, 148, 149, 151, 154, 186, 191, 202
Lane, John, 30, 216
Lane, William, 214
Langford, Banjamin, 143, 158, 164, 170, 172, 173, 177
Lannum, John, 263
Larue, Jacob, 187, 251
Larue, William, 251,
Lawson, Robert, 37, 40, 45, 76, 260
Laxton, Jesse, 228
Lee, James, 7
Leach, I., 229
Leach (Leatch), James, 8, 10, 202
Leach (Leatch), John, 30, 36, 62, 123, 167, 189, 202, 206, 234 260
Leath, Willis, 19, 20, 83, 102, 103, 107, 130, 187, 200, 216
Leary, James, 4, 15
Leib, Daniel, 85, 121, 122, 247, 255, 258, 261
Leib, Jacob, Jr., 92
Leib, John, 34, 76, 82, 98, 121, 122, 132, 133, 164, 178, 191, 208, 226, 236, 239, 241, 242
Lemar, Rosanna, 254
Lemar, William, 142, 187, 239, 254
Lenard, William, 147
Leonard (Linart, Lynart), Jacob, 33, 34, 76, 120, 122, 181, 184, 191, 195, 204, 205, 209, 211, 213, 214, 219, 229, 246, 260
Lewallen (Luallen), Charles, 112, 148

Luallen, John, 40, 111, 120, 143, 148, 158, 164, 170, 177, 215, 243, 245, 260
Luallen, Richard, 6, 18, 111, 140, 143, 165, 182, 184, 188, 202, 208, 236, 239, 250
Lewis, Jacob, 250, 252, 254
Lewis, Willoughby, 31, 62, 66
Linder, Isaac, 1, 10, 51
Little, Thomas, 37, 40, 48
Lively, John, 143, 158, 260
Lohery, John, 74, 115, 207
Lohery, William, 67, 100, 114, 115, 144, 145, 149, 150, 154, 156, 177, 192, 204, 208, 222, 242
Long, I., 7
Long, James, 19
Love, Hezekiah, 136
Low, Aquilla, 140, 49, 200, 201
Lowe, Isaac, 20, 83, 92, 98, 102, 103, 106, 109, 110, 140, 149, 182, 237, 247
Lowe, John, 50
Loy, John, 28, 47, 53, 58, 80, 142, 147, 225, 247, 256
Lucas, Elizabeth, 156
Lynch, George, 141
Lynn (Linn), John, 105, 126, 261

M

Maclin, Carter, 230, 231
Maclin, Benjamin Parker, 198, 199, 230, 231
Maclin, James Zachfield, 198, 231
Maclin, Landon Carter, 198, 199, 231
Maclin, William, 198, 199, 230, 231
Malaby, John, 169, 175, 178, 184, 189, 197
Malaby, Sarah, 155
Manley, Ansil, 33, 50, 119, 142
Marsh, Daniel, 241
Markey, Solomon, 226
Marshall (Martial), Richard, 76, 83, 93, 95, 96, 128, 139, 142, 187, 200, 204, 206, 212, 216, 248
Marshall, Samuel, 85, 86, 126
Marshall, William, 214
Martin, Jesse, 1, 4, 6
Massey (Macey), Charles, 5, 31
Massingale, John, 137
Mattox, Daniel, 146, 260
Mayberry, George, 90

Mayberry, Isaac, 34, 59, 69, 75, 79, 92, 93, 98, 111, 133, 134, 136, 142, 148, 149, 152, 158, 164, 165, 188, 182, 236, 250, 252, 260

Mayberry, Jacob, 67, 93, 95, 96, 101, 224

McAdoo, John, 9, 10, 11, 14, 21, 22, 24, 29, 30, 31, 32, 49, 55, 58, 61, 76, 88, 91, 97, 111, 112, 113, 114, 120, 121, 122, 129, 138, 140, 147, 148, 159, 165, 181, 188, 200, 201, 210, 212, 248, 251

McAdoo, William, 179, 219, 243, 245

McCampbell, James, 42, 74, 77, 82

McCart, Robert, 127, 139, 142, 154

McClain, Thomas, 96, 120, 134, 135

McClung, Charles, 153, 216

McCormick, Charles, 8, 28, 87, 97, 121, 136, 160, 168, 252,

McCormick, William, 43

McCorry, Sarah, 198

McCorry (McCurry), Thomas, 47, 198, 230, 259, 261

McCoumous, Stephen, 215

McCoy (McKoy), Samuel, 1, 3, 10, 76, 259

McDaniel, James, 141

McEntire (McIntyre), John, 20, 26, 179

McEntire, John F., 125, 126, 175, 181, 189, 197, 219, 229

McEntire, Wm. F., 113

McFall, Patrick, 223, 247, 250

McIntyre, Malcolm, 10

McKamey (McAmey), Andrew, 10, 92, 98, 116, 127, 130, 138, 148, 149, 151, 154, 159, 225, 252, 256

McKamey, Isaac, 103

McKamey, John, 10, 34, 142, 212, 257

McKamey, Wm., 2, 6, 10, 13, 14, 17, 19, 21, 23, 25, 27, 31, 32, 37, 44, 53, 56, 58, 76, 78, 79, 81, 87, 114, 133, 139, 142, 151, 156, 157, 162, 170, 175, 185, 187, 188, 200, 201, 202, 203, 208, 209, 210, 211, 212, 216, 217, 219, 220, 225, 234, 241, 245, 248, 249, 251, 254, 255, 257

McKnight, Andrew, 140, 162, 168, 191, 192, 194, 195, 196, 209, 211, 212, 213, 215

McMinis, Isaac, 8

McPeters, Joseph, 36, 37, 38, 40, 41, 47, 52, 53, 54, 65, 67, 70, 72, 75, 86, 88, 100, 116, 118, 124, 125, 141, 145, 163, 189

McWhorter, Hance, 1, 2, 4, 10

McWhorter, John, 11, 22, 27, 51

McWhorter, Moses, 79

McWhorter, Quin, 22

Medlin, Hardy, 34, 35, 37, 40, 226

Medlin, Richard, 35, 37, 40, 46, 48, 103

Melton, William, 116

Menefee, Thomas, 10, 15, 28, 74, 76, 126, 141, 142, 248, 262

Mercer, James, 49

Mercer, John, 49

Mildom, James, 11

Millikin, Hugh, 47, 101, 104, 106, 110, 125, 126, 184, 189, 208, 214

Millikin, James, 216

Millikin, Julius, 101, 104, 146, 170, 187, 200, 239, 247, 255, 258

Miller, Brummett, 19

Miller, John, 4, 17, 147, 179, 181, 202, 234

Miller, Mary, 82, 202

Miller, William, 147

Mills, Her, 168

Mills, Mary, 89

Minor, Joseph, 164, 189

Mitchell, William, 240

Monger, Henry, 113, 142

Monger, Peter, 243, 245

Montgomery (McGomery), Hugh, 11, 26, 47, 59, 190, 199, 213, 214

Moore, George, 214

Moore, Jacob, 263

Morton, Quin, 1, 18, 22, 24, 31, 57, 62, 74, 82, 87, 88, 91, 92, 95, 96, 97, 100, 118, 120, 125, 134, 135, 138, 148, 154, 156, 157, 161, 162, 165, 168, 170, 172, 175, 176, 179, 186, 188, 192, 195, 200, 201, 203, 209, 210, 211, 214, 216, 220, 226, 233, 238, 241, 242, 243, 244, 249, 250, 252, 257, 262

Moser, Abraham, 148, 174

Moser, Jacob, 10, 76, 226, 263, 264

Moss, Reuben, 201

Murphy, William, 78

Murray, James, 11, 13, 17, 19, 21, 24,

Mynatt, James, 247, 255

Mynatt, Wm. C., 8, 64, 100

N

Nation, Thomas, 226
Newberry, James, 37, 40, 45, 46, 48, 148, 150, 151
Newman, James, 262
Newman, John, 141, 237, 239, 248
Newport, Ezekiel, 141
Nichol (Niccol), 10, 113, 206, 219, 224, 260
Nickle, Edward, 99
Norman, Aaron, 11, 13, 15, 17, 19, 24, 21, 126
Norman, Eli, 243, 245
Norman, Henry, 34, 92, 98, 141, 143, 158, 177, 260
Norman, Isaac, 10, 76, 126, 143, 158, 184, 248
Ogle, Boston, 27

O

Ogle, Boston, 27
Oliver, Charles, 194
Oliver, Charles Y., 13, 33, 34, 65, 85, 115, 117, 122, 127, 174, 179, 181, 199, 200, 219, 236, 245, 249, 253, 254, 257, 259, 264
Oliver, Douglass, 13, 17, 19, 21, 23, 32, 33, 34, 43, 55, 64, 76, 81, 82, 85, 86, 115, 124, 139, 160, 162, 176, 178, 187, 242, 248, 257
Overton, Joseph, 53, 58, 62, 65, 67, 68, 70, 73, 121, 122, 130, 133
Oliver, Lunsford, 83, 142, 187
Owens, Elias, 235, 257

P

Paine, John, 14, 189, 224
Panky, Stephen, 4
Pore, Peter, 153
Park, James, 32, 37, 54, 72, 73, 74
Parks, William, 54, 56
Parks, John, 34, 41, 63, 113, 92, 98, 120, 122, 125, 126, 130, 132, 133, 134, 167, 187, 248
Parks, Joseph, 187, 225
Parks, William, 32, 37, 73, 74, 198, 230
Parker, Benjamin C., 8, 10, 14, 32, 37, 54, 62, 72, 73, 74, 134, 170, 177, 198, 199
Parsons, Thomas, 81, 97, 117, 248
Patterson, John, 89, 236, 239
Patterson, Mary, 128, 156, 207
Patterson, Robert, 236, 239
Patterson, William, 236
Patton, Jesse, 187, 189, 206
Patton, Robert, 166
Peak (Peek), Jacob, 2, 76, 83, 93, 95, 96, 120, 131, 142, 144, 187, 215, 225, 227, 245, 248, 258
Peak, Molly, 245
Pearce, Robert D., 167
Peck, Noah, 127, 139, 140
Peters, Henry, 92, 98, 179, 181, 187
Peters, Thomas, 260
Peters, Tobias, 10, 13, 76, 99, 179, 181, 187, 200, 216, 212
Pettit, Jonas, 34, 187, 200, 216
Petty, William, 258
Piles, William, 73
Pore, Peter, 153
Portwood, Page, 10, 15, 54, 76, 127, 142, 184, 193, 194, 205, 260
Potter, Benjamin, 179, 250, 254
Powers, Jesse, 209, 211, 222, 240
Price, Charles, 57, 116, 187, 215, 224, 225
Prior, Green, 259
Prior, Samuel, 187, 200, 216, 176
Pruitt (Prewit), David, 47, 88, 95, 103, 105, 124, 125, 126, 146, 163, 186, 177, 191, 193
Pryor, Samuel, 176, 187, 200, 216

Q

Qualls, Richard, 8

R

Ragan, Daniel, 136
Ragan, James, 53, 58, 67, 70, 73, 179, 181
Ragland, Reuben, 123
Reavis, Thomas S., 8, 12, 36, 50, 63
Rector, John, 50, 108, 127, 138, 172, 173, 178, 181, 189, 226, 233, 242
Rector, Lewis, 179, 190
Reed, J., 6
Reed, James, 3, 140, 149
Reed, John, 17, 24, 32, 38, 41, 44, 52, 53, 70, 74, 86, 90, 104, 110, 116, 167, 260
Reeds Mill, 138
Reed, Thomas, 5

Reynolds, Gideon, 165, 175, 192, 212
Reynolds, Thomas, 11, 13, 17, 19, 21
Rhea (Ray, John, 11, 46, 88, 90, 101, 106, 109, 143, 158, 188, 208, 251, 260
Ridenhour, Henry, 168
Ridenhour, John, 187, 200, 206, 209, 211, 212
Robbins, Isaac, 2, 100, 135
Robbins, Michael, 41, 56, 57, 101, 145
Robbins, Samuel, 10, 27, 40, 45, 46, 48, 100, 140, 162, 168, 191, 192, 194, 195, 196, 209, 211, 212, 213, 215, 250
Roberts, Collins, 92, 98, 102, 108, 116, 171, 176, 178, 181, 189, 191, 236
Roberts, Moses, 13, 239
Roberts, Polly, 24, 135
Roberts, Reuben, 53
Roberts, William, 53, 91, 104
Robertson, James, 85
Robertson, John, 170
Robertson, Joseph, 23, 76, 243, 245
Robinson, Elizabeth, 152
Robinson, Irvine, 58
Robinson, James, 153
Robinson, John, 147, 155
Robinson, Joseph, 32, 43
Roddy, Jesse, 26
Ross, James, 247, 255, 256, 258
Ross, Robert, 146, 235, 240, 241, 260
Roysdon, Robert, 128, 139, 187, 205, 219, 227
Russell, Gilbert C., 11
Russell, William, 92, 98, 132, 142, 226, 234, 236, 239, 241

S

Salter, Robert, 119, 201
Sartain, Henrietta, 195
Sartain, Isaac, 143, 158, 165, 188, 216, 247
Sartain, John, 52, 262
Scarbrough, David, 113, 187
Scarboro (Scarbro, Scarburough), James, 2, 10, 13, 113, 162, 187, 216, 243, 260
Scarbroough, John, 13
Scarbrough, Rachael, 2, 129, 204, 206, 216, 217
Scarbrough, Sarah, 178
Scarbrough, William, 10, 56

Scott, Alexander, 30, 70, 86, 111
Scott, John, 9, 29, 30, 33, 70, 108, 112, 122, 125, 126, 129, 136, 142, 146, 170, 171, 184
Scott, William, 9, 10, 30, 38, 54, 70, 75, 76, 86, 133, 153, 171, 191, 193
Scurlock, Samuel, 13
Scruggs, James, 120, 122, 243, 245
Seiber, Philip, Jr., 247, 255, 260
Severs, Philip, 37, 40, 45, 48, 76, 83, 143, 158, 177, 206, 219, 245
Severs, Robert, 222
Severs, Saml., 108, 110
Severs, William, 37, 40, 45, 46, 48, 93, 95, 96, 100, 128, 140, 146, 147, 148, 165, 188, 204, 206
Sewall, James, 71
Shannon, John, 226, 233
Sharp, William, 34, 50, 76, 113, 170, 205, 206, 208, 209, 248, 254, 259
Shelton, Thomas, 69, 72, 118, 125, 145, 196
Shepheard (Shepherd), James, 120, 125, 129, 135, 154, 152, 153, 155, 164, 170, 172, 186
Shepherd, John, 88, 90, 225
Shetter, George, 59, 92, 98, 187
Shinliver (Chinliver), Charles, 29, 34, 181, 252, 260
Shulbread, James, 119
Silvey, William, 209, 211
Simpson, John, 16, 64, 71, 91, 103, 105, 124, 146, 163, 191, 193
Sinclair, Joseph, 5, 10, 13, 21, 22, 27, 40, 72, 76, 79, 81, 85, 92, 98, 100, 105, 124, 162, 172, 176, 190, 192, 210, 223, 225, 230, 233, 235, 237, 238, 241, 242, 243, 245, 247, 248, 250, 257, 263
Sinclair, Joseph, Jr., 203, 209, 249, 263
Slover, Aaron, 34, 100, 121, 122, 125, 126, 130, 132, 133, 135, 179, 181, 205, 219, 229, 248
Smith, David, 263
Smith, George, 142, 251, 252
Smith, John, 23, 32, 143, 158, 255
Smith, Layton, 86
Smith, Simeon, 143, 82, 158, 182
Smith, William, 18, 25, 81
Snodgrass, John, 169
Still, Truman, 208
Sutherland (Southerlin), George, 31, 34, 65, 76, 79, 113, 127, 165, 183, 186, 187, 188, 225, 228, 252

Sutherland, Jacob, Jr., 247
Sutherland, John, 5, 8, 19, 34, 36, 46, 54, 74, 79, 80, 99, 113, 171, 179, 190
Sutherland, John Jr., 66, 67, 157
Spaw, Christian, 247
Spesard, (Spysard), John, 225
Stanley, Rhode, 67, 74, 91, 130, 179, 181, 195, 243, 245, 250
Stephen, Lewis, 28, 47, 80
Stewart, Andrew, 2, 36, 46, 62, 77, 104, 117, 126, 129, 153, 164, 172, 186, 253
Stewart, James, 2, 10, 11, 37
Stewart, John, 2, 10, 37, 50, 62, 77, 117, 126, 134, 169, 175, 176, 178, 184, 196, 197, 214, 215, 218
Still, James, 100, 123, 202
Still, Truman, 189, 226, 227, 260
Stonecypher, Daniel, 247, 255, 258, 260
Stooksberry, Jacob, 207, 221
Stooksberry, James, 152
Stout, David, 1, 2, 4, 6
Stout, Joseph, 258
Stout, Samuel, 119
Stutler, Jacob, 247

T

Taber, John, 148, 149, 151, 154, 173, 184, 208, 247, 255
Taber, William, 53, 173
Taylor, George, 100, 135
Taylor, James, 100, 128
Taylor, John, 40, 139, 167, 179, 181, 182, 187, 202, 261
(Taylor), John Cooper, 92, 98
Taylor, Saml., 34, 139, 187
Taylor, Walter, 135, 167, 209
Teague, William, 35, 49, 51, 66, 72, 87, 93, 94
Terry, John, 4, 18, 21
Tevis, Robert, 65, 211, 222, 240
Tindall, Jeremiah, 44
Tipton, Betsy, 132
Tipton, Briant, 112, 114, 117, 223
Tipton, Jonathan, 223
Tipton, Shaderick, 37, 40, 45, 46, 48
Thomas, John, 53, 58, 73, 89
Thompson, Elizabeth, 31
Thompson, John, 28, 31
Thompson, William, 15, 18, 28, 46
Todd, James, 47

Todd, Joe, 166
Tovera, John, 37, 76, 179, 181, 204, 208, 219, 211, 212, 214
Trammell, Dennis, 41, 50, 54, 65
Travis, George, 3
Trigg, William, 42, 104
Triplett, John, 1, 4, 6, 142, 246, 250, 252
Trowel, James, 243, 245
Tunnell, Calvin, 246
Tunnell, James, 5, 120, 122, 127, 189, 214, 206, 219
Tunnell, John, 10, 76, 83, 92, 98, 107, 158, 164, 170, 172, 173, 177, 204, 206, 219, 224, 239, 248
Tunnell, Robert, 238
Tunnell, William, 1, 10, 16, 31, 53, 127, 143, 158, 188, 190, 225
Tunnell, William, Jr., 76, 99, 179, 260
Turpin, Martin, 143, 158

U

Underwood, James, 3, 54, 65, 69, 81, 94, 114, 134, 174, 195, 213
Underwood, John, 1, 3, 8, 9, 11, 13, 20, 25, 26, 29, 30, 33, 40, 43, 52, 58, 63, 74, 75, 77, 83, 88, 89, 91, 92, 98, 111, 112, 118, 140, 144, 145, 152, 154, 157, 162, 164, 177, 187, 191, 195, 203, 204, 208, 216, 217, 220, 221, 222, 223, 236, 249, 252, 253, 254, 259, 262, 263
Underwood, William, 1, 2, 6, 9, 15, 21, 22, 23, 25, 44, 79, 86, 91, 113, 148, 176, 186, 196, 197, 203, 208, 214, 218, 223, 241, 248
Usher, John, 255
Ussery, Samuel, 49

V

Vandergriff, Leonard, 142
Vowel, Man Page, 37, 91, 92, 93, 95, 96, 98, 106, 109, 110, 115, 116, 178, 181, 207, 224, 227

W

Walker, Mark, 258
Walker, West, 123
Wall, Daniel, 181, 187, 200, 216
Wallace, David, 5, 120, 122, 123, 125, 126, 186

Wallace, John, 123, 188, 201, 209, 214, 247
Wallace, Samuel, 123,
Warrick (Warwick), John, 34, 76, 99, 240
Watson, William, 23
Weaver, Jacob, 32, 35, 49, 51, 62, 66, 72, 87, 93, 94, 121, 122, 130, 133, 142, 234, 263
Webb, Culberth, 246
Webb, John, 11, 13, 15, 17, 19, 21, 24
Wheeler, Benjamin, 41, 56
White, Abraham, 204
White, Absolom, 81, 108, 178, 189, 204, 206, 217, 216, 233
White, George, 127, 139, 154, 226
White Hugh L., 42
White, James, 174, 243, 245, 250
White, John, 2, 206, 219, 229
White, Moses, 42, 82
White, Philip, 226, 233, 241
White, Robert, 37, 40, 45, 46, 48
Whitson, Charles, 17, 24, 32, 38, 44
Wilhite, Ezekiel, 145
Williams, Alexr., 18, 28
Williams, Edward, 205, 219, 224, 226 229
Williams, Rebecca, 15, 18
Williams, Reuben, 34, 99, 113, 108, 135, 171, 187, 260
Williams, Samuel, 191, 206, 219, 229, 237
Williams, William, 2, 4, 6, 19, 235, 236, 257
Wilson, Bendogo, 226
Wilson, C., 6
Wilson, Jeremiah, 18
Wilson, Robert, 57, 186, 204, 219
Wilson, Thomas, 49, 86, 126, 184, 187, 194, 225
Woods (Wood), George, 70, 112, 121
Woods, James, 204, 206, 209
Wood, John, 130, 132, 133
Wood, Obadiah, 4, 6, 10, 15, 29, 30, 53, 58, 62, 66, 67, 70, 73, 75, 86, 103, 111, 112, 226, 227, 233
Woods, Sampson, 1
Woodward, Edward, 128, 139, 142
Worthington (Wortherington), Betsy, 237
Worthington, James, 102, 105, 107, 150, 210, 235, 237
Worthington, Letty, 237
Worthington, Polly, 237

Worthington, Samuel, 55, 76, 83, 93, 95, 96, 99, 179, 190
Worthington, William, 101, 235
Wright, John, 169
Wright, Thom., 187, 236, 260
Wright, William, 142

Y

Young, Robert, 188
Young, William, 188
Young, Willie, 14, 27, 32, 104, 108, 210, 260
Young, Wiley, 23, 181, 184, 186, 191

ANDERSON COUNTY

COURT MINUTES
1810 - 1813

(P. 1) At a Court of pleas and quarter Sessions opened and held for the County of Anderson at the Court House in Clinton upon the second Monday of October in the year of our Lord One thousand eight hundred and ten.
Present William Underwood, Alexander Gastin, Robert Dew & Sam,l McCoy, Esquires.--

John Underwood Sheriff returned the venire facias, to-wit.- William Griffith, Quin Morton, Thomas Adair, John Gamble, William Boyd, David Stout, John Kitchin, Hance C. McWhorter, Robert Gilbreath, Mitchel Holt, Jesse Martin, William Tunnel, Sen,r, and John Triplet.

Ordered by the Court that John Gamble, John Kitchen, & Michael Holt & William Tunnel, Sen,r be each fined in the sum of two dollars for their non attendance as Jurors to this term

A deed from Sampson Wood, to Isaac Linder was proved in open Court and ordered to be registered.

A deed from John Kerby to Samuel Frost was acknowledged in open Court and ordered to be registered.

(P. 2) Rachel Scarbrough, Administratrix of James Scarbrough, deceased, rendered into Court the amount of sales of the estate of James Scarbrough, deceased:

Larkin Bowling, Esq.	)	Present,
Charles Scarbro	)	William Underwood, Robert Dew,
vs	)	Alexander Gastin
James Stewart	)	William McKamey
John Stewart &	)	& Arthur Crozier, Esq^{rs}
Andrew Stewart	)	

Whereupon came a jury, tow-t, William Griffith, Thomas Adair, William Boyd, David Stout, Hance C. McWhorter, Robert Gilbreath, Jacob Peak, Abraham Jones, Isaac Linder, Isaac Robbins, John Hoskins, William Williams, who being duly elected, tried and sworn, on their oaths do say they find the defendant hath paid the debt in the declaration mentioned as in pleading he hath alledged

Therefore it is considered by the Court that the plaintiff take nothing for his writ but for his false clamour be in mercy and that the defendant go hence without day and recover against the defendant his costs by him about his defence in his behalf expended

An assignment from John White to Craven Johnson on a lot and certificate was proved in open Court

(P. 3) Ordered that James Brumley be bound to James Underwood until he attain to the age of twenty one years, at the end of which time he is to give him a horse, Saddle and bridle to the value of fifty dollars & have him taught to read, write and figure as far as the rule of three, also when he attains the age of twenty one to give one full suit of decent clothes besides his wearing apparel

    A deed from George Travis to John Carwile for three hundred acres of land was proved in open court by John & James Underwood and ordered to be registered

    Court then adjourned till tomorrow at nine o'clock

    TUESDAY, OCT, 9th, 1810

    The Court met according to adjournment. Present, Arthur Crozier, Samuel McCoy & Robert Dew, Esq^{rs}.

    A deed from Patrick Campbell to David Hall for fifty acres of land was proved in open Court and ordered to be registered.

    James Reed returns one thousand acres of land subject for Taxes the present year lying on the North side of Clinch.

(P. 4) William Hogshead) This day came the plaintiff by his proper person
        vs.) and on motion by the said plaintiff it was or-
Larkin Bowling) dered by the Court that Judgement be entered a-
        gainst said defendant for the sum of twelve dollars eighty two and a half cents and also his costs- it appearing to the Court that the said plaintiff paid the above mentioned sum of twelve dollars eighty two and one half cents for security for the said defendant, and be the defendant in Mercy, &c—

William Hogshead) This day came William Hogshead by his attorney into open
    Vs.) Court and ordered a non suit Therefore it is consided-
Thomas Hill) ed by the Court that the defendant recover of the plain-
        tiff his costs about his defence in this behalf expended.

John Terry) This day came the plaintiff by his Attorney, Stephen Heard,
    vs.) and filed his declaration and the defendant having been ar-
Robert King) rested and not appearing tho solemnly called, came not, Where-
    upon it is considered by the Court that Judgement be entered against the defendant. (P. 5)

Andrew Breden)
    vs) Present the same Court as before.
James Leary)

    Whereupon came a Jury (to-wit) Larkin Bowling, Samuel Hall, John Miller, Obediah Wood, Stephen Panky, William Williams, William Boyd, David Stout Hance C. McWhorter, Robert Gilbreath, Jesse Martin & John Triplet, who being duly elected tried and sworn, upon their oaths do say they find he hath paid the debt as in his pleading he hath alledged,

    Therefore it is considered by the Court that the plaintiff take nothing (P. 5) for his suit, but for his false clamour be in mercy, &c and that the defendant go hence without day and recover against the plaintiff his costs by him about his defence in this behalf expended from which judgment the defendant prays an appeal and gives John Sutherland & John Parks as securities on being filed an appeal granted.

    A deed from David Wallace to Robert Dew was acknowledged in open Court and ordered to be registered

A deed from Robert Macey to Stephen Heard was proved in open Court by Charles Macesy & James Tunnell for one town lot & ordered to be registered.

A bill of sale from Thomas Reed to Joseph Sinclair for a negro fellow was proved in open Court and ordered to be recorded. (P. 6)

T. Reed)
  vs) In this case, Charles Whitson surrenders himself in discharges
C. Whitson) of his bail and John Kirby & Stepehn Heard came into open
           Court & undertook for him that he show, pay the costs and damages if there be costs in the action or they would do it for him or surrender his body into custody in discharge of the bond.

Ordered by the Court that John Hoskins be appointed a Constable in Capt. Breden,s Company who then took the necessary oath and entered into bond with John Parks and Andrew Breden prays writs for the faithful performance of the same.

William Underwood Agent for Walter Alves returns five thousand eight hundred, eight and a half acres of Land subject to Tax for the present year

Bumgarner)
  vs) Present Robert Dew, William McKamey & Alexander Gaston, Esq^{rs}.
Wm. Hogshead)

Whereupon came a Jury, to-wit: William Griffith, Thomas Adair, William Boyd, David Stout, Hance C. McWhorter, Robert Gilbreath, John Triplet, Jesse Martin, William Williams, Obediah Wood, Richard Lewallen & Simon Derrick who being duly elected tried and sworn upon their oaths do say that the defendant did not assume as plaintiff hath alledged.

Therefore it is considered by the Court that the plaintiff take nothing for his suit, but for his false clamour be in mercy &c- and that the defendant go hence without day and recover (P. 7) against the plaintiff his costs and charges in defence Expended.

Thomas Parsons proved two days attendance as Constable of the Jury

J. Long & J. Brummitt) In this case the defendant made oath that he had
  vs) discovered that a number of witnesses living in
John Miller) the state of Kentucky would be material in this cause, therefore it is ordered by the Court that Didimus Potestaten issue to take the depositions of James Long & others by giving ten days notice.
The plaintiff then filed an affidavit upon which it is ordered by the Court that they take the deposition of James Lea and James Brummit by giving ten days notice also.

John Underwood) In this case it is ordered by the Court that judgment
  vs) be entered up against said defendant for forty two
Kames Kirkpatrick) dollars and forty two cents. It appearing to the satisfaction of said Court that the plaintiff paid that amount as being security for the said James Kirkpatrick and be the defendant in mercy &c (P. 8)

Administrator of) In this case it is ordered by the Court that
James Cunningham, deceased) John Underwood Sheriff of ----County Expose
  vs) to sale the lands of William Hogshead lying
William Hogshead) upon Clinch river adjoining the land of Ben-

jamin C. Parker and Richard Qualls.

Susannah Delk) In this case the attorney for the defendant entered a
vs) rule to quash the proceedings had before Jaret Harben,
Thomas Reaves) Esqr, and for reason thereof he says that Susannah Delk
is the wife of Jourdan Delk and ought not to have and
maintain her action in her own proper name. Therefore it is considered by
the Court that the rule be made absolute and that the defendant recover
from the plaintiff the amount of his costs in his defense expended and be
the plaintiff in Mercy &c and the defendant go hence without day.

John Sutherlin) The same Court as above.
vs) Whereupon came a Jury, to-wit, Thomas Emmerson, William
John Kirby) C. Mynot, William Kelly, Isaac McMinnis, Samuel Anderson, William Hogshead, George Baumganer, James Leath,
Charles McCormick, (P. 9) John Scott, William Scott & John Brown, who
being duly elected tried and sworn upon their oaths do say that they came into Court and declared that they could not agree in their verdict-by the consent of the parties and with the assent of the Court, one of the Jurors to-wit aforesaid was withdrawn and prevents the rest of the Jurors from rendering their verdict and therefore it is considered by the Court that they are discharged and the cause is continued until the next Court for a new trial to be had thereon.-

The Court then adjourns till 9 o'clock tomorrow-

WEDNESDAY, OCT. 10th, 1810.
The Court met according to adjournment, Present Arthur Crozier, John McAdoo, William Underwood, Esq^{rs}.

John Underwood Sheriff reported to the Court that the jail in Anderson County was insufficient, protested against the same as being insufficient for the safe keeping of prisoners.

(P. 10) The following persons were appointed Jurors to the Circuit Court to be held at Clinton on the fourth Monday of February next (viz) William McKamey, Samuel McCoy, Benjamin C. Parker, Arthur Crozier, John McKamey, Goodlow Dossett, Joseph Gallaher, James Scarbro, Samuel Davidson, William Niccol, William Tunnel, Sen,r., Andrew McKamey, Tobias Peters, Joseph Sinclair, Enoch Foster, Joseph Day, Paul Harmon, John Leach, James Leach, William Scott, Thomas Menefee, Aaron Jenkins, Isaac Norman, John Gordon, Malcom McIntyre, Obediah Wood, Andrew Breden, Johnson Heath, Hance McWhorter, Samuel Dunn, Page Portwood, John McAdoo, Jacob Moser (Hynes Creek), Marmaduke Bookout, William Scarbrough, Elijah Hendon, Thomas Dixon, John Tunnel, John Day & Isaac Linder-

James Harbison, John Stewart) In this cause the defendants being solemnly
and James Stewart) called- came not- Whereupon it is considered by the Court that the plaintiff recover
vs) of the defendants the sum mentioned in the
William Hogshead) venire facias and also the costs attending
the Judgement & be in Mercy &c

A deed from Squire Hendrix to Childress was acknowledged in open Court and ordered to be recorded. (P. 11)

Larkin Bowling J. P. In this case on motion of the plaintiff,s counsel
vs) that a rule should be entered to show cause why a
James Stewart) new trial should be granted- said rule was ordered

to be entered which rule on solemn argument was discharged

A Bill of Sale from Hugh Montgomery to Gilbert C. Russel for three negroes was proved in open Court and ordered to be recorded

Ordered by the Court that James Epperson be Overseer of the Road in place of John Rhea and have the same bounds & hands-

Ordered that the following persons are appointed Jurors to next County Court (to-wit) Amos Dowlin, Paul Chiles, Aron Norman, Thomas Landrum, John King, John Hibbs, Constant Claxton, William Ashlock, George Hawkins, Thomas Reynolds, Peter Clair, James Murry & John Webb, Samuel Dunn, Page Portwood, John McAdoo, Jacob Moser (Hynes Creek).

James Mildom) In this case on motion of the plaintiff,s counsel to amend
vs) the writ- upon solemn argument by the counsel on both
John McWhorter) sides it is ordered by the Court that the plaintiff amend
his writ agreeable to the act of assembly in that case moved and provided (P. 12)

The Court then adjourned till tomorrow nine o'clock.

THURSDAY, OCT. 11th, 1810.
The Court met according to adjournment. Present Michael Clardy, John McAdoo and Arthur Crozier, Esquires.

A deed from John Underwood Sheriff to Mary Kirkpatrick was acknowledged in open Court and ordered to be recorded-

Susannah Delk) In this case it was moved by the plaintiff --- that the
vs) Court reconsider the declaration of this cause as it was
Thomas Reaves) determined upon the second day of this term and upon solemn argument it was granted and upon solemn argument it was considered by the Court that the declaration of the Court as heretofore be the same. It was then moved by the counsel of the plaintiff that he have leave to amend and upon argument it was not granted.

The Court then adjourned till Court in course.

ARTHUR CROZIER, C. A. C.

(P. 13) At a Court of pleas and quarter Sessions opened and held for the County of Anderson at the Court House in Clinton upon the second Monday of January in the year of our Lord one thousand eight hundred and eleven.
Present Arthur Crozier, Douglas Oliver, Joseph Sinclair, and William McKamey, Esquires.

John Underwood Sheriff returned the venire facias, (to-wit) Amos Dowlin, Paul Chiles, Aron Norman, Thomas Landrum, Constant Claxton, William Ashlock, George Hoskins, Thomas Reynolds, James Murray & John Webb.

A deed from Arthur Crozier to David Clarkston was acknowledged in open Court.

John Hoskins Constable of this day offered his resignation which was received by the Court and ordered to be recorded.

A deed from Seth Johnson to Douglas Oliver was proven in open Court by Charles Y. Oliver & Elliot Johnson.

A deed from John Scarbrough to James Scarbrough was proven in open Court by Samuel Scurlock and Tobias Peters.

Ordered by the Court that John Lieb, Junr be Overseer of the Road in place of Moses Roberts and have the same bounds and hands that was assigned to said Roberts.

(P. 14) Ordered by the Court that Craven Johnson be bound as Overseer of the Road to extend so as to include the plantation whereon Willie Young and John Payne now live.

On application of Matthew Heath it is ordered by the Court that S,d Heath be Administrator of the goods and chattels, lands and tenements of Johnson Heath, Deceased, and that letters of administration issue accordingly- said Matthew Heath having given bond and security for the due execution of the same.

Ordered by the Court that John Hoskins have leave to turn the road so as to leave his house on the South side of said road-

On petition of Benjamin C. Parker ordered by the Court that the road leading from John McWhorter,s lane to Eagle Ford be discontinued.

Court then adjourned until tomorrow Nine Oclock.

TUESDAY, JANUARY 15TH, 1811.
Court met according to adjournment. Present John McAdoo, William McAmy and Alexander Gastin, Esq^rs

Richard C. Cobb)
vs) Appeal
Stephen Heard) The Appellant October 1810 dismissed his appeal-At this term the Apeller petitioned for a proceeding to issue to the Justice granting the Judgment which was awarded. (P. 15)

Andrew Braden)
vs) Original Writ
James Leary) This cause was this day dismissed and the defendant assumed to pay all lawful costs.

Smith)
vs) Certiorari
Hogshead) Rule to dismiss the Certiorari and Supersedias

A Deed from Walter Alves to Abraham Jones proven in open Court by William Underwood and John Gibbs.

William Thompson)
vs) Case
Alec & Rebbecka Williams) This day came the parties and also their attorneys-

Whereupon came a Jury (to-wit) Amos Dowlin, Paul Chiles, Aaron Norman, Constant Clackston, William Ashlock, George Hoskins, Obediah Wood, Peter Clair, Page Portwood, John Webb, Jacob Clodfelter & Thomas Menefee, who being elected, tried and sworn upon their oaths do say the Defendants are not guilty as in pleading they have alledged- Therefore it is considered that the defendants go hence without day and that they recover of the plaintiff their costs in their behalf in the suit expended from which judgment the plaintiff prayed an appeal to the next Circuit Court for the County of Anderson.

(P. 16) John Simpkins was recommended & appointed Constable gave bond and security and took the oath prescribed by law.

Ordered by the Court that Matt Heath be appointed Administrator of the estate of Johnson Heath on Thursday the 14th day of February next.

Ordered by the Court that Britton Cross be bound as Overseer of the Road Begin at John Hoskins and run from thence to William Tunnell,s and on Poplar Creek thence down the south side of said creek to Zachariah Key,s, thence across to where Phillips trace intersects the road leading from Clinton to Kingsport from thence to the Pilot Knob thence along the North side of said knob to Clinch River thence up the North side of said river And that said Cross have all the hands in said bounds for the purpose of working on the road except John Hoskins.

Matt Heath, Administratorof the estate of Johnson Heath returned the following inventory of said estate,

3 head of horse Beast	1 drawing knife
3 head of cattle	1 auger
15 head of hogs	1 chest
3 feather beds & furniture	6 pewter plates
2 kittles	1 dish
1 pot	2 basons
1 oven	2 hoes
1 Skillet	1 cowhide
1 plough	2 kegs
1 ax	1 washing tub
1 Pail	1 piggin & churn

Sworn to in open Court

Ordered by the Court that Kinza Johnson support ----- Asherst from this term of Court until the next term

Court then adjourned until tomorrow morning at nine oclock

WEDNESDAY JANUARY 16TH 1811.
Court met according to adjournment. Present Douglas Oliver & Robert Dew, Esquires.

John Reed)
  vs) Case
Charles Whitson) Present Douglas Oliver, Robert Dew & William McAmy, Esquires.

This day came the parties & their attorneys, whereupon came a Jury (to-wit), Amos Dowlin, Paul Chiles, Aaron Norman, Constant Clarkston, William Ashlock, George Hoskins, Thomas Reynolds, Peter Clair, James Murry, John Webb, Samuel Dunn & John Miller, who being Elected tried & sworn upon their oaths do say that the defendant is guilty as charged in the Plaintiff,s declaration and he is not justified as in pleading he hath alleged and they do assess the damages to fifty Dollars besides Costs.

Therefore it is considered by the Court that the Plaintiff recover against the (p. 18) Defendant the fifty dollars damages aforesaid assessed also his costs by him about his suit in this behalf expended and the defendant in mercy &c

A Deed from John Terry to Richard Campbell proven in open Court by William Smith and Thomas Adcock.

Ordered by the Court that Henry Etter be overseer of the road in the place of Samuel Dunn and have the same Bounds & hands.

Ordered by the Court that Robert Dew Coroner be allowed five Dollars for holding an inquest over the dead body of Jeremiah Wilson.

William Thompson)
    vs) Motion for appeal withdrawn
Alex & Rebbecah Williams) Motion for a new trial granted

Richard Lewallen & William Lemar)
    vs) Richard Lewallen by his attorney moved the
Thomas Hart & Quin Morton) Court for Judgment against Thomas Hart, William Lemar & Quin Morton on a Replevy Bond, which Judgment was granted for fifty one dollars and eight cents also the further sum of ---- for costs and charges

On this motion, Court adjourned until tomorrow morning at 9 oclock.

(P. 19) THURSDAY JANUARY 17, 1811.
Court met according to adjournment. Present Arthur Crozier, Douglas Oliver and William McKamey.

David Ayres, Adm^r)
    vs) Stay Bond.
John Sutherland) Judgment on the Stay Bond for Plaintiff rendered by the Court for one hundred and thirty seven dollars and fifteen cents together with eleven dollars six and a fourth cents damage besides his Costs in his behalf expended.

James Long)
    vs) Certio.
Brummett Miller) This day came the parties and a Jury, to-wit, Amos Dowlin, Paul Chiles, Aaron Norman, Constant Clarkson, William Ashlock, George Hoskins, Thomas Reynolds, Peter Clair, James Murray, John Webb, Isaac Frields and William Williams, who being elected tried and sworn upon their oaths do fine for the Defendant.

David Ayres, Adm^r)
    vs) Stay Bond
John Sutherland & A. Crozier) Judgement for the Stay Bond for plaintiff rendered by the Court for one hundred & ninety five dollars and ninety four & one half cents, also all lawful Costs.

(P. 20) A Deed from Isaac Lowe to Willis Leath acknowledged in open Court.

William Hogshead)
    vs) On Motion of Plaintiff Judgment was ordered against Sheriff
Larkin Bowlin) of Campbell County for the amount of the execution originally issued from this Court in this cause to the said ---- as Sheriff of said Campbell County in consequence of said election not being returned in time

William Hogshead)
    vs) On Motion of the plaintiff as security Judgment
John & James Kirkpatrick) was obtained against said John & James Kirkpatrick for one hundred and twenty five dollars

Ordered that a road leading from the top of Chestnut Ridge crossing Clinch River at Robertson's Ferry to the county line be discontinued.

William Hogshead)
    vs) On Motion of plaintiff for John McIntyre Judgment was or-
John McIntyre) dered by the Court for said Hogshead and said McIntyre and for eleven dollars & Costs.

    Ordered by the Court that Hugh Barton dep and John Underwood Sheriff be allowed fifty four dollars each for ex officio services for the year 1810.

John Terry)
    vs) Case
Robert King) This day came the parties and thereupon came a Jury (to-wit)
    Amos Dowlin, Paul Chiles, Aaron Norman, Constant Clarkston, William Ashlock, George Hoskins, Thomas Reynolds, Peter Clair, James Murray, John Webb, Isaac Frields, & John Green who being elected tried and sworn upon their oaths do find for the plaintiff his damages and assess six hundred dollars besides Costs,
    Therefore it is considered by the Court that the defendant recover against the defendant six hundred dollars damages aforesaid assessed also his costs by him about his suit in this behalf expended and the defendant in mercy &c----

Arthur Crozier)
    vs) Case
Richard C. Cobb) Present Wm. Underwood, Alexander Gastin, John McAdoo, Joseph Sinclair, Douglas Oliver & Wm. McAmy, Esquires.
    This day came the parties by their attorneys- Whereupon came a Jury (towit) Amos Dowlin, Paul Chiles, Aron Norman, Constant Clarkston, William Ashlock, George Hoskins, Thomas Reynolds, Peter Clair, James Murray, John Webb, Isaac Frields and John Green, who being duly elected tried and sworn upon their oaths do say that the defendant did assume and take upon himself in manner and form as the (P. 22) plaintiff against him hath complained & do further say the horses named in the plaintiffs declaration was not lent for the purpose of being on horse race as defendant in pleading hath alleged, and he asserts his damage to be one hundred & eighty dollars besides his Costs.
    Therefore it is considered by the Court that the plaintiff recover against the said defendant one hundred & eighty dollars the damages by the Jury aforesaid assessed also his costs by him about his suit in this behalf expended & said Def^t. in mercy &c prays an appeal- reasons filed Bond given & appeal granted.

    John McAdoo returns one hundred acres of land on Clinch River for Elliott Grills for the year 1810.

William Underwood)
    vs) On Motion of the plaintiff,s council it was
Quin Morton & John McWhorter) ordered by the Court that said Judgment be rendered against Quin Morton & John McWhorter

his security for the sum of one hundred and thirty three dollars & fifty cents together with lawful interest since the thirteenth of September eightteen hundred & nine also the further sum of --- for costs and charges about said suit expended.

(P. 23) Ordered by the Court that the following persons take the list of polls and property subject to Taxes for the year 1811, towit, and that the taxes be the same as they were last year-

    Cpt. Park,s Company   Alex^r Gastin, Esq.
    Cpt. Braden,s   "   Arthur Crozier, Esq.
    Cpt. Tunnel,s   "   Sam,l. Galbreath, Esq.
    Cpt. Davidson,s "   Douglas Oliver, Esq.
    Cpt. Scruggs,s "   Robert Dew, Esq.
    Cpt. Morton,s   "   Sam,l McCoy, Esq.
    Cpt. Bruten,s   "   Jarret Harben, Esq.

Ordered that there be paid to Kinza Johnson twenty four dollars for the support of Molly Ashurst being the amount due from July term to the present.

Ordered that the following persons be Jurors for April term next "to-wit" Joseph Robertson, Wiley Young, John Hoskins, William Horton, John Fry, Simon derrick, George Brummet, William Watson & John Smith

FRIDAY JANUARY 18TH 1811
Court met according to adjournment. Present Alexander Gastin, William McKamey & William Underwood, Esquires- (P. 24)

Quin Morton)
  vs   ) Came a Jury, towit, Amos Dowlin, Paul Chiles, Aaron Norman,
Richard C. Cobb) Constant Claxton, William Ashlock, George Hoskins, Thomas
                Reynolds, Peter Clair, James Murray, John Webb, John Claxton & Christopher Bailey, who being duly elected tried and sworn upon their oaths do say they fine for the plaintiff as his damages one hundred dollars also his Costs expended- appeal prayer by the defendant reasons filed bond given appeal granted-the above case was tried by consent of the parties-

Polly Roberts)
  vs   ) Ordered that Polly Roberts be allowed ten dollars from John
John Hibbs) Hibbs annually until a certain child begotten by said Hibbs
           on the body of Polly Roberts arrive to the age of five years and the said allowance to be paid quarterly to John McAdoo.

John Reed   )
  vs   ) The Defendant in this case by his Attorney moved for a new
Charles Whitson) trial and upon argument before the Court it was granted.

(P. 25) Edward Freels)
       vs   O Present Wm. Underwood, Wm. McKamey & Alexander Gastin,
    Joab Dodd) Esquires.
                Whereupon came a Jury (to wit) the same as before, who being duly elected tried and sworn upon their oaths do say they fined for the plaintiff & assess his debt and damages to one dollar and twelve and a half cents also further sum of ---- costs and charges about said suit expended and be the defendant in mercy &c-

Smith
  vs   ) On Certiorari
Wm. Hogshead)

In this case it is ordered that the Certiorari be set aside and a procedento issued the Justice who awarded the Judgment to proceed as if no writs of certiorari had issued

Hugh Barton returns one town lot subject to tax for the year 1810.

John Underwood returns one town lot subject to tax for the year 1810.

(P. 26) John Underwood, Esqr Sheriff of Anderson County returned the list of lands and town lots upon which the tax remained unpaid.

Name	Year	Acres	Tax
James Davidson	for year 1809	540 Acres	$ 2 93-1/3
Jesse Roddy	" 1810	200 "	75
James Davidson	" 1810	400 "	1 89½
Gabriel Keith	" 1810	150 "	58½
Lucy Clack	" 1810	50 "	18½
John McEntire, Senr.	" 1808	5000 "	23
Hugh Montgomery	for 1808-1809-10	two town lots not in Clinton	
	Not given in		double tax

John Underwood Sheriff of Anderson County do certify that the taxes remain due and unpaid on the land & lots as stated above and that the owners thereof have no goods and chattles to distrain so as to make the taxes &c in his county.

Ordered by the Court that William Smith be Overseer in place of Thomas Adcock and have the same bounds and hands &c---
ARTHUR CROZIER   C. A. C.

(P. 27) At a Court of Pleas and Quarter Sessions began and held for the County of Anderson at the Court House in Clinton on the second Monday in April it being the eighth day of April one thousand eight hundred and eleven.
Present William McAmey, Sam McCoy and Joseph Sinclair, Esquires.
Samuel McCoy Esqr returned a list of the taxable property and polls in Capt. Mortins Company and ordered by the Court to be recorded.

Robert Dew, Esqr. returned a list of the taxable property and polls in Capt. Scruggs Company and ordered by Court to be recorded.

Ordered by the Court that John McWhorter be released from his bond given as a ferriage bond.

Ordered by the Court that Boston Ogle be appointed Overseer of the Road in the room of William Thompson, dec,d, and have the same bounds and hands.

Ordered by the Court that Willie Young be overseer of the road in the room of Craven Johnson and have the same bounds & hands.

Ordered by the Court that Elijah Hendon be appointed overseer of the road in the room of David Hall & have the same bounds & hands

(P. 28) Ordered by the Court that John Clarkston be appointed Constable in Capt. Breadens Company who entered into bond and security as the Law requires and took the necessary Oaths &c.

Ordered by the Court that the right hand road leading from Portwood,s to Thomas Menefee,s will be discontinued to where it intersects the Emery road.

    Ordered that Jacob Jackson be appointed Overseer of the Road in the room of Elijah Frost and work on the road leading to Thomas Menefees Mill to the top of the Chestnut Ridge.

John Loy   )
   vs   ) Attachment- Continued.
Lewis Stephens)

William Thompson   )
By his Father & Next friend)
    vs   ) Case
Alex^r R. Williams   ) This day came John Thompson by his attos. moved the Court to be appointed plaintiff in the room of William Thompson, Dec,d, the former plaintiff in this case who gave bond & security for the prosecution of said suit- on which the motion was granted by the Court.

(P. 29) Ordered by the Court that Charles McCormick be allowed two dollars and forty cents for repairing the Court House.

    Samuel Gilbreath, Esqr. returned the taxable property and Polls in Capt. Tunnel,s Company, and ordered by the Court to be recorded.

    On petition of Craven Johnson- It is ordered by the Court that Sam,l Dunn, Constant Clarkston, Charles Shinliver, Kinza Johnson, George Hoskins, John Asherst and William Ashlock or a majority of them be appointed to review the road leading from Coal Creek to Emery, Beginning at the branch at the end of Sam,l. Dunns lane to the fork of the road, where the road turns off to go to Clinton from the Valley road.

John Scott   )
  vs   ) Ordered by the Court that all matters and things in dispute
Obediah Wood) between the parties be submitted to the arbitrament and a-
                  ward of Aron Jenkins, John McAdoo, John Underwood and Stephen Heard or a majority of them whose award shall be made a Judgment of the Court. (P. 30)

John Scott   )
  vs   ) Ordered by the Court that all matters and things in dispute
Obediah Woods) between the parties be submitted to the arbitrament and
                  award of Aron Jenkins, John McAdoo, John Underwood and Stephen Heard or a majority of them, whose award shall be made a Judgment of the Court.

Alexander & Wm. Scott)
    vs   ) Ordered by the Court that all matters and things in
Obediah Wood   ) dispute between the parties be submitted to the arbitrament and award of Aron Jenkins, John McAdoo, John Underwood & Stephen Heard, or a majority of them, whose award shall be made a Judgment of the Court.

    Ordered by the Court that Larkin Bowling be overseer of the road in the room of John Lowe & have the same bounds & hands.

George Baumgardner)
    vs   ) Appeal- This cause is continued until the next term
Arthur Crozier   ) of this Court on affidavit of the Plaintiff.

Ordered by the Court that John Leach be overseer of the road in the room of Benjamin Bowling and have the same bounds & hands.

(P. 31) Ordered by the Court that George Sutherland be appointed a commissioner to settle with the Clerk, Sheriff and Treasurer in the room of Joseph Hart.

John Thompson returns one Black poll as taxable property for the present year as agent for Elizabeth Thompson.

William Tunnel, Sen,r. Agent for Charles Massey returns two hundred acres of land as taxable property for the present year.

Court then adjourned until tomorrow morning 9 oclock.

TUESDAY APRIL 9TH 1811.
Court met according to adjournment. Present Arthur Crozier, William McAmey & John McAdoo, Esqrs.

Quin Morton was qualified as Deputy Clerk to this Court, as the Law directs.

A Deed from Quin Morton to Willoughly Lewis was acknowledged in open Court & ordered to be registered.

(P. 32) Jarrott Harbin, Esq. returned a list of the taxable property & Polls in Capt. Bruton,s Company and ordered to be recorded.

James & William Park)
    vs   ) In Debt.
Benjamin C. Parker   ) John McAdoo, Arthur Croqier and Wm. McAmey, Esqrs.
                          present. This day came the plaintiffs by their atto. and moved the Court to amend the writ by the clerks signing his name officially to the writ, after the words, and of American Independence the thirty fifth, which was on solemn argument granted.

Ordered by the Court that Kinza Johnson supply Charles and Milly Asher with nesessarys of life for the insuing three months.

John Reed   )
    vs   ) Case
Charles Whitson) John McAdoo, Joseph Sinclair, A. Gastin, D. Oliver & J.
                   Harben, Esq,rs.
This day came the Parties by their Attorneys and a Jury (to wit) Joseph Robinson, Willie Young, John Hoskins, Wm. Horton, John Fry, Kinza Johnson, Jacob Weaver, John G. Durrett, George Brummett, John Smith, Lewis Campbell (P. 33) and Charles Y. Oliver who being elected tried and sworn the truth to speak upon the issue joined upon their oaths do say the Defendant is guilty of speaking the words in Manner and form as charged in the plaintiffs Declaration & they assess the plaintiffs damage by reason thereof to one dollar besides costs.
Therefore it is considered by the Court that the plaintiff recover of

the Defendant the sum of one dollar aforesaid assessed by the Jury also the further sum of --- for costs and charges in this behalf expended & the defendant in mercy &c from which judgment the plaintiff by his atto prays an appeal to the next Circuit Court to be holden for the County of Anderson.

Douglas Oliver Esq. returned a list of the taxable property and Polls in Capt. Davidson,s Company.

A Deed from Jacob Linder to John Scott was proved in open Court.

John Underwood, Sheriff of Anderson County, gave bond & Security for the collection of the taxes due for the present year. (P. 34)

Ordered by the Court that Henry Norman be appointed overseer of the road in place of John H. Chapman and have the same bounds & hands.

The following persons are appointed Jurors to the next Circuit Court to be holden for the County of Anderson at Clinton on the fourth Monday of August next. (To wit) Alexander Gastin, Douglas Oliver, David Hall, John Sutherland, George Sutherland, John McAmey, John Parks, John Cooper (over the river), Sam,l Taylor, Alexander Gilbreath, Junr., Abram Hagler, Thomas Gilbreath, John Kirby, Arthur Crozier, Thomas Dixon, Reuben Williams, Saml. Gilbreath, Samuel Dixon, Charles Y. Oliver, Wm. Lamar, John Leib, Junr., Nathan Hail, Jarrott Harbin, Thomas Hart, George Hoskins, Isaac Brazletom, Henry Butler, Anson Manley, Elijah Frost, John Bounds, Michael Clardy, Hardy Medlin, Wm. Sharp, Jacob Linard, Aron Slover, Charles Shinliver, John Warrick, Isaac Brazleton, --Mayberry & Richard Campbell.

Alexr. Gastin, Esq. returned a list of the taxable property & polls in Capt. Parks Compnay.

Adkins)
  vs) Certiorari
Delk) Cont,d on affidavit of the plaintiff.

A Deed from Henry Harless to Jonas Pettit was proven in open Court.

(P. 35) A Deed of gift from Joseph Griffy to James Griffy was proven in open Court by Jarrott Harben.

Jacob Weaver)
  vs) Attachment
W. Teague) In this cause William Teague and Hardy Medlin & Richard Medlin his security came into open Court & acknowledged themselves indebted to Jacob Weaver in the sum of eleven hundred & twenty dollars to be void on condition that the above bound William Teague shall abide by & perform the Judgment which shall be rendered against him in this case or render his body to prison in Execution of the same.

Court then adjourned until tomorrow Morning nine Oclock. (P. 36)

WEDNESDAY APRIL 10TH 1811.
Court met according to adjournment. Present A. Crozier & Jarrott Harbin, Esquires.

Joseph McPeters)
  vs) Certiorari
Dennis Trammel) Rule to quash & continued.

John Sutherland)
    vs   ) Appeal
John Kirby   ) Continued.

John Leach   )
    vs   ) On Motion of John Leach by attorney it appearing to the
Dennis Condray) satisfaction of the Court that an execution did issue in
favor of John Leach returnable to this term against White & Dougherty directed to the Sheriff of Claiborne County-which writ was not returned by said sheriff agreeable to the tener of said writ.

    Therefore it is considered by the Court that the plaintiff recover of the defendant & his securities the sum of forty four dollars for the amount of said execution together with the costs of this motion and the Def,t in Mercy---

(P 37)

Thomas Reavis   ) Certiorari
    vs   ) Continued by
Jourdan & J. Delk) Consent

John Stewart .)
    vs   )Case
John Hoskins)Continued as on affidavit of plaintiff.

James Stewart)
    vs   ) Certiorari
John Stewart) On Motion of the plaintiff by his attorney- Judgment is awarded against John Stewart & his securities for the sum of thirty four dollars which sum said plaintiff paid as security for said defendant.

    Therefore it is considered by the Court that the sum of thirty four dollars aforesaid also the further sum of --- for the costs of this motion and the defendant in Mercy &c---

Andrew Stewart)
    vs   ) Certiorari
John Stewart) Continued

Thomas Adair)
    vs   ) Appeal
John Green) Continued by Consent.

(P. 38) Ordered by the Court that Wm. McKamey Esqr. take a list of the Taxable property & Polls in Capt. Breaden,s Company and report the same to the next term of this Court.

    The following persons are appointed as jurors to the next term of this Court (to wit) Richard Medlin, Hardy Medlin, Robert White, Phillip Harless, Saml Robins, Man Page Vowell, Samuel Robins, Thomas Little, Phillip Seavers, Richard Haynes, William Severs, Richard Haynes, William Seavers, Shaderick Tipton, James Newberry and Robert Lawson.

    Ordered by the Court that George Hoskins be Overseer of the Road in the room of John Tovera and have the same bounds.

James & William Parks)
    vs   ) In Debt
Benjamin C. Parker   ) Oyer prayed of the original writ, plea in abatement filed and Demurrer joinder

Joseph McPeters)
    vs   ) Appeal
J. Reed   ) Continued by Consent

John McPeters)
    vs   ) Appeal
John Reed   ) Continued

(P. 39) John Reed)
       vs   ) Case
   Charles Whitson) On motion of the plaintiff by his attorney a rule is entered for a new trial and granted by the Court & Motion for appeal withdrawn.

John Crozier)
    vs   ) Debt.
Wm. Scott   ) This day came the defendant in his own proper person and confessed Judgment for one hundred and twenty two Dollars sixty two & one half cents and execution stayed by consent until the first day of January one thousand eight hundred & Twelve.
    Therefore it is considered by the Court that the plaintiff recover against the defendant one hundred & twenty two dollars & sixty two and one half cents aforesaid in form aforesaid, also the further sum of ---- Costs by him about his suit in this behalf expended and the defendant in Mercy &c--
    Court then adjourned until Court in course.
                          ARTHUR CROZIER Chairman

(P. 40) At a Court of Pleas and quarter Sessions begun and held for the County of Anderson at the Court house in Clinton on the second Monday of July, it being the 8th day of July 1811.
    Present Joseph Sinclair, Michael Clardy & Jarrott Harben, Esqrs.

    John Underwood, Esquire, Sheriff returns the following persons as Jurors to this term (to wit) Richard Medlin, Hardy Medlin, Robert White, Phillip Harless, Samuel Robins, Thomas Little, Philip Severs, Wm. Severs, Richard Haynes, Shaderick Tipton, James Newberry & Robert Lawson.

Joseph McPeters)
    vs   ) Appeal
John Reed   ) Rule to Quash

    A Deed from Robert Lawson to Joseph Chapman for eighty four acres of land was acknowledged in open Court & ordered to be registered.

    A Bill of Sale from Michael Clardy, Senr. to Michael Clardy, Junr., was proven in open Court & ordered to be recorded.

    A deed from John Lewallen to John Taylor was proven in open Court & ordered to be registered. (P. 41)

John Crozier)
    vs   ) Certioari
Rich C. Cobb) Rule to dismiss the writs of certiorari Suspended.

Benjamin Wheeler   )
    vs   ) Appeal
Thomas & Samuel Dixon) Rule to dismiss the appeal.

Rowland Chiles)
vs) Certiorari
Michael Robins) Rule to dismiss the certiorari & supersedeas

Joseph McPeters)
vs) Certiorari
Dennis Trammel) William Doherty, Bail for certiorari in place of John Reed.

Aron Jenkins)
vs) Stay Bond
John Bradley & Others) Whereas it appears to the Court that heretofore a
Judgment was obtained in the County Court of Anderson
by Aron Jenkins against John Bradley for three hundred & twenty one dollars
sixty seven and one half cents debt & costs upon which execution issued on
the twentieth day of April one thousand eight hundred & ten and whereas on the
28th day of June one thousand eight hundred & ten, John Bradley to procure a
stay of the Execution entered into bond with John Parks and Joel Dyer his Securities and thereupon procured a stay of the said Execution until the twenty
eighth day of June one thousand eight (P. 42) hundred and eleven.
    Therefore on motion of the defendant by James McCampbell his attorney,
it is considered by the Court that he recover against the said John Bradley
and John Parks and Joel Dyer his securities the said sum of three hundred &
twenty one dollars sixty seven and a half cents debt & costs aforesaid also
the further sum of forty three dollars and the interest thereon until this
date-together with costs in this behalf expended and the defendants in mercy
&c.---

William Trigg Exec,r.)
  of William King, Dec.) This day came the defendant in his own proper per-
vs) son as well as the Plaintiff by Samuel Anderson
Aaron Jenkins) his attorney and the said Defendant confesses Jugts.
for Sixty Dollars and the Plaintiff grants a stay
of Execution until the first day of January 1812.
    Therefore it is considered by the Court that the Plaintiff recover of
the defendant the aforesaid sum of sixty Dollars also the further sum of -----
for costs and charges in this behalf Expended.

Hugh L. White &)
Moses White) In Debt.
vs) This day came the plaintiff by Thomas Emmerson his attorney
Arthur Crozier) as well as the Defendant, in his own proper person & the
defendant confessed Judgment for Three hundred and five
dollars and seven cents with a stay of execution for nine months. (P. 43)
Whereupon it is considered by the Court that the Plaintiff recover of
the defendant the sum of Three hundred and five Dollars & seven cents aforesaid together with the sum of ----for costs & charges in this behalf expended--

    A Deed from John Underwood to William McCormick was acknowledged in open
Court and ordered to be registered.

    Ordered by the Court that the bounds belonging to Joseph Robinsons road
on the south side of Clinch River be added to Elijah Hendon,s Bounds- Beginning at the county line on Clinch River thence along said line to where Davis's
road crosses said line thence with said road crosses Bull Run, thence along
said road until it crosses the Emmery road thence up a draft to the Chestnut
Ridge Meeting House to intersect the bounds given David Hall.

Ordered by the Court that Arthur Crozier, John Gibbs & Douglas Oliver be inspectors of the next General Election for this County.
Court then adjourned till tomorrow Morning 9 oclock, (P. 44)

TUESDAY JULY 9TH 1811.
Court met according to adjournment.
Present, Arthur Crozier, William McKamey and Jarrott Harbin, Esquires.

William McKamey, Esqr. returned the Tax list of Taxable property in Capt. Braden,s Company.

John Crozier)
   vs) Certiorari
Richard C. Cobb) This day came the Plaintiff by Thomas Emmerson his Atto. and entered a Rule to dismiss the writs of certiorare & supersedeas and shewing sufficient cause to the Court the Court was opinion that the writs of certioari should be dismissed and presedento awarded and the defendant pay all costs in this behalf expended &c--

A Relinquishment from Jeremiah Tindall and Thomas Gott to James Hill for a negro named Patience was proved in open Court by the oath of William Underwood.

John Reed)
   vs) Case:
Charles Whitson) This day came the Parties by their attorneys- whereupon came a Jury (to wit) Richard Medlin, (P. 45) Robert White, Philip Harless, Saml. Robins, Thomas Philip Severs, William Severs, Richard Haynes, Shaderick Tipton, Robert Lawson, James Newberry and Jacob Jackson, who being duly Elected tried and sworn the truth to speak upon the issue join,d upon their oaths do say that the Defendant is not guilty of speaking the words in manner & form as charged in the Plaintiff,s declaration. Therefore it is considered by the Court that the Pftff. take nothing by his writ but for his false clamour be amerced & the Defendant go hence without day and recover of the Plaintiff his costs by him about his suit in this behalf Expended &c--

Ordered by the Court that Nathaniel B. Buckingham, William Cobb & Rebecca Cobb have leave to administer on the Estate of Richard C. Cobb Deceased who entered into Bond and Security and was qualified as the Law requires, and letters of Administartion issued accordingly.

William Davidson, Senr. returns 392 acres of Land as Taxable for the present year.

A Deed from William Ashlock for 25 acres of Land to John Hoskins was acknowledged in open Court.

Edward Freelds returns five Black Polls and 238 acres of Land as Taxable for the present year. (P. 46)

Henry Adkin)
   vs) Certiorari
Susannah Delk) This day came the parties by their attorneys- Whereupon came a Jury (to wit) Richd. Medlin, Robert White, Philip Harless, Saml Robins, Thomas Little, Philip Seavers, Richard Haynes, Shaderick Tipton,

John Green, James Newberry, & Jacob Jackson, who being Elected tried and sworn the truth to speak upon the issue joined upon their oaths do say they find for the plaintiff the sum of ten dollars besides costs. Therefore it is considered by the Court that the plaintiff recover of the defendant the aforesaid sum of ten dollars also his costs by him in this behalf expended and the Deft. in mercy &c----

William Thompson by his)
  Brother & Next Friend) This day came the defendant by his attorney and
        vs) withdraws his plea of Justification---Whereupon came
Alexr & R. Williams) the Plaintiff by his Attorney and dismisses his action and therefore it is considered by the Court that the defendant recover of the Plaintiff his Costs by him in this behalf Expended.

John Sutherland)
    vs) Appeal
John Kirby) This day came the parties by their attornies and consents to the following Jury (to wit) Lewis Campbell, Andrew Stewart, Ephraim Branham, John Rhea (P. 47) Robert Lawson, Hugh Milican, David Pruet, Joseph McPeters, William Doherty, Henry Adkins, James Todd, and John Hoskins who being duly sworn the truth to speak upon the issue join,d upon their oath do say they find for the Plaintiff the sum of four dollars and sixteen cents. - Therefore it is considered by the Court that the Plaintiff recover of the defendant the sum of four dollars and sixteen cents aforesaid, also his costs by him in this behalf Expended and the Defendant in mercy &c---

    A Bill of Sale from Hugh McGomery to Thomas McCurry was proved in open Court by the oaths of Athur Crozier & Hugh Barton.

Jonas Frost)
  vs) This day came the plaintiff by his attorney & dismisses
Richard C. Cobb) his action and assumes the payment of all costs thereon.
        Therefore it is considered by the Court that the Defendant do recover of the Plaintiff the sum of --- for costs & charges in this behalf Expended &c---

John Loy)
  vs) Continued.
Lewis Stephens)
  (P. 48)
Thomas Adair)
  vs) Certiorari
John Green) This day came the parties by their attos- whereupon came a Jury (to wit) Richd. Medlin, Robert White, Samuel Robbins, Philip Harless, Thomas Little, Phillip Severs, Wm. Severs, Richard Hays, Shaderick Tipton, Joshua English, James Newberry and Jacob Jackson who being duly Elected tried and sworn the truth to speak upon the issue joined upon their oaths do say they find for the Plaintiff and assess his debt to four dollars.
    Therefore it is considered by the Court that the plaintiff recover of the defendant the sum of four dollars aforesaid assess,d by the Jury aforesaid also the further sum of ---costs and charges in this behalf expended and the defendant in mercy &c---
    Court then adjourned until tomorrow morning 9 oclock.

    WEDNESDAY JULY 10, 1811.
    Court met according to adjournment. Present Arthur Crozier, John Mc-

Adoo and Robert Dew, Esquires.

William Scott)
vs) This day came the plaintiff by his attorney and dismisses
John Armstrong) his action and the Defendant assumes the payment of all
costs thereon. (P. 49) Therefore it is considered by the
Court that the plaintiff recover of the defendant his costs in this behalf expended.

Jacob Weaver)
vs) This day came the Plaintiff, by Thomas Emmerson, his attorney-
Wm. Teague) On affidavit moved the Court for a commission to take the deposition of John Mercer, James Mercer, ----Kilgore, who lives or resides in the County of Caldwell and State of Kentucky-
Therefore it is ordered by the Court that the Clerk of this Court issue a Didemus Potastatem directed to any two Justices of the Peace to take the depositions of said witnesses for said County of Caldwell the Plaintiff giving the Defendant Twenty days notice of the place and time of taking said depositions.

A Deed from Samuel Ussery to Thomas Ketcherside for 100 acres of Land was proved in open Court by the oaths of Alexander Gastin & Thomas Wilson.

Ordered by the Court that the present Commissioners reexamine a settlement made by the former Commissioners with the Sheriff for the year 1809 and if they should find any mistake in said settlement the County is to pay the Expense and if not the Sheriff to pay the expense and they report the same to next Court.

Joseph Carter & Others)
vs) Stay Bond
Jacob Butler) On motion of the Plaintiff by his attorney, It is ordered by the Court that Judgment be entered against the Defendant (P. 50) for the sum of Twenty four dollars and sixteen cents which appears to be the ballance together with the Interest thereon up to this day.-- Therefore it is considered by the Court that the Pltff recover of the Defendant, Ansel Manley & John Rector his securities the aforesaid sum of Twenty four dollars and sixteen cents aforesaid also the costs of this motion & Judgment.

Ordered by the Court that George Sharp son of John Sharp be overseer of the road from Byrums fork through the Indian Gap to the forks of the road in place of Adam Cobb and that he have the same bounds & hands.

Thomas Reavis)
vs) Continued on affidavit of the Defendant
Jourden & John Delk)

John Stewart)
vs) This day came the Plaintiff by his attorney and dismisses his
John Hoskin) and assumes the payment of all costs thereon.- Whereupon it is considered by the Court that the Defendant recover of the Plaintiff his costs in this behalf Expended &c -

Dennis Trammell)
vs) This day came the Pltff by his attorney and dismisses his
John Lowe) action and assumes the payment of all costs thereon.

Wherefore it is considered by the Court that the Defendant recover of the Plaintiff his costs in this behalf expended &c- (P. 51)

George Baumgartner)
    vs) Appeal
Arthur Crozier) Cont,d by Consent

John & Arthur Crozier)
    vs) This cause is dismissed at the Defts. costs- There-
John Asherst) fore it is considered by the Court that the Plaintiffs recover of the defendant his costs in this behalf Expended-

John Dew Lessee of)
Arthur Crozier)
    vs) Ejectment
Richard Few with notice) This day came the Plaintiff by his attorney and the
  to Isaac Linder) defend,t being solemnly called came not,- Wherefore
it is considered by the Court that the Plaintiff re-
cover of the Defendant his term yet to come in premises mentioned------
Pltf declaration and also his costs by him in this behalf Expended and the defendants in mercy &c-

Jacob Weaver)
    vs) Att.
W. Teague) Pleas Issue Demurrer & Joinder continued

Henry Adkins)
    vs) This day came the Defendant by her Att° prayed and appealed
S. Delk) filed her reasons entered into bond with security and the
appeal granted.

    Four deeds from John McWhorter to John Crozier was proved in open Court by the oaths of Stephen Heard & Quin Morton. (P. 52)

John Kirby)
    vs) Attachment
Thomas Adair) This day came the Plaintiff by his Attorneys and the Defend-
any being solemnly called came not- Whereupon it is considered by the Court that Judgment be entered against the Defendants by Default
and a writ of inquiry awarded and the cause continued until the next term of
this Court.--

Thomas Adair)
    vs) Certiorari
John Green) On motion of the Defendant by his Att° it is ordered by the
Court that the Plaintiff in this cause pay one half of the
witnesses attendance.

John Underwood Admor)
of John Sartain Dec.)
    vs) This day came the plaintiff by his atto and entered
Quin Morton & Others) a Rule to shew cause why the writ should be amended
by inserting after the words Twenty five cents,
which the word, to him they owe & - after solemn argument it was the opinion
of the Court that the rule should be made absolute.

Joseph McPeters)
   vs   ) Apl. This day came the plaintiff by his attorney and dis-
John Reed   ) misses his (P. 53) Suit, and assumes the payment of all
costs thereon.- Whereupon it is considered by the Court that the defendant recover of the Plff his costs in this behalf Expended &c-

Joseph McPeters)
   vs   ) Appeal
John Reed   ) This day came the Plaintiff by his Attornies- dismisses his action- Whereupon it is considered by the Court that the Defendant recover of the Plff. his costs in this behalf Expended.

    Ordered by the Court that the following persons be Jurors for next term to-wit, John Loy, John Thomas, James Robinson, John H. Chapman, Joseph Overton, James Kirkpatrick, John Fry, John Hackworth, Malon Hibbs, Andrew Braden, Wm. Horton, Obediah Wood & James Ragan.-

    Ordered by the Court that William Tunnell, Senr. Andw. Braden, Reuben Roberts, John Leib, Junr., William Tunnell, Junr., John Tunnell and William Roberts be a jury of review, to view the road from where Wm. Taber now lives down the Buckhorn Valley past Braden,s Plantation from thence past William Tunnell Senr and from thence past where Reuben Roberts lives from thence the best and nearest way to where it will intersect the road leading by William McKamey,s and that they report to next Court.

(P. 54)   John Clarkston proved three days attendance as Constable to the Jury at this Term.

Joseph McPeters   )
   vs   ) Cert,o.
Dennis Trammell) This day came the Plff. by his Attorney and entered a Rule to dismiss Certiorari- The Rule being solemnly argued, was discharged by the Court.

    Ordered by the Court that Thomas Dixon, William Scott, Samuel Frost, John Southerland, John Cooper, Page Portwood and Arthur Crozier be a Jury of review to view and lay off a road leading from some where near Portwood,s field between the Scotts and Frosts and pass the place owned by A. Crozier and from thence the nearest and best way to intersect the road leading from Beaver Creek to John Southerland,s and they report to next Court.

James & Wm. Parks)
   vs   ) Crozier, Dew, McAdoo & Gastin, Esqrs.
Benjamin C. Parker) In this case the Demurrer came on to be argued, after a lengthy and solemn argument, it was considered by the Court demurrer be sustained and the Defendant answer same.

    James Underwood proved three days at October term 1810 five days at January term three days at April Term 1811 and three days at the present Term as Constable to the Court.

(P. 55)   Ordered by the Court that Douglas Oliver, John Parks, William Boyd, Samuel Worthington, Britton Cross & Elijah Hendon be a Jury of review to view a road from the North side of Clinch at Southerland,s ferry the nearest & best way to intersect the Emmery road & they report to next Court.

Ordered by the Court that James Epperson be overseer of the road in the room of John Rhea and have the same bounds.

Ordered by the Court that Thomas Dixon, John McAdoo, Stephen Heard, Charles Kirkpatrick & Wm. Hogshead be a Jury of review to view the road from Clinton to Isaac Mayberry,s ferry to the fork of the road where the road where the road turns off to the Eagle Bent, and report to next Court.

Court then adjourned until tomorrow morning 9 o,clock.

THURSDAY JULY 11TH- 1811-
Court met according to adjournment.
Present Arthur Crozier, John McAdoo & Alexr. Gaston, Esqrs.   (P. 56)

William Scarborough)
    vs) It appearing to the satisfaction of the Court that
Thomas Johnston) A Capias ad respondendum was return,d to the Court
against Thos. Johnston in favor of William Scarborough and the Plff. having failed to file his declaration in due time-
    Therefore it is considered by the Court upon the motion of Saml. Anderson that a suit be entered against said Plff. also Judgment for all Lawful Costs thereon.

James & William Parks)
    vs) Demurrer Joined to the second plea & Issue on the
Benj,n. C. Parker) first plea

Rowland Chiles)
    vs) Cert.
Michael Robins) This day came the plaintiff by his Attorney and entered a
Rule to dismiss the Certiorari- on solemn argument it is considered by the Court that the Certiorari be dismissed and that the Defendant pay all Costs thereon-

Benjamin Wheeler)
    vs) Robert Dew, Alexr. Gaston, Wm. McKamey, Esqrs.
Thomas & Saml. Dixon) Appeal-
This day the Defendant came by his attorney and entered a rule to dismiss the appeal- Which rule was made absolute by the Court. (P. 57) Whereupon it is considered by the Court that the Plff. pay all costs thereon ' a Bill of exceptions was prepared by the Plaintiff and signed by the Court.

Rowland Chiles)
    vs) Att.
Michael Robins) On motion of the plaintiff by his attorney a presendo is
awarded.

Robert Wilson (or Scarborough) returned 120 acres of land as Taxable property for the present year.

Arthur Crozier entered into bond & security for the purpose of keeping a ferry near Clinton.

Robert Dew handed the Court his resignation as Justice Peace which resignation was excepted by the Court and ordered to be entered of Record.

Joseph Hart & Wynn Dix)
vs) Came this day the Plaintiffs by their attorney and
Charles Price) the Defendant being solemnly called came not-
Whereupon It is considered by the Court that Judgment be entered against the Defendant for the debt in the Declaration mintioned also his Costs in this behalf Expended &c-

(P. 58)   Court then adjourned until Court in Course.
                            ARTHUR CROZIER, C. A. C.

MONDAY
State of Tennessee) At a Court of Pleas and Quarter Sessions begun and held
Anderson County   ) for the County aforesaid at the Court House in Clinton
                     on the second Monday of October it being the 14th day
of October 1811-
    Present John McAdoo, Wm. McKamey and Arthur Crozier, Esqrs.

    John Underwood Esq. Sheriff of the County of Anderson returned the following persons as Jurors to this Term (to wit), John Loy, John Thomas, Irvine Robinson, John H. Chapman, Joseph Overton, James Kirkpatrick, John Fry, John Hackworth, Malon Hibbs, Andw Braden, Wm. Horton, Obediah Woods, James Ragan,
(P. 59)
    Joseph R. Henderson Attorney was qualifyed in open Court as the Law requires----

    A Deed from John McGomery Carrick to George Shetler for 640 acres of Land was proved by the oath of James Guthrie one of the subscribing witnesses who also swears that he saw James Hutcherson subscribe his name as a witness to said deed and he believes he is not an inhabitant of this State.

    On application of Isaac Mayberry, it is ordered by the Court that his ferry on Clinch River be disanull,d-

    Court then adjourned until Tomorrow Morning 9 o,clock.

    TUESDAY OCTOBER 15TH, 1811-
    Court met according to adjournment. Present the same Court as yesterday-

    The Administrators of Richard C. Cobb, Deceased, returned the following Inventory of said Cobbs Estate, to-wit,
        17 negroes   28 head of horses   25 head of hoags
    four Beds and furniture, five Bead steads, 1 set of Smiths tools, one desk and Book case, two Tables, one large trunk, Eleven chairs, Two shott Guns, one Rifle Gun, mould & wipers, (P. 60) one Brace of Pistols, one pair of Stalyards, Two saddles, three Bridles, one pair of saddle bags, 1 steel mill, one coffee mill, Two cotton wheels, one flax wheel, one check reel, one looking glass, one box with 14 panes of glass, two pair of plates for a horse, Six books for Acts of Assembly, four Bottles, two decanters, one flask, nineteen plates, two pitchers, eight Tumblers, one Salt Celler, one peper box, one cream pott, one sugar dish, Six Silver Teaspoons, three Tea cups, four saucers, one bowl, 1 wooden ditto, Tea Canister, 1 sugar canister, 5 tin pans, 1 Butter Bason, 1 Tin Buckett, 1 Bread Baskett, 8 tin custard pans, six knives and forks, 1 Pewter dish, 1 cloth Brush, 1 coffee Pott, two Table spoons, 1 Course Comb, 1 fine ditto, 1 candlestand & snuffers, 1 slate, 1 loom, 4 Slays, 2 pr. Harnesses, 1 pair temples, 4 Shuttles, 1 funnel, 1 large Kettle, 3 potts, 3 ovens, 1 skillet, 2 potracks, 3 pr pothooks, 3 washing

tubs, 4 poles, 4 peggins, 2 churns, 1 cooler, 3 soap stands, 2 Hogsheads, 9
Barrels, 1 fat stand, 1 Gudgin, 1 reddle, 1 sifter, 3 syths, 1 waggon, 2
pairs hind gears, 1 pair cart wheels, 1 pair working bars, 1 spool fraim, 21
spools, 1 curry comb, 16 Ducks, 1 pr. cotton cards, 1 grid iron, and two straw
baskets, 2 bells, 1 iron, 1 handsaw, 5 augurs, 3 Gimbletts, 5 ploughs, 2 pr.
Gears, 2 foot addzs, 1 drawing knife, 1 tin ladle, 3 axes, 2 mattocks, 5 weed-
ing hoes, 3 clevises, 2 chains, 3 files, 1 stone auger, 1 stone hammer, 2 pow-
der horns, 1 Blowing ditto, 1 case razors & box, 1 shovel, 1 flesh fork, 1
set fire dogs, 1 Iron ladle, 1 Crock, 2 Smoothing Irons, 1 Loom Brush, 1 nutmeg grater-

(P. 61) TUESDAY 15TH OCTOBER 1811-
1 Iron wedge, 1 grindstone, 1 melting ladle, 1 Small Harrow, 1 Earthen Still

Nath,l B. Buckingham)
William Cobb   ) Admins.
Rebecca Cobb   ) Adminx.
    The Administrators of the Estate of Richard C. Cobb deceased returned
the foregoing Inventory of the property of said Estate within the time limit-
ed by Law-
    Whereupon it is ordered by the Court that said administrator proceed to
sell so much of the Estate as is perishable or may be necessary to discharge
the debts due from said Estate according to Law.

    Ordered by the Court that John McAdoo have leave to Administer on the
Estate of Saml. Dixon, Deceased, who gave bond & security as the Law directs
and was qualifyed accordingly and returned the following Invontory of said
Estate, towit- 4 head horse beasts, 4 Head of Cattle, 1 plough, 1 pair horse
gears, 1 ax, 1 Hoe, 12 head of Hogs, crop of corn quantity not known, 1 silver watch, 1 pistol, 1 Bed &c, 2 Bead steads, 1 pott, 1 trunk, 1/2 dox.
plates, 1/2 doz. knives & forks, 1 tea pott, cups & saucers, 1 Dish, 1 Bason
& 2 Chairs, 1 looking glass, 1 Cotton wheel, 6 table spoons, 1 pr. Cards, 1
iron candlestick, 1 candle moul containing 3 lites, 1 tea pott, 1 pitcher,
1 Bread Basket, 3 bake pans, 1 small drawing knife, 1 umbarella, 1 morocco
pockett book-
    The above is a true Invontory of the Estate of Saml. Dixon-Dec. so far
as has come to my knowledge.
    John McAdoo-Admr. of the Estate of Saml. Dixon, Deceased-

(P. 62) Stephen Heard Plaintiff)
        Against   ) In Case
Wm. Boyd- Defendant   ) In this cause
    This day came the Pltff into open Court and dismisses his suit and the
defendant came into open Court and assumed upon himself the Payment of all
the Costs- Whereupon it is considered by the Court that the plaintiff recover of the defendant his costs in this behalf Expended and said Deft. in mercy &c-

    A deed from Isaac Linder to Arthur Crozier for 132 acres of land was
proved by the oaths of Quin Morton & Benjamin C. Parker & ordered to be registered.

Andrew Stewart)
    vs   ) Certio.
John Stewart   ) A. Crozier, McKamey & Gastin
    This day came the parties by their attorneys and a Jury, towit, Joseph

Overton, John Fry, Malon Hibbs, Wm. Horton, Obediah Wood, Joshua English, Robert Dew, Wm. Boyd, John Leach, Willoughly Lewis, Benjamin Candra, & Jacob Weaver, who being elected tried and sworn the truth to speak upon the issue joined upon their oaths do say they find for the plaintiff Twenty nine dollars and seventy five cents-

Thereupon it is considered by the Court that the plaintiff recover against the Defendant & his securities the sum of twenty nine dollars and seventy five cents with interest thereon at --p. cent from the time of rendering the judgment by the justice aforesaid assessed by the Jury, also his costs (P. 63) by him in this behalf Expended and the Defendant in mercy &c- Upon which Judgment the said Deft. by the attorney filed his reasons in arrest of Judgment.

Thomas Reavis)
vs) Certiorari
Jourden & Thomas Delk) This day came the Parties by their Attornies and the Jury as above except John Claxon in the room of Josua Inglish- Whereupon the Plaintiff by his attorney dismisses his suit-

Therefore it is considered by the Court that the Defendants go hence and recover of the Plaintiff their Costs in this behalf Expended &c-

Thomas Reavis)
vs) Certiorari
Jourden & John Delk) In this cause the plaintiff by his council entered a rule to set non suit aside.

A Bill of Sale from Michael Clardy Senr. to Michael Clardy Junr. was proved in open Court by the Oaths of John Underwood & John Parks two of the subscribing witnesses and ordered to be recorded.

Thomas Reavis)
vs) Forfeiture
Jourden & John Delk) In this cause it appearing to the satisfaction of the Court that George Adkins and Ephraim Branham was legally summoned to appear at this term to give evidence on behalf of the Plaintiff who being solemnly called came not-

Therefore on motion of the Plaintiff by his Atto. (P. 64) It is considered by the Court that the Plaintiff recover of the said George Adkins and Ephraim Branham one hundred and twenty five dollars each unless the said George Adkins and Ephraim Branham do appear at next term of this Court and shew sufficient cause why they did not attend-

Which forfitures is ordered to be set aside on the said Adkins and Branhams paying Costs.

Ordered by the Court that Nathan Hail be overseer of the road from Sacrbrough,s ferry to Douglass Oliver,s.

Ordered by the Court that the property of Saml. Dixon, deceased, be sold on the 9th November next.

Ordered by the Court that the road leading from Clinton to Mayberry's ferry turn out immediately above where Stephen Heard now lives and intersect the old road beyond what is called Crockitts Cabbin and about one hundred yards on the side of a bald ridge according to the Jury of reviews report.

Joseph Doherty)
    vs   ) A. Crozier, D. Oliver & Alexr. Gaston, Esqrs.
Sarah Brinley) Motion for Judgment vs. Constable & securities.
                This day came the plaintiff by Wm. C. Mynatt his attorney and moved for Judgment against John Simpkins constable and (P. 65) his securities and on solemn argument on both sides the Court takes time to advise until tomorrow.

Court then adjourned until tomorrow morning 9 o,clock.

WEDNESDAY OCTOBER 16TH 1811
Court met according to adjournment.
Present A. Gastin, M. Clardy & Saml. McCoy, Esquires.

Joseph McPeters)
    vs   ) Certiorari
Dennis Trammell) Same Court as above.
               This day came the Parties by their attornies- Whereupon came a Jury, to wit, John H. Chapman & others- the Plaintiff because he will not contend comes into Court by his attorney and dismisses his suit- Therefore it is considered by the Court that the Defendant go hence without day and recover of the Plaintiff his Costs about his suit in this behalf Expended &c-

A Deed for 300 acres of Land from Robert Tevis to James Epperson was proved in open Court by the oaths of James Underwood & Joseph Overton two of the subscribing Witnesses and ordered to be registered.

Ordered by the Court that Charles Y. Oliver, Thos. Hart, George Southerland, be allowed Ten dollars & 16 cents each for their services as Commissioners to settle with the public officers of this County for the last year.

(P. 66) Jacob Weaver)
        vs   ) On Demurrer
   William Teague) This day came the Plaintiff by his Attorney and moved the Court for the argument of the Demurrer to come this day on which motion was on argument set aside.

James & Wm. Parks)
    vs   ) Demurrer
Benjamin C. Parker) This day came the Plaintiffs by their attornies and moved the Court for the argument of the Demurrer to come on this day-which motion was on argument set aside.

George Baumgartner)
    vs   ) Appeal-
Arthur Crozier   ) Clardy, McKamey & Gastin, Esqrs.
               This day came the parties by their attornies- whereupon came a Jury, to wit), John H. Chapman, William Horton, Obediah Wood, John Sutherland, Junr., James Kirkpatrick, Willoughly Lewis, Benjamin Condra, John Fry, Edward Freelds, Elijah Frost, Joseph Overton, and John Kitchen who being duly elected tried and sworn the truth to speak upon the issue joined upon their oaths do say they fined for the Plaintiff Eighteen dollars forty five and three fourth cents- Therefore it is considered by the Court that the Plaintiff recover of the Defendant the sum of eighteen dollars and forty five and (P. 67) three fourth cents as aforesaid assessed by the jury aforesaid also his costs by him about his suit in this behalf Expended and the Defendant in mercy &c,

from which Judgment the Defendant prays an appeal to the next Circuit Court to be holden for the County of Anderson- filed his reasons gave bond & security as the law requires and appeal granted.

William Doherty)
vs) Trespass
Joseph McPeters) This day came the Parties by their attornies, Whereupon came a Jury to wit, Malon Hibbs, James Ragan, Henry Goodman, John Hibbs, Jacob Butler, Solomon Fry, Jacob Mayberry, William Lohery, Samuel Frost, Christopher Bailey, Thomas Dixon and Rhodes Stanley, who being duly elected tried and sworn the truth to speak upon the issue joined upon their oaths do say the Defendant is guilty of the trespass &c in manner and form as charged in the Plaintiffs declaration and they assess the plaintiffs damages to fifty cents- Therefore it is considered by the Court that the plaintiff recover of the Defendant the sum of fifty cents aforesaid assessed by the Jury aforesaid also his Costs by him in this behalf.Expended and the Defendant in mercy &c-

William Doherty)
vs) In case
Joseph McPeters) This day came the parties by their attornies and a jury towit, John H. Chapman, Wm. Horton, Obadiah Woods, John Southerland, Junr., James (P. 68) Kirkpatrick, John Hackworth, Benjamin Condra, John Fry, Edward Frields, Elijah Frost, Joseph Overton & John Kitchen, who be- duly elected tried and sworn, the truth to speak upon their oaths, do say the Defendant is guilty of the Trespass in manner & form as the Plaintiff against him hath declared, and they do assess the Plaintiffs damages to fifty dollars.

Therefore it is considered by the Court that the Plaintiff recover of the Defendant fifty dollars aforesaid in form aforesaid assessed by the Jury aforesaid also his Costs by him about his suit in this behalf Expended and the said Defendant in mercy &c from which Judgment the Defendant prays an appeal.

A Deed from Wm. Hogshead to Robert Burton and Archebald Henderson for 85 acres of Land was acknowledged in open Court and ordered to be registered.

Court then adjourned until tomorrow morning at 9 o,clock.

(P. 69) THURSDAY 17TH OCTOBER 1811---
Court met according to adjournment, Present Samuel McCoy, Jarrott Harben & Michael Clardy, Esqrs.

Thomas Shelton)
vs) Appeal
Joseph McPeters) This day came the Plaintiff by his attorney and the Defendant being solemnly called came not- Therefore it is considered by the Court that the Plaintiff recover of the Defendant the sum of forty four dollars sixty two and one half cents besides costs and said Defendant in mercy &c

Aaron Jenkins came into open Court and made oath that that he did not directly nor indirectly give any order or orders to the sheriff of Rutherford County in this State to stay or stop an execution issued from this Court against John Bradley, John Parks, and Joel Dyer, said Bradley,s securities on a stay bond-

James Underwood)
    vs   ) Ordered by the Court that all matters in contraversy be
Isaac Mayberry) submitted to the former arbitrators or a majority (P. 70)
of them in this cause and they report their award to the
next term of this Court which shall be a judgment of said Court.

Alexander Scott by)
Wm. Scott   )
    vs   ) Ordered by the Court that all matters of dispute in
Obadiah Woods   ) this cause be submitted to the arbitrament of the former arbitrators or a majority of them appointed by the
Court to arbitrate this cause and that they return their award to the next
term of this Court which award shall be a Judgment of the Court.

John Scott)
   vs   ) Same order as above—
George Woods)

John Scott)
   vs   ) Same as above—
Obadiah Woods)

Joseph McPeters)
   vs   ) Appeal-
John Reed   ) This day came the parties by their attornies, whereupon
came a Jury, to-wit,

1. William Horton   5. James Kirkpatrick   9. James Sewell
2. John H. Chapman   6. Joseph Overton   10. Christopher Bailey
3. Obadiah Woods   7. John Hackworth   11. Simon Derrick
4. James Ragan   8. John Fry   12. John Kitchen

who being elected tried and sworn the truth to speak upon their oaths do
say they find for the Plaintiff and assess his debt to twenty dollars- therefore it is considered by the Court that the Plaintiff recover of the Defendant
Twenty dollars aforesaid also his costs by him in this behalf Expended and
the said Defendant in mercy &c—

Joseph Doherty)
    vs   ) Motion for Judgment.
John Simpkins &) In this case the Court having taken time to advise and it
his Securities   ) this day came on to be argued- it is considered by the
Court that the motion be overruled from which Judgment
the Plaintiff prayed an appeal filed his reasons entered into bond with security and appeal granted. (P. 72)

Jacob Weaver)
   vs   ) On Demurrer
William Teague) This day came the parties by their attornies and the Demurrer being solemnly argued it is considered by the
Court that the Demurrer be sustained.

    Court then adjourned &c

    FRIDAY 18TH OCTOBER 1811—
    Court met according to adjournment. Present Alexander Gastin, Jos.
Sinclair & A. Crozier, Esqrs.

Thomas Shelton)
   vs   ) Rule to shew cause why the Judgment should be set aside
Joseph McPeters)

James & William Park)
   vs   ) On Demurrer
Benjamin C. Parker) On solemn argument it is considered by the Court that the Demurrer be sustained--

Jacob Weaver)
   vs   ) Attachment
Teague) Continued on affidavit of the Defendant

John Dew Lessee of)
  Jacob Butler   ) Ejectment
   vs   ) This day came the parties by their attornies (P. 73)
Edward Frields) Whereupon came a Jury, towit, John H. Chapman, James Ragan, Obadiah Wood, William Horton, James Kirkpatrick, Joseph Overton, John Thomas, Malon Hibbs, Barnabas Butcher, John Bounds, William Piles, John Fry.
     Jury withdrawn by consent and cause continued.

James & William Park)
   vs   ) In Debt.
Benjamin C. Parker) This day came the parties by their attornies- Whereupon came a Jury, towit,

1. John H. Chapman   5. James Kirkpatrick   9. Barnabas Butcher
2. James Ragan   6. Joseph Overton   10. John Bounds
3. Obadiah Wood   7. John Thomas   11. William Piles
4. William Horton   8. Malon Hibbs   12. John Fry,

who being duly Elected tried and sworn the truth to speak upon the issue joined upon their oath do say the Defendant hath not paid the debt in the declaration mentioned and by reason of the detention of that debt they assess the Plaintiffs damages to four hundred and fifty nine dollars, forty six and one half cents. Therefore it is considered by the Court that the Plaintiffs do recover of the Defendant the sum of Eleven hundred and ninety two dollars twenty seven and one half cents the debt in the declaration mentioned also the further sum of four hundred and fifty nine dollars and forty six and one half cents damages (P. 74) aforesaid in manner & form aforesaid assessed by the Jury aforesaid also their Costs by them in this behalf Expended and said Defendant in mercy &c-

John Reed)
   vs   ) Certiorari
John Loughery) This day came the Defendant by his attorney and the Plaintiff being solemnly called came not- Therefore on motion of the Defendant by Stephen Heard his attorney it is considered by the Court that a non suit be entered, and the Defendant go hence without day and recover of the Plaintiff his costs in this behalf Expended &c-

James & William Park)
   vs   0 This day came the Defendant by James McCampbell his
Benjamin C. Parker) attorney and prayed the Court to grant him a writ of Error in this cause- filed his reasons- entered into bond together with Arthur Crozier, Quin Morton, John Southerland & Thomas Menefee his securities and writ of Error granted.

John Underwood, Admr.   )
    vs   ) On Demurrer-
Quin Morton, Geo. Sutherlin,) On solemn argument the Demurrer was sustained.
Rhode Stanley & Arthur Crozier)

(P. 75)   James Underwood)
              vs   ) Ordered by the Court that all matters in dispute
Isaac Mayberry   ) in this cause be submitted to the arbitrament of
                        the former arbitrators or a majority of them appointed to arbitrate this cause and that they return their award to the next term of this Court, and their award shall be a Judgment of the Court--

John Scott   )
   vs   ) Ordered by the Court that all matters and things in dispute
Obadiah Wood   ) between the Parties be submitted to the arbitrament and award
                of Aron Jenkins, John McAdoo, John Underwood & Stephen Heard
or a majority of them and they return their award to the next term of this
Court which award shall be made a judgment of the Court--

John Scott)
   vs   ) Same order as in the above case.
Geo. Wood   )

Alexander Scott   )
by William Scott)
     vs   ) Same order as in the above case.
Obadiah Wood   )

William Doherty)
   vs   ) This day came the Defendant by his attorney and withdrew
Joseph McPeters) his motion for appeal and prays a new trial in this cause
                 which was granted by the Court.

(P. 76) Ordered by the Court that the following persons be Jurors to the next Circuit Court for this County.

1. William McKamey
2. John McAdoo
3. Geo. Southerland
4. Joseph Sinclair
5. John Tovera
6. William Tunnell, Junr.
7. Henry Farmer (P. Creek)
8. Kinza Johnson
9. Jacob Leynart
10. Thomas Menafee
11. Samuel Frost
12. Aaron Jenkins
13. Joseph Robertson
14. John Leib, Senr.
16 Page Portwood
17. Jacob Butler
18. Samuel McCoy
19. Josua English
20. Robert Lawson
21. Ephraim Branham
22. James Hill
23. Marmaduke Bookout
25. John Warrick
26. Isaac Norman
27. Jacob Moser
28. John Farmer
29. Douglass Oliver
30. Alexander Gaston
31. Jacob Peak
32. Robert Gilbreath
33. Samuel Davidson
34. Joseph Golleher
35. William Gamble
36. Tobias Peters
37. William Scott

    Ordered by the Court that the following persons be appointed Jurors to the next term of this Court.

1. Phillip Severs
2. Josua Frost
3. Richard Marshall
4. John Tunnell
5. William Craighead
6. Britton Cross
7. David Hicks
8. Craven Johnson
9. Constant Clarkston
10. Saml. Worthington
11. John Bounds
12. Phillip Harless

(P. 77)

Andrew Stewart)
    vs   ) Certiorari
John Stewart   ) Motion to arrest Judgment

         This day came the Parties by their attornies and the reasons in arrest of Judgment being solemnly argued it is considered by the Court that they be set aside.

Joseph Carter)
    vs   ) Motion for Judgment
John Underwood &) This day came the Plaintiff by James McCampbell, his attorney and moved the Court for Judgment against John Underwood Sheriff and his securities and it appearing to the satisfaction of the Court that an Execution was issued from this Court at the instance of Joseph Carter against Jacob Butler for the sum of Twenty Eight Dollars & six cents and that said Execution was put into the hands of John Underwood Sheriff of Anderson County and that said Sheriff has failed to return the same- Therefore it is considered by the Court that the Plaintiff recover of the said John Underwood Sheriff aforesaid and -----his securities the aforesaid sum of Twenty Eight dollars and six cents also the costs of this motion

(P. 78) Ordered by the Court that John Bounds have leave to administer on the Estate of Wm. Murphy, deceased, that is remaining in this State, and who was qualifyed and gave bond & security as the law requires-

    Ordered by the Court that the present Commissioners or a majority of them reexamine a settlement made by the former Commissioners with the Sheriff of this county for the year 1809 if they should find any mistake in said settlement the County is to pay the costs and if not the Sheriff to pay the Costs and report to next Court, the Commissioners to give said Sheriff five days notice of the time and place of Examination.

    James Underwood proved 5 days attendance as Constable to the Court at this Term.

    Court then adjourned until tomorrow morning 9 o'clock.

(P. 79) SATURDAY 19TH OCTOBER 1811---

    Court met according to adjournment, Present Joseph Sinclair, Wm. Underwood, Alexander Gastin & William McKamey.

    A deed acknowledged in open Court by John Southerland and George Southerland, and ordered to be recorded.

Isaac Mayberry   )
    vs   ) Isaac Mayberry This day came by his Atto. Stephen Heard
William Hogshead   ) and moved the Court for Judgement against William Hogshead, Moses McWhorter, John Kirkpatrick, and James Kirkpatrick, his securities, and it appearing to the satisfaction of the Court that the said Isaac Mayberry & William Hogshead security did pay the said Hogshead ninety
Moses McWhorter   )
John Kirkpatrick   )
& Jas. Kirkpatrick)

dollars- Therefore it is considered by the Court that the Plaintiff recover of the Deft. William Hogshead, Moses McWhorter, John Kirkpatrick and James Kirkpatrick the sum of ninety dollars aforesaid, to be levied of the goods and Chattles, Lands and tenements of the Defendant Wm. Hogshead and if not sufficient to be found then one fourth part of the said sum of ninety dollars to be levied of the goods and Chattles, lands and Tenements of each of the other Defendants also all Costs- (P. 80)

John Loy)
vs) Attachment
Lewis Stephens) This day came the Plaintiff by his Attorney and the Defendant being solemnly called came not but made default
Therefore it is considered by the Court that the Plaintiff recover of the Defendant the sum of one hundred Dollars the debt in the declaration mentioned also his costs in this behalf Expended &c and said Defendant in mercy &c--

Ordered by the Court that William Boyd be overseer of the ferry road from the Meeting House near John Southerlands to where the said ferry road intersects the Emmery road on the north side of Clinch River and have John Southerlands hands and his own.

Ordered by the Court that Jacob Jackson be overseer of the road from the upper end of Crozier,s lane to the ferry bank in place of that part of the road leading to the Eagle Bent ford which has been disannulled-

Court then adjourned until Court in course---
ARTHUR CROZIER- C. A. C.

(P. 81)
State of Tennessee) At a Court of Pleas and Quarter Sessions began and
Anderson County) held for the County of Anderson at the Court House in
Clinton on the second Monday of January, it being the 13th day of January Instant 1812.
Present William McKamey, Douglass Oliver and Joseph Sinclair, Esquires.

Ordered by the Court that Carter Hendrix be permitted to retail Spirits for the Term of Twelve months in the County of Anderson he having given bond and security as the Law directs-

Ordered by the Court that Absolom White be Overseer of the road in the room of William Smith and have the same bounds & hands.

Ordered by the Court that James Underwood be appointed Constable in Captain Scruggs,s Company who entered into bond with security and was qualified accordingly.

Ordered by the Court that John Gamble be overseer of the road in the room of Reuben Gholson and have the same bounds and hands-

Ordered by the Court that Thomas Parsons be appointed Constable in Captain Davidsons Company who entered into bond with Security & was qualified accordingly.

(P. 82) MONDAY JANUARY 13TH 1812.
Ordered by the Court that John Hoskins be overseer of the road in the room of John Leib, Junr and have the same bounds and hands.

Ordered by the Court that Simeon Smith be overseer of the road in the room of Britton Cross and have the same bounds and hands.

A Plat and Certificate of an entry of Land for fifty acres of Land the Transfer of the same from William Gardenhire to John Gamble was proved in open Court by the oaths of Moses White and James McCampbell, the Subscribing witnesses thereto.

The Transfer of a Plat and Certificate for fifty acres of land from William Gardenhire to Moses White was proved in open Court by the oaths of John Gamble and James McCampbell the Subscribing Witnesses thereto—

A deed for 120 acres of Land from George Gallaher to Mary Miller was proved in open Court by the oaths of Douglass Oliver and John G. Durrett, and ordered to be registered—

Samuel Davidson, Edward Hawkins and Quin Morton was qualifyed according to Law having produced their Commissions to the Court as Justices of the peace for the County of Anderson. (P. 83)

Jacob Peak)
vs) Appeal
Stephen Heard) Rule to Quash the proceedings of the Justice of the Peace.

John Underwood returned the following Venire Facias, towit, Philip Severs, Josua Frost, Richard Marshall, William Craighead, Britton Cross, Craven Johnson, Constant Claxon, Samuel Worthington, John Tunnell, David Hicks, John Bounds, & Philip Harless, (out of which was not summoned by the sheriff) the following persons, towit, John Tunnell, David Hicks, John Bounds & Philip Harless—

Isaac Low assignee of)
Willis Leath)
vs) Debt.
William Boyd & Luncford) This day came the Defendant in his own proper per-
Oliver) son and confessed Judgment for seventy two dollars
and Twenty three cents besides costs——Whereupon tho the Plaintiff by his attorney stays Execution six months.
Therefore it is considered by the Court that the Plaintiff recover of the Defendant the sum of Seventy two dollars and twenty three cents aforesaid also his costs by him about his suit in this behalf expended and the Defendant in mercy &c——

Nathaniel B. Buckingham one of the administrators of the Estate of Richard C. Cobb Deceased returned the amount of the sales of the perishable property of said Estate which amounts to thirteen hundred Eighty Eight dollars and Eighty six cents as appears from (P. 84) said return, which return was signed as follows towit—
      Errors Excepted—
       Natl B Buckingham
       William Cobb
       Rebecca Cobb

Ordered by the Court that the road leading to Kentucky by Piles Turnpike continue to go as does at present except the part that goes through old Mr. Butler,s field which part is to go the best way leaving his house to the left hand, the owner of said Plantation aforesaid to make this alteration by order of the Court—

Court then adjourned until 9 O'clock Tomorrow morning.

(P. 85) TUESDAY JANUARY 14TH 1812--
Court met according to adjournment- Present Samuel Gilbreath, Joseph Sinclair, Saml. Davidson, Edward Hawkins, Alexr. Gastin, & Arthur Crozier-Esquires---

Robert H. Adams, Esq. produced his License and was qualifyed as an Attorney---

A deed from Douglas Oliver to Charles Y. Oliver for 100 acres of Land was acknowledged in open Court and ordered to be registered-

James Robertson was excused by the Court for not attending as Juror at last Term-

A deed from Douglas Oliver to Charles Y. Oliver for 100 acres of Land was acknowledged in open Court and ordered to be registered-

Charles Y. Oliver was elected Sheriff for the County of Anderson for the Two succeeding years who entered into Bond and Security and was qualifyed accordingly.--

Samuel Anderson was Elected Solicitor for the County Court of Anderson and was qualifyed accordingly.---

Daniel Leib was Elected Coroner for the County of Anderson for the two succeeding years who entered into bond and security and was qualifyed accordingly.-

Ordered by the Court that Ephraim Branham be released from the payment of any Costs on a <u>forfiture</u> taken against him at last Term of this Court, which forfiture was set aside by said Branhams paying Costs.

(P. 86) A deed from Layton Smith to Leonard Coffin for 200 acres of Land was proved in open Court by the oaths of Alexander Gastin, Samuel Marshall and Thomas Wilson the Subscribing Witnesses thereto and ordered to be registered--

Ordered by the Court that George Hoskins be appointed Constable in Captain Tunnells Company, who entered into bond with Security and was qualifyed accordingly.

Samuel McCoy one of the Justices of the Peace for the County of Anderson gave into Court his resignation which was received-

Ordered that all the hands from the lower end of John Haskin,s field work on the road that he is appointed Overseer of--

Alexander Scott by)
William Scott   ) This cause is continued by consent, on the Rule of
     vs   ) next Court.
Obadiah Woods   )

Joseph McPeters
     vs
John Reed   Appl) Douglas Oliver, Arthur Crozier, William Underwood, and

Edw. Hawkins, Esqrs.- Present-

This day came the Plaintiff by Stephen Heard Esquire, his attorney, and moved the Court for judgment against the Defendant by default.

On solemn argument the said Plaintiff was (P. 87) overruled by the Court- Whereupon it is considered by the Court that the Plaintiff take nothing by his motion but for his false clamor be in mercy and that the Defendant go hence without day and recover of the Plaintiff the Costs of his motion--

Ordered by the Court that the following tax be laid for the present year.

	Cents
Towit on every Poll	31-1/4
" " every hundred acres of land	31-1/4
" " each Town Lott	31-1/4
" " Each Black Poll	62-1/2

And on every stud horse the season of one mare

Court then adjourned until tomorrow morning 9 o'clock--

WEDNESDAY JANUARY 15TH 1812.

Court met according to adjournment- Present, William McKamey, Samuel Gilbreath and Quin Mortin, Esquires--

Charles McCormick was appointed Constable in the Town Company who gave bond & security and was qualifyed accordingly--

Ordered by the Court that Charles McCormick attend as Constable to the Court for the present Term--   (P. 87)

Jacob Weaver)
   vs   ) Attachment
William Teague) This cause is laid over until tomorrow by consent--

Willaim Doherty)
   Vs.   ) Case
Joseph McPeters) Continued on affidavit of Defendant.--

John Kirby)
   vs   ) Attachment, on writ of Enquiry
Thomas Adair) This day came the parties by their Attornies, -Whereupon came
              a Jury towit, Wm. Craighead, Craven Johnson, William Doherty,
John Kitchens, John Shepard, John Rhea & Jacob Jackson, who being duly sworn diligently to enquire into the Damages in this Case upon their oath do say that the Plaintiff hath sustained one hundred and twenty three dollars damages-
Therefore it is considered by the Court that the Plaintiff do recover of the Defendant the sum of one hundred & twenty three dollars aforesaid assessed by the Jury aforesaid also his Costs by him about his suit in this behalf expended and the Defendant in mercy- &c.-

John Underwood, Admr.   )
        vs   ) In Debt.
Quin Morton, Rhode Stanley,   ) This day came the parties by their attornies-
George Sutherland and   ) whereupon came a Jury, to wit, William Craig-
Arthur Crozier   ) head, Craven Johnson, Constant Clarkston, Rich-
                                  ard Cravens, William Doherty, John Kitchens,
John Shepard, John Rhea, Jacob Jackson, Joshua Frost, David Prewet and John Reed who being duly Elected tried and sworn the truth to speak upon the issue

Joined upon their oaths do say the Defendants have paid Twelve Dollars and Eighty two cents part of the debt in the declaration mentioned and that they have not paid Two hundred and Eighty Eight dollars and forty three Cents the residue of said debt in said Declaration mentioned and they assess the Plaintiff,s damages by reason of the detention thereof to thirteen dollars- Therefore it is considered by the Court that the Plaintiff do recover of the Defendants the sum of Two hundred and Eighty Eight dollars and forty three cents the residue of the debt in the declaration mentioned also the damages aforesaid in form aforesaid assessed by the Jury aforesaid besides his Costs in this behalf Expended and said Defendants in mercy &c writ of error prayed to the Circuit Court for this County.

John McAdoo, Admr. of the Estate of Saml. Dixon, Dec,d. returned the amount of sales of said Estate which was two hundred dollars and twenty five cents.

(P. 89) Ordered by the Court that John Underwood be entitled to the following allowances towit:

For furnishing Locks for the P. Jail	$18..00
For Ex Officio Services for the year 1811--	50..00
Summoning & furnishing a guard over John Thomas	2..50
	$70..50

Ordered by the Court that the Clerk of this Court be allowed Fifty dollars for his ex officio services for the year 1811-

An additional Inventory of the Estate of Richard C. Cobb, Deceased, was returned to this Court by Nathaniel B. Buckingham one of the Admrs of said Estate- of Twenty five head of hogs.

Henry Farmer)
vs) In case
John Patterson) This day came the Plaintiff in his own proper person and dismisses his suit and assumes upon himself the payment of all Costs thereon--Therefore it is considered by the Court that the Defendant recover of the Plaintiff his costs in this behalf expended &c-

The last Will and Testament of Mary Mills Deceased was proved in open Court as the law requires and ordered to be recorded.- (P. 90)

Jacob Butler Lessee)
vs) In Ejectment
Edward Frields) This day came the Parties by their Attornies.,
Whereupon came a Jury towit, William Craighead, Craven Johnson, Constant Claxton, Richard Cravens, Wm. Doherty, John Ketchins, John Shepard, John Rhea, Joshua Frost, David Prewitt, John Reed and Jacob Jackson, who being Elected tried and sworn the truth to speak upon the Issue Joined upon their oaths do say the Defendant is guilty of the Trespass in the Plaintiff,s declaration of Ejectment mentioned and they assess the Plaintiffs damages to six cents besides Costs- Therefore it is considered by the Court that the Plaintiff do recover of the Defendant his term yet to come in the premises in the Pltfs declaration mentioned also --his damages aforesaid assessed by the Jury aforesaid & also his Costs by him about his suit in this behalf Expended and the Defendant in mercy &c-

A Bill of Sale from George Mayberry to William Boyd was proved in open Court by Edward Frields & ordered to be recorded-

John Hoskins and George Hoskins came into open Court and executed their bond as Securities for Rebecca Ashlock, to keep the County from being at any expence, or charges for a Bastard child she has-

(P. 91) John Underwood, Admr.)
            vs   ) In this cause the Defendants Except Rhode
    Quin Morton & Others   ) Stanley prayed a Writ of Error in this
                                             cause who gave bond and Security and writ
of Error allowed by the Court and the said Rhode Stanley after being Solemnly summoned to join with the other Defendants in prosecuting said Writ of Error and wholly refusing so to do--Therefore it is considered by the Court that the said Rhode Stanley be severed from the rest of the Defendants and they be permitted to prosecute said writ of Error themselves-

William Roberts)
    vs   ) In case
John Clarkston) This day came the Plaintiff by his attorney and dismisses
                   his suit and assumes upon himself the payment of all Costs-
Therefore it is considered by the Court that the Defendant recover of the Plaintiff his costs in this behalf expended.-

Ordered by the Court that the following persons take a list of Taxables &c required by the late Act of the Assembly- towit-

Arthur Crozier	for	Capt. Marshall Company
Quin Morton	"	the town company
John McAdoo	"	Scruggs Company
Saml. Gilbreath	"	Tunnells "
Saml. Davidson	"	Davidson Company
William Underwood		Mortin "

(P. 92) Ordered by the Court that the following persons attend as Jurors at next Term towit-

1. Samuel Dunn
2. Man Page Vowel
3. John Cooper (Taylor)
4. Jacob Clodfelter
5. Britton Cross
6. James Hicks
7. Robert Hays
8. Jacob Leib, Junr.
9. Isaac Brazleton
10. John Tunnell
11. Collins Roberts
12. Zachariah Key
13. Andw. McKamey
14. William Russell
15. Wm. Lamar
16. John Fry
17. Isaac Mayberry
18. John Garner
19. David Hall
20. Henry Norman
21. John Underwood
22. John Parks
23. Wm. Griffith
24. Isaac Loe
25. Henry Peters
26. George Shetter

Court then adjourned until tomowwow morning 9 o'clock.

THURSDAY JANUARY 16TH 1812-
Court met according to adjournment- Present Joseph Sinclair, Samuel Gilbreath and Quin Morton, Esquires-

Joseph Hart)
   vs)   Motion for Judgment
William Hogshead) This day came the Plaintiff by his attorney, and moved
moved the Court for Judgment against the Defendant for
Eight dollars Twelve and one half cents paid by him as Security for said Defendant (P. 93) and said Plaintiff produced a receipt from the clerk of this county for the amount of Eight dollars Twelve and one half cents aforesaid.

    Therefore it is considered by the Court that the Plaintiff do recover of the Defendant the sum of Eight dollars Twelve and one half cents <u>togather</u> with the Costs of this motion & the defendant in mercy &c-

Jacob Weaver)
   vs)   Attachment
William Teague) This day came the parties by their attornies- Whereupon came
a Jury, towit, Joshua Frost, Richard Marshall, William Craighead, Craven Johnston, Constant Claxton, Samuel Worthington, Jacob Peak, John Cooper, Jacob Mayberry, Man Page Vowell, Wm. Severs, Isaac Mayberry, who being duly Elected tried and sworn upon their oaths do say that the Defendant did assume upon himself in manner and form as the Plaintiff is his declaration hath Complained and they assess the Plaintiffs damages to Five hundred and ninety nine dollars and thierty two cents besides Costs.

    Therefore it is considered by the Court that the Plaintiff do recover of the Defendant five hundred and ninety nine dollars & thirty two cents the damages aforesaid assessed by the Jury aforesaid in form aforesaid, also his costs by him about his suit in this behalf expended & the Defendant in mercy &c (P. 94) from which Judgment the Defendant prayed an appeal, tendered security which was not declared good by the Court-

Jacob Weaver)
   vs)   Attachment
William Teague) On motion of James Underwood by his attorney it is ordered
by the Court that James Underwood aforesaid be allowed fourteen dollars for keeping two horses Twenty eight days and recover the same of said Teague--

    Ordered by the Court that Robert Gilbreath be a Commissioner to settle with the officers of this County in the room of Charles Y. Oliver.

    Ordered that the Commissioners appointed to settle with the County Officers, be the Commissions to settle with the Town Commissioners.

    Ordered by the Court that Micajah Frost be allowed three dollars for killing a wolf agreeable to an act of assembly.

John Claxton)
   vs)   Certiorari
Wm. Lohery) Continued by consent

Same)
   vs)   Certiorari
Jacob Mayberry) Cont. by consent

David Prewet)
   vs)   Case continued by consent
John Simpkins)

Smith & Neilson surviving)
partners of Wm. King Decd.)
  vs   ) Continued by consent
Quin Morton   )

Jacob Peak)
  vs   ) Certiorari
Stephen Heard) Continued by consent

Joseph Hart)
  vs) Appeal
John Hibbs) This day came the parties by their attornies- Whereupon came
      a Jury towit. Joshua Frost, Richard Marshall, Wm. Craighead, Craven Johnson, Constant Claxton, Samuel Worthington, Jacob Peak, John Cooper, Jacob Mayberry, Man Page Vowell, William Severs & William Bounds, who being duly Elected tried and sworn the truth to speak upon the issue Joined upon their oath do say that they find for the Plaintiff thirty four dollars twenty one and one fourth cents-

  Therefore it is considered by the Court that the Plaintiff do recover of the Defendant thirty four dollars twenty one & one fourth Cents aforesaid also his costs by him about his suit in this behalf expended and the Defendant in mercy &c--

(P. 96) Joseph Hart)
    vs) Appeal
  John Hibbs) Rule for a new trial

William Trigg for the use)
of Barton & Sutherland)
  vs   ) Appeal-
Andrew Stewart   ) This day came the parties by their attornies-
      Whereupon came a Jury towit, Joshua Frost, Richard Marhsall, Wm. Craighead, Craven Johnson, Constant Clarkston, Samuel Worthington, Jacob Peak, John Cooper, Jacob Mayberry, Man Page Vowell, William Severs and William Bounds, who being duly Elected tried and sworn the truth to speak iupon the issue joined upon their oaths do say they find for the Plaintiff five dollars and ninety five cents besides Costs-

  Therefore it is considered by the Court that the Plaintiff do recover of the Deft. five dollars and ninety five cents aforesaid also his Costs in this behalf expended and said Defendant in mercy --from which Judgment the Defendant prayed a new trial. On solemn argument a new trial was granted by the Court.

  James Underwood proved two days attendance as constable to the Court at this Term.

  Thomas Parsons proved Two days attendance as Constable to the Court at this Term.

Thomas McClain)
  vs   ) Certiorari
Quin Morton) Rule to dismiss certiorari cont.

(P. 97) Court adjourned until Tomorrow morning 9 O'clock.

  FRIDAY JANUARY 17TH 1812---
  Court met according to adjournment.

Present A. Crozier, John McAdoo, and Quin Morton, Esquires.- also Joseph Sinclair & Samuel Gilbreath.

Ordered by the Court that that the sheriff notify Thomas Parsons to attend next Circuit Court and next County Court as Constables of said Courts.-

Joseph Hart)
   vs) Motion
William Hogshead) Rule to shew cause why the Judgment be set aside.

ARTHUR CROZIER C. A. A.

(P. 98) State of Tennessee)
    Anderson County) At a Court of Pleas & quarter Sessions began and held at the Court House in Clinton on the second Monday of April- it being the 13th Instant 1812.

Present Arthur Crozier, Wm. McKamey, Joseph Sinclair & William Davidson, Esquires.

Charles Y. Oliver Esquire Sheriff returned the following Venire Facias for this Term towit.

1. Saml. Dunn
2. Man Page Vowel
3. John Cooper (Taylor)
4. Jacob Clodfelter
5. Britton Cross
6. Robert Hays
7. John Leib, Junr.
8. Isaac Brazleton
9. John Tunnell
10. Collins Roberts
11. Zachariah Key
12. Andrew McKamey
13. William Russell
14. Wm. Lamar
15. John Fry
16. Isaac Mayberry
17. John Garner
18. David Hall
19. Henry Norman
20. John Underwood
21. John Parks
22. William Griffith
23. Isaac Low
24. Henry Peters
25. George Shetter

Out of which was drawn as Grand Jurors, towit,

1. John Underwood (foreman)
2. Samuel Dunn
3. Britton Cross
4. John Leib, Junr.
5. John Tunnell
6. Zachariah Key
7. William Russell
8. William Lamar
9. Isaac Mayberry
10. John Garner
11. David Hall
12. William Griffith
13. Henry Peters

(P. 99) MONDAY APRIL 13TH, 1812—

Ordered by the Court that Robert H. Adams be appointed <u>Soliscitor</u> Pro Tem for this Term---

Isaac Brazleton and George Shetter were excused from serving as Jurors at this Term----

Ordered that Elijah Whitton be overseer of the road in the room of John Thomas & have the same bounds & hands--

Ordered that Saml. McCoy, George McCray, John Worrick, Christopher Baker, Jacob Stout, John Philpot and David Stout, be appointed a Jury of review to view the road leading from Cloud,s ford on Clinch river to the Knox County line that part of the road from the top of the Chesnut ridge to the line aforesaid and report to next Court.

Ordered by the Court that William Scott be overseer of the road in the room of Jacob Jackson and have the same bounds & hands.

Ordered by the Court that John Cooper be overseer of the road in the room of Elijah Hendon and have the same bounds & hands.

Ordered by the Court that John Sutherland Senr., William Boyd, Saml. Worthington, Abraham Hagler, William Nickle, Matthew Hawkins, Edward Hawkins, William Tunnell Junr., and Tobias Peters be appointed a Jury of review to view the roads, towit, from the top of the black oak ridge near Reuben Williams, field to where the said (P. 100) two roads intersect and report to next Court—

Samuel Gilbreath and Quin Morton, Esquires, returned the Tax lists for the present year.-

Ordered by the Court that William Severs be overseer of the road from Shinlivers machine to James Taylors and the following persons to work on said road for the Term of six months, Aron Slover, ----Beach, Saml. Robbins, Isaac Robbins, James Still, Jeremiah Hibbs, George Taylor, William Craighead, ---- Hall, William Edwards, James Shepherd, and ----Deaton.

The Jail of Anderson County reported by the Commissioners in repair and the key delivered to the Sheriff of said County.

Court then adjourned until Tomorrow morning 9 o'clock.

TUESDAY APRIL 14TH, 1812—
Court met according to Adjournment. Present Arthur Crozier, Joseph Sinclair, Michael Clandy & Samuel Davidson, Esquires-----

William Doherty)
    vs   ) Case- continued on affidavit of the plaintiff
Joseph McPeters)

John Clarkston)
    vs   ) Certiorari
William Lohery) This day came the Parties by their attornies- whereupon
                came a Jury (Rmc101) towit, Charles Kirkpatrick, John Hoskins, Jacob Clodfelter, James Hicks, Robert Hays, John Fry, Michael Robbins, John Kirby, John Rhea, William Worthington, Julus Millikin, & Hugh Milliken who being duly elected tried and sworn the truth to speak upon the issue joined upon their oaths do say they find for the Defendant-
Therefore it is considered by the Court that the Plaintiff take nothing by his action but for his false clamour be in mercy &c and that the Defendant go hence without day and recover of the Plaintiff his costs by him about his defence in this behalf expended- from which Judgt the Pltf prays an appeal-

Samuel Davidson Esquire returned a list of the Taxable property & polls in Capt. Davidsons company-

John Clarkston)
    vs   ) Certiorari
Jacob Mayberry) This day came the Plaintiff by his Attoney and dismisses
his suit & assumes upon himself one half of the costs and
the defendant comes into Court by his attorney and assumes upon hiself the
payment of the other half of the Costs.

    Therefore it is considered by the Court that the Plaintiff pay one half
of the Costs and the Defendant pay the other half of the Costs in this behalf expended--

(P. 102) State   )
          vs   ) Presentment
  James Worthington) This day came the Defendant and Britton Cross and
acknowledged themselves Indebted to the State of
Tennessee in the sum of one hundred Dollars each to be levied of their respective goods and chattles Lands- Tho to be void on condition that said
James Worthington doth make his personal appearance from day to day at this
Term to answer a charge of the State preferred by the Grand Jury against him
and not depart the Court without leave-

Same)
  vs) This day came Britton Cross & Zachariah Key into open Court and ac-
Same) knowledged themselves Indebted to the State of Tennessee in the sum
of Twenty five dollars each to be levied of their respective goods
& chattles, lands & Tenements- To be void on condition they make their personal appearance from day to day at this Term to give evidence on behalf of
the State in the above case and not depart the Court without leave--

Same   )
  vs   ) Presentment
Willis Leath) This day came Willis Leath, Collins Roberts, and Isaac Low-
and acknowledged themselves Indebted to the State of Tennessee
in the sum of one hundred dollars each to be levied of their respective goods
and chattles, lands & Tenements, (P. 103) To be void on condition the said
Willis Leath doth make his personal appearance from day to day at this Term
to answer a charge of the State preferred by the Grand Jury against him and
not depart hence without leave of the Court-

State   )
  vs   ) This day came Henry Peters into open Court and acknowledged
Willis Leath) himself Indebted to the State of Tennessee in the sum of fifty dollars to be levied of his goods & chattles &c- To be void
on Condition that he make his personal appearance from day to day at this
term to give evidence on behalf of the State against Willis Leath and not depart the Court without leave-

David Prewit)
    vs   ) Case
John Simpkins) This day came the Parties by their Attornies, Whereupon came
a Jury (towit). Aron Jenkins, John Cooper, Collins Roberts,
Isaac Low, Andrew McKamey, Wm. Hogshead, Obadiah Wood, Richard Medlin, James
Childress, Willis Leath, Anderson Frields, & John Scott who being duly elected tried and sworn the truth to speak upon the issue joined upon their oaths
do say they find for the Plaintiff and assess his damage to Eleven dollars
& fifty cents besides Costs-

Therefore it is considered by the Court that the plaintiff do recover of the defendant (P. 104) Eleven dollars & fifty cents, the damages aforesaid assessed by the Jury aforesaid, also his Costs by him about his suit in this behalf expended and the Defendant in mercy &c-

William Trigg for the use of)
Barton & Sutherland   ) Appeal
         vs   ) This day came the Parties by their Attornies
Andrew Stewart   ) and a Jury towit James Kirkpatrick, James
                              Hicks, Charles Kirkpatrick, Julus Milliken,
Hugh Miliken, William Roberts, John Hoskins, Jacob Clodfelter, John Reed, Wm. Frields, Willie Young, & Andrew Braden who being Elected tried and sworn the truth to speak upon the issue joined upon their oath do say they find for the Plaintiff and assess his damage to Six dollars two and one half cents besides Costs--

Therefore it is considered by the Court that the Plaintiffs do recover of the Defendant Six Dollars two and one half cents the damages aforesaid assessed by the Jury aforesaid also his Costs by him in this behalf expended and the Defendant in mercy &c-

Arthur Crozier Esquire returned the Tax list for Captain Marshall,s Compy. for the present year.

Ordered by the Court that John Ashurst be overseer of the road in room of Willie Young and have the same bounds & hands. (P. 105)

Micajah Frost produced a grown wolf scalp and proved in open Court that he killed the same since the last Term of this Court (in this County) Ordered by the Court that he be allowed $3.00.

Ordered by the Court that John Lin be overseer of the road in room of Joel Holbert & have the same bounds & hands.-

Court then Adjourned until Tomorrow Morning 9 o,clock,

WEDNESDAY APRIL 15TH 1812-
Court met according to adjournment. Present Wm. McKamey, Joseph Sinclair & Michael Clardy, Esqrs.-

David Prewit)
    vs   ) This day came the Defendant by his attorney and on affi-
John Simpkins) davit entered a rule for a new Trial in this cause & new
                Trial granted by Court-
Ordered by the Court that no rule be entered unless the party praying such Rule shew sufficient cause by affidavit.

State   )
    vs   ) Indictment on A. B.
James Worthington) This day came Robert H. Adams, who prosecutes for the
                    State and the Defendant having heard the Bill (P. 106)
of Indictment read- because he will not contend says he is guilty in manner & form as charged in said Bill and puts himself upon the grace and mercy of of the Court.

Whereupon it is considered by the Court that for such his offence he be fined the sum of fifty cents and pay the Cost of this prosecution-

State)
vs) Indictment on Affray
Hugh Barton) This day came Robert H. Adams who prosecutes for the people
of the State and the Defendant having heard the Bill of Indictment read says he is not guilty in manner & form as charged in the bill aforesaid and puts himself upon the Country- whereupon came a Jury towit:

    1. Man Page Vowel   7. Hugh Milican
    2. John Cooper   8. Joseph Keny
    3. Jacob Clodfelter   9. Charles Kirkpatrick
    4. James Hicks   10. John Rhea
    5. Robert Hays   11. William Carrel
    6. Isaac Low   12. Andrew Braden   of Travis

who being elected tried and sworn the truth to speak upon the issue/joined upon their oath do say the Defendant is guilty in manner and form as charged in the Bill of Indictment.

    Therefore it is considered by the Court that for such his offence he be fined twenty five cents and pay the costs of this prosecution- reasons in arrest of Judg,t. filed.

    Absolom White returned one stud horse as Taxable for the present year at $1.50.

(P. 107) State)
        vs) Recognizance
  Wm. Bounds) This day came William Bounds and John Tunnell into open
Court and acknowledged themselves indebted to the State in the sum of one hundred dollars.-To be void on condition said William Bounds makes his personal appearance from day to day to answer a charge exhibited against him by the Grand Jury and not depart the Court without leave.

State)
vs) Indictment on A. & B.
James Worthington) This day came Robert H. Adams who prosecutes for the
people of the State and the defendant having heard the Bill of Indictment read because he will not contend says he is gulty in manner and form as charged in said Bill and puts himself upon the grace and mercy of the Court, Whereupon it is considered by the Court that for such his offence he be fined Six and one fourth cents and pay the Costs of this prosecution.

State)
vs) Indictment A. & B.
Willis Leath) This day came Robert H. Adams who prosecutes for the people
of the State and the Defendant having heard the Bill of Indictment read and because he will not contend says he is guilty in manner & form as charged in the Bill of Indictment and puts himself on the grace and mercy of the Court.

    Therefore it is considered by the Court that for such his offence he be fined Seventy five cents & pay the Costs of this Prosecution-- (P. 108)

State)
vs) Indictment A & B
William Bounds) This day came Robert H. Adams who prosecutes for the people of the State and the Defendant having heard the Bill

of Indictment read because he will not contend says he is guilty in manner and form as charged in said Bill and puts himself upon the grace & mercy of the Court- Therefore it is considered by the Court that for such his offence he be fined six and one fourth Cents and pay the costs of this prosecution and may be taken &c-

Whereupon John Bounds Senr. comes into Court and agrees that if said Defendant doth not pay said fine & costs that he will do it for him.-

State)
vs) Indictment A & B
John Rector) This day came Robert H. Adamds, who prosecutes for the people of the State and the Defendant having heard the Bill of Indictment read because he will not contend says he is guilty in manner and form as charged in said Bill-

Therefore it is considered by the Court that for such his offense he be fined the sum of seventy five Cents and that he pay the costs of this prosecution--

State)
vs) Indictment on Affray
James Childress) This day came Robert H. Adams, who prosecutes for the people of the State and the Defendant having heard the Bill of Indictment read says that he not guilty in manner and form as charged in the Bill of Indictment and of this he puts himself upon the country- whereupon came a jury towit-

1. Willie Young   7. Thos. Dixon
2. Wm. Hogshead   8. John Kirkpatrick
3. Reuben Williams   9. Jas. Kirkpatrick
4. Absolom White   10. Jas. Blackborn
5. John Scott   11. Collins Roberts
6. Saml. Severs   12. John Fry

(P. 109) who being duly elected tried and sworn the truth to speak upon this issue of Travis upon their oath do say the Defendant is not guilty in manner and form as charged in the Bill of Indictment.

State)
vs) Indictment on Affray
William Childress) This day came Robert H. Adams who prosecutes for the for the people of the State and the Defendant having heard the Bill of Indictment read says he is not guilty in manner and form as charged in the Bill of Indictment and puts himself upon the Country.

Whereupon came a jury towit.

1. Man Page Vowell   7. Hugh Miliken
2. John Cooper   8. Chas. Kirkpatrick
3. Jacob Clodfelter   9. Jo Kemy
4. James Hicks   10. John Rhea
5. Ro. Hays   11. Wm. Carrell
6. Isaac Low   12. Andw. Braden-

who being elected tried and sworn the truth to speak upon the issue of Travis upon their oath do say the Defendant is not guilty in manner & form as charged in the Bill of Indictment-

Ordered by the Court that Richard Medlin be allowed six dollars for supporting Elizabeth Hutchins until the next Term of this Court.

(P. 10) State)
     vs) Indictment Affray
John Kerby) This day came Robert H. Adams who prosecutes for the people of the State, and the Defendant having heard the Bill of Indictment read says he is not guilty in manner and form as charged in the Bill of Indictment and of this he puts himself upon the country. Whereupon came a jury towit.

1. Man Page Vowell   7. Hugh Miliken
2. John Cooper   8. Chas. Kirkpatrick
3. Jacob Clodfelter   9. Jo Keeny
4. James Hicks   10. John Reed
5. Saml. Severs   11. Wm. Carrell
6. Isaac Low   12. Andw. Braden-

who being duly elected tried and sworn the truth to speak upon the issue of Travis upon their oaths do say the Defendant is not guilty in manner & form as charged in the Bill of Indictment-

Same)
     vs) Indictment Affray
Jesse Henderson) This day came Robert H. Adams, who prosecutes for the people of the State and the Defendant having heard the Bill of Indictment read says he is not guilty in manner & form as charged in the Bill of Indictment & of this he puts himself on the country.

    Whereupon came a Jury (towit) (Same as above) who being elected tried and sworn upon their oaths do say the Defendant is not guilty in manner & form as charged in the bill of Indictment.

(P. 111) John McAdoo, Esqr. returned tax list of Capt. Scruggs Company for the present year.

William Underwood, Esqr. returned tax list of Capt. Mortin,s Company for the present year.

James Underwood)
     vs) Continued by consent
Isaac Mayberry)

    A deed from Rich,d. Lewallen & Robert Burton to William Lamar for 200 acres of land was proved in open Court by John Lewallen & Charles Lewallen two of the Subscriving Witnesses thereto & ordered to be registered--

Alexander Scott by his)
Father & Next friend) In this cause John Underwood, John McAdoo & Aron
     vs) Jenkins, Arbitrators, to whom was referred the
Obadiah Woods) matter in dispute having this day heard the parties and their Testimony respecting the matters in dispute between them do award that in this cause that the Plaintiff dismiss his suit and that the Defendant pay the Costs which award is confirmed by the Court.
    Therefore it is considered by the Court that the Plaintiff recover against the Defendant his costs in this behalf expended and the Defendant in mercy &c- (P. 112)

John Scott)
     vs) In this cause John Underwood, John McAdoo & Aron Jenkins,
Obadiah Woods) Arbitrators, to whom was referred the matters in dispute

having this day heard the parties and their Testimony respecting the matters in dispute between them do award, that in this Cause that the Plaintiff dismiss his suit and that he pay the Costs thereon which award is confirmed by the Court.- Therefore it is considered by the Court that the Plaintiff take nothing by his suit but for his false clamor be in mercy and that the defendant go hence with day and recover of the Plaintiff his Costs by him about his defense in this behalf expended.

John Scott)
vs) In this case John Underwood, John McAdoo, and Aron Jenkins,
George Woods) Arbitrators, to whom was referred the matters in dispute,
having this day heard the parties & their Testimony respecting the matters in dispute between them, do award that in this Cause that the Plaintiff dismiss his suit and that he pay the costs thereon, which award is confirmed by the Court.

Therefore it is considered by the Court that the Plaintiff take nothing by his writ but for his false clamor be in mercy and that the Defendant go hence without day and recover of the Plaintiff his costs about his defence in this behalf expended. (P. 113)

Ordered by the Court that John McAdoo, Admr. of the Estate of Sam,1. Dixon deceased proceed to sell the Corn & fodder belonging to said Estate within Sixty days from this time.

State)
vs) Indictment A & B
Briant Tipton) This day came Robert H. Adams who prosecutes for the people
of the State and the Defendant having heard the bill of Indictment read because he will not contend says he is guilty in manner and form as charged in said Bill and puts himself on the grace and mercy of the Court, Whereupon it is considered that by the Court that for such his offence he be fined seventy five cents and pay the costs of this prosecution.

Ordered that the following persons be jurors to next Circuit Court (to-wit)

1. Edward Hawkins
2. Arthur Crozier
3. Saml. Gilbreath
4. John G. Durrett
5. Reuben Williams
6. John Parks
7. Alexr. Gilbreath, Junr.
8. Robert Gilbreath
9. Wm. Nichol
10. Jas. Scarbro
11. Thos. Dixon
12. Abram Hagler, Senr.
13. William Boid
14. George Sutherland
15. John Sutherland
16. Henry Monger
17. John McAdoo
18. John Gibbs
19. David Scarboro
20. Malon Hibbs
21. Wm. F. McEntire
22. Michael Clardy
23. Reuben Gholston
24. Andw. Braden
25. Wm. Sharp
26. Wm. Underwood

(27) Jas. Hill

Court then adjourned until tomorrow &c.

(P. 114) THURSDAY 16TH APRIL 1812-
Court met according to adjournment. Present Wm. McKamey, Arthur Crozier, & John McAdoo, Esquires-

State)
vs) Ordered by the Court that the Defendants fine in this case
Briant Tipton) be reduced to six and one fourth cents-

State)
vs) This day the reasons in arrest of Judgment came on and there
Hugh Barton) being no opposition, It is ordered by the Court that the Judgment heretofore rendered in this Cause be arrested—

Ordered by the Court that Charles McClung be released from the payment of the Tax on 3780 acres of Land for the present year of 1811—It appearing to the Court there was that quantity of Land more than ought to have been returned in this county--

State)
vs) Bastardy
William Lohery) John Cooper surrendered the body of William Lohery into open Court, in discharge of himself as bail in this Cause-
And said Lohery ordered in Custody of the sheriff until he gives further security.

(P. 115) Charles Y. Oliver gave Hugh Barton, Douglas Oliver & William Lamar as securitys for the Collection of the publick Tax for the present year who entered into bond accordingly--

State)
vs) Bastardy
Wm. Lohery) William Lohery tendered to Court John Lohery, John Fry, and Man Page Vowell, as his securitys for the maintenance of a bastard child begotten by him on the Body of Polly Patterson which Security is received by the Court and they entered into Bond accordingly.

State)
vs) Recognizance
John Lohery) This day Andrew Braden, Britton Cross and David Hall came into open Court and acknowledged themselves indebted to the State in the sum of fifty dollars each, to be void on condition they make their personal appearance from day to day at this Term to give evidence on behalf of the State in this case & not depart the Court wihout leave.

State)
vs) Indictment-
William Lohery) This day came Robert H. Adams Esqr. who prosecutes for the people of the State and the Defendant hearing the Bill of Indictment read because he will not contend saith he is guilty, in manner & form as charged in the Bill of Indictment and puts himself upon the (P. 116) grace & mercy of the Court- Whereupon it is Considered by the Court that for such his offence he be fined Six & one fourth cents, and that he pay the Costs of this prosecution and may be taken &c

State)
vs) Indictment A & B
John Lohery) This day came Robert H. Adams who prosecutes for the people

of the State and the Defendant having heard the Bill of Indictment read because he will not contend says that he is guilty in manner & form as charged in said Bill.

Whereupon it is considered by the Court that for such his offence he be fined six and one fourth cents and pay the Costs of this prosecution and may be taken &c.

Whereupon Saml. Dunn comes into open Court and agrees if the Defendant doth not pay the Costs in this case he will do it for him.— Therefore it is considered by the Court that the State do recover of John Lohery & Saml. Dunn the Costs of the above prosecution &c.

Joseph McPeters)
vs) Appeal
John Reed) This day came the parties by their attorneys, whereupon came a jury towit, Wm. Hogshead, Charles Price, Andw. Braden, Thos. Hope, William Melton, Collins Roberts, John Fry, Andw. McKamey, Man Page Vowell, John Cooper, Jacob Clodfelter, & James Hicks, who being elected tried and sworn the truth to speak upon this issue joined upon their oaths do say they find for the Deft. (P. 117)

Therefore it is considered by the Court that the Plff. take nothing by his suit but for his false clamour be in mercy and the Defendant go hence without day and recover of the Plaintiff his costs about his defense in this behalf expended.

John Stewart for the use)
of Stephen Heard)
vs) Cont. on the rule of last Term—
Andrew Stewart) The Travis Jurors was then discharged—

Thomas Parsons proved four days attendance as Constable to the Travis Jury at this Term.

A deed from Charles Y. Oliver Shff. to Arthur Crozier for 320 acres of Land was acknowledged in open Court and ordered to be registered.

A deed from Arthur Crozier to Sampson David for 320 acres of Land was acknowledged in open Court & ordered to be registered.

State)
vs) In this case all the parties released their costs— Whereupon it is ordered by the Court that the Defendant be released from his imprisonment and all costs in this cause.
Briant Tipton)

(P. 118) Thomas Shelton)
vs) Appeal—
Joseph McPeters) This day came the parties by their attornies and the rule to set aside the Judgment by default being solemnly argued it is considered by the Court that the rule be made absolute and the cause continued.—

Smith & Neilson Surveying Partners)
of Wm. King Deceased)
vs) Demurrer
Quin Morton) This day came the parties by their

Attos. and the Plaintiffs Demurrer to the Defendants first plea coming on to be argued, On solemn argument it is considered by the Court that the Demurrer be sustained.

John Underwood Esquire Collector of the County and Publick Tax for the County of Anderson for the year 1810 and 1811 returns to Court the following Lists of Lands on which the Taxes have not been paid and the owners of which have no goods or chattels within this county which he can distrain for said Taxes. (P. 119)

Name	Acres	Year	Amount of Taxes
Samuel Stout	800 acres	1811	$3.00
Charles Hogshead	220	1811	.82½
James Shulbread	812½	1811	4.4½
Robert Salters Heirs	1685	1811	6.31½
James Creswell	340	1810 & 1811	2.55
Hugh McGomery	2 Town Lots	1810 & 1811	2.00

Ordered by the Court that said Tracts of Land be sold agreeable to Law to discharge the said taxes and costs.

Thomas Butler to William Butler--
A Deed for 420 acres of Land was proved in open Court by the oath of Ancil Manley who also swore that he saw Caleb Manley sign said deed as a witness thereon who is since dead and said deed is ordered to be registered.

Court then adjourned until Tomorrow Morning 9 O'clock--

(P. 120) FRIDAY APRIL 17TH, 1812-------
Court met according to adjournment. Present John McAdoo, Arthur Crozier & Quin Morton Esqrs.

Thos. McClain)
    vs   ) Certiorari
Quin Morton) Continued by Consent

Jacob Peak   )
    vs   ) Certiorari
Stephen Heard) This day came the Plaintiff by his attorney and dismisses his suit and the Deft. assumes upon himself the payment of one half of the Costs thereon- Therefore it is considered by the Court that the Plaintiff pay one half of the Costs and the Defendant pay the other half of the Costs, and the Defendants attorney charges no tax fee in this cause.

Joseph Hart)
    vs   ) This day came the Defendant by his attorney and the rule to
Wm. Hogshead) set aside the Judgment rendered at last Term was made absolute.

Ordered by the Court that the following persons be jurors at the next Term of this Court towit, Saml. Frost, John Scott, Peter Monger, John Fry, John Parks, Hugh Dixon, Jas. Kirkpatrick, Jas. Tunnell, James Scruggs, David Wallace, William Ashlock, John Lewallen, Constant Clarkson, Enoch Foster, Jacob Lenard, Daniel Leib, (P. 121) Aaron Slover, Jacob Weaver, John Wood, John Farmer, Moses Farmer, John McAdoo, Junr., George Woods, John Leib, Junr., Joseph Overton & Carter Hendrix.

Ordered by the Court that the Clerk of this Court do Certify to the Circuit Court Judges of the State of Tennessee that William Hogshead has resided in this County several years previous to this time, that the Court believes him to be a person of good reputation and that he has attained the age of twenty one years-

The Grand Jurors was then discharged.

Charkes McCormick proved five days attendance as Constable to the Grand Jury.

Court then adjourned until Court in Course

(P. 122)   ARTHUR CROZIER C. A. C.

State of Tennessee) At a Court of Pleas and Quarter Sessions began and held
Anderson County   ) for the County of Anderson at the Court House in Clinton
                     on the second Monday of July 1812 being the 13th day of
said month---
Present Arthur Crozier, John McAdoo and Edward Hawkins, Esqrs.

Charles Y. Oliver, Esqr. Sheriff of the County aforesaid returned the following Venire facias towit. Saml Frost, John Scott, John Fry, John Parks, Hugh Dixon, James Kirkpatrick, James Tunnell, James Scruggs, David Wallace, William Ashlock, Constant Clarkston, Enoch Foster, Jacob Lenard, Daniel Leib, Aaron Slover, Jacob Weaver, John Wood, John Farmer, Moses Farmer, John McAdoo, Junr., George Wood, Carter Henry, John Leib, Junr., Joseph Overton & Peter Monger--

Out of which was drawn as grand jurors (towit)
1. Jacob Lenard (Foreman)   7. John McAdoo, Junr.
2. Moses Farmer   8. Jas. Tunnell
3. James Kirkpatrick   9. Daniel Leib
4. Tom. Ashlock   10. Saml. Frost
5. Constant Clarkston   11. John Fry
6. Peter Monger   12. George Wood and John Lewallen.-

Robert Gilbreath entered into bond with Security as a commission to settle with the County officers.-

(P. 123) MONDAY 13TH JULY 1812--

John Farmer for Reuben Ragland returned 100 acres of land as taxable property for the present year and the year 1811--

Ordered that James Still be overseer of the road in room of John Leach and have the same bounds & hands.

Two deeds from John Wallace, Senr. to David & Saml. Wallace for 100 acres Each was acknowledged in open Court & ordered to be Registered--

A deed from Hugh Lackey to William Johnson for 51½ acres was proved by the oaths of West Walker and John Hickey.

Matthew Hill produced a wolf scalp and proved he killed the said wolf in January last.

John Leach returned one poll & 100 acres of Land as Taxable for the present year---

Carter Hendrix excused from serving as a Juror at this Term.

David Prewitt returned one poll Taxable for the present year.

Joseph Keeny, Junr., returned 525 acres of land & one Poll as Taxable for the present year.

Court then adjourned until Tomorrow Morning 9 o'clock.
(P. 124)

TUESDAY JULY 24TH, 1812--
Court met according to adjournment- Present Douglas Oliver, Joseph Sinclair, & Samuel Davidson Esquires--

Ordered that John Kirby be overseer of the road in the room of Henry Etter and have the same bounds & hands.

Ordered by the Court that Hugh Barton Administer on the Estate of Benjamin C. Parker Deceased who entered into bond with security and was qualifyed accordingly and returned into open Court the following Inventory (towit) 3 cows & 2 calves one three year old stear one 2 year old heifer 1 yearling 1 Bull 300 doz. of wheat & rye 380 Bushels of corn to be paid by Thomas Dixon out of the present crop 1 Sorrel mare 1 three year old horse 1 two year old Colt 1 Bay Horse 3 axes 4 Hoes 1 Mattock 1 silver watch 1 Coulter plough, 170 doz. of oaths, 2 clevises 2 horse collars 2 sickles 2 mobby stands, 2 Sythes, 1 wheel, 2 augers, 1 candle stick, 1 drawing knife, 1 hammar, 1 handsaw Sythe anvil 1 chissel 1 Padlock 1 looking glass 1 wedge 2 pr traces 2 Sets of Harness & back bands 1 pr. Shears 6 pewter plates 1 dish 1 coffee pot, 1 pepper box, 2 flat irons 1 nutmeg grater 2 tables 1 trunk 3 knives & forks 1 coffee mill 4 blankets 1 bedtick 2 dutch ovens 1 pot 1 tin Buckitt 1 pr fire tongs 1 churn 2 plates 1 salt sellar 1 grrind stone hemp not cleaned- 80 head hogs 1 blind bridle 1 spade 1 pr. Steelyards-- (P. 125)

Wm. Doherty)
     vs   ) Cont. on affidavit of Defendant---
Joseph McPeters)

David Prewit)
     vs   ) Continued on affidavit of Plaintiff and the Defendant by
John Simpkins) his attorney moved the Court for a commission to take the
             deposition of Sarah Brinley, Whereupon it is ordered by the Court that a Commission issue accordingly the Defendant giving the Plaintiff twenty days notice of the time & place of taking said deposition.

Thomas Shelton)
     vs   ) Appeal
Joseph McPeters) Cont. on affidavit of Deft.

Smith King & Neilson)
          vs   ) This day came the parties by their attornies, and
Quin Morton   ) a Jury towit. John Scott, John Parks, Hugh Dixon,
                        David Wallace, Enoch Foster, Aaron Slover, James
Shepheard, John Hoskins, Hugh Milikin, John F. McEntire, David Prewit and Jacob Jackson who being duly elected tried and sworn the truth to speak upon

the issue Joined upon their oaths do say the Defendant hath paid the Debt in the Declaration mentioned except the sum of one hundred & Eighteen Dollars and Seventy two cents and they assess the Plaintiffs damages by reason (P. 126) of the detention of that sum to forty dollars & thirty cents.

Therefore it is considered by the Court that the plaintiff recover of the defendant the sum of one hundred & Efghteen dollars and seventy two cents together with forty dollars & 30 cents the damages aforesaid assessed by the Jury aforesaid also their costs in this behalf expended and the Defendant in mercy --&c--

A deed from Thomas Menifee to Samuel Marshall for 24 acres of Land was proved in open Court by the oaths of Thos. Wilson & Alexander Gastin--

Ordered by the Court that George Sutherland be allowed Seven dollars for a Registers Book Furnished by him-

Ordered by the Court that Samuel Marshall, Isaac Norman, Aaron Norman, Thomas Ketcherside, Paul Chiles, Aaron Jenkins, & Thomas Wilson be appointed a Jury of review to view the Emery road from the ford of the Copper Ridge to intersect the road that leads by Thomas Menifees and report to this Court--

Ordered by the Court that John Linn's bounds as overseer of the road be extended as to include John Kirk, Thomas Kirk & Elijah Kirk--

John Stewart for the use of)
Stephen Heard) This day came the parties by their attornies
vs) and a Jury, towit, John Scott, John Park, Hugh
Andrew Stewart) Dixon, David Wallace, Enoch Foster, Aaron Slover, John Gibbs, John Hoskins, Hugh Milikin,
John F. McEntire, David Prewit, (P. 127) and Page Portwood who being duly elected tried and sworn the truth to speak upon the Issue Joined upon their oaths do say the Defendant did not assume upon himself in manner and form as the Plaintiff against him hath complained-

Therefore it is considered by the Court that the Plaintiff take nothing by his writ but for his false clamor be in mercy and that the Defendant go hence without day and recover of the Plaintiff his Costs by him about his defense in this behalf expended--

Ordered by the Court that George Sutherland, Thomas Hart and Charles Y. Oliver be allowed the sum of Eight dollars each for their services as commissioners to settle with the Public officers for Anderson County for the year 1809--

A deed from George Gordon to James King for 200 acres of land was proved in open Court by the oaths of William Tunnell & James Tunnell & ordered to be registered.

Ordered by the Court that Hardy Medlin be allowed two dollars & fifty cents for furnishing Elizabeth Hutchins with clothing--

Ordered by the Court that the following persons be Jurors at the next Term of this Court towit.

1. John Landrum 2. John Rector
3. Henry Butler 4. Andw. McKamey
5. Noah Peck   6. Moses Brown

7. Nathan Hale
8. Saml. Taylor
9. Geo. White
10. Austin Hackworth
11. Abraham Hagler
12. Robert MaCart

(P. 128)

13. Joseph Black
14. Thos. M. Ashley
15. Jo. Keeny Senr.
16. John Taylor
17. Wm. Lamar
18. Robert Roydon
19. Edward Woodward
20. Rich,d Marshall
21. Wm. Hancock
22. Solomon Alred
23. Phillip Harless
24. Matthew Hill
25. Thomas Landrum
26. Thomas Carnall--

Ordered by the Court that Mary Patterson be allowed Nine dollars from William Lohery for supporting a child begotten on her body by said Lohery up to this day, and Ten dollars per year for two years to come from this day- and the same to be paid into the hands of the Clerk of this Court quarterly.

Ordered by the Court that George Sutherland and Thomas Hart be allowed ten dollars & twenty five cents each for setling with the Publick officers of this County for the year 1811--

Ordered by the Court that John Carwile be allowed one dollar and fifty cents annually.

Jesse Roddy by Saml. Gilbreath returns 200 acres of land as Taxable for the present year.

Ordered by the Court that Joseph Keeny Junr. be overseer of the road in the room of Larkin Bowling and have the same bounds and hands.

Ordered by the Court that Jermiah Hibbs be overseer of the road in the room of William Severs and have the same bounds & hands.

Court then adjourned until tomorrow morning 9 O'clock--

(P. 129)

WEDNESDAY JULY 15TH, 1812--
Court met according to adjournment.
Present Arthur Crozier, John McAdoo and Quin Morton, Esquires--

John McAdoo Administrator of the Estate of Saml. Dixon Deceased returned the following amt. of Sale--towit

300 W. Cotton...	$12.00
117 Bushels Corn	40.65
2 Stacks of Fodder	2.25
for clearing 1 acre of land	8.00
for wheat	2.00
	$64.90

A Transfar of five acres of land from John Brandham to Rachel Scarbrough was proved in open Court by the oath of James Anderson & Daniel Johnson the Subscribing Witnesses thereto.--

James Shepheard)
     vs   ) On affidavit of the Plaintiff, It is ordered by the
Andrew Stewart) Court that a Commissioner issue to any two Justices of
the Peace for the County of Cumberland and State of Kentucky to take the depositions of----Elliott who resides in the said county of Cumberland aforesaid the Plaintiff giving the Defendant thirty days notice of the time and place of taking Elliotts deposition.

Arthur Crozier Esquire was elected Treasurer of the county of Anderson for the two succeeding years who was qualifyed & entered into bond with security according to Law.

(P. 130) Ordered by the Court that the Emery road be altered according to the report of the Jury of review which are as follows towit to leave the old road on the right hand at the foot of the Copper ridge and taking the ro road that leads to the meeting house to where it intersects the road that passes Thomas Menifees thence into said road.

State   )
  vs   ) <u>Maliscious</u> Mischief
John Scott) This day came Samuel Anderson Esquire who prosecutes for the
people of the State and the Defendant having heard the Bill of Indictment read says he is not guilty in manner & form as charged in said Bill of Indictment and of this he puts himself upon the country -

Whereupon came a Jury towit. John Parks, Hugh Dixon, Enoch Foster, Aaron Slover, Jacob Weaver, John Wood, John Farmer, Willis Leath, Joseph Overton, Andrew McKamey, William Butler, and Rhode Stanley, who being duly elected tried and sworn the truth to speak upon this issue of Travis upon their oaths do say the Defendant is guilty in manner & form as charged in the Bill of Indictment,

Therefore it is considered by the Court that for such his offence he be fined the sum of one dollar & be imprisoned twenty four hours and that he pay the Costs of this prosecution, from which Judgment the Deft. prays an appeal filed his reasons entered into bond with Security as the Law requires and appeal granted----

(P. 131) Ordered by the Court that William Gamble be overseer of the road in the room of Jacob Peak and have the same bounds & hands.

Nathaniel Hart by William Underwood his agent returns 5000 acres of Land Taxable for the present year.

William Sharp was qualified as a Justice of the Peace for the County of Anderson.

State   )
  vs   ) Recognizance
Wm. Brumley) Ordered by the Court that the Defendant be discharged from
his Recognizance and that he pay all Costs thereon.

State   )
  vs   ) Recognizance
John Brumley) In this case it is ordered by the Court that the Defendant
be discharged from his Recognizance and that he pay all Costs thereon----

State

State)
vs) Recognizance
Austin Brumley) In this case it is ordered by the Court that the Defendant
be discharged from his recognizances & that he pay all costs
thereon--

State)
vs) Recognizance
Patty Frost) In this case, It is ordered by the Court that the Defendant
be discharged from her recognizance & that she pay all Costs
thereon. (P. 132)

State)
vs) Recognizance
Betsy Tipton) In this case it is ordered by the Court that the Defendant be
discharged from her recognizance and that she pay all Costs
thereon.

Ordered by the Court that Fanny Horton and John Parks have leave to administer on the Estate of William Horton Deceased, who entered into bond with Security and was qualifyed according to Law.

State)
vs) Presentment
John Asher) This day came Samuel Anderson Esqr. who prosecutes for the people of the State as well as the Defendant by his attorney, Whereupon came a Jury towit, John Leib, Hugh Dixon, Enoch Foster, Aaron Slover, Jacob Weaver, John Wood, Andrew Braden, William Russell, Jacob Jackson, James King, John Kerby, & Finchem Hall, who being Elected tried and sworn the truth to speak upon this issue of Travis, upon their oaths do say the Defendant is not guilty in manner and form as charged in the Bill of Indictment.
Therefore it is considered by the Court that the Defendant go hence &c--

Court then adjourned until Tomorrow morning 9 o'clock--

(P. 133) THURSDAY JULY 16TH 1812--
Court met according to adjournment. Present Wm. McKamey, Saml. Davidson and Saml. Gilbreath Esqrs.

On Motion of Arthur Crozier Esqr. Trustee for the County of Anderson, It is considered by the Court that the said Arthur Crozier Trustee as aforesaid have Judgment against John Underwood Late Sheriff of the county aforesaid and his Securities for the sum of Seventy Eight dollars thirty six & three fourth cents, It being a ballance of the Tax collected by said Underwood as Sheriff of the county aforesaid for the year 1809 also the costs of this motion---

State)
vs) Presentment
William Scott) This day came Saml. Anderson Esqr. who prosecutes for the State as well as the Defendant by his attorney. Whereupon came a Jury towit Isaac Mayberry, John Parks, Hugh Dixon, David Wallace, Enoch Foster, Aaron Slover, Jacob Weaver, John Wood, John Farmer, John Leib, Joseph Overton & John Hibbs, who being elected tried and sworn the truth to speak upon this issue of Travis upon their oaths do say the Defendant is guilty in manner & form as charged in the bill of (P. 134) Indictment.

Therefore it is considered by the Court that for such his offence he be fined the sum of six & one fourth cents and that he pay the Costs of this prosecution.

Fanny Horton Administratrix and John Parks Admr of the Estate of William Horton Dec, returned an Inventory of the Estate of William Horton, Deac and the same is ordered to be sold the 15th day of August next by giving twenty days notice.

James Underwood)
    vs   ) Continued by Consent.
Isaac Mayberry)

John Stewart for the use of)
    Stephen Heard   ) This day came the Plaintiff by his attorney
        vs   ) and on affidavit entered a rule for a new
    Andrew Stewart   ) trial in this cause, and the said Rule coming
                                 on to be argued- It is considered by the
Court that the said Rule be discharged--

Thomas McClain)
    vs   ) Certiorari
Quin Morton   ) Rule to dismisss Certiorari
        This day came the parties by their Attornies and the Rule to dismiss the Certiorari being Solemnly argued, It is considered by the Court that the said Rule be discharged--- (P. 135)

Thomas McClain)
    vs   ) Certiorari
Quin Morton   ) This day came the Plaintiff by his attorney and dismisses
                      his suit and assumesupon himself the payment of all Costs.
Therefore it is considered by the Court that the Defendant go hence without day and recever of the Plaintiff his costs in this behalf expended.

Rhode Stanley returns one hundred acres of land and 1 free poll taxable for the present year--

Ordered by the Court that the road leading to Stogdens Valley (the part of it near Reuben Williams) be continued the old way agreeable to the report of the Jury of review made to this Court--

Ordered by the Court that the following persons work under Jermiah Hibbs, overseer of the road towit, Elijah Beach, Aaron Slover, Walter Taylor, Isaac Robbins, George Taylor, Zadock Deaton, William Blagg, Wm. Craighead, Finchin Hall, Wm. Edwards & James Shepheard. (P. 136)

Polly Roberts)
    vs   ) Sci fa-
John Hibbs   ) On Demurrer- This day came the parties by their attornies
                      and the Defendants demurrer to the Plaintiffs Sci fa being solemnly argued, It is considered by the Court that the demurrer be overruled and Execution awarded vs the Defendant for Ten dollars besides Costs-
    Therefore it is considered by the Court that the Plaintiff recover of the Defendant Ten dollars being the amount due by virtue of an order of court for one year ending the 17th January last, also all costs in the behalf expended.

Isaac Mayberry)
vs) This day came the Plaintiff by his attorney and releas-
William Hogshead) ed all of a Judgment rendered some time agao in favor
of the Plaintiff vs. the Defendant except fifty two
dollars and costs.

State)
vs) This day came the Defendant and withdrew his appeal, Where-
John Scott) upon the Court ordered him to be released from his imprisonment.

Ordered by the Court that Rhode Stanley be appointed Guardian for John Sartin a minor who entered into bond with security accordingly---

A deed from Charles McCormick to Daniel Ragan for one acre of land was acknowledged in open Court. (P. 137)

Hezekiah Love)
vs) This day came Stephen Heard in his own proper person and
Stephen Heard) confess,s Judgment for four dollars- Therefore it is
considered by the Court that the Plaintiff recover of the
Defendant the four dollars aforesaid also the Costs of this Judgment.

John Massingale)
vs) Certiorari
Robert Hays) This day came the Defendant by Stephen Heard Esqr his attorney and the Plaintiff being Solemnly called to come
into court & prosecute his certiorari came not-
Therefore it is considered by the Court that the Defendant go hence without day and recover of the Plaintiff his costs by him about his defense in this behalf expended &c-

Agreeable to the Act of General Assembly passed at Knoxville the 1st day of November 1811, I, Hugh Barton, Clerk of the Court of Pleas & Quarter Sessions for the county of Anderson have proceeded to take the aggregate number of the Taxable Inhabitants in the County aforesaid who are over the age of twenty one years & who will be entitled to vote for Members of the general assembly at the next Election and find the aggregate number to be 488 agreeable to the returns of the Justice of the peace for said county.

Court then adjourned until Tomorrow morning 9 o'clock.

FRIDAY 17TH JULY 1812-
Court met according to adjournment. Present A. Crozier, John McAdoo, & Quin Morton, Esqrs.

Ordered by the Court that the Court of Knox County in this State be requested to cause to be opened a road from the county line between the two Counties to go by Reeds Mill on Beaver Creek to where they may think proper to cross Holston River on a direction to Maryville or Blount County, - a road to intersect the same in this County is very much wanting, Ordered that the chairman of this court sign a copy of this order and forward it to the first county court to be holden for Knox County.

Ordered by the Court that the sheriff of this county notify two constables to attend each Court in such manner that no Constable shall attend only by rotation-

Court then adjourned until Court in Course.

ARTHUR CROZIER, C. A. C.

(P. 139)

State of Tennessee- At a Court of Pleas and Quarter Sessions began and held for the County of Anderson at the Court House in Clinton the second Monday of October 1812, being the 12th day of said month. Present- Douglas Oliver, Samuel Gilbreath, A. Crozier, and William McKamey Esquires.

Charles Y. Oliver Esquire of the County of Anderson returned the Venire facias to this Session 1812 towit.

1. John Landrum
2. John Rector
3. Henry Butler
4. Andw. McKamey
5. Noah Peck
6. Moses Brown
7. Nathan Hale
8. Saml. Taylor
9. George White
10. Robert McCart
11. Joseph Black
12. Thomas M. Ashley
13. Joseph Keeny Senr.
14. Austin Hackworth
15. Abram W. Hagler
16. John Taylor
17. Wm. Lamar
18. Robert Roysdon
19. Edward Woodward
20. Richard Marshall
21. Wm. Hancock
22. Phillip Harless
23. Matthew Hill
24. Thomas Landrum
25. Solomon Alread
26. Thomas Carnell

Out of which was drawn Grand Jurors towit.

1. Joseph Keeny (Senr) Foreman
2. Solomon Alred
3. Henry Butler
4. Ro. Roysdon
5. Phillip Harless
6. John Taylor
7. Joseph Black
8. Austin Hackworth
9. Nathan Hale
10. John Rector
11. Wm. Hancock   (P. 140)
12. Noah Peck & Thomas Carnell

MONDAY 12TH OCTOBER 1812--
who being sworn and charged & retired to consider of their presentment.

A deed from Richard Lewallen to Walter Taylor for 100 acres of land was acknowledged in open Court and ordered to be registered.-

A deed from Isaac Brazleton to Thomas Dixon for 300 acres of land was acknowledged in open Court and ordered to be registered.

A deed from Thomas Eskridge attorney in fact for James Reed to Isaac Low for 1000 acres of land was proved in open Court by the oaths of Aquilla Low & Nathan Hale --

Samuel Robbins)
vs) In this cause John Underwood Robert Dew and James Cogbourn
Andrew McKnight) surrendered the Body of the Defendant Andrew McKnight in Custody of the Sheriff in discharge of themselves as bail.

John McAdoo Esquire resigned his office as Justice of the Peace--

Ordered by the Court that Malon Hibbs be discharged from payment of Tax for the present year it appearing to the satisfaction of the Court that he is exempt by reason of his age.

(P. 141) Ordered by the Court that William Severs have leave to Administer on the Estate of James McDonald Dec,d.

Whereupon he entered into bond and Security and was qualified accordingly and returned the following inventory of said Estate towit, one mare, one yearling, colt, one cow and calf, one yearling, some flax not cleaned, two shirts, two pair of overalls, one coat, two waist coats, one pair of stockings, one razor, some thread-- It is ordered by the Court that said property be sold the 27th Instant.

Ordered by the Court that Gabrial Prewit be overseer of the road in the room of Henry Norman and have the following bounds and hands towit. Beginning at the foot of the Chestnut Ridge to extend to the top of the Copper Ridge at the Knox county line to include James Kirkpatrick thence to the Pine Ridge opposite to the Chestnut Ridge Meeting House thence to cross said ridge including George Lynch, Leonard Coffman and the hands that resides at Thomas Menefees.

William Doherty)
    vs   ) By consent of the parties, It is ordered by the Court
Joseph McPeters) that this Cause be submitted to the arbitrament of John
                  Newman, Ezekiel Newport, Joshua English and John
(P. 142) Triplett and if they cannot agree they the said arbitrators are to choose a fifth man and the award of a majority of the arbitrators is to be a Judgment of the Court which award is to be returned to the next Term of this Court.

Ordered by the Court that James Cogbourn be discharged from the payment of a Poll Tax for the present year it appearing to the Court that he is upwards of fifty years of age.

Ordered by the Court that Leonard Vandegriff be discharged from the payment of the Tax on one town lot, It appearing to the satisfaction of the Court that he has not a town lot--

Ordered by the Court that the following persons be excused from serving as Jurors at this session towit. Robert McCart, Edward Woodward, and Richard Marshall--

Ordered by the Court that the following persons be jurors to the next Circuit Court towit---

1. William Wright
2. John Scott
3. Page Portwood
4. Thomas Menefee
5. Thos. Dixon
6. John McKamey
7. Wm. Butler
8. Wm. Griffith
9. Wm. Russell
10. Ro. Gilbreath
11. Zach. Kee
12. Ansil Manley
13. Wm. McKamey
14. Saml. Dunn
15. John Cooper
16. Carter Hendrix
17. Henry Monger
18. John Loy
19. Ro. Dew
20. Wm. Lemar

21. Geo. Smith
22. John Fry
23. Jacob Weaver
24. Lunsford Oliver
25. Jacob Peak
26. A. Crozier

(P. 143) Ordered by the Court that the following persons be Jurors to the next County Court towit.

1. Michael Hostler
2. Wm. Tunnell
3. John Tunnell
4. John Smith
5. Simeon Smith
6. Constant Claxton
7. Henry Norman
8. Edward Freels Senr.
9. Isaac Norman
10. Richard Lewallen
11. John Lewallen
12. Leonard Coffman
13. David Claxton
14. Philip Severs
15. John Lively
16. James Davidson
17. Benj. Langford
18. Joel Epperson
19. Jesse Hoskins
20. Marmaduke Bookout
21. Isaac Sartin
22. Isaac Mayberry
23. John Rhea
24. Martin Turpin
25. Matt. Heath
26. David Hall

Court then adjourned until Tomorrow 9 O'clock.

TUESDAY 13TH OCTOBER 1812-
Court met according to adjournment.
Present William McKamey, Edward Hawkins & Arthur Crozier————

(P. 144) It was ordered by the Court at last Session that Joseph Keeny Junr. should be overseer of the road in the room of Larkin Bowling- A copy of which order was returned to this Court by the Sheriff in the following words towit, Came to hand 16th September 1812 left a copy of the within at the house of Joseph Keeny Jnur. the 25th Sept. 1812——

It was ordered by the Court at last Session that William Gamble be overseer of the road in the room of Jacob Peak a copy of which order was returned to the Court by the Sheriff in the following words towit, Came to hand 17th Sept. 1812- Delivered a Copy the 26th Sept. 1812-

John Underwood)
   vs   ) This day came the Plaintiff by Thomas Emmerson Esquire
William Lohery) his Attorney and dismiss,d his suit and assumes upon himself the payment of all costs thereon- Therefore it is considered by the Court that the Plaintiff take nothing by his writ but for his false clamor be in mercy and that the Defendant go hence without day and recover of the Plaintiff his Costs by him about his defense in this behalf expended. (P. 145)

John Underwood)
   vs   ) This day came the parties by Thomas Emmerson Esq. his at-
Wm. Lohery   ) torney and dismiss his suit and assume upon himself the payment of all costs thereon- Therefore it is considered by the Court that the Plaintiff take nothing by his writ but for his false clamor be in mercy and that the Deft. go hence without day and recover of the Plaintiff his costs in this behalf expended---

Thomas Shelton)
    vs   )   In this cause appearing to the satisfaction of the court
Joseph McPeters)   that Joseph Doherty, Ezekiel Wilhite & Jarrot Harbin
was legally summon to appear and givee evidence in this cause who being solemnly called came not- Whereupon it is considered by the court that the said Joseph Doherty, Ezekiel Wilhite & Jarrot Harbin forfeit and pay said Shelton one hundred and twenty five dollars each according to act of assembly in such cases made and provided and a sc facias awarded &c.

Thomas Shelton)
    vs   )   This day came the Parties by their attornies. Whereupon
Joseph McPeters)   came a Jury towit, John Landrum, Moses Brown, Zeadock
Deaton, John Hibbs, Robert Dew, William Boynter, Henry Etter, Michael Robbins, Robert (P. 146) Ross, John Scott, Kinza Johnson & Julus Milliken who being duly Elected tried and sworn to try the matters in dispute upon their oaths do say that they fined for the Defendant. Whereupon it is considered by the Court that the Plaintiff take nothing by his suit but for his false clamor be in mercy and that the Defendant go hence without day and recover of the Plaintiff his costs by him about his defense in this behalf expended &c ----

    An assignment of a plat and certificate from Wm. Gardenhire to Daniel Mattox for twenty two acres of land was proved in open Court by the oaths of Luncford Oliver and Thomas H. Carrell the Subscribing Witnesses thereto---

State)
   vs   )   This day came the Defendant and having heard the Bill of
William Severs)   Indictment read because he will not contend says that he
is guilty in manner & form as charged in the Bill of Indictment.- Therefore it is considered by the Court that for such his offense he be fined the sum of Six and one fourth Cents and that he pay the Costs of this prosecution.

David Prewit)
    vs   )   This cause is cont,d on affidavit of William Doherty.-
John Simpkins)

(P. 147)   State)
            vs   )   This day came Thomas Hope into open Court and acknowl-
    John Roberson)   edged himself Indebted to the State of Tennessee in the
sum of one hundred Dollars to be levied of his goods & chattles &c. To be void on condition he doth make his personal appearance from day to day at this term to prosecute and give evidence on behalf of the State in this cause and not depart the Court without leave.

    Ordered by the Court that William Miller aged 15 years and three months be bound to John Miller as an apprentice to the Black-Smiths business until he is twenty one years of age said John Miller to give said apprentice Education (towit) reading, <u>riting</u> and Cyphering as far as the Double rule of three together with a Horse Saddle and Bridle to be worth fifty dollars when he becomes of age.

    Ordered by the Court that William Severs, William Lamar, John Loy, John Gibbs, Jaconb Linard, John McAdoo Senr., Thomas Hart, John Garner, and

David Hall, be appointed a Jury of review to view the two roads, Beginning at the top of the Black Oak Ridge at Reuben William,s field to where said roads intersect and report to next Court which is the best and nearest road-

(P. 148)   James Newberry)
      vs   ) This day came William Severs and surrendered in-
   John Hibbs) to Court the body of John Hibbs, the Deft. in dis-
          charge of himself as Bail. Whereupon said Defend-
ant tendered Malon Hibbs and Thomas Landrum as counter security who was rec,d. &c and entered into bond &c—

 Ordered by the Court that John McAdoo Junr. be overseer of the road in room of Richard Lewallen and that William McAdoo, Saml. Moore, John Lewallen, Charles Lewallen, Negro Aaron and William Hogsheads hands work under him as overseer.

 Court then adjourned until Tomorrow morning 9 O'clock.

 WEDNESDAY 14TH OCTOBER 1812.
 Court met &c. Present William Underwood, Quin Morton, & Matthew Hawkins-

State   )
 vs   ) A. & Battery
William Lohery) This day came Samuel Anderson who prosecutes for the peo-
       ple of the State as well as the Defendant who having heard the Bill of Indictment read says he is not guilty in manner & form as charged in the Bill of Indictment- Whereupon came a Jury towit, John Landrum, Moses Brown, Thomas Landrum, Andw. McKamey, Isaac Mayberry, John Taber, Thomas Hope, John Bounds, Abram Moser, Constant Claxton, James Epperson, (P. 149) & Zeadock Deaton who being duly elected tried and sworn the truth to speak up- on the issue joined upon their oaths do say the Defendant is guilty of the assault and Battery as charged in the Bill of Indictment.
 Therefore it is considered by the Court that for such his offence he be fined the sum of one dollar and pay the costs of this prosecution-

 George M. Campbell agent for the heirs of Doherty returns —— acres of land a Taxable for the present year.

 A power of attorney from James Reed to Thos. Eskredge was proved in op- en Court by the oath of Aquilla Low.

State   )
 vs   ) Tipling
William Lohery) This day came the Defendant by his attorney and moved the
       Court to quash the Bill of Indictment and upon solemn ar- gument the motion was overruled by the Court.
 Whereupon came the Parties and a Jury towit, John Landrum, Moses Brown, Thomas Landrum, Andw. McKamey, Isaac Mayberry, John Taber, Thomas Hope, John Bounds, Isaac Low, Constant Claxton, Thomas Dixon, and Thomas Hart, who be- ing elected tried and sworn the truth to speak upon this Issue Joined upon their oaths do say the Defendant is guilty in manner and form as Charged in the Bill of Indictment.
 Therefore it isconsidered by the Court that for such his offence he be fined the sum of one (P. 150) dollar and that he pay the Costs of this prosecution &c

James Newberry)
    vs   ) This day came the Plaintiff by his attorney and dismiss,s
John Hibbs   ) his suit. Whereupon came the Defendant in his own proper
person and assumes upon himself the payment of all costs thereon.- Therefore it is considered by the Court that the Plaintiff recover of the Defendant his costs by him about his suit in this behalf expended and said Defendant in mercy &c.

State   )
    vs   ) A. & Battery
James Worthington) This day came Samuel Anderson Esquire who prosecutes
for the people of the State as well as the Defendant by his attorney and the Defendants Demurrer to the Bill of Indictment being solemnly argued, It is considered by the Court that the Demurrer be overruled. Whereupon came the Defendant in his own proper person because he will not contend says he is guilty in manner and form as charged in the Bill of Indictment and puts himself upon the grace and mercy of the Court as charged in the Bill of Indictment-

Therefore it is further considered by the Court that for such his offence he be fined Six and one fourth Cents and pay the Costs of this prosecution.

State   )
    vs   ) Assault
William Lohery) This day came Samuel Anderson for the people of the state
as well as for the Defendant by his attorney and the Defendant Demurrer to the Bill of Indictment being Solemnly argued, It is considered by the Court that the Demurrer be (P. 151) overruled and the Defendant having heard the Bill of Indictment read says he is not guilty in manner & form as charged in the Bill of Indictment.

Whereupon came a Jury towit, John Landrum, Moses Brown, Thomas Landrum, Andw. McKamey, John Taber, Thomas Hope, John Bounds, Matthew Hill, John Hibbs, Saml. Hibbs, Henry Butler, and James Newberry who being duly elected tried and sworn the truth to speak upon the Issue Joined upon their Oaths do say the Defendant is guilty in manner and form as charged in the Bill of Indictment.

Therefore it is considered by the court that for such his offence he be fined the sum of fifty cents and pay the Costs of this prosecution &c-

Court then adjourned until Tomorrow at 9 O,clock.

THURSDAY 15TH OCTOBER 1812--
Court met &c- Present Arthur Crozier, Jo Sinclair, Edward Hawkins and William McKamey, Esquires--- (P. 152)

Elizabeth Robinson)
    vs   ) This day came the Defendants by their attorney and the
Thomas Hope and) Plaintiff being solemnly called to come into Court and
William Boyter   ) prosecute her suit came not, Therefore it is considered by the Court that a non suit be entered and that the Defendant go hence without day and recover of the Plaintiff their Costs by them about their Defence in this behalf expended.----

James Stooksberry is released from payment of his Poll Tax for the present year he being over age.-

State)
vs) This cause is continued on affidavit of the Defendant
James Shepheard) until next Court. Whereupon came the said James Shepheard, Hugh Barton and Joseph Minor and acknowledged themselves indebted to the state of Tennessee in the following sums towit said Shepheard in the sum of one hundred dollars, and said Barton & Minor in the sum of fifty dollars each to be levied of their respective goods and Chattles lands & tenements. To be void on condition said Shepheard doth make his personal appearance at next term of Court of Pleas and Quarter Sessions to be held for the county of Anderson & not depart the Court without leave---

James Underwood)
vs) Continued on affidavit of the Plaintiff----
Isaac Mayberry)

(P. 153) State) Tipling-
vs) This day came Samuel Anderson who prosecutes for the people of the State and the Defendant having heard the Bill of Indictment read because he will not contend says he is guilty in manner and form as charged in the Bill of Indictment and puts himself on the grace and mercy of the Court, Therefore it is considered by the Court that for such his offence he be fined the sum of one Dollar & pay the Costs of this prosecution----

William Scott)
vs) Certiorari
William Hogshead) Continued

James Shepheard)
vs) Continued on affidavit of the Defendant
Andrew Stewart)

Charles McClung)
vs) This day came the Plaintiff by attorney and Discontinued his suit and assumes upon himself the payment of all Costs thereon. Whereupon it is Considered by the Court that the Defendants go hence without day and recover of the Plaintiff their Costs by them about their suit in defence in this behalf expended &c--

(P. 154) The Grand Jury was then discharged.

John Underwood)
vs) Appeal
William Lohery & wife) This day came the Parties by their attornies, Whereupon came a Jury towit, John Landrum, Moses Brown, Thomas Landrum, Andw. McKamey, Matthew Hill, George White, John Taber, Constant Claxton, Thomas Dizney, Matthew Hawkins, Ro. McCart, and John Bounds Junr. who being duly elected tried and sworn to try the matter in dispute upon their oaths do say they find for the Plaintiff and assess his damage to forty Dollars besides Costs-
Therefore it is considered by the Court that the Plaintiff recover of

the Defendants forty dollars the damages aforesaid assessed by the Jury aforesaid also his Costs by him about his suit in this behalf expended and the said Defendants in mercy &c.-

State)
vs) This day came Andrew Stewart and Quin Morton and acknow-
James Shepheard) ledged themselves indebted to the State of Tennessee in the sum of fifty dollars each to be levied of their respective goods and chattles &c. To be void on Condition that said Andw. Stewart doth make his personal appearance at the next session of this Court to prosecute on behalf of the State in this cause and not depart the Court without leave.---

(P. 155) State)
vs) This day came Sarah Malaby and Elizabeth Edwards
James Shepheard) and acknowledged themselves indebted to the State of Tennessee in the sum of fifty dollars each. To be void on Condition the said Sarah, and Elizabeth doth make their personal appearance at the next Sessions of this Court to give evidence on behalf of the State in this cause and not depart the Court without leave.

State)
vs) This day Thomas Hope and Paul Chiles and acknowledged them-
John Robinson) selves Indebted to the State of Tennessee in the following sum towit said Hope in the sum of one hundred Dollars and said Chiles in the sum of fifty dollars to be levied of their respective goods and Chattles lands and tenements. To be void on Condition that said Thomas Hope do make his personal appearance at next Sessions of this Court to prosecute and give evidence on behalf of the State in this Cause without leave and that said Chiles appear and give evidence on behalf of the State in this Cause and not depart the Court without leave.---

Court then Adjourned until Tomorrow morning nine O'clock--

(P. 156) FRIDAY 16TH OCTOBER 1812---

Court met &c. Present Arthur Crozier, William McKamey and Quin Morton Esquires---

John Crozier)
vs) This day came the Defendant into open Court and confessed
Stephen Heard) Judgment for one hundred and forty six dollars and Sixty one Cents the amt. of the debt and interest up to this time. Therefore it is considered by the Court that the Plff. do recover of the Defendant one hundred and forty six dollars and Sixty one cents aforesaid also his Costs by him about his suit in this behalf expended with stay of Execution nine months and said Defendant in mercy &c-

Mary Patterson)
vs) Sci fa.
William Lohery) In this cause it appearing that the Scire facias was legally made known to the Defendant commanding him to shew cause if any he can why Judgment should not be awarded against him and the Defendant being solemnly called came not. Therefore it is considered by the Court that the Plaintiff recover of the Defendant the sum of nine dollars the amount of the sum in the Scire facias mentioned also all Costs thereon-

A deed of trust from Elizabeth Lucas to Hugh Barton for four negroes & one house & lott in Clinton was proved in open Court by the Oaths of George (P. 157) Sutherland and John Sutherland Junr. the Subscribing Witnesses thereto and ordered to be recorded--

On motion of Arthur Crozier Esquire Trustee for the County of Anderson- It is considered by the Court that the said Arthur Crozier Trustee aforesaid have Judgment against John Underwood late collector & Sheriff of the said County aforesaid and his Securities for the sum of one hundred and Sixty one dollars and thirty five cents being the <u>ballance</u> due the County of Anderson aforesaid by said John Underwood collector and Sheriff aforesaid for Tax Collected by him for the year Eighteen hundred and Eleven and that said Underwood pay the Costs of this motion.

Ordered by the Court that the following rates be Observed by the Ordinary Keepers in Anderson County towit.

Breakfast Supper or Dinner
Coffee or tea to be furnished for Breakfast..............25 cents
Horse Feed...12½ "
Ditto per day & night Corn & Hay..........................25
Peach Brandy whiskey per half pint.......................08-2/3
Metheglin or Cyder per Qt.................................06¼
Rum or Wine per half pint................................25
Lodging..06¼

Court then adjourned until Court in Course
ARTHUR CROZIER C. A. C.

(P. 158) State of Tennessee-
At a Court of Pleas and Quarter Sessions begun and held for the County of Anderson at the Court House in Clinton on the second Monday of January 1813- Present Wm. McKamey, Edwrad Hawkins & Quin Morton- Esquires--

Charles Y. Oliver Sheriff of the County of Anderson returned the following Venire facias towit.
Michael Hosler, Wm. Tunnell, John Tunnell, John Smith, Simeon Smith, Constant Claxton, Henry Norman, Isaac Norman, Edward Frields, Senr., Richard Lewallen, John Lewallen, Leonard Coffman, Henry Atter, Phillip Severs, John Lively, James Davidson, Benjamin Langford, Joel Epperson, Jesse Hoskins, Marmaduke Bookout, Isaac Sartain, Isaac Mayberry, John Rhea, Martin Turpin, Matt. Heath & David Hall executed on all of the persons named therein----
Out of which was drawn as Grand Jurors towit, William Tunnell, foreman, David Hall, Isaac Mayberry, Richard Lewallen, Edward Frields, Senr. Isaac Sartin, Constant Claxton, Leonard Coffman, Isaac Norman, Martin Turpin, John Rhea, John Smith & Joel Epperson who being sworn and Charged &c retired to inquire of their Presentments.-

Simeon Smith was as appears from the sheriffs return summoned as a Juror to attend at this Court & being Solemnly called came not, Whereupon it is considered (P. 159) by the Court that he forfeit & pay $5 agreeable to act of Assembly in such case made and provided unless he appear at the next Term of this Court & shew cause Why Exceution should not be Awarded against him and that a Scire facias issue accordingly----

Samuel Severs was appointed by the Court overseer of the road in room of George Hoskins and have the same bounds & hands.--

Andrew McKamey was appointed by the Court overseer of the road in room of John Dunnivan & have the same Bounds and hands.---

James King was appointed by the Court overseer of the road in room of John Hoskins & have the same bounds and hands.--

Spencer Keith was appointed by the Court overseer of the road in room of John Gamble and have the same bounds and hands.--

John McAdoo Administrator of the Estate of Samuel Dixon Deceased returned an Additional Am't. of Sales of nine dollars eighty seven & one half Cents (P. 160)

Simon Derrick returns 100 acres of Land for Taxable for the year 1812--

Hugh Barton returns two Town Lotts for Taxable for the year 1812-

Charles Haskell is permitted by the Court to retail Spirits he having given bond and security as the Law requires- for the present year.

Douglass Oliver is permitted by the Court to retail Spirits, he having given bond and security as the Law directs- for the present year.

John Bounds)
   vs   ) Charles McCormick constable for the County of Anderson re-
John Davis) turned him into Court an Execution issued by Arthur Crozier
one of the Justices of the Peace for Anderson County, whereby It appears from the return of said Charles McCormick Constable aforesaid he could find no goods & chattles of said John Davis, and levied the same on two hundred acres of land more or less as the property of said John Davis.
Whereupon it is considered by the Court that the sheriff of our said County of Anderson Advertise and sell the said two hundred Acres of Land, (P. 161) according to law to Satisfy said execution amounting to thirty one Dollars and Twenty five cents, also all the costs thereon.

Robert H. Adams is allowed by the Court Twelve Dollars and fifty Cents for his Services, as Soliscitor Pro Tem at April Sessions 1812----

Samuel Anderson County Soliscitor is allowed thirty seven dollars & fifty Cents for the Present Sessions-

Charles Y. Oliver is allowed by the Court fifty dollars for his Ex officio services up to this time including the Present Sessions--

Hugh Barton Clerk is allowed by the Court fifty dollars for his Ex officio services for the last year.

Quin Morton is allowed Eighteen dollars for Books furnished the Circuit & County Court.

(P. 162) Matt. Heath is appointed constable in Captain Millers Company gave bond and security and was qualified &c.

Samuel Robbins)
     vs   )   This day came Joseph Day and surrendered to Court the
Andw. McKnight) body of Andrew McKnight the Defendant in discharge of
                    himself as bail. -Whereupon came Quin Morton & John Underwood and entered themselves bail in room & stead of said Joseph Day----

    Arthur Crozier, Douglass Oliver, & Quin Morton is appointed commissioners to settle the Estate of James Scarbrough Deceased with Rachel Scarbrough the administratrix---

    Ordered by the Court that the same tax be laid for the present year that was last year, But the Jurors is not to be paid for attending---

    Court then adjourned &c.

    TUESDAY JANUARY 12TH 1813--
    Court met &c. Present Wm. McKamey, Edw. Hawkins & Joseph Sinclair, Esq.

(P. 163) William Doherty)
          vs   )   Rule of Reference set aside, and cause contin-
   Joseph McPeters)   ued.

David Prewit)
    vs   )   This day came the Pltf. by his attorney and dismiss,s his
John Simpson)   suit and assumes upon himself the payment of all Costs ex-
              cept the Attornies Tax fee.- Whereupon came the Defendants by his Attorney and assumes the payment of the Tax fee--
    Thereupon it is considered by the Court that the Defendant go hence without day and recover of the Plff. the Costs of this suit except the tax fee aforesaid and that the Plff. recover of the Defendant the Tax fee &c.

  State   )   )
    vs   ) Reco.) This day came John Bounds Senr. into open Court &
John Davis)   ) acknowledged himself Indebted to the State of Tenn-
                       essee in the sum of two hundred dollars to be lev-
ied of his goods & Chattles lands & tenements-----To be void on condition the said John Bounds do make his personal appearance from day to day at this Court to prosecute & give evidence in this cause and not depart the court without leave. (P. 164)

James Underwood)
    vs   )   This day came the Plff. by his Atto. and suffers a non
Isaac Mayberry)   suit to be entered in this cause- Whereupon It is con-
                sidered by the Court that the Deft. go hence without day and recover against the Plaintiff the Costs by him about his defence in this behalf expended &c--

John Shepheard)
    vs   )   Forfeiture Recognizanee
Andw. Stewart)   In this cause it appearing to the satisfaction of the
               Court that James Underwood was legally summoned to appear and give evidence in this cause who being solemnly called came not- Therefore It is considered by the Court that the said James Underwood forfeit and pay one hundred and twenty five dollars agreeable to act of assembly in such cause made & provided unless he make his personal appearance at the next term of this Court & shew sufficient cause why execution

should not be awarded & Scire Facias Issue accordingly--the above forfeiture is set aside.

James Shepheard)
vs) This day came the Parties by their Attos.- Whereupon came
Andw. Stewart) a Jury towit- Henry Atter, Michael Hosler, James Davidson, Benjamin Langford, Matt. Heath, John Tunnell, John Lewallen, Jesse Hoskins, Joseph Minor, Thomas Dixon, John Leib, Junr., & John Dunevan, who being duly elected tried and sworn the truth to speak upon the Issue (P. 165) Joined upon their Oaths do say they find for the Plff. ninety one Dollars and fifty cents damages-

Therefore it is considered by the Court that the Plaintiff recover of the Defendant Ninety one Dollars and fifty Cents the damages aforesaid also his Costs by him about his suit in this behalf expended-&c. Whereupon came the Defendant by his attorney & entered a Rule for a new trial which is granted---

State)
vs) Recognizance
Gideon Reynolds) This day came into open Court John Hoskins & acknowledged himself Indebted to the State of Tennessee in the sum of Two hundred dollars to be levied of his goods & Chattles lands & tenements. To be void on Condition the said John Hoskins do make his personal appearance from day to day at this Court to prosecute and give evidence in this Court & not depart the Court without leave.

State)
vs) Recognizance
John Hoskins) This day came into open Court John Hoskins & Quin Morton & acknowledged themselves Indebted to the State of Tennessee in the sum of One hundred dollars each to be levied (P. 166) of their respective goods & Chattles lands & tenements to be void on condition the said John Hoskins do make his personal appearance from day to day at this Court to answer a Charge of the State exhibited by the Grand Jury against him and not depart the Court without leave.

Ordered by the Court that John McAdoo Senr., William Lamar, Isaac Mayberry, Thomas Hart, George Sutherland, Wm. Severs, Richard Lewallen, Thomas Dixon, & Isaac Sartin, review the road from Clinton to intersect the road that leads from Fraziers to John Rhea,s & report the nearest & best way to next Court.

Ordered by the Court that Joe Todd, a boy of twelve years old be bound unto Robert Patton, said Patton to learn him the hatters business, reading, writing and Cyphering as far as the rule of three and to give said Boy one hundred dollars when he arrives to the age of 21 years for which time he is bound, fifty dollars of which is to be paid in Hatters tools and the other fifty dollars in a horse- said Patton is at all times bound to keep said boy comfortably clothed & to give him a good suit of Clothes at the time of his freedom.

Ordered by the Court that Kinza Johnson be allowed twenty dollars for supporting Charles and Milly Asher up to this time.

(P. 162) John Taylor returns fifty acres of land as Taxable for the last year.

Thomas Adcock released from the payment of his Poll Tax for last year being over age.

A deed from Robert D. Pearce to Isaac Brazleton for 100 acres of land was proved in open Court by the oaths of John D. Hart & John Dunnevan.

A deed from Walter Taylor to Elijah Beach for 100 acres of land was acknowledged in open Court.

John Parks one of the Admrs. of Wm. Horton Deceased Estate returned amount of sales said Estate.

State)
vs) This day came Saml. Anderson Esquire who prosecutes for the
John Leach) people of the State and the Defendant having heard the Bill
of Indictment read because he will not contend says he is guilty in manner & form as Charged in Bill of Indictment & puts himself on the grace & mercy of the Court- Whereupon it is considered by the Court that for such his offence he be fined 6¼ cents & pay the costs one half of the prosecution of this suit & John Reed the prosecutor comes into open Court and assumes upon himself the other half of the costs.- Whereupon, It is further considered by the Court that the State recover of said John Reed one half of the Costs of this prosecution. (P. 168)

Saml. Robbins)
vs) Cont. on affidavit of the Plff.
Andw. McKnight)

Wm. Hogshead)
vs) Attachment
Her Mills) Charles McCormick constable in and for this County returns
here into court the attachment and it appearing to the Court from the return of said McCormick Constable that the Defendant hath no goods & chattles in this County and said attachment was levied on six hundred and forty acres of Land the property of the Defendant- Whereupon it is considered by the Court that the Sheriff of this County Advertise and sell said six hundred & forty acres of land according to Law to satisfy the Judgment rendered by Quin Morton one of the Justices of the Peace for said County on said attachment which said Judgment amounts to Eighteen Dollars also to satisfy all Costs thereon.-

State)
vs) This day came Saml. Anderson who prosecutes for the peo-
Henry Redenhour) ple of the State and the Defendant who prosecutes for
the people of the State and the Defendant having heard the Bill of Indictment read because he will not contend says he is guilty in manner & form as Charged in the bill of Indictment & puts himself upon the grace & mercy of the Court.
Therefore, It is considered by the Court that for such his offence he be fined the sum of 6¼ cents, and that he pay the costs of this prosecution.

(P. 169) A power of attorney from John Snodgrass to Hugh Dixon was proved in open Court by the oath of Quin Morton & ordered to be recorded.

John Wright was appointed constable in Capt. Marshalls Company gave bond and security & was qualifyed &c.

John Malaby)
    vs   )   <u>Attachment</u>
J. Stewart) In this Case Isaac Mayberry who is summoned as Garnishee and being this day sworn to declare upon oath what he is indebted to the said John Stewart or what effects of his he has in his Possession or what other Persons he knows is Indebted to the said Stewart or has effects of his in their hands- Deposeth and saith that John Stewart put into his hands in the Spring of the year 1811- a note of one hundred dollars on John F. McEntire to be paid in a Horse, he further saith that said Stewart was Indebted to him something tho he does not know to what amount and that he was to pay himself out of that note and that the <u>ballance</u> If any he was to return to said Stewart & his family & further the said Mayberry knows not of any person who is Indebted to the said Stewart or any of his effects in their hands & further saith not----

    Court then adjourned until Tomorrow &c----&c----

(P. 170) WEDNESDAY 13TH JANUARY 1813--
    Court met according to adjournment.
    Present- William McKamey, Sam,l. Davidson, & Quin Morton- Esquires-

State)
    vs   ) This day came Samuel Anderson who prosecutes for the peo-
James Shepheard) ple of the State and the Defendant having heard the bill of Indictment read says he is not guilty in manner & form as Charged in the Bill of Indictment, and puts himself upon the Country, Whereupon came a Jury towit, Henry Atter, Michael Hosler, James Davidson, Benjamin Langford, Matt. Heath, John Tunnell, John Lewallen, Jesse Hoskins, William Hancock, Phillip Harless, John Scott, & Julias Milliken who being duly elected tried and sworn the truth to speak upon the Issue Joined upon their oaths do day the Defendant is not guilty in manner & form as charged in the Bill of Indictment.

    Arthur Crozier, William Sharp & Quin Morton the commissioners appointed on yesterday by the Court to settle with Hugh Barton, Admr. of the Estate of Benjamin C. Parker Dec,d. have proceeded to make said settlement and find that Hugh Barton Admr. aforesaid hath paid $8.6½ cents more than the amount of sales of property administered--

State)
    vs   )   <u>Discontinued</u>
John Robertson)

(P. 171) Ordered by the Court that the same Jury who was appointed to view the two roads. Beginning at Reuben Williams field on the Black Oak Ridge. Report to next Court agreeable to the order of the last Court.

State)
    vs   ) This day came the Defendant by his attorney and motioned the
David Hall) Court to Quash the Bill of Indictment and arguments having been heard thereon, It is considered by the court that the said Bill of Indictment be Quashed.

    A deed from John Sutherland for 100 acres of land to Sam,l. Edmundson was acknowledged in open Court and ordered to be registered--

Wm, Scott)
vs) Certiorari
Wm. Hogshead) Cont,d. on affidavit of John Scott.

State)
vs) This day came the Defendant by his attorney and motioned
Collins Roberts) the Court to Quash the Bill of Indictment and argument
being heard thereon, It is considered by the Court that
said Bill of Indictment be Quashed from which Judgment Saml. Anderson Solicitor for the county prayed an appeal to the next Circuit Court to be held for the County of Anderson filed his reasons & appeal granted by the Court.--

(P. 172) State)
vs) This day came Saml. Anderson who prosecutes for the peo-
) ple of the State and moved the Court to Tax the Defend-
James Shepheard) ant with the Costs On Solemn argument, It is considered
by the court that the State recover of the Defendant the
Costs of this prosecution.

Court then adjourned until Tomorrow Morning 9 O,clock.

THURSDAY 14TH JANUARY 1813.
Court met &c--Present Joseph Sinclair, Arthur Crozier & Quin Morton, Esquires--

State)
vs) This day came Saml. Anderson, Esqr. who prosecutes for the
Andrew Stewart) people of the State and the Defendant having heard the Bill
of Indictment read says he is not guilty in manner and form
as charged in the Bill of Indictment. Whereupon came a Jury towit, Henry Atter, Michael Hostler, James Davidson, Benjamin Langford, Matt. Heath, John Tunnell, Britton Cross, George Hensley, Richard Campbell, John Rector, John Bounds, Senr. & Thomas Hope, who being duly Elected tried and sworn the truth to speak upon the issue joined upon their oaths do say the Defendant is guilty of the assault & Battery in manner & form &c--- (P. 173)

John Fry)
vs) Appeal
Stephen Heard) In this cause the rule taken at last Court is Dismissed
and the cause continued.

Mary Kirkpatrick returns 300 acres of land as Taxable Property for last year.

Ordered by the Court that Elijah Beach be overseer of the road in room of Jeremiah Hibbs removed & have the same bounds & hands.

State)
vs) This day came Samuel Anderson who prosecutes for the peo-
William Taber) ple of the State and the defendant having heard the Bill
of Indictment read says he is not guilty in manner & form
as charged in the said Bill of Indictment and puts himself upon the Country-
Whereupon came a Jury towit, Henry Atter, Michael Hosler, James Davidson,

Benjamin Langford, Matt. Heath, John Tunnell, Britton Cross, George Hensley, Richard Campbell, John Rector, John Bounds, & Thomas Hope, who being duly elected Tried and sworn the truth to speak upon their oaths do say the defendant is guilty in manner & form as charged in the Bill of Indictment-

Therefore it is considered by the Court that for such his offence he be fined Six and one fourth Cents, and pay the Costs of this prosecution. Whereupon comes John Taber into open Court & acknowledges himself bound to pay said Costs (P. 174) charged in the Bill of Indictment therefore It is Considered by the Court that for such his offence he be fined six and one fourth cents & pay the Costs of this prosecution----

An assignment of a Platt and Certificate from Rich,d Campbell to James White was acknowlegded in open Court.

Ordered by the Court that Abraham Moser take the children of ----- Keller and keep them until next Court, At which time he is to bring them into Court for the purpose of having them bound under direction of the Court.

Charles Y. Oliver sheriff of the County of Anderson acknowledged the Execution of Deed for Six Town Lotts in the town of Clinton to James Underwood.

State)
vs) John Hoskins makes affidavit that he is not ready for trial
John Hoskins) and the Cause is continued. Whereupon came the said John
Hoskins and Libston Bailey and acknowledged themselves indebted to the state of Tennessee in the sum of one hundred dollars each to be levied of their respective goods & chattles lands & tenements- To be void on condition the said John Hoskins do make his personal appearance at the next term of this Court to answer a charge of the State exhibited against him by the Grand Jury & not depart the Court without leave. (P. 175)

State)
vs) This day came John Hoskins into open Court and acknowl-
Gideon Reynolds) edged himself indebted to the State of Tennessee in the
the sum of one hundred & fifty dollars to be levied of his goods & chattles lands & tenements. To be void on Condition he do make his personal appearance at the next term of this Court to give evidence & prosecute in this cause and not depart the Court without leave.

State)
vs) On Motion, It is considered by the Court the prosecutor
John Davis) John Bounds Senr. is Tax with the Costs of this prosecution.

Same)
vs) On motion, It is considered by the Court the prosecutor John Bounds
Same) Senr. is Tax with the Cost of this prosecution.

John Malaby)
vs) Attachment
John Stewart) John F. McEntire who was summoned as garnisher in this
cause was solemnly called came not- It is considered by the Court that Judgment be entered against said McEntire unless at the next term of this Court he comes & shews cause why Execution should not issue against him and that Scire facias Issue accordingly-

(P. 176) Court then adjourned until Tomorrow Morning 9 O,clock.

FRIDAY 15TH JANUARY 1813.

Court met &c- Present William McKamey, Quin Morton & Joseph Sinclair Esquires-

John Stewart for the use of)	
William Underwood)	Prayed
vs)	Oyer of the covenant &
William Hogshead)	writing declared on.

State) Forfeiture against-
vs)
Collins Roberts) The Defendant being bound in Recognizance to appear at this Court to answer a Charge of the State, being solemnly called came not. Therefore It is considered by the Court that he forfeit & pay the State the sum of one hundred dollars the sum named in the Recognizance unless he appears at next Court and shew cause to the Contrary & that Scire facias Issue accordingly.

Same)
vs) Forfeiture Recognizance
Sampl. Pryor &) In this cause it appearing to the satisfaction of the
Douglass Oliver) Court that Sam,l Pryor & Douglass Oliver was bound in recognizance for the appearance of Collins Roberts at this Court, who being solemnly called to bring into Court the body of said Collins Roberts failed so to do.

Therefore it is considered by the Court that they forfeit their Recognizance agreeable to act of Assembly in such Cases made & provided in such cases & Scire facias Issue accordingly. (P. 177)

John Underwood)
vs) Contd. by Consent-
Wm. Lohery)

Ordered by the Court that James Kirkpatrick be overseer of the road in room of Gabriel Prewit & have the same bounds & hands.

Lewis Harmon for the)
use of Wm. Parks) This day came the parties by their attornies-
vs) Whereupon came a Jury towit. Henry Atter, Michael
Hugh Barton Admr. of) Hosler, James Davidson, Benjamin Langford, Matt.
Benj. C. Parker) Heath, John Tunnell, John Lewallen, Marmaduke Bookout, Phillip Severs, Henry Norman, David Hall, & LeonardCoffman who being Elected tried and sworn well & truly to try the Issue Joined upon their oaths do say that the Defendant hath fully administered all & singular the goods & chattles rites and credits of Benjamin C. Parker, Deceased which have come to his hands to be administered as in pleading he hath alledged--

Whereupon the prayer of the Plaintiff, It is considered by the Court that the Plff. recover against Defendant the debt in the Declaration mentioned together with two hundred & forty four dollars & 3 cents for his damages by reason of the detention of their Debt and their Costs by him expended to be levied of the goods & chattles rights & credits of the said Benjamin C. Parker when the same shall come to the hand of said Defendant to be administered & the Deft. in mercy &c-- (P. 178)

Sarah Scarbrough)
    vs   ) Cont. by Consent
Absolom White)

John Malaby)
    vs   ) Attachment Cont.
John Stewart)

    Ordered that the following persons take list of Taxable property for the year 1813-

    Gastin................... Capt. Bradens
    McKamey.................. " Tunnells
    Gilbreath .... " Davidsons
    Hawkins.................. " Millers
    Morton................... " Scruggs
    Underwood................ " Marshalls.

    A deed of trust from Gabriel prewit to William Tunnell was acknowledged in open Court--
    John Gibbs, Douglass Oliver & John Leib Junr. be Judges of the next congressional Election----

    Ordered by the Court that Lewis Freeman be overseer of the road in room of Absolom White.

    Ordered that the following persons be Jurors to next County Court (towit) Charles Shinliver, Jacob Lenard, Man Page Vowell, Willie Young, William Arthur, Henry Farmer, John Tovera, John Rector, (P. 179) Collins Roberts, Micajah Frost, John Gamble, Tobias Peters, Henry Peters, Austin Hackworth, Aaron Slover, John Taylor, John Garner, Moses Farmer, James Ragan, William McAdoo, John F. McEntire, Josua Frost, John Miller, John Wallace, Rhode Stanley, & David Hall.

    Charles Y. Oliver sheriff of the county of Anderson reports the following Tracts of Land as Taxable property for the year 1812- towit, Robert Salter,s Heirs in Henderson & Co. Survey in the Hickory Valley) $7.10¾
James Shulbread 825 Ditto   Ditto   8.50
    Also the following is returned has not been given in for the year 1812 towit.
    4000 acres of land North East half of Lott H. in Henderson & Company's Clinch Survey
    George Gordon 200 acres Poplar Creek
    Benjamin Potter 100 acres Cole Creek
    Quin Morton returns into Court 300 acres of land as the property of James Hannah Dcd. as Taxable for the present year 1812--

    Ordered by the Court that Matthew Hawkins, John Sutherland, Saml. Worthington, Wm. Boyd, William Tunnell Junr., Jacob Butler, & Lewis Rector be a Jury of review to view the road Beginning at the corner of James Childress fence to Intersect (P. 180) the road near Collins Roberts,s fence View Report &c to next term of this court. It is understood they are to view old and new roads

    Court then adjourned until next Court in Course.
                                         ARTHUR CROZIER C. A. C.

(P. 181) MONDAY APRIL 12TH 1813.

At a Court of pleas and quarter sessions opened and held at the Court House in Clinton in the County of Anderson on the second Monday in April 1813 Present Arthur Crozier Samuel Galbreath & Edward Hawkins Esqrs

Charles Y. Oliver Sheriff returned the following Venire Facias (towit) Charles Chinliver, Jacob Leinard, Manpage Vowell, Wiley Young, Henry Farmer Junr John Tovera, John Rector, Collins Roberts, Micajah Frost, John Gamble, Tobias Peters, Henry Peters, Austin Hackworth, Aaron Slover, John Taylor, John Garner, Moses Farmer, James Ragen, John McAdoo Senr, John F. McEntire, Joshua Frost, John Miller, Rode Stanley & Danl Wall.

John Tovera, Tobias Peters, Henery Peters, John Taylor were excused for attending as Jurors at this term.

Micajah Frost Rode Stanley & Daniel failed to attend.

The following were chosen Grand Jurors (towit) John McAdoo Senr foreman, John Gamble, John Rector, Aaron Slover, Austin Hackworth, Manpage Vowel, Charles Shinliver, John F. McEntire, John Miller, Joshua Frost, Henery Farmer Junr, James Ragen & John Garner.

Ordered that Joseph Black be overseer in the place of John Cooper (over the river) and have the same bounds & hands-

(P. 182) A Deed from Joseph Keeny to John Taylor for seventy five acres of land was proved in open Court by the oaths of Wm. Hogshead, & Richard Luallen and ordered to be registered

Simeon Smith excused for his non attendance as a juror at last term-

A Deed from Isaac Low to Gabriel Hackworth was proved in open court for two hundred and fifty six acres by Austin Hackworth and James Scarbro and oredered to be registered-

Saml. Galbreath Esqr. returned into Court the tax list Tunnels Company for the present year—

Ordered by the Court that Isaac Mayberry be overseer of the road in place of James Epperson and have the same Bounds & hands—

John Hollin brought into Court two grown wolf Scalps, and made oath that he killed the wolves in Anderson County in the year 1813 Ordered by the Court he be allowed agreeable to Law—

Ordered that Wm. Wortherington be overseer of the road in place of Simeon Smith and have the same bounds & Hands-

(P. 183) Ordered by the Court that George Sutherlin, Thomas Hart & Robert Galbreath be allowed each the sum of eleven dollars for settling with the County officers and Hugh Barton one dollar for furnishing paper wafers &c-

Jeremiah Hatfield brought into open Court three grown wolf scalps and made oath that he killed the wolves in Anderson County sometime in the year 1813 Ordered that he be allowed agreeable to law.

William Doherty)
    vs   )   This day came the plaintiff by his atto. J. McCampbell
Joseph Doherty)   and moves the court for judgment against Wm. Doherty and
                   it appearing to the satisfaction of the Court that the
Wm. Doherty was security for said Joseph Doherty and did pay for the said
Joseph Doherty Eighteen dollars and fifty cents— therefore it is considered
by the Court that plaintiff recover of the defendant the sum of Eighteen dollars and fifty cents and the defendant in mercy &c—

    The following Jury of review to view the road from the forks of the
Road in the wolf valey leading towards Thomas Reed's mill where it will strike
the (P. 184) line between Knox County and this some where near Paul Chiles
plantation or if they have reviewed it in Knox County before this order is
carried into effect this Road is to Join it Joshua Frost Aaron Jenkins, David
Hall, Thomas Wilson, Paul Chiles, page portwood, Isac Norman John Scott &
Saml Frost appointed a Jury of review to view the same and that they make report to this Court—

John Malaby)
    vs   )   present Joseph Sinclair Alexander Gastin & Edwrad Hawkins
John Stewart)   Esqrs.
              Whereupon came a Jury towit Jacob Lenard, Moses Farmer,
Wiley Young, William Doherty, John Taber, Charles Kirkpatrick, Robert Galbreath, Richard Luallen, Thomas Hope, Hugh Millican, Constant Clarkson &
John Bounds who being empannelled tried and sworn to say what damages the
Plaintiff hath sustained in the premises, do say they find the Plaintiff hath
sustained damages to the amount of thirty four dollars forty six and three
fourth cents besides his Costs— Whereupon it is considered by the court that
the plaintiff do recover of the Defendant the sum aforesaid in form aforesaid
assessed and also his Costs about his suit in this behalf expended and be the
Deft in mercy &c—

    Court then adjourned until tomorrow 9 o,clock.

(P. 185) TEWSDAY APRIL 13 1813
    Court met according to adjournment— Present Arthur Crozier William
Underwood and Edward Hawkins Esqrs.

    Thomas Hart, William Severs, David Hale, John McAdoo Senr. and William
Lemar who in pursuance of an order of the County Court of Pleas and Quarter
Sessions and to us directed met upon the 27th of March and viewed the two
roads agreeable to the order to us directed begining at the top of the Black
Oak Ridge at Reuben Williams field and we are of the opinion that the old
road is the best and most convenient way which report was by the court—

    John Gibbs Esq. who was appointed a Justice of the Peace came into open
Court and took the oaths of office agreeable to law—

    George Sutherland and Thomas Hart who was appointed Commissioners came
into Court entered into Bond and security for the purpose of setling with the
officers of Anderson County.

    William McAmey Esqr— Returned the tax list of Cpt. Tunnels Company for
the year 1813

(P. 186) A deed from Thomas Dixon Senr. to Hugh Dixon and Thomas Dixon Junr.

to John Hoskins was proved in open Court by Thomas Hart and George Sutherland for three hundred acres of land to be registered-

James Shepheard)
vs) This day came the parties by their attorn- whereupon came
Andrew Stewart) a jury towit

Jacob Leinard, Moses Farmer, Wilie Young, David Pruit, David Wallace, John Hoskins, Thomas Landrum, John Bounds, John Wallace Junr- Charles Kirkpatrick, Robert Wilson & Peter Clair who being duly elected tried and sworn the truth to speak upon the Issue Joined upon their oaths do say they find for the pltf Seventy dollars Damages-

Therefore it is considered by the Court that the plaintiff recover of the defendant seventy Dollars the damages aforesaid assessed By the Jury aforesaid also his costs by him about his suit in this behalf expended and be the Defendant in mercy &c-

Quin Morton Esqr- returned the tax list of Capt. Miller,s Company for the year 1813-

Edward Hawkins Esqr. returned the tax list of Cpt. Davidsons Company for the year 1813

William Underwood Esqr- returned the tax list for Cpt Scruggs Company for the year 1813

(P. 187) Ordered by the Court that the following Persons be Jurors to the next County Court (towit) Henry Peters, Tobias Peters, Daniel Wall, John Taylor, John Tovera, Abreham Hagler, James Hill, George Shetter, Clinging Kincade, Richard Martial, Robert Roysdon, Charles Price, Julius Millican, John Redenhour, John H. Chapman, Jones Pettit, James Scarbro, Jacob Peek, Edward Freels, George Hudson, Willis Leath, Samuel Prior, Obediah Ashlock, John Freels, & John Dunevan-

Ordered by the Court that the following persons be jorors to the next Circuit Court (towit) Samuel Frost, Alexander Gastin, Edward Hawkins, SamuelGalbreath, David Scarbro, Michael Clardy, John Gibbs, Jesse Patton, George Sutherlin, Gabriel Hackworth, Douglas Oliver, Nathan Hale, John Underwood, Samuel Dunn, Thomas Wilson, Jacob Larew, Aron Jenkins, Thomas Wright, William Lemar, Thomas Hart, John Parks, Joseph Parks, William McAmey, Samuel Taylor, Jacob Butler, Ruben Williams & Luncford Oliver-

Delia Blackburn)
vs) On Motion by Saml. Anderson Esqr, It is ordered that
James Deaton) James Deaton pay to Delila Blacburn two dollars and fifty
Cents quarterly for the term of five years for the support of a child begot By the said Deaton upon the said Delila Blackburn-

(P. 188) Ordered that Quin Morton, William McAmey, and Kinza Johnson do take the deposition of Elliot Grills at the house of Wm Tunnel Senr. to establish the first and second corner in an eighteen hundred and fifty acre survey granted to Robert Young on the Brushy fork of poplar creek and joined above by a Nineteen Hundred and fifty acre Survey granted to George or Robert Gordon on or near the plantation where Joseph Parks now lives formerly owned by Arthur Crozier- given notice according to law &c-

In pursuance of an order to us directed we met upon 6th February last and viewed the road from Clinton to where Wm. Edwards now lives from thence to Clinch River past where John Ray now lives from tence to the Road that leads to Frazier (?) past a field of Isaac Mayberry,s- on said Road and marked the same- Signed John McAdoo Senr- Wm. Lemar, Thomas Hart, George Sutherlin, William Severs, Richard Luallen, Thomas Dixon & Isaac Sartin-

John Wallace Junr be appointed overseer of the road in place of Richard C. Cobb Deceased and have the same bounds and hands-

Ordered that William Edwards be overseer of the road from his house to the River at Ray,s Ford and have John Edwards and all the hands in the bend of the River commonly known as Parkers hands-

(P. 189) Wm. Doherty)
vs) This day came the parties by there attr- where-
Joseph McPeters) upon came a Jury (towit) Collins Roberts, Jesse Patton, Truman Still, John Pain, Absolom White, John McEntire, James Tunnel, Hugh Millican, John Taylor, William Edwards, Joseph Minor and John Rector- who being duly elected tried and sworn the truth to speak upon there oaths do say they fine for the plaintiff and assess his damages one hundred and thirty dollars- Therefore it is considered By the Court that the Plaintiff recover of the Defendant one hundred and thirty dollars the damages aforesaid assessed By the Jury aforesaid also his Costs By him about his suit expended and be the defendant in mercy &c-

John Mallaby)
vs) Motion By Defendant Atto. to set aside the Judgment by
John F. McEntire) Default By Showing Cause &c-

Ordered by the Court that John Taylor by overseer of the Road in place of John Leach and have the same bounds and hands.

Ordered by the Court that Phillips Allbright be allowed the sum of thirty dollars yearly to be paid as compensation for supporting Elizabeth Huchings. (P. 190)

Nathanl. B. Buckingham))
& William Cobb) adminrs.) This day came the plaintiff by their
Rebecca Cobb) Adminx of) attorney Wm. C. Mynat and moved the
Richard C. Cobb, Deceased) Court for Judgment vs. Hugh Mont-
vs) gomery for the sum of fifty eight
Hugh Montgomery) Dollars and forty one cents and they
) having produced him into Court a
receipt Specifying they had paid that Sum on account of Richard C. Cobb Deceased being security for said Hugh Montgomery-

Therefore, It is considered by the Court that the Plaintiffs recover of the Defendant fifty Eight Dollars and forty one cents aforesaid also their Costs about their motion in this behalf expended and said Defendant in mercy &c-

Court then adjourned til tomorrow nine o,clock-

WEDNESDAY APRIL 14TH 1813-
Court met according to adjournment- Present Samuel Galbreath, Joseph Sinclair and John Gibbs Esqrs.-

In pursuance of an order to view the Roads from the Corner of James

Childres fence to intersect the Emery road at Collins Roberts fence the Jurors met according to appoint and viewing both roads are of opinion the old Road is the best Mathew Hawkins, Lewis Rector, Saml. Wortherington, John Sutherland and William Tunnel-

(P. 191) State)
    vs) In this Case the forfeiture taken against the defend-
Collins Roberts) ant was set aside & he assumed the payment of the costs accruing thereon.

Ordered by the Court that John Underwood be appointed overseer of the Road instead of William Scott and have the same Bounds and hands.

State)
    vs) Present Samuel Galbreath, Edward Hawkins & John Gibbs,
John Hoskins) Esquires--
    Whereupon came a Jury towit Jacob Lenart, Collins Roberts, Moses Farmer, Wiley Young, Andrew Breden, John Leib Senr, William Doherty, Thomas Landrum, David Pruitt, John Simpkins, Andrew McKnight & Saml Robbins who being empannelled tried and sworn do say they find the Defendant Guilty in manner and form as charged in the Bill of Indictment whereupon it is considered by the Court that the defendant be fined in the Sum of fifty cents Besides the Costs & be in mercy-- (P. 192)

State)
    vs) Present Quin Morton, John Gibbs, Alexander Gaston and Ed-
Gideon Reynolds) ward Hawkins Esquires---
    Same Jury as above, who being empannelled tried and sworn do say they find the defendant guilty in manner and form as charged in the Bill of Indictment----Whereupon it is considered by the Court that the Defendant be fined in the sum of six cents and one fourth of a cent besides the Costs & be in mercy &c---

Quin Morton, Arthur Crozier & Douglas Oliver who were appointed Commissioners to settle with Rachel Scarbro Admix of the Estate of James Scarbro deceased returned the Settlement to Court --

John Underwood)
    vs) This Cause was Continued by the Consent of the parties
William Loughery) until next Term.---

William Scott)
    vs) In this Case the parties refered the matter in dispute
William Hogshead) to the arbitrament of Robert H. Adams & William C. My-
natt whose award was to be made a Judgment of the Court, who say they consider that the plaintiff recover of the defendant three dollars besides his Costs- (P. 194)

Samuel Robbins)
    vs) In this case Quin Morton surrendered the defendant in open
Andrew McKnight) Court in discharge of himself as Bail-----

Charles Oliver Sheriff entered into Bond with Security for the Collection of the Taxes assessed for the year 1813.

We the Jurors appointed to this Term have viewed the road agreeable to

to the order to us directed Begining at the County line on the Copper Ridge
running by Andrew Letts thence across Bull Run by said plantation where
Nathaniel davis formely lived thence by Joshua Frost thence in the Wolf Valley to the forks of the road to be the nearest and best way –

Given under our hands this 14th April 1813– Aron Jenkins Page Portwood
Thomas Wilson Paul Chiles Joshua Frost

Ordered that Joshua Frost be overseer and have following bounds (towit)
Begining at Pruitts including ----------from thence across to the Bull Run
Ridge thence down the River to the County line thence up the Copper ridge to
said road thence to include Julias Millican thence to include John H. Chapman and Fips thence to the beginning–

Court then adjourned to tomorrow Morning nine Oclock

(P. 195) THURSDAY 15TH APRIL 1813

Court met according to adjournment– present Arthur Crozier Quin Morton & Edward Hawkins Esqr–

Saml Robbins)
vs) This day came James Underwood & Jacob Lenard and under-
Andrew McKnight) took for the Defendant to pay and satisfy the Judgment of
the Court or render his body in discharge of the same if
he should be cost in his suit &c–

Henrietta Sartin Adminx.)
vs) In this Case the Defendants being solemnly called,
John Underwood & Rode) came not, Whereupon it is considered by the Court
Stanley, Adminrs.) that the Plaintiff recover of the Defendant the
sum of one hundred and Seventy Six dollars, twenty
two cents & one half of a cent besides his Costs except one hundred and five
dollars which has been already paid And be the defendants in mercy &c––

Rowland Chiles)
vs) This Cause was continued By the Consent of the parties
William Hogshead)

(P. 196) Samuel Robbins)
vs) In this case on motion of the Defendant,s Counsel
Andrew McKnight) it is ordered that a Rule to Shew cause why a
new trial should be granted––which Rule on Solemn
argument was made absolute––

T. & W. Allen for the use of)
James Harper)
vs) This case was continued by consent of counsel–
Thomas Dixon)

John Stewart for the use of)
William Underwood) In this case a Demurrer having been filed
vs) by the Plaintiff, and having been Solemnly
William Hogshead) argued this day, it is considered by the
Court that the demurrer should be sustained
after solemn argument having been had thereon and the defendant &c––

Thomas Shelton)
vs) On Scire facias
James Harbin) In this case it is ordered by the Court that the Judgment
by default against defendant be set aside, and that the Defendant pay the Costs of said Scire facias---

Ordered by the Court that the Jury be discharged----

(P. 197) White & Lynch for the)
use of John Underwood) On Scire facias
vs) In this case the Plaintiff demurred &
Larkin Bowling) the Court agreed to take an advisari
until next Term----

John Malaby)
vs) On Scire facias
John F. McEntire) In this case the Defendant had leave to enter a Rule to
shew cause why a Judgment by default should be set aside, and after solemn argument it is ordered by the Court the Rule be made absolute, and the defendant pay the Costs of said Scire facias------

Charles McClung)
vs) In this case Thomas Butler being solemnly called to re-
Thomas Butler &) plevy the property attached came not Whereupon it is
Jacob Butler) considered by the Court that the Plaintiff recover a-
gainst the said Thomas Butler debt in the declaration
mentioned also his cost about his suit his damages by him sustained in this behalf expended and be the defendant in mercy &c----- (P. 198)

White & Lynch)
vs) This day the Plaintiffs Came by their Attorney & two Scire
John Stewart) facias,s having been returned not found And the defendant
John Stewart not appearing tho solemnly called, It is considered by the Court that the Plaintiffs have Execution against the said John Stewart of the Judgment in the Scire Facias mentioned ----

Lewis Harmon for the)
use of William Park) In this cause the Plaintiff having suggested to the
vs) court that real Estate had descended from said Benj-
The Admor of Benj. C.) amin C. Parker to Elizabeth Bryan, wife of William
Parker, Deceased) H. Bryan, and Sarah McCorry wife of Thomas McCorry
and Benjamin Parker Maclin, William Maclin, James
Zachfield Maclin and Landon Carter Maclin Heirs at Law of said Benjamin C. Parker--- On motion of said Plaintiff a writ of Scire facias is awarded him, against the said William H. Bryan, & Elizabeth his wife, Thomas McCorry, Sarah his wife Benjamin Parker Maclin, William Maclin, James Zachfield Maclin & Landon Carter Maclin, returnable to the next Term of this Court to shew cause why Execution should not be Issued against (P. 199) the real estate descended to them from said Benjamin C. Parker for the amount of the Judgment in this cause, and appearing to the Court that the said Benjamin Parker Maclin, William Maclin, James Zachfield Maclin & Landon Carter Maclin are minors under the age of Twenty one years, John McCampbell is appointed their Guardian to defend the Scire facias hereby awarded against them.-----

John Aldridge proved that he killed a grown wolf in Anderson County in the present year ordered he be allowed agreeable to Law.

Charles Y. Oliver Collector who having heretofore reported four thousand acres of land in Henderson & Co Survey on Clinch River which having reference to the former entry at January term 1813 having Received other information which he believes to be correct it is therefore ordered by the Court that only he advertise 2000 acres in the place of 4000 which appears to be the quantity that ought to have been reported-
ARTHUR CROZIER C. A. C.

(P. 200) At a Court of Pleas and Quarter Sessions opened and held for the County of Anderson, at the Court House in Clinton, on the second Monday of July, in the year of our Lord one thousand eight hundred and thirteen--
Present Arthur Crozier, Quin Morton, William McKamey, Douglas Oliver & Joseph Sinclair Esquires-

Charles Y. Oliver Esquire Sheriff returned the Venire Facias (Executed) of whom the following were appointed grand Jurors (towit) Tobias Peters, Foreman, Edward Freels, John H. Chapman, Abraham Hagler, Samuel Prior, George Hudson, Jonas Pettit, Obadiah Ashlock, Daniel Wall, John Freels, Julius Millican, Willie Leath, & James Scarbro who being empannelled, charged & sworn retired to enquire-

The following are Traverse Jurors (towit) John Tovera, Clinging Kinkaid, Richard Martial, John Ridenour-----

A deed from Josiah Hannah & others to Jacob Huffstedler for two hundred Acres of Land was proved in open Court by Aquilla Lowe & John Huffstedler & ordered to be Registered-

(P. 201) A Deed from Josiah Hanna & others to John Huffstedler for one hundred Acres of Land was proved in open Court by Aquilla Lowe & Jacob HuffStedler and ordered to be registered-

Ordered by the Court, that James Wood & Sally Wood have leave to administer on the Estate of John Lanum deceased, who gave Bond with John Wallace & Enoch Foster Securities & were qualified as the Law requires-

Ordered by the Court that Arthur Crozier, Quin Morton & William McKamey Esquires be appointed to settle with John McAdoo administrator of the Estate of Samuel Dixon deceased & that they make report accordingly----

Ordered by the Court that John Cress be over seer of the road in stead of William Gamble & have the same Bounds & hands-----

Reuben Moss agent for Robert Salter, returns one thousand and twenty five acres of Land Subject to Tax for the present year----

(P. 202) Mary Miller returned two black poles Subject to Tax for the present year.-

Jacob Huffstedler Returned two hundred acres of land subject to taxation for this present year-

Ordered by the Court that Rhodes Stanley be excused for not having attended as a Juror at the last Term-

Ordered by the Court that Thomas Landrum be released from the payment of the tax on a Negro Boy returned on the List of William Underwood Esquire-

Ordered by the Court that John Taylor overseer have the following hands to work under him (towit) John Keeney, John Leach, Michael Asher, James Still, Neely Gibbs, James Leatch, John Harmon, Sam Hibbs & John Miller---

The Court then adjourned until tomorrow morning 9 O,clock.

(P. 203) TUESDAY 13TH JULY 1813.

The Court met according to adjournment- Present Arthur Crozier, William Underwood, & William McKamey Esquires---

Jane Breden by her next friend)
vs) In this case, on the suggestion of the plaintiffs
Joseph Sinclair Junr) attorney, that Joseph Sinclair is a minor, It is therefore ordered by the Court, that Joseph Sinclair the Elder be appointed his guardian, pendente Lite--

Ordered by the Court that Clinging Kinkaid be excused from attending as a juror at this term.---

William Hogshead produced in open Court his Licence to practice as an Attorney and was sworn accordingly.---

Ordered by the Court that Arthur Crozier & John Gibbs be appointed to settle with the administrators of Richard C. Cobb deceased, and make report to Court.----

White & Lynch for the use of)
John Underwood) Present Quin Morton, William McKamey and Edward Hawkins Esqrs.- (P. 204)
vs) Whereupon came a Jury who being duly sworn
Larkin Bowling) (towit) Isaac Horton, William Craighead, John Leatch, William Lamar, William Severs, Jesse Haskins, John Hoskins, Robert Wilson, Isaac Freels, James Woods, John Tovera, & Richard Marshal say on plea alledging the Death of Charles Crobaugh, that he is not dead.

Rachel Scarbro)
vs) Same Court and Jury as above, except Isaac Freels & Robert
Absolom White) Wilson, in whose stead are Jacob Linard & John Tunnell who being duly sworn say they find for the Plaintiff and assess her damage to fifteen dollars, Eighteen and one half cents---
Whereupon it is considered by the Court that the Plaintiff do recover the sum aforesaid as also her Costs about her suit in this behalf expended and be the defendant in mercy &c.-----

John Underwood)
vs) In this case Hugh Barton surrendered the defendant in open
William Lohrey) Court, in discharge of himself as Bail---

Ordered by the Court that John Kirk be overseer instead of John Lynn and have the same Bounds & hands.----

(P. 205) Walter Alves returned Ten thousand Seven hundred and ninety nine acres of Land subject to Tax for this present year.--

The following persons are appointed to attend as Jurors at the next Term of this Court (towit) William Ashlock, Jacob Lynart, Craven Johnson, Joseph Keeney Senr. Aaron Slover, Jesse Hoskins, Philip Severs, James Tunnell, William Nichols, Richard Campbell, William Gamble, Samuel Williams, William Craighead, Robert Roysdon, John White, Elijah Frost, Elijah Hendon, Reuben Golson, James Caldwell, Robert Wilson, John McEntire Junr, William McAdoo, James Hill, Jesse Bookout, Edward Williams & Charles Heskell---

Page Portwood returned one white pole Subject to Tax for the present year----

William Sharp returned one white and four black polls, four hundred acres of land & one Stud Horse (Season $2) subject to tax for this year

Elijah Frost returned one hundred & forty acres of Land for Tax for this year-- (P. 206)

Rachel Scarbro)
    vs   ) In this Case the Defendant,s Attorney entered a Rule to
Absolom White) shew cause why a New trial should be granted-

A deed from Richard Lewallen to John Leatch for one hundred and fifty acres of Land was acknowledged in open Court and ordered to be registered--

A deed from John Hoskins to William Ashlock for one hundred acres of Land as acknowledged in open Court and ordered to be registered--

John & William Allen)
    vs   ) Present Arthur Crozier, Quin Morton, William Sharp
Thomas Dixon) & M. Clardy, Esquires-
    Whereupon came a Jury (to wit) Isaac Horton, William Craighead, John Leatch, William Lamar, William Severs, Jesse Hoskins, John Hoskins, James Wood, Jesse Patton, John Tunnell, Richard Marshal & John Ridnour who being duly sworn do say they find for the plaintiff the debt in the Declaration mentioned & assess his damage by reason of the detention thereof to Sixty two dollars & costs- Whereupon it is considered by the Court that the Plaintiff do recover his Debt & damages aforesaid, also his costs about his suit expended & be the Deft. in mercy--&c-- (P. 207)
From which judgment the defendant prayed an appeal, filed his reasons, and gave Bond with Security whereupon the appeal was granted-----

Ordered by the Court that Jacob Stukesbery (April 1814) be allowed thirty dollars annually payable Quarter-yearly for the support & maintenance of Elizabeth Hutchings Instead of Phillip Allbright who has refused to keep said woman---

Mary Patterson)
    vs   ) Bastardy- In this case the Deft- & John Loughery, John
William Loughery) Fry and Manpage Vowell his Securities confessed Judgment for Seven dollars and fifty cents besides the Costs.

Mary Patterson)
    vs   ) Bastardy- In this case the defendant & his Securities
William Lohery) John Lohrey, John Fry & Man Page Vowell confessed Judgment for Twelve dollars and fifty cents maintenance of

a child begotten on the body of the said Mary Patterson by the said William Lohrey---

(P. 208) John Fry, Assee)
       vs   ) Present Arthur Crozier, M. Clardy, William Mc-
   Stephen Heard) Kamey & Wm. Sharp Esquires-
                       Whereupon came a Jury (to wit) Thomas Dixon Senr, Hugh Dixon, Jesse Bounds, John Leib Junr, John Taber, Hugh Milican, Elijah Frost, Andrew Breden, Samuel Edmondsun, John Rhea, Trueman Still, John Tovera who being duly sworn say they find for the Plaintiff fifteen dollars his debt, also Eighty Eight cents for his damages by reason of the detention thereof-

    Whereupon it is considered by the Court that the Plaintiff recover his Debt, damages & Costs about his suit in this behalf expended & be the said defendant in mercy &c---

John Underwood)
     vs   ) Continued by Consent.
William Lohrey)

Rachel Aultum)
   vs   ) In this case on motion of Deft,s Atto. Rule to shew cause
John Fry   ) why Proceedings before Justice should be quashed which
                 rule is withdrawn-

    The Court then appointed John McAdoo, Saml Galbreath & William Underwood Inspectors of the insuing Election for members to the Legislature & governor---

    Ordered by the Court that John McAdoo Junr be overseer of the Road instead of Richard Luallen & have the same Bounds & hands--

(P. 209) Ordered by the Court that Walter Taylor be overseer instead of Joseph Keeney Junr. & have the same bounds and hands.----

    The Court then adjourned until Tomorrow 9 Oclock.

WEDNESDAY 14TH JULY 1813-
    The Court met according to adjournment- Present Arthur Crozier, William McKamey, William Sharp, Quin Morton, Edward Hawkins & Alexander Gastin Esquires-

  State   )
     vs   ) Present as above-
Joseph Sinclair Junr) Whereupon came a Jury (to wit) John Tovera, John
                           Ridenhour, William Silvey, James Wood, Jacob Linard, Andrew McKnight, James Deaton, Samuel Robbins, William Ashlock, John Bounds, Jessie Powers & John Wallace Junr. who being duly sworn say they find the Defendant Guilty in manner & form as charged in the Bill of Indictment- Whereupon it is considered by the Court that he be fined Six & one fourth cents & Costs & be in mercy &c--

(P. 210) Arthur Crozier & William McKamey who were appointed to settle with John McAdoo administrator of Samuel Dixon deceased, Report that there remains in the hands of the Administrator one hundred & thirty Eight dollars forty three and three fourth Cents.----

Ordered by the Court that the following allowance be made to the Commissioners (to wit) Arthur Crozier Seven dollars, John Leib, Senr., nine dollars, Hugh Barton Eight dollars, Quin Morton Seven dollars, John Leib Junr, five dollars, John McAdoo, Senr Five dollars & Joseph Sinclair two dollars.

Ordered by the Court that Willie Young, Kinza Johnson, Andrew Breden Craven Johnson, Samuel Dunn, Constant Claxon & Jesse Hoskins be appointed a Jury to review the Road from Clinton to William McKameys, to injure as little as possible the plantations of John Leib and John Kirby, and that they make report to next Court---

State)
vs) Present Quin Morton, William McKamey, William Sharp &
James Worthington) M. Clardy, Esquires-
Whereupon came a Jury (to wit) the same as in Sinclair,s case, except Page Portwood in place of William Ashlock & John Wallace Instead of Jesse Powers, who being duly sworn say they find the defendant guilty in manner & form as charged in the Bill of Indictment-
Whereupon it is considered by the Court that he be fined Twenty five cents & Costs & be in mercy &c--   (P. 211*

Rowland Childs)
vs) In this case the Defendant comes into open Court & confess-
Wm. Hogshead) es Judgment for Two dollars & twelve & one half Cents-
Therefore it is considered that the plaintiff recover against the defendant the sum aforesaid & also his costs & the Deft. in Mercy-

Robert Tevis)
vs) Present Alexander Gastin, William McKamey & Quin Morton
Jesse Powers) Esquires- Whereupon came a Jury (to wit) John Tovera, John Ridenour, William Silvey, James Wood, Jacob Linard, Andrew McKnight, James Deaton, Samuel Robbins, William Ashlock, John Bounds, John Wallace, Junr. & Page Portwood who being duly sworn say they find the Defendant hath paid the Debt in the declaration mentioned except the sum of forty dollars & assess the Plaintiffs damage, by reason of the detention of that sum to Eleven dollars & fifty Cents.-
Whereupon it is considered by the Court, that the plaintiff do recover his debt & damage aforesaid, also his Costs about his suit in that behalf expended, and be the said defendant in mercy &c---

State)
vs) Present Quin Morton, William McKamey, Alexander Gastin &
Joseph Denison) Edward Hawkins, Esqrs.- Same Jury as above, who being duly sworn say they find the Defendant guilty in manner & form as charged in the Bill of Indictment- Whereupon it is considered by the Court that he be fined Six & one fourth Cents & Costs & be in mercy-&c-

(P. 212) Oeredered by the Court that John McAdoo be appointed the Guardian of Harriett Dixon who gave Bond with William Lamar security---

Arthur Crozier & John Gibbs Esquires who were appointed to settle with the Administrator of Richard C? Cobb deceased, returned the Settlement into Court----

Ordered by the Court that John G. Durrett be appointed overseer of the road instead of John McKamey, and have the same bounds & hands---

The Court then adjourned until tomorrow 9 O,clock.

THURSDAY 15TH JULY 1813.
The Court met according to adjournment- Present William McKamey, Quin Morton, and Arthur Crozier Esquires-

Samuel Robbins)
    vs   ) This day came the parties by their attornies- Whereupon
Andrew McKnight) came a Jury (to wit) John Tovera, John Ridenour, Richard
                  Martial, Danl. Wall, Abraham Hagler, Tobias Peters, Obediah Ashlock, John Davis, Absolom White, William Silvey, Malon Hibbs & Gideon Reynolds, who being duly sworn say they find the defendant not guilty-
Wherupon it is considered by the Court that the defendant go hence without day & the plaintiff be amerced for his false Clamor-

(P. 213) The Heirs of James Hanna by Joseph Sinclair Senr. returned 200 acres of land as Taxable for the year 1811-

Sam Robbins)
    vs   ) In this case Jacob Linart surrendered the defendant in
Andrew McKnight) open Court in discharge of himself and James Underwood
                  as Bail, prayed in custody &c---

The Court being satisfied that there is due from Anderson County to Hugh Montgomery the sum of (P. 214) fifty five dollars and Seventy five Cents which sum ought to have been placed to his credit on a note of hand on which the administrators of Richard C. Cobb as security have been sued on and paid the amount due thereon,
It is therefore ordered by the Court that the said sum of fifty five dollars and seventy five cents be refunded and paid to the said Hugh Montgomery out of any monies in the hands of the trustee of the County--

Ordered that Peter Clair have his mark recorded which is two crops and two overbits.--

John Davis)
    vs   ) Continued as on affidavit of the Defendant--
John Bounds)

John Stewart for the use of)
   William Underwood   ) Present Arthur Crozier, Quin Morton & Alex-
         vs   ) ander Gastin, Esqrs.--
William Hogshead   ) This day came the parties by their attornies
                                        and thereupon came a Jury (to wit) John
Wallace, Senr., John Fry, Jacob Linard, Leonard Coffman, John Hibbs, Hugh Millican, James Tunnell, George Moore, Henry Etter, William Lane, John Tovera, & William Marshall who being elected tried & sworn the truth to speak upon the issue joined upon their oaths do say that the defendant hath not kept and performed his covenant and that he hath broken the same as the plaintiff against him hath (P. 215) complained and that the said John Stewart did not assign to the said defendant the note on Stephen McCaumus for Seven hundred pounds of salt petre in manner & form as the said defendant in his fourth plea has alledged and they assess the plaintiff damage by reason of the breach of the Covenant in the declaration mentioned to eighty

three Dollars besides his Costs But because the Court are not yet advised what Judgment to render on the demurrer of the plaintiff to the third plea of the defendant therefore the rendition of Judgment is this cause is deferred until the decision of the said demurrer--

Charles Price & Jacob Peak who were summoned as Jurors to attend this term tho solemnly called came not--

Samuel Robbins)
  vs   ) John Luallen & William Carrol who was summoned as witness-
Andrew McKnight) es in this cause was solemnly called came not it is considered by the Court that Judgment be entered against said Luallen & Carrol unless at the next term of this Court they come and shew cause why Execution should not issue against them and that Scire facias issue accordingly-

Court then adjourned until tomorrow 9 o,clock.

FRIDAY 16TH JULY 1813.
Court met according to adjournment- Present Arthur Crozier, William McKamey and Quin Morton, Esqrs.-

State)
 vs) In this cause the <u>Soliscitor</u> by the Consent of the Court
Jacob Coburn) suffered a Nolli prosequi to be entered.-

Charles McClung)
  vs) This day came the Plaintiff by his atto. as well as the
Thomas Butler &) Deft. Jacob Butler by his atto. and, Thereupon came a
Jacob Butler) Jury (to wit) Richard Marshall, Willis Leath, James Scarbro, Obediah Ashlock, Daniel Wall, Tobias Peters, Jonas Pettitt, Julius Millikin, Isaac Sartin, Saml Pryor & George Hudson who being Elected tried and sworn the truth to speak upon the Issue joined upon their oaths do say the Defendant Jacob Butler hath not paid the debts in the Declaration mentioned as in pleading he hath alleged and they assess the Plaintiffs damages by reason of the detension thereof to two hundred & four Dollars & fifteen cents besides his Costs, and the Defendant Thomas Butler having failed to appear and replevy the property attached and plead to this action,

Therefore it is considered by the Court that the Plaintiff (P. 217) recover of the Defendants Eleven hundred and fifty Dollars the debts in the declaration mentioned together with two hundred & four dollars & fifteen cents the damages aforesaid assessed by the Jury aforesaid also his costs by him about his suit in this behalf expended- &c--

Rachel Aultum)
 Vs) Appeal
John Fry) Continued and by consent of the parties the deposition of Samuel Koyl is to be taken -------------esse this day at the Store House of Barton & Sutherland before Arthur Crozier & William McKamey, Esqrs.-

White & Lynch for the use of)
 John Underwood   ) Sci Fa
   vs   ) Continued
Larkin Bowling   )

Same)
vs) Certiorari
Same) Continued

John Hoskins)
vs) Sci Fa
Heard & McCormick) Continued

Rachel Scarbro)
vs) A Rule for a new trial in this cause was discharged by
Absolom White) the Court

(P. 218) John Stewart for the use)
of Wm. Underwood) Demurrer
vs) Continued
Wm. Hogshead)

John Davis)
vs) Its appearing to the Court that the Judicial attach-
John Bounds, Junr.) ment awarded in this cause at the last Term has not
been issued on motion of the Plaintiff It is ordered
that a Judicial attachment against the Defendants Estate Issue returnable
to the next term of this Court-

The Court adjourned until Court in Course.
(P. 219) ARTHUR CROZIER C. A. C.

State of Tennessee) At a Court of Pleas and Quarter Sessions began and held
Anderson County) for the County aforesaid at the Court House in Clinton
on the second Monday of October 1813 being the 11th day
of said month--- Present Arthur Crozier, Wm. McKamey, Saml. Davidson & Edward Hawkins Esquires-

Charles Y. Oliver Sheriff of County of Anderson returned the following Venire facias (to wit) William Ashlock, Jacob Linard, Craven Johnson, Jo. Keeney, Senr., Aaron Slover, Jesse Hoskins, Phillip Severs, Jas. Tunnell, Wm. Nichol, Richard Campbell, Wm. Gamble, Saml. Williams, Wm. Craighead, Robert Roysdon, John White, Elijah Frost, Elijah Hendon, Reuben Gholson, James Caldwell, Robert Wilson, John F. McEntire, Wm. McAdoo, James Hill, Jesse Bookout, Edwrad Williams & Charles Heskell, Executed on all but Chas. Heskell & Ro. Wilson- out of which was drawn as Grand Jurors (to wit) John F. McEntire foreman, Aaron Slover, Edward Williams, Reuben Gholson, Jacob Lenard, William Ashlock, Phillip Severs, John White, Wm. Craighead, Saml. Williams, Richard Campbell, Craven Johnson & Elijah Frost who being sworn and charged retired to consider of their presentments.

James Hill who was summoned as a Juror at this term was called & came not-

William Gamble was excused as serving as a Juror at this Court-

(P. 220) MONDAY 11TH OCTOBER 1813-
Andrew Braden, Saml. Dunn, Jesse Hoskins, Craven Johnson, and Constant Clackson who was appointed a Jury of review at last Term, returned the folowing report (to wit) the road leading from William McKamey to Clinton the way it now goes until it comes to John Kirby's fence after passing Cosway

leaving the old road to the right and intersect it again at the creek as marked thence along the old road to near Hugh Dixons then leaving the old Road to the right crossing the branch and to run through Dixons orchard leaving said Dixons house on the Right to Intersect the old Road immediately below said Dixons.

Court then adjourned until tomorrow Morning 9 O,clock.

TUESDAY 12 TH OCTOBER 1813.
Court met according to adjournment. Presnt Samuel Davidson, Edward Hawkins and Quin Morton, Esqrs.-

White & Lynch for the use of)
   John Underwood   ) Sci Fa
       vs   ) Demurrer
   Larkin Bowling   ) This day came the parties by their Attorneys and the Demurrer being solemnly argued, It is considered by the Court that the Demurrer be sustained and that the Plaintiff have Execution against the Defendant of the Judgment in the writ of Sci Fa mentioned. (P. 221)

White & Lynch for the)
use of John Underwood) Certiorari
     vs   ) Continued by Consent
Larkin Bowling   )

Ordered by the Court that Jacob Stooksberry be allowed Seven dollars & fifty Cents the Amt. of a county claim which he hath made oath that he lost.

Ordered by the Court that John Gibbs Esqr. received William Keelings allowance in the room of William Underwood---

Ordered by the Court that Joseph Keeny Junr. be allowed six dollars for supporting Molly Ashurst three months-

Ordered by the Court that William Keeling be allowed twelve dollars for his support for three months past.

Ordered by the Court that William Underwood be allowed Twenty four dollars for supporting William Keeling from Janury Court until Huly Court last.

(P. 222) John Kirby was appointed Constable in Capt. Bradens Company who gave bond and security & was qualified accordingly.

John Hoskins   )
   vs   ) Continued
S. Heard & C. McCormick)

Robert Tevis)
   vs   ) Continued
Jesse Powers)

Same)
  vs) Continued
Same)

John Underwood   )
    vs   ) Continued
William Lohery   )

Rachel Aultum)
    vs   ) Appeal
John Fry   ) Continued

    Francis M. Ashley orphen of William Ashley Deceased came into open Court and chose Thomas M. Ashley his guardian who entered into bond with security & was appointed by the Court—

(P. 223)

Joseph Sinclair)
    vs   ) Continued by Consent and time to plead so as not to
Patrick McFall) delay trial

William Underwood)
    vs   ) Continued
Wm. Hogshead   )

Thomas Hill   )
    vs   ) Appeal
John Underwood) Continued

John Davis   )
    vs   ) Continued as on affidavit of the defendant—
John Bounds Senr.)

Nathaniel Hart by Robert Houston Returns 5000 acres of land as Taxable the present year.

    Ordered by the Court that Samuel Anderson be allowed Thirty seven Dollars and fifty Cents for his ex officio services at April, July and the present Sessions

    Ordered by the Court that Jonathan Tipton, son of Brian Tipton, be bound unto Arthur Crozier until he becomes to twenty one years of age and said Crozier binds himself to have said boy (School,d, towit Reading writing and Cyphering as far as the rule of three, (P. 224) also to Furnish said boy in comfortable Cloathing and victuals.

    Ordered by the Court that Edwrad Williams the fined the sum of five dollars for contempt. to the Court and that he remain in Custody of the Sheriff until said fine and Costs are paid,
    Whereupon Charles Oliver comes into Court and enters himself security for the payment thereof— which security is received by the Court.

    Ordered by the Court that Christopher Bailey be fined the sum of five dollars for contempt to the Court and that he remain in Custody of the Sheriff until said fine and Costs are paid Whereupon Man P. Vowell comes into Court and enters himself security for the payment thereof which security is received by the Court

    Charles Price was excused for his non attendance as a Juror at last term—

    Court then adjourned until tomorrow morning at 9 Oclock.

(P. 225) WEDNESDAY 13TH OCTOBER 1813

Court met according to adjournment &c- Present Joseph Sinclair, William McKamey & Edwrad Hawkins Esqrs-

Barton and Sutherland)
vs) This day came the parties by their Attos.
Jacob Mayberry) Whereupon came a Jury (to wit) Wm. Nichols, Jesse Hoskins, Jesse Bookout, Elijah Hendon, Andrew Braden, John Tunnell, Man P. Vowell, Enoch Foster, John Paine, John Davis, Charles Price and John Bounds Junr, who being duly Elected tried and sworn the truth to speak upon Issue Joined upon their oaths do say they cannot agree in their verdict, Whereupon came the parties by their Attorneys and consented to a miss Trial--

Ordered by the Court that the following persons be Jurors to the next Circuit Court (to wit)

Arthur Crozier, Joseph Sinclair, Samuel Davidson, Robert Galbreath, Wm. Tunnell, William Griffith, Andw. McKamey, George Sutherland, Jos. Parks, Jacob Peak, David Hall, Alexr. Gastin, Thomas Wilson, John Spysard, Thomas Gallion, Abraham Hagler, Enoch Foster, John Gibbs, Charles Price, Joseph Gallaher, Austin Hackworth, John Gamblem Saml. Frost, and John Loy--

(P. 226) Ordered by the Court that the following persons be Jurors at next County Court (to wit) William Russell, John Landrum, John Rector, William Butler, John Dunevan, George Hundson, George White, Phillip White, Thomas Carnell, Isaac Frields, John Shannon, Hardy Medlin, Solomon Markey, James Hicks, Henry Etter, Obadiah Wood, Abner Farmer, Bendogo Wilson, Abraham Hagler, Truman Still, Joseph Keeney Junr- John Garner, John Leib Junr & Britton Cross--

William Childress proved by his own oath that he killed a grown wolf in the County of Anderson in the month of September last and produced the scalp in open Court--

Ordered by the Court that the fines imposed on Edward Williams and Christopher Bailey on yesterday be remitted-

John Davis)
vs) Continued by
John Bounds Junr.) Consent

A Deed from Thomas Nation to Jacob Moser for 135 acres of land was acknowledged in open Court--

A Deed from Saml. Taylor to John Taylor for 120 acres of land was acknowledged in open Court--

A deed from John Brumley & Mary his wife to -----Brumley for 133 acres was acknowledged (P. 227) separately in open Court.

State)
vs) Recog-
John Clarkson) This day came Samuel Anderson Esqr. who prosecutes for the people of the State and the Defendant having heard the Bill of Indictment read says he is not guilty in manner and form as charged in said bill and puts himself upon the Country- Whereupon came a Jury (towit)

Thomas Dixon Senr, Robert Roysdon, Obadiah Wood, John Bounds Senr, William Childress, Jacob Peak, Truman Still, Britton Cross, Kinchen Hall, James Childress, John Edwards & Thomas Vowell who being duly Elected tried & sworn the truth to speak upon the Issue Joined upon their oaths do say the Defendant is guilty in manner and form as charged in the Bill of Indictment

 Whereupon the Defendant by his attorney comes and enters a Rule to shew cause why a new trial should be granted and said Rule being solemnly argued the same is made absolute

 Whereupon the defendant John Clarkson, together with Constant Clarkson, and Stephen Heard comes into Court and acknowledged themselves Indebted to the State of Tennessee in the following sums (to wit) John Clarkson in the sum of Two hundred Dollars & said Constant Clarkson and Stephen Heard jointly and severally in the sum of Two hundred Dollars to be levied of their respective goods and chattles lands and tenements- But to be void on condistion (P. 228) that said John Clarkson dorth make his personal appearance at the next Court of pleas and Quarter Sessions to be held for the County of Anderson to answer a charge of the said State exhibited against him and not depart the Court without leave.

Same)
vs) Recog.
Same) This day came into open Court Absolom Johnson, George Sutherland and Jesse Laxton and acknowledged themselves indebted to the State of Tennessee in the following sums (to wit) said Johnson in the sum of two hundred Dollars and said Sutherland & Laxton in the sum of one hundred dollars each to be levied of their respective goods & chattles lands & tenements- Tho to be void on condition said Johnson doth make his personal appearance at the next Court of pleas and quarter sessions to be held for the County of Anderson to prosecute & give evidence in a case wherein the State is Plaintiff and John Clarkson is Defendant and not depart the Court without leave-

Same)
vs) This day came Jesse Laxton and Thomas Laxton and acknowledged themselves indebted to the State of Tennessee in the sum of one hundred
Same)
dollars each to be levied of their respective goods & chattles lands & tenements tho to be void on condition said Jesse & Thomas make their personal appearance at the next Court of pleas and quarter sessions to be held for the County of Anderson to give evidence in a case wherein the State is Plaintiff & John Clarkson is Defendant and not depart the Court without leave---

(P. 229) State)
vs) Recog-
Isaac Coburn & I. Leach) This day came Jacob Lenard & Aron Slover and acknowledged themselves indebted to the State of Tennessee in the sum of fifty dollars each to be levied of their respective goods and chattles lands and Tenements Tho to be void on Condition the sd. Lenard and Slover dorth make their personal appearance at the next Court of Pleas and Quarter Sessions to be held for the County of Anderson to give evidence in the above case and not depart the Court without leave-

State)
vs) This day came Samuel Anderson Esqr. who prosecutes
Leonard Vandegriff) for the people of the State and the Defendant having heard the Bill of Indictment read says he is not guilty in manner and form as charged in said Bill and puts himself upon the

County - Whereupon came a Jury (to wit) Aaron Slover, Edward Williams, Reuben Gholson, Jacob Linard, William Ashlock, John F. McEntire, John White, William Craighead, Samuel Williams, Richard Campbell, Craven Johnson, & Elijah Hendon who being duly Elected tried and sworn the truth to speak upon the issue joined upon their oaths do say the defendant is not guilty in manner and form as charged in the Bill of Indictment- therefore said defendant is discharged by the Court-

State)
vs) This day came Saml. Anderson Esqr who prosecutes for the
James Everett) people of the State and the defendant having heard the
Bill of Indictment read says he not guilty in manner and form as charged in said Bill Whereupon came the same Jury as above and brought in a verdict as above- (P. 230)

Rebecca Ashlock)
vs) On motion of the Plaintiff by her Attorney It is order-
Jesse Hoskins) ed by the Court that said Rebecca Ashlock be allowed
Twenty dollars pr year to be paid Quarterly by Jesse Hoskins for the term of five years commencing from the time that a certain child was born of Rebecca Ashlock begotton on her body by said Jesse Hoskins and that said allowance be paid into the hands of William Ashlock and that said Hoskins pay all Costs that have accrued in this case.

Court then adjourned until tomorrow morning 9 Oclock.

THURSDAY 14TH OCTOBER 1813-
Court met according to adjournment-
Present Arthur Crozier, Joseph Sinclair, & Alexr Gastin Esqrs.

Lewis Harmon for the use of)
William Parks)
vs)
William H. Brian & Elizabeth his wife) In this case it appearing
Thomas McCorry & Sarah his wife and) to the Court that the orig-
Benjamin Parker Maclin, William Maclin,) inal writ of Scire facias
James Zachfield Maclin, & Landon Carter) has been made (P. 231)
Maclin, Heirs of Benjamin C. Parker Deceased) known to Thomas McCorry and
) Sarah his wife and John
McCampbell who was heretofore appointed Guardian for the said Benjamin Parker Maclin, William Maclin, James Zachfield Maclin & Landon Carter Maclin who were minors, and it also appearing to the Court from the return of the Sheriff on said writ of Scire facias & also on the Alias writ of Scire facias Issued in this cause that the said William H. Brian & Elizabeth his wife are not Inhabitants of this State and the said Defendants not appearing altho solemnly called-

Therefore on motion of the Plaintiff It is considered by the Court that Judgment be entered in favor of said Plaintiff against the real Estate which descended from the said Benjamin C. Parker deceased to the said Defendants for the amount of ---- the Judgment obtained by him against Hugh Barton administrator of the said Benjamin C. Parker in the Scire facias mentioned and that the said Pltf. have Execution of his said Judgment against the real estate of the said Benjamin C. Parker which descended to the said Defendants as heirs at law of the said Parker. And it is considered that the Plaintiff recover of the Defendants his costs about his suit in this behalf expended--

(P. 232) Ordered by the Court that David Clarkson be authorized to take of support the Base born children of Susanna Argabright until next term of this Court for which he is to have a reasonable allowance, & that the Sheriff deliver a copy of this order to said Clarkston.

John Davis)
vs) Ordered by the Court that a Subpoena Ducesticum Issue
John Bounds Junr.) in favor of the Defendant for Arthur Crozier to bring in an Execution Issued by him against John Davis in favor of John Bounds Senr. to be used as evidence for the said Defendant at next Court.

Court then adjourned until Court in Course.
ARTHUR CROZIER C. A. C.

(P. 233) State of Tennessee) At a Court of Pleas & Quarter Sessions open-
Anderson County) ed and held for the County of Anderson aforesaid on the second Monday being the 10th day of January 1814- There were present Samuel Galbreath, Joseph Sinclair, Edward Hawkins, & Quin Morton Esqrs---

The Sheriff then returned the Venire facias of whom the following were appointed Grand Jurors (Viz)

1. Henry Atter
2. George Hudson
3. John Shannon
4. John Dunaven
5. John Garner
6. Britain Cross
7. Philip White
8. Thomas Carnel
9. John Landrum
10. John Rector
11. Absolom White
12. Abner Farmer
13. Obadiah Wood

who being sworn and charged retired to enquire---

Ordered by the Court that William McKamey, Saml. Dunn, & Quin Morton be appointed Commissioners to settle with the Administrator of Oliver Dodson deceased to report at next October term----

Isaac Lowe Esquire was qualified as a Justice of the Peace, & took his seat--

Samuel Anderson Esquire Solicitor prefered his resignation to the Court they then proceeded to elect Robert H. Adams Solicitor---

(P. 234) The following persons are Traverse Jurors (to wit) Joseph Keeny Junr. William Russell, & William Butler---

A Bill of sale from Silas Bennett to Reuebn Brown was proved in open Court by William McKamey and ordered to be registered.

Ordered by the Court that George Gollaher have leave to administer on the estate of John Jones deceased who entered into Bond with security, in the sum of one thousand dollars, had an order to sell and report to next court.-

Ordered by the Court that Jacob Weeaver be appointed a Constable in Capt. Miller,s Company, who gave Bond and Security and was qualified as the Law requires--

A Bill of Sale from James Robertson to John Miller for a negro woman was proved in open court by George Sutherland & oredered to be recorded.-

To deeds of conveyance from Solomon Massengale to John Miller, one containing 201 & the other 187 acres of land was proved in open Court and ordered to be registered---

State)
vs) In this case the Defendant submitted to Court & was fined
John Leatch) six and one fourth cents & that he pay the costs of this prosecution-

(P. 235) Ordered by the Court that William Worthington have leave to administer on the Estate of James Worthington deceased who entered into Bond with security as the Law requires.---

Ordered by the Court, that John White be overseer of the Road in place of Lewis Freeman & have the same Bounds and hands.-----

Simon Derrick)
vs) On motion of Plaintiff,s Attorney A Rule was entered to
Robert Ross) shew cause why the Writs of Certiorari & Supersedeas should be quashed.

The Court then adjourned untill Tomorrow morning 9 O'clock.----

TEWSDAY 11TH JANUARY 1814.
Court met according to adjournment. Present Joseph Sinclair, Saml. Galbreath, Edward Hawkins & Michael Clardy Esqrs.

Wm..Williams for the)
use of John Childs) Continued by Consent
vs) time to declare so as not
Elias Owens) to delay trial

(P. 236) White & Lynch)
for the use of John Underwood) This day came the parties by their Attos-
vs) Whereupon came a Jury (to wit) Joseph
Larkin Bowling) Keeny Junr, William Russell, William Butler, John Leib Junr, Elijah Frost, Thos.
Wright, Isaac Mayberry, Saml. Hall, William Patterson, Robert Patterson, Richard Luallen & John Patterson who being duly Elected tried and sworn the truth to speak upon the issue joined upon their oaths do say they fined for the defendant upon which verdict the Plff. prayed an appeal the appeal granted and entered into bond and security for the appeal.

Charles Y. Oliver was Elected Sheriff for the County of Anderson for the two succeeding years who entered into bond with security and was qualified accordingly.

Ordered that Thos. Parsons be appointed Constable in Cpt. Davidson,s Company who gave bond and security and was qualified as the law requires.

Ordered that the tax for the present year be the same as it was last year.-

Ordered that William Williams be overseer of the road beginning at the forks of the Emmery and Piles Turnpike road near Collins Roberts field on to the County line on said road and have the same hands that William Gamble had as overseer in addition to the hands that the said Williams now has also Alexander Galbreath Junr-

(P. 237) Ordered that Lettie Wortherington be Guardian for Saml., William, Polly, Betsy, Thomas & Kitty Wortherington, children of James Wortherington Deceased who entered into bond and security as the Law requires.---

Ordered that Charles Y. Oliver Shff. be allowed fifty dollars and Hugh Barton clerk be allowed fifty dollars for the Ex officio services for the year 1813.-

Ordered that the following Justices take a list of the Taxable property for the year 1814- (to wit)

```
Michael Clardy, .....................in Cpt. Martials Company
Saml. Galbreath, .....................  "  Cpt. Tunnels Company
Joseph Sinclair......................  "   "   Breadens    "
John Gibbs ..........................  "   "   Fosters     "
Isaac Lowe ..........................  "   "   Millers     "
Saml. Davidson ......................  "   "   Davidsons   "
John Newman..........................  "   "   Griffith    "
```

Court then adjourned till tomorrow nine O'clock.

(P. 238) WEDNESDAY 12TH JANUARY 1814----
Court met according to adjournment- Present- Samuel Galbreath, Quin Morton, Edward Hawkins, Joseph Sinclair, & Alexander Gastin, Esquires--

Stephen Heard having produced his receipts from the Treasurers for having paid his Tax as clerk, It is ordered by the Court that he be allowed out of the Treasury of Anderson County the sum of fouteen dollars & eighty cents----

Robert Tunnell)
vs) In this case the Plaintiff dismissed his suit & the Defend-
Henry Atter) ant came into Court & assumed payment of the costs-

State)
vs) In this case the Defendant & his securities being solemnly
John Clarkson) called came not, whereupon it is considered by the Court
that their Recognizance be certified---

(P. 239) State)
vs) Same Court
Jonathan Coburn) Whereupon came a Jury towit, Joseph Keeny, Junr., Wm.
Butler, Wm. Russell, John Leib Junr., Robert Patterson, Aquilla Claxon, John Tunnell, Constant Claxon, Aaron Jenkins, William Lamar, Richard Luallen & Moses Roberts, who being duly sworn say the Defendant is not Guilty.---Whereupon it is considered by the Court that the defendant go hence without day---

Ordered by the Court that John Newman Esquire take the list of taxable property and Polls in Capt. Griffith,s Company---

State)
vs) In this case the Defendant submitted & is fined in the
Julius Milliken) sum of six and one fourth cents & that he pay the Costs
of this prosecution.

John Davis)
vs) Same Court and Jury except John Patterson & Henry Farmer, who
John Bounds) being duly sworn say they find for the Plaintiff and assess
his damage to twenty (P. 240) five dollars— Whereupon it
is considered by the Court that the Plaintiff do recover the sum aforesaid,
also his Costs, and be the Defendant in mercy &c—

Ordered by the Court that William Mitchell be overseer in place of
John Warwick and have the same bounds & hands—

Robert Tevis)
vs) In these cases the Pltff dismisses his suits & assumes the
Jesse Powers) payment of the costs &c— Therefore it is considered by the
court that the Defendant go hence and recover of the Plaintiff his costs by him about his defense in these behalfs expended.

Simon Derrick)
vs) In this case the Certiorari & Supersedeas were dismissed &
Robt. Ross) other writs of Supersedeas & Certiorari granted.—

Ordered by the Court that Malon Hibbs be released from the payment of
his poll tax—

Court then adjourned til Tomorrow 9 O'clock.

(P. 241) THURSDAY JANUARY 13TH 1814—
Court met according to adjournment.— Present Wm. McKamey, Joseph Sinclair, Saml. Galbreath, and Quin Morton, (Esquires).

Isaac Brazleton)
vs) Appeal
Thos. & Hugh Dixon) Motion by Defendant,s Atto. to quash the proceedings
before the Justice of the Peace upon argument the
motion was not granted.

John Davis)
vs) Same Court as above.
John Bounds Junr.) This day came the parties by their attos.— Whereupon
came a Jury (to wit). Joseph Keeny Junr., William Rus-
sell, William Butler, John Leib Junr., Thos. Dixon Senr., Alexander Cole,
John Garner, Danl. Marsh, Robert Ross, John Landrum, Phillip White & Abner
Farmer, who being duly elected tried and sworn the truth to speak upon the
issue joined upon their oaths do say they fine for the Pltff. and assess his
damages to seventeen dollars— Whereupon it is considered by the Court that
the plaintiff do recover the sum aforesaid also his Costs, & be the defendant
in mercy &c.—

Thomas Hill)
vs) Continued
John Underwood) The deposition of ————— is to be taken in the County
of Madeson, Mississippi territory, first given thirty
days notice.

William Underwood)
    vs   )   This day came the defendant into open Court and confessed
William Hogshead)   Judgment for sixty dollars.-Therefore it is considered
                   by the Court (P. 242) that the Plaintiff do recover
of the Defendant the aforesaid sum of Sixty dollars also his costs by him about his suit in this behalf expended and be the defendant in mercy &c with a stay of Execution for Eleven months.

    Ordered that George Hoskins be appointed Constable who gave bond and security and was qualified as the law requires.

Isaac Brazleton   )
    vs   )   Present: Joseph Sinclair, Saml. Galbreath, Quin Morton
Thos. & Hugh Dixon)   Douglas Oliver & Alexander Gastin Esqrs.
                   This day came the parties by their Attos. Whereupon
came a Jury (to wit)   The same as before except John Rector in the place of John Leib Junr. who being duly elected tried and sworn the truth to speak upon the Issue Joined upon there oaths do say they fine for the Plaintiff the sum of thirty dollars and forty five cents debt and interest also the further sum of ---for costs and charges by him about his suit in this behalf expended.

    Whereupon it is considered by the Court that the plaintiff do recover the sum aforesaid and be the Defendant in mercy &c.

John Underwood)
    vs   )   Cont. by Consent
William Laughery)

    Quin Morton Esqr. was appointed chairman of the Court pro tem.

(P. 243) THURSDAY JANUARY 13TH 1814.-
    Ordered by the Court that Elizabeth Henderson be bound to Thomas Dixon Senr. & that he the said Thomas Dixon Senr. enter into Indentures at the next term of this Court.

    Ordered by the Court that the following persons be jurors to the next County Court (towit) Michael Hagler, Edward Freels, John Hoskins, Alexander Galbreath, Henry Butler, Jacob Butler, Samuel Dunn, William Ashlock, Jesse Hoskins, Thomas Dickson, Road Stanley, Paul Childs, Joseph Robertson, Eli Norman, James Scarbrough, Thomas M. Ashley, Peter Monger, James White, James Trowel, John Hackworth, John Farmer, William McAdoo, John Luallen, Jacob Clodfelter, Saml. Edmondson & John Scruggs.

    Court then adjourned till Tomorrow nine O'clock.

FRIDAY JANUARY 14, 1814.
    Court met according to adjournment. Present: Joseph Sinclair & Quin Morton & Michael Clardy Esquires.

(P. 244) Samuel Frost the clerk then proceeded to read the minutes- Court then adjourned until Court in course.
                              QUIN MORTON C. A. C.
                                       Pro tem.

(P. 245) At a Court of Pleas & Quarter Sessions opened and held for the County of Anderson at the Court House in Clinton on the second Monday of

April (being the 11th day of said month) There were present- Joseph Sinclair, Alexander Gastin, and William McKamey Esquires.-

Charles Y. Oliver Sheriff returned the Venire Facias executed of whom the following were appointed Grand Jurors (to wit) Joseph Robertson, William McAdoo, Eli Norman, John Luallen, James Trowel, John Scruggs, Jacob Clodfelter, Samuel Edmondson, Peter Monger, Jacob Butler, Michael Hostler, William Ashlock, & Edward Frields,-

The following are Traverse Jurors (viz) John Hoskins, Thomas Dixon, Rhodes Stanley & James White.

The last Will & Testament of William Johnson was proved in open Court by Jacob Peak, & Molly Peak and ordered to be recorded---

(P. 246) Ordered by the Court that George Hoskins be overseer of the Road in stead of Philip Seiber and have the same bounds & hands--

Ordered by the Court that Jacob Linard have leave to administer on the Estate of John Aldridge deceased, who entered into Bond with security had leave to sell the property of the deceased, giving twenty days notice & a credit of twelve months--

Ordered by the Court that Calvin Tunnell be appointed Overseer of the Road in place of William Worthington & have the same bounds & hands.

A deed from John Triplett, to Culberth Webb for sixty acres of Land, was acknowledged in open Court and ordered to be registered.---

Ordered by the Court that William Gamble & Evan Evans have leave to administer on the Estate of John Gamble deceased, who have leave to sell at twelve months the credit. (P. 247)

Joseph Sinclair)
    vs   ) In this case Isaac Sartin acknowledged himself security
Patrick McFall) instead of Thomas Dixon Junr.

Robert Galbreath gave Bond and security as the Law requires as a Commissioner to settle with the County Trustee or Treasurer & officers of court, sheriff &c.-

An assignment of a Platt & Certificate from George Hoskins to John Taber for fifteen acres of land was acknowledged in Open Court.---

The following characters were appointed Jurors to attend at the next County Court (towit) Daniel Stonceypher, Daniel Leib, Julius Millikan, Gabriel Keith, William Edwards, Joseph Homesley, Philip Seiber Junr., Christian Spaw, Leonard Coffman, Thomas M. Ashley, John Hackworth, Isaac Lowe, Daniel Beets, James Wyatt, Jacob Stutler Junr., William Davidson, Saml. Dunn, James Ross, Moses Brown, Enoch Foster, John Wallace Junr., Francis Irwin, John Loy, Solomon Alred, Zachariah Key & John Taber.----

(P. 248) Ordered by the Court that George Hoskins have leave to resign his appointments as Constable.

Ordered by the Court that the following persons be appointed Jurors to the ensuing Circuit Court (to wit) Robert Galbreath, Samuel Galbreath, Jacob Peak, Alexander Gastin, William McKamey, John McAdoo Senr., Michael

Clardy, Joseph Sinclair, Arthur Crozier, John Gibbs, Matthew Hawkins, William Sharp, John Newman, Douglas Oliver, William Underwood, Samuel Davidson, Hugh Barton, Thomas Menefee, Aaron Jenkins, Richard Marshall, Thomas Parsons, Senr., Henry Farmer, Junr., Isaac Norman, Aaron Slover, John Parks, & John Tunnell--

The Court then adjourned until Tomorrow nine O'clock.

(P. 249) TUESDAY 12TH APRIL 1814--
The Court met according to adjournment--
Present Arthur Crozier, Quin Morton & Edward Hawkins, Esquires.--

John Underwood)
    vs) In this case the parties agreed to a continuance-
William Laughery)

Jane Breaden by her next friend)
    Andrew Braden) This case was continued, the continuance
    vs) was set aside & the following agreement
Joseph Sinclair Junr.) took place between the parties. (Viz)
That the matters in dispute should be submitted to Arthur Crozier, William McKamey, Aaron Jenkins & Charles Y. Oliver, and if they cannot agree, they are to choose a fifth man, and return their award to the next term of this Court which shall be made a Judgment thereof. (P. 250)

Joseph Sinclair)
    vs) Present Arthur Crozier, Quin Morton & Edward Hawkins-
Patrick McFall) Esquires.- Whereupon came a Jury (towit) Jesse Hoskins,
Rhodes Stanley, James White, Jacob Lewis, Jared Harbin & Joseph Hatfield, Fielding Griffith, George Baumgertner, Benjamin Potter, Samuel Robbins, John Triplett & Isaac Mayberry who being duly sworn say they find for the Defendant-
Whereupon it is considered by the Court that the Plaintiff take nothing by his writ & pay the costs attendant on & incurred on said suit & be in mercy &c. A Rule was then entered to shew cause why a new trial should be granted.

Ordered by a Majority of the Court that Arthur Crozier Treasurer be allowed the sum of one hundred, seventy seven dollars & fifty cents in his present settlement with the Commissioners Vouchers to that amount having been consumed by fire.

Richard Luallen)
    vs) In this case the Platiff didmissed his suit.-
John Triplett &)
Benjamin Potter)

(P. 251) Ordered by the Court that Thomas Dixon Junr be overseer of the Road in place of James King & have the same bounds & hands.-

Ordered by the Court the Road leading from Clinton to John Rhea,s ferry be discontinued.

Ordered by the Court that the Road leading from Clinto to William

McKamey,s be altered in the following manner, (Viz) leaving the old road immediately after crossing Poplar Creek to the right hand, then taking up a Ridge to the top on the north side of John Kirby,s Plantation, & keep the extreme right thereof till intersect the old Road at said Kirby,s orchard field.--

  Ordered by the Court that George Smith be Overseer of the Road in the place of Thomas Hart & have the same Bounds & hands---

  Ordered by the Court that William Edwards, Jacob Larue & William Larue work under John McAdoo Junr. overseer of the road--

(P. 252) Ordered by the Court that Thomas Hart, Robert Galbreath & George Sutherland be allowed the sum of Eleven Dollars each, for their services as Commissioners for the present year, and that Hugh Barton be allowed one Dollar for furnishing Paper, &c--

John Hoskins)
 vs   ) In this case the Defendant confesses Judgment for the
Stephen Heard &) amount of the Costs & the Costs accruing on Scire facias--
Chas. McCormick)

  Ordered by the Court that John Hoskins be overseer of the road in the place of Andrew McKamey and have the same Bounds & hands--

Thomas Hill)
 vs   ) Present Arthur Crozier, Quin Morton & Matthew Hawkins
John Underwood) Esquires--
  Whereupon came a Jury (towit) Jesse Hoskins, Thos. Hart, Charles Shinliver, Jacob Lewis, Jared Harbin, Joseph Hatfield Junr, Fielding Griffith, Isaac Mayberry, George Smith & James Blackburn who being duly sworn say they find for the Plaintiff & assess his damage to fifty dollars besides his costs-- Whereupon it is considered by the Court that the Plaintiff recover the Debt aforesaid by costs & be the Defendant in mercy &c--

(P. 253) Richard C. Cobbs Admors)
    vs   ) Continued on the affidavit of the De-
   John Underwood   ) fendant--

David Hicks)
 vs   ) In this case the Plaintiff by his attorney dismissed his
Andrew Stewart) suit & assumed the payment of costs--

Samuel Frost)
 vs   ) In this case the Plaintiff dismissed his suit, & Defend-
John Underwood) ant assumed one half of the Clerks & Sheriffs fees & State Tax & the Plaintiff to pay the Ballance.

Simon Derrick)
 vs   ) This case was continued by consent.
Robert Ross)

  Ordered by the Court that Charles Y. Oliver have the collection of the public Tax for the year 1814 who gave Bond & Security as the Law requires.--

 State   )
  vs   ) In this case Constant Clarkson & S. Heard assumes the pay-
John Clarkson) ment of the Costs of conviction and of 3 Sci fa,s-- & the

forfeitures of the Recognizances are remitted-

Court adjourned till Tomorrow 9 O,clock.

(P. 254) WEDNESDAY 13TH APRIL 1814-

Court met according to adjournment. Present William McKamey, William Sharp, & John Newman Esqrs.

State vs Jacob Lewis & Joseph Hatfield	In this case it is ordered by the Court that Benjamin Potter Prosecutor pay costs.

Thomas Hill vs John Underwood	The Defendant prayed an appeal which was granted entered into bond and security and filed his reasons.

Ordered by the Court that William Lamar administer on the Estate of Rosanna Lemar who entered into bond and security.-

(P. 255) At a Court of Pleas & Quarter Sessions opened and held for the County of Anderson at the Court House in Clinton on Monday the Eleventh day of July in the year of our Lord one thousand Eight hundred and fourteen- There were present: Arthur Crozier, Joseph Sinclair, & William McKamey Esquires.-

Charles Y. Oliver Sheriff returned the Venire facias executed, of whom the following are granted Grand Jurors, (Viz) Enoch Foster foreman, Moses Brown, John Taber, Julius Milikin, William Davidson, Philip Seiber, Daniel Beets, Joseph Homesley, John Hackworth, William Edwards, Jacob Huffstutler, Thomas M. Ashley, & James Wyatt, who being empanneled sworn and charged retired to inquire.

The following are Traverse Jurors (Viz) Zachariah Key, James Ross, Daniel Stonecypher, Solomon Alred, Leonard Coffman, & Daniel Leib.-

Ordered by the Court that John Smith have leave to administer on the Estate of John Usher who gave Bond and security as the Law requires, returned an inventory of said Estate and had leave to sell the same on giving twenty days notice.-

(P. 256) Ordered by the Court that David Huffstutler have leave to administer on the Estate of Joseph Chapman Deceased, gave bond & security as the Law requires, returned an inventory of said Estate & had leave to sell the same, on giving twenty days notice.--

Ordered by the Court that David Clarkson,s mark be recorded which is a Swallow fork & Underbit in the left ear and a slope in the right ear.

William Gamble Administrator of the Estate of John Gamble deceased, returned the amount of the sales of said Estate.--

Ordered by the Court that Robert Lawson,s mark be recorded which is an underbit in each ear--

Ordered by the Court that John Loy have leave to keep an ordinary, or

House of public entertainment, who gave Bond & security as the Law requires-

Ordered by the Court that James Ross have his mark recorded which is a smooth Crop in the right ear and two slits in the left ear.--

Ordered by the Court that John Hoskins be overseer of the road in place of Andrew McKamey & have Brazleton,s former hands and Bounds.--

Ordered by the Court that Ayers Goad have his mark recorded which is, an under bit in the right & slit in the left ear.

(P. 257) Ordered by the Court that John Reed have his mark recorded which is, a swallow fork & under & over bit in each ear--

Ordered by the Court that William Copeland have a resurvey, it appearing that there was a mistake in the former survey; the Grant is No. 324 dated 8th March 1793 & 17 year of American Independence; Beginning on the 2nd Corner of the said Survey, on a White oak, corner to Joseph Sinclair,s land, thence north with his line 80 poles to a Stake, thence West 230 poles to a Stake, thence South to the river, thence up the river to the beginning of the original survey.-

John Bounds Junr. & William Bounds each returned one white Poll subject to taxation for the present year.--

Ordered by the Court that Elijah Beach have his mark recorded which is, a Crop off the right ear, and an under bit in the left ear.--

A deed from John McKamey to Douglas Oliver for 150 acres of Land was proved in open Court by Charles Y. Oliver & Stephen Heard & ordered to be registered.--

Ordered by the Court that Valentine Ball be released from the payment of the Tax on 200 acres of Land for the year, it having been given in thru mistake.--

William Williams for the)
use of John Chiles) Present Arthur Crozier, Joseph Sinclair, William
vs) McKamey, Quin Morton & Edward Hawkins Esquires-
Elias Owens) This day came the parties by their att. and
(P. 258) Thereupon came a Jury (Viz). Zachariah Key, Julius Milikin, Daniel Beets, Joseph Homesley, John Hackworth, Jacob Huffstutler, James Wyatt, Solomon Alred, Leonard Coffman, Daniel Leib, Danl. Stonecypher, & James Ross who being duly sworn say they find for the Plaintiff and assess his damages to ninety six dollars and twenty five cents besides his costs.
Whereupon it is considered by the Court that the Plaintiff recover of the Defendant ninety six dollars and twenty five cents the damages aforesaid assessed by the Jury aforesaid also his costs by him about his suit in this behalf expended & the Deft. in mercy &c.-

A deed from Mark Walker to John Carroll was acknowledged in open Court & ordered to be registered.--

A deed from Joseph Stout to Drury Carroll was proved in open Court for 200 acres of land by John Carroll & William Petty & ordered to be registered.

John Garner one white & one black poll subject to taxation for the present year.

Ordered by the Court that Jacob Peak, Joseph Gollaher, and Abraham Hagler Senr. be appointed to set apart a portion of the Crop, agreeable to an Act of Assembly in such case made and provided, for the support & maintenance of Elizabeth Gamble widow & relict of John Gamble deceased, for one year.—

(P. 259) Green Prior)
vs) This day came Larkin Bowling in his own proper per-
Larkin & Joseph Bowling) son into open Court & with the consent of the
Plaintiffs Attorney confessed Judgment for twenty five dollars and fifty cents, & also for all the Costs appertaining to the above mentioned Suit.— And ordered by the Court that the Plaintiff recover against the Deft. twenty five dollars and fifty cents & also his costs by him in this behalf expended & the Deft. in mercy &c.—

The Court then adjourned till tomorrow 9 O,clock.

TUESDAY 12TH JULY 1814.
Court met according to adjournment. Present: Arthur Crozier, Quin Morton, & William McKamey Esquires.—

Admors of Richd. C. Cobb decd.)
vs) This case was continued on affidavit of Deft
John Underwood)

Ordered by the Court that Isaac Horton be overseer of the Road instead of George Sharp & have the same Bounds & hands.—
Also ordered that Saml. McKoy be overseer of the Road leading to Jacksborough, from his house to Cloud,s ford, & have the Bounds & hands that the former Overseer had.

A deed from Charles Y. Oliver Sheriff to Thomas McCorry for 3,490 acres of Land, known by the name of Parker,s Bend, was acknowledged in open Court & ordered to be registered.—

(P. 260) Thomas Wright returned one white poll subject to taxation for the present year.—

Simon Derrick)
vs) Present: Arthur Crozier, John Gibbs and William Underwood
Robert Ross) Esquires.—
This day came the parties by their Attornies and whereupon came a Jury (to wit) Andrew Braden, John Rhea, Isaac Mayberry, Craven Johnson, John Leach, Thos. Wright, Page Portwood, Zachariah Key, Danl. Stonecypher Solomon Alred, Leonard Coffman, & Daniel Leib, who being duly sworn say they find for the Defendant.—
Whereupon it is considered by the Court that the plaintiff be amerced for his clamour, & that the defendant go hence without day.—

Ordered by the Court that the following persons be appointed as Jurors to attend at the next term of this Court (to wit)
Saml. Dunn, Thos. Craig, John Reed, William Doherty, Robert Lawson, Willie Young, Jacob Linard, Charles Shinliver, Alexander Cole, John Cooper Farmer,

James Scarbrough, John Garner, Henry Norman, Daniel Mattox, Abraham W. Hagler, Thomas Kernall, Reuben Golstone, Thomas Peters, William Nichol, William Gamble, Reuben Williams, Thomas Boteler, Philip Seiber, Senr., John Lively, John Farmer & William Tunnell Junr.

Samuel Galbreath gave his resignation as a Justice of the Peace.-

Ordered by the Court that John Luallen be overseer of the road in place of Elijah Beach & have the same Bounds & hands.-

Micajah Frost returned 30 acres of land & one Black poll subject to taxation for the present year & Truman Still one white poll.

(P. 261) Walter Alves returned 10,999 acres of land subject to tax for the year 1813---

Ordered by the Court that Saml. McCoy be allow,d the sum of forty dollars, for the ensuing year (to be paid quarterly) for maintaining Priscilla Hutchings.

Ordered by the Court that Hugh Dixon be overseer of the road instead of John Kirby & have the same Bounds & hands.-

Ordered by the Court that John Kirk be overseer of the Road in place of John Lynn, & have the same bounds & hands.

Ordered by a majority of the Court that Stephen Heard be allow,d the sum of fifteen dollars & 75 cents for certificates to Jurors---

Ordered by the Court that Hugh Barton take charge of the Court House & have the same repaired or amended.

Ordered by a majority of the Court that Hugh Barton be allow,d the sum of 8 dollars for blank Books furnished for the use of this County---

Ordered by the Court that Neely Guest be Overseer of the Road in place of John Taylor & have the same Bounds & hands.-

Thomas McCorry returns 3490 acres of land liable for taxes for the year 1813-1814.

(P. 262) Ordered by the Court that Arthur Crozier be allowed seven dollars, thirty three & one third Cents, for monies paid by him to the County for Estrays taken up by John Sartain which appear to have been proved by owners & taken away---

Ordered by the Court that the Land of John Crawford levied on by James Newman Constable be exposed to sale to satisfy a Judgment which William Hogshead recovered against said John Crawford for the sum of nine dollars, Ballance on a note.---

Ordered by the Court that Thomas Menefee be overseer of the road in the place of James Kirkpatrick & have the same Bounds & hands.---

Ordered by the Court that Arthur Crozier be overseer of the Road in place of John Underwood & have the same bounds & hands.-

A deed from John Kirby to John Underwood was acknowledged in open Court and ordered to be registered.-

Court then adjourned till Tomorrow 9 O,clock.

Charles McClung returns 2020 acres of land liable for taxes for the present year.-

(P. 263) **WEDNESDAY 13TH JULY 1814-**

Court met according to adjournment. Present Arthur Crozier, Joseph Sinclair & Quin Morton Esquires.-

Jane Braden by her next friend
vs
Joseph Sinclair Junr.

This day came the parties by their attornies and the arbitrators to whom all matters in dispute between the parties in this suit were heretofore referred returned into Court their award whereby they find that the Defendant did speak the words laid in the declaration without justification and therefore they award that the Deft. pay all the costs of this suit and fifteen Dollars damages.- Therefore it is considered by the Court that the said award be confirmed and that the Plaintiff recover against the Defendant fifteen dollars the damages aforesaid and also her costs by her about her suit in this behalf expended and the Deft. in mercy &c.-

Enoch Foster Guardian for the Estate of John Lannun
vs
Jacob Moser

Ordered that Charles Y. Oliver sheriff expose to sale a tract of land which is returned levied on by Jacob Weaver a constable by virtue of two executions issued in these cases & that he sell the same according to law to satisfy said executions, which Tract consists of 135 acres lying in the Big Valley on the road on Dry Buffalo

The Same
vs
The Same

(P. 264) Whereupon the defendant now lives it appearing by the said return that there are no goods & chattles to be found to satisfy said Executions.

David Smith
vs
Jacob Moser

Matthew Heath a constable for this county returned to Court an execution issued in this cause by William Sharp- Esq- A Justice of the Peace for this County on a Judgment obtained by the plaintiff against the defendant with the following return thereon "No goods and chattels of the Defendants found in my County to make the within mentioned Judgment and costs but levied the within execution on one tract of land of the defendant containing 135 acres on the road leading from Clinton to Tazewell on dry Buffalo whereon Jacob Moser now lives" and on motion of the plaintiff- it is ordered that the sheriff of this County sell the said land according to law to satisfy said Execution.

A deed from Thos. Kelly to Douglass Oliver for 40 acres of land was proved in open Court by Charles Y. Oliver who also made oath that he seen John Jones one of the subscribing witnesses who is since dead subscribe his name as a witness to the same-

Court then adjourned until Court in Course-

ARTHUR CROZIER C. A. C.

www.ingramcontent.com/pod-product-compliance
Lightning Source LLC
Chambersburg PA
CBHW080126020526
44112CB00036B/2580